Praise for *It's Easier to Reach Heaven than the End of the Street*

"A fascinating account... Emma Williams is an honest, fair-minded, humane, highly intelligent young woman with a passion for justice who turns out to be an elegant, perceptive, delightful writer."

—Arthur Schlesinger Jr.

"A sustained masterpiece of the contemporary genre. It deserves to be read very widely: Nothing I have read during the last decade about the Israel-Palestine conflict in journalistic reportage, political analyses, histories, personal stories, or novels comes close to its brilliance in exposing the accumulating human debris of this monstrous 'situation.' Williams's writing in this memoir displays the tenacity of Anna Funder, the intrepidity of a Ryszard Kapuscinski, the politically gendered sensitivity of Nadine Gordimer, the reconciliatory instincts of Desmond Tutu, and the literary competence of Joyce Carol Oates. It's a joy to read."

—Les Rosenblatt, *Arena* magazine

"The best account I've read of the tragedy that took the Palestinians and Israelis hostage."

—Daniel Ben Simon

"What Emma Williams has to tell us in this riveting and moving memoir is of two peoples living in a time of terror, fear, anger and death. Her humanity and empathy allow her to see both peoples in all their individuality, rather than as political footballs...It is one of the most significant contributions to establishing the day-to-day reality of the time."

—Linda Grant

"Emma Williams has pulled off an amazing literary and journalistic feat—a study of modern Israel that shows the best and the worst on each side of the tragedy, and which engages our sympathy with both. She writes beautifully."

—Boris Johnson

"Brilliant and moving... one of the best of recent books about Israel and Palestine."

—William Dalrymple, *New Statesman*

"[A] brilliant memoir... she succeeds like few others in her ability to view the situation through the eyes of Jew and Arab... Drawing our sympathy now to one, now to the other, she envies those with a 'one-eyed view,' undisturbed by the layers of complication... Her eye for detail conveys the situation more painfully than statistics... What she has produced is a human document; sensitive, compassionate, and superbly written. The exemplary notes, maps, and glossary... help to make this memoir more illuminating and instructive than many a pundit's tome."

—Theo Richmond, *The Spectator*

"Short of a crash course in Nablus or a Gaza refugee camp, I recommend Emma Williams's expatriate memoir of Jerusalem in the second intifada as an initial exposure to the dispiriting reality behind the propaganda, theirs and ours... Israelis and Palestinians are like angry twins joined at the hip. [This book] is an engrossing exploration of what that means."

—Eric Silver, *Jewish Chronicle*

"This book must be one of the most honest accounts of those terrible years. It's proportionate, subtle and comprehensive... biased towards nobody but the voices of moderation and hope."

—*The Guardian*

"This is a clever book, in the best sense of the word. Emma Williams deftly weaves two stories into one, using a personal journey through the grinding Israeli-Palestinian conflict to explore its larger dynamics and personalities... The book's strength lies in its many conversations, which capture the relentless determination of what Williams rightly describes as 'two extraordinary peoples' to remain blind to the plight of the other... A valuable, highly readable contribution."

—*The Australian*

"Many books have been written about the Israeli-Palestinian conflict... What makes Emma Williams' memoir unique is the honesty of her observations on ordinary life: what it is like to live with occupation and suicide bombers…The beauty of this book is that, as the author's political awareness grows, so does that of the reader. She explains the conflict in simple terms, without getting bogged down by the tedious chronology that weighs down other Jerusalem memoirs. Yet everything is here."

—*Daily Telegraph*

"This intelligent, incisive account… and her cool analysis of the humanity and hypocrisy at the heart of the Israeli/Palestinian fighting is striking."

—*The Times*

"Compelling… extraordinary and insightful account of the Israeli-Palestinian conflict."

—*Harper's Bazaar*

"Our choice of the best recent books."

—*Sunday Times*

"Emma Williams has gone to great lengths to talk to both sympathetic and unsympathetic Israelis, chronicling the human cost of Palestinian suicide bombings as well as of Israeli incursions, curfews, punitive shellings and bombings. … A reader only vaguely aware of the reality behind the headlines will find much that is observant and saddening in her vivid portrait of this tribal dispute."

—*The Independent*

"Williams is an excellent recorder of dialogue on both sides of the political divide. Her purpose is to illuminate the plight of each community… It makes grim reading, but it is all true."

—*Sunday Times*

"On one level, it is a personal memoir… On another level, it strikes in a more profound way, keeping at front and centre the people afflicted by the conflict and making tangible the fear to which many are condemned. It also provides the political and historical context of the events of the last six years, lightly told."

—*Financial Times*

"As well as telling the story of her family's two-and-a half-year stay in Jerusalem, it offers a careful and accessible explanation of the background to 'the situation.' ...Williams, who studied history at Oxford before taking a degree in medicine, wanted to explain the difficulties of ordinary life that fail to make the news, but which, over years, fuel much larger events... She got to know the situation first-hand, from both sides.... Williams manages to be scrupulously even-handed about one of the most contentious situations in the world."

—*The Scotsman*

"The insanity of the Israel-Palestine conflict is a constant background in global affairs, but how do we assess its impact on those who have to endure it? Emma Williams' account of that experience provides a rare glimpse into its day-to-day reality... Her direct and punchy style fits the atmosphere of constant tension she describes, and brings it to the surface of our conscience."

—*Canberra Times*

"Emma Williams' Jerusalem memoir is a vivid account of the quotidian existence of Israelis and Palestinians in each other's hostile midsts... a poignant response to the usual misinformation about the Palestinians."

—*The Oldie*

"[Williams's] experience, recorded with painstaking honesty, will be welcomed by anyone who wants to understand the complexities of the Israeli-Palestinian conflict... In the midst of denial and the language of force, Williams's own voice seeks truth, moderation and dialogue."

—*New Statesman*

"[Charles] Glass wrote that Williams could 'do anything.' What she does best is toe the extremely valuable line of impartiality while describing the daily life of people in hell."

—*Sunday Times*

It's Easier to Reach Heaven
than the End of the Street

A JERUSALEM MEMOIR

by Emma Williams
foreword by Brian Urquhart

OLIVE
BRANCH
PRESS

An imprint of Interlink Publishing Group, Inc.
www.interlinkbooks.com

First American edition published in 2010 by

OLIVE BRANCH PRESS
An imprint of Interlink Publishing Group, Inc.
46 Crosby Street, Northampton, Massachusetts 01060
www.interlinkbooks.com

Originally published in Great Britain by Bloomsbury Publishing Plc, London

Library of Congress Cataloging-in-Publication Data
Williams, Emma.
It's easier to reach heaven than the end of the street : a Jerusalem memoir /
by Emma Williams. —1st American ed.   p. cm.
First published in Great Britain in 2006 by Bloomsbury Publishing, London.
Includes bibliographical references.
ISBN 978-1-56656-789-3
1. Arab-Israeli conflict--1993- 2. Arab-Israeli conflict--1993---Social
aspects. 3. Al-Aqsa Intifada, 2000- 4. Williams, Emma. 5. Americans--Jerusalem--
Biography. 6. Women physicians--Jerusalem--Biography. 7. Jerusalem--Biography.
8. Jerusalem--Social conditions--21st century. 9. Ram Allah--Social conditions--
21st century. 10. Tel Aviv (Israel)--Social conditions--21st century. I. Title.
DS119.76.W55 2009   956.05'3092--dc22
[B]   2009034228

The maps on pages viii, x, and 280 are based on maps produced by OCHA, the
United Nations Office for the Coordination of Humanitarian Affairs. The maps
were redrawn by HLStudios.

Cover image: Arab brother and sister in the city of old Jerusalem © Mikhail Leavit

Printed and bound in the United States of America

To request our free 48-page full-color catalog, please call us toll-free at
1-800-238-LINK, visit our website at www.interlinkbooks.com, or e-mail us at
info@interlinkbooks.com.

For Anat, Intisar, and Rita

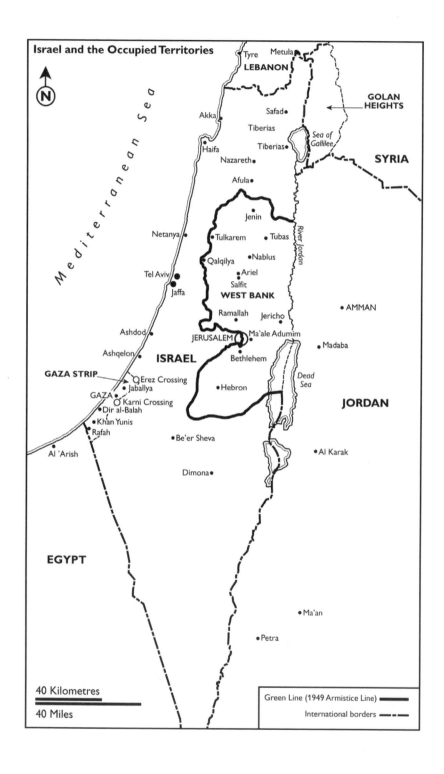

Israel and the Occupied Territories

N

Mediterranean Sea

LEBANON

Tyre

Metula

GOLAN HEIGHTS

Akka

Safad

Tiberias

Sea of Gallilee

Haifa

Tiberias

SYRIA

Nazareth

Afula

Jenin

Netanya

Tulkarem

Tubas

River Jordan

Qalqilya

Nablus

Ariel

Tel Aviv

Salfit

Jaffa

WEST BANK

AMMAN

Ramallah

Jericho

Ashdod

JERUSALEM

Ma'ale Adumim

Madaba

Ashqelon

ISRAEL

Bethlehem

Dead Sea

GAZA STRIP

Erez Crossing

Jaballya

Hebron

GAZA

Karni Crossing

Dir al-Balah

JORDAN

Khan Yunis

Rafah

Be'er Sheva

Al Karak

Al 'Arish

Dimona

EGYPT

Ma'an

Petra

40 Kilometres

40 Miles

Green Line (1949 Armistice Line)

International borders

Contents

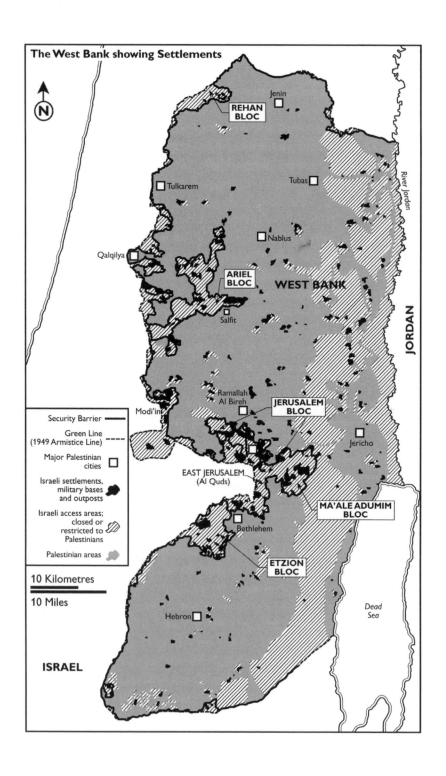

The West Bank showing Settlements

N

REHAN
BLOC

Jenin

Tulkarem

Tubas

Nablus

Qalqilya

ARIEL
BLOC

WEST BANK

Salfit

Ramallah
Al Bireh

JERUSALEM
BLOC

Modi'in

Security Barrier

Green Line
(1949 Armistice Line)

Major Palestinian
cities

Israeli settlements,
military bases
and outposts

Israeli access areas;
closed or
restricted to
Palestinians

Palestinian areas

10 Kilometres

10 Miles

EAST JERUSALEM
(Al Quds)

Jericho

MA'ALE ADUMIM
BLOC

Bethlehem

ETZION
BLOC

Hebron

ISRAEL

River Jordan

JORDAN

Dead
Sea

Foreword

When I reviewed the British version of Emma Williams's book in the *New York Review of Books* three years ago, I hoped that it would soon be available in the United States in an American edition. The book had been very well received by British, Australian, and other reviewers. Almost of all them commented on the combination of the beauty of the prose, the lucid understanding of the political issues, and the emotional horror of the conflict with the author's clear-sighted balance. They recognized that it was the manifest intention of the writer to see the conflict from both sides, not in a way that involved sitting on the fence but truly getting to grips with how painful the situation is for both peoples involved in the Israeli-Palestinian conflict.

I am delighted that this updated version is now available in the US. Due not least to President Obama's call for real progress through purposeful negotiation, the Israeli-Palestinian conflict is once again in the forefront of international attention. The significance of a book of this kind is therefore even greater than it was three years ago, a time when it was clear to all that under the Bush administration there was going to be no movement on the peace process. This updated version has even more relevance now than the first edition had then.

Emma Williams provides a personal and highly perceptive account of working daily with both Israelis and Palestinians during a three-year period of extreme violence and emotion, the second Intifada. Because she has a strong affection and respect for the people of both sides, her account is of particular interest, and value, to those who are part of the search for a resolution, as well as to all those interested in this longstanding human tragedy.

Williams, her husband, a UN official, and their three small children (a fourth was born in Bethlehem at the height of the violence) arrived in Jerusalem four weeks before the Intifada started

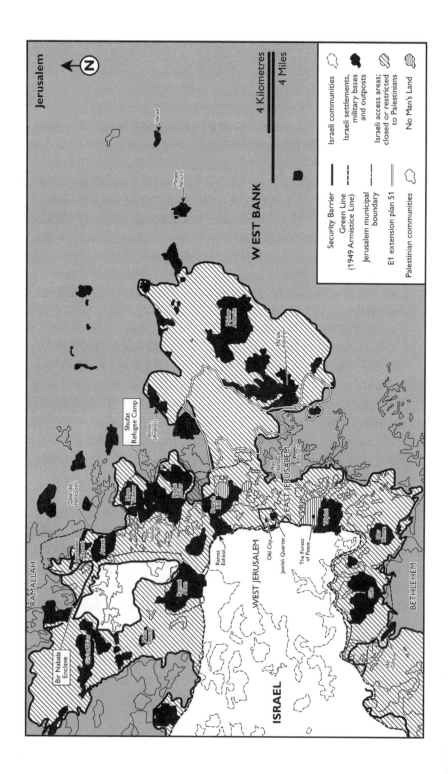

Jerusalem

N

WEST BANK

ISRAEL

WEST JERUSALEM

EAST JERUSALEM

RAMALLAH

BETHLEHEM

Bir Nabala
Enclave

Qalandia
checkpoint

Shufat
Refugee Camp

Almon
(Anatot)

Ma'ale
Adumim

Mishor
Adumim

Vered

Mizpe
Yericho

Ramat
Eshkol

Old City

Jewish Quarter

The Forest
of Peace

Ras
al-Hamis

Abu Dis

Gilo

Har
Homa

Talpiot

Neve
Ya'acov

Pisgat
Ze'ev

Beit
Hanina

Ramot
Allon

Neve
Samuel

French
Hill

4 Kilometres

4 Miles

	Security Barrier
	Green Line (1949 Armistice Line)
	Jerusalem municipal boundary
	E1 extension plan 51
	Palestinian communities
	Israeli communities
	Israeli settlements, military bases and outposts
	Israeli access areas; closed or restricted to Palestinians
	No Man's Land

and insisted on staying on as a family. They thus shared, to an unusual degree, the very different anxieties and hardships of ordinary Israelis and Palestinians. Though it is unusual and not easy to arrange, this sharing of experience is invaluable if UN officials are fully to understand and to play a positive role in helping to resolve issues that fuel violence and conflict.

A medical doctor, Williams worked by day in Palestinian hospitals on the Mount of Olives and near Ramallah. Her husband worked mostly in Gaza and the West Bank. At night they returned, sometimes with difficulty, to their children—at school during the day—and their house in a largely Arab part of Jerusalem. The couple had a great many Israeli friends with whom they would spend time in the evenings and on the weekends.

They experienced at first hand the violence—suicide bombings, Israeli military counter-measures, checkpoints, and innumerable disruptions of normal life, increasingly irrational reactions on all sides, hatred and the insatiable desire for revenge, and, last but not least, having to explain it all to three young children. They also witnessed many acts of heroism, decency, and understanding.

The result is not only an intimate, moving, and revealing book about two extraordinary peoples whose lives and futures are now in the balance, but also an important contribution to understanding the conflict, its history, and current status. Emma Williams's account of what the Israeli-Palestinian conflict means for ordinary people on both sides, how they react to it, what they fear and what they hope for, could well, in the long run, be far more useful than all the partisan rhetoric, the hatred, the myths, and the lust for revenge that inevitably lead, over and over again, to extreme violence.

Meanwhile, this beautifully written book will certainly help outside observers to understand better the people of both sides and their struggle. Is it too much to hope that it might also help Israelis and Palestinians to see each other in a less baleful light, as they must do if they are to avoid a shared, and terminal, calamity?

—*Brian Urquhart*

Introduction

Just over the Hill

The first I heard of the plan to move our young family from New York to Jerusalem was on an October night's drive along the Sawmill Parkway to Connecticut.

"How'd you like to live in Jerusalem for a couple of years?"

Andrew and I had been married for eight years. Soon after our wedding in Britain I'd joined him in Pakistan where I worked as a junior surgeon in a Pakistan hospital, and we moved to New York in 1992.

Now it was late October, 1999. Andrew was at the wheel of a rented car. We'd stood in line for burgers and milkshakes at the Red Rooster in Brewster and the smell of French fries hung stale in the car air.

"Might be good." I needed more information. "What's up?"

"The main UN office for the Middle East peace process is setting up a unit for regional politics out there, helping with the negotiations that are looking encouraging. The lead guy has asked if I'd be interested in heading it."

"When?"

"Starting in a couple of months. We'd see in the new millennium in New York, and be out there some time after that."

The new millennium. Newspapers, websites, and conversations obsessed with Y2K and the impending end of electronic interaction. Seven years in New York had been light and young. We'd built ourselves a home in a Chelsea loft and filled it with three children. They were now five, two, and six months old. Archie could handle moving schools without too much trouble; Xan and Catriona would take it in stride. And I had swapped clinical medicine for research and public health. There'd be plenty of work to do out there.

"Great. Let's go for it."

The weekend was bright with the colors of a New England

fall, so much more vibrant than a veiled old England autumn. The children buried themselves in leaves and tried to redirect a small stream ambling down the hillside. Andrew and I played visions of a Holy Land life in each other's heads, and drove back to the city halfway out of it already.

The reality of relocation was not so streamlined. The UN machine moved slowly, and Andrew didn't start his new post until April 2000. We waved goodbye to him and stayed on in New York to see out the school year, finish my work projects, and pack up our loft.

Friends were full of advice about where to live, which schools to choose, and how to cope with the natives (definitions varied). I heard about our new location directly from Andrew when he reached it. His reports about our new rental accommodation in a tiny village in Jerusalem caused problems for me when I relayed them in conversations back in New York. Apparently he'd found a house for us that couldn't exist, in an area we shouldn't contemplate, and he'd chosen a school—the Lycée Francais—from a different culture that would only confuse our children. At a party on Gracie Square Peter Jennings questioned me about the location of the Palestinian village in central Jerusalem. Edward Said explained to him that it was in "No Man's Land," that is, the area in Jerusalem lying between two threads of the Green Line, the 1949 Armistice Line (I made a mental note to find out about these complications, and their history). At a book party I was told that I must find an apartment in Ramallah, as that was where all the fun was to be found, not in stodgy Jerusalem. No, no, no, others insisted: Tel Aviv was the only place to live, with way too much religion in Jerusalem. On a bench in Union Square a friend told me that to live in a Palestinian area was to ask for trouble; why not choose one of the nice areas of West Jerusalem, like Rehavia or near Emek Rephaim, or even one of the up and coming areas like Bakaa? None of the names meant anything to me yet. As for the French school system, why burden children with the francophone way of thinking? There was a perfectly good American school in the center of town, wasn't there?

New York's confidence was as solid as its concern, but not always shored up by the reality 6,000 miles away. My confusion at the contradictions was to morph into an automatic resignation; I would stop the retort that rose automatically and bite it back until I'd seen for myself what was happening on the ground. I was to find that contradiction became a pattern and the general way of things.

The house that Andrew found, through a French-Israeli friend—Ofer—who lived in Jaffa, was in a village in Jerusalem after all. We did live in a Palestinian area, but found it no trouble. I grew accustomed to the names of places, and to love them. The French school served us well and was a good choice, though there was a suicide bombing at its gate one morning. And we added to the family: a baby boy, born in Bethlehem, four days before Christmas.

Six years later we were back in New York. Six years; a large slice of a family's life, but a brief moment in the story of the Mideast. A moment in which there had been an intifada, an attack on the US homeland, and the inauguration of two wars. New York's assuredness had shifted and realigned. A moment of profound change, and opportunity, of failure, and pain. For us it was a moment of watching people's futures sawn off by extremism and violence, observing diplomacy fail and anti-Semitism and Islamophobia grow, witnessing hope cemented into despair. It was our moment of riding the roller coaster euphemistically known as "the situation."

"The situation": that's what those on the ground call it. On the face of it, the situation is straightforward. It's a conflict between two peoples, Israeli and Palestinian, over land: the Holy Land. In reality, it's a maelstrom, a tragedy of our times, a shameful failure of the modern world. And it looks so different from over there, on the ground, that the view from New York verges dangerously on fantasy.

We walked into the situation in August 2000, a month before it blew up; the calm before the continuing storm. We quit on the first night of George Bush's invasion of Iraq, in March 2003, the bombs falling on Baghdad as I sat waiting with my four children in a large airplane on the tarmac of Tel Aviv airport, hoping we would not end up as collateral damage of the onslaught a few hundred miles away.

A few hundred miles. That's a big distance in Israel. Many of Israel's enemies are much closer, and the gap between protection and defenselessness painfully narrow. There's no Atlantic barrier, no island safety for Israelis, who inhabit a sliver of land with undefined, changing borders. I heard the fears all too painfully in a conversation with an IDF general, Amos Gilad, military strategist in the Israeli Ministry of Defense. He had described to a friend of mine, Peter, his straightforward vision of the future: to turn the seven major Palestinian cities into isolated "microcosms." That would contain the problem. This was to be the strategy, he had said, "this year and for all years."

Peter told me about their conversation over coffee one morning in the Jerusalem winter of 2002, after we had dropped our respective children at the school next door to the café. An Australian ex-soldier turned UN political officer, Peter wondered aloud at the idea of "microcosms" and their effects on people's lives. Roni, the café owner, switched channels to find the news. There had been another terror attack, and Roni translated for us.

"We'll never be free," he said. "This country is shit, we'll never be free from terror."

"This is my point," said Peter. "How do we, they—Israelis and Palestinians, but it affects the rest of us too—get out of here? Everyone is trapped, in different ways, but trapped all the same by the situation." The question stuck, as it always did, in the freeze of frustrated silence. The two of us left Roni's coffee shop in that same silence, heading out into the damp Jerusalem chill to start work.

Later, when I went to see General Gilad myself, I asked him about "the situation" and, remembering Peter's troubling question, how we might get out of it. Major General Amos Gilad, by now head of the Israeli government's military-political unit, held court in Tel Aviv at the Kyria, the left ventricle of the Israeli defense ministry. I had driven down from Jerusalem with a slow leak in a tire through sluggish traffic on Route 1, and an Israeli in the lane next to me had pointed out my flattening tire with a look of sympathy. I was going to be late if I stopped so I didn't.

Tel Aviv was bright in the Mediterranean sun, as bright as it had been buzzing when I had seen it the night before, the clubs pounding music and the people filling the streets, gathering in the balmy night air. Now, out of the morning rush hour, I drove cautiously through the security procedures into the Kyria, an awesome complex in the center of the city. I wished I had stayed the night in Tel Aviv instead of heading back to Jerusalem, but the two cities are less than forty miles apart and the pull of Jerusalem is strong. I had submitted all my details to the ministry and been given clearance for my visit. That same week an Israeli-Arab* journalist had also been given clearance to visit the Kyria to interview an official; the soldiers on guard were jumpy and when he reached into his pocket for his ID they thought he was a terrorist and beat him up, breaking his legs. I was glad General Gilad had sent one of his uniformed assistants to escort me through the complex to his office.

I had first met the general at a party in Tel Aviv. Guarded by security men, all shaven-headed with coiled listening pieces in one ear, he was talking to Norway's ambassador, Mona Juul, who introduced me. He was genial, relaxed, telling me about female pilots in the Israeli air force and the military's worries in case they were shot down and captured by Arabs. "You don't want to know what they do to women if they capture them. And I'm not going to tell you," he said slowly, looking straight at me. "But these girls insist on being pilots, and we are," he laughed, "a democracy. Sometimes too democratic, I think."

*Those Palestinians who took Israeli citizenship after the creation of Israel in 1948 refer to themselves as Palestinian Israelis or '48 Arabs. Jewish Israelis and most foreigners refer to them as Israeli Arabs.

Now, in the Kyria, a girl in khaki fatigues was leading me through the complex of buildings and corridors. She handed me over to the general in his office; he smiled and shook my hand firmly. He was charming: "You know, I was in New York, but I came back because I wanted to see you." We both laughed at his flattery. "Why don't you sit here?" the palm of his hand offering the corner in an elbow of sofas. "Coffee?" He glanced at one of the uniformed girls in the outer office.

His office was small, unpretentious. Israelis are not particular about putting on a show; they are informal and unstuffy. Nor did the general need any trappings to give the impression of power. He sat at the protected heart of a vast army, equipped with the latest, most invincible land, sea, and air weaponry, conventional and nuclear. Ursine, solid, and gray-haired, he radiated power: it hung off his civilian clothes. His unraised voice was frank as he laid out Israel's policy toward the Palestinians.

"You have to understand the deep motives in this situation." He leaned back. "It was Rabin who sent me to Arafat," the general said, "and eventually I reached a deep insight of the Palestinian leader. We developed a chemistry. But we got him wrong, in a way that doesn't contribute to the image of Jews as geniuses. One of our most critical mistakes."

A young woman came in with cups of coffee. She set them down on the low table between us.

General Gilad thanked her and carried on. "One of our most critical mistakes was dealing with this guy. My assessments irritated some politicians." He chuckled, but went on more seriously, explaining that, tragically, the Palestinians don't recognize Israel as the homeland of the Jewish people. He looked down at my notepad, pausing while I wrote, and then explained that Arafat believed demographic trends dictated that Israel was temporary, and accepted Israel on that basis only. The general added his resentment at Palestinians' making "no attempt to understand Israelis, how we feel, what our concerns are."

His words conjured up the image of Arafat, the short man in his military gear, keffiyeh placed painstakingly on his strange head. I tried to picture the two men together, working out each other's deep motives.

The general was telling me how Palestinians wanted all Jews out of the West Bank and Gaza Strip, and that their ideas were not based on mutual recognition; they want an independent Palestinian state without Jews. "Unlike Israel, of course, which is one fifth Palestinian." And they want us "to take back the refugees as well." He broke off, mildly angry.

I had questions, but he was explaining in his own way.

"The Hashemite Kingdom is, of course, two thirds Palestinian," he was saying about Jordan. "Amman is almost entirely Palestinian." And then: "As for women, you know that to them women are less than donkeys and dogs. An Arab of 75 came to me asking for fertility treatment—he had a 25-year-old wife! You can *buy* women in their society."

I thought of men buying women, that it's not impossible to buy anyone, anywhere.

"You remember the suicide bombing by the woman at Erez?"

I nodded.

"She was having an affair with her husband's boss, a Hamas man. Her family left her no choice. Either she died 'with honor'— as a suicide bomber—or she got killed."

"How did we get here, though? Into this terrible situation?"

"In 2000, Arafat decided to use terror to break us. He was confident he would break us with their terror. This was the correct assessment I presented before Camp David.

"Israel suffers far more from terror than any previous people. Israelis are remarkable people—they show unbelievable resistance. People don't understand what it's like. We were briefing a delegation and I was explaining to them that I was never sure whether I would see my wife alive each night. At that very moment my daughter called me to say that there had been a suicide bomb in

Herzliya. My mother, my wife, and my daughter had left the scene *one minute* before it went off. The Hungarian delegate said to the Russian, '*Now* I understand, and I'm leaving.'"

I thought back to my own narrow escape from a suicide bombing, and the cold horror of knowing how close the three children and I (pregnant with our fourth) had been.

"They failed," the General was saying, "the Palestinians, because we don't do revenge, we don't do atrocities, we don't do rape—the Russians in April and May 1945 ordered their soldiers to rape German women. Even torture—I don't think there is any here because it's against the law. As for assassinations, the British are so hypocritical..." He tutted. "But it is intolerable to have so many casualties."

I wondered for a moment whose casualties he meant. Then I realized he was talking about the spring of 2002, when 129 Israelis were killed in suicide bombings and other attacks.

"Let me tell you, in March 2002 we opened a new chapter."

"Operation Defensive Shield?" Israel's April 2002 invasion of Palestinian cities, most famously Jenin.

"Yes. We are weak in propaganda, I'm not sure why. Saeb Erekat said 700 were killed, but in fact only 53 died—I've got the names. And we saved the hospital in Jenin—I financed generators for them: 1 million shekels. And we arranged the hospitalization of the wounded. The director of the hospital lied when he said the hospital was hit."

I let these facts roll out: by now I'd lived in Jerusalem for some time. I asked him where he thought the situation was going.

"You have to understand this, we are dealing with an entity that will *never* accept us."

He let this sink in, and then added: "The Holocaust was so cruel" and that Palestinian attitudes reminded so many Israelis of this. "I'm not sure if I have the answer as to where we are going. You don't understand the *hatred*. Do you know how many Palestinian workers turn on their Israeli bosses and kill them?"

I didn't. He continued. "And this hatred comes from incitement. The incitement is terrible, unbelievable. In 2000 Arafat could have had all the settlements removed, but he wants only the final solution."

I looked at him. He had not used the phrase thoughtlessly.

The incitement, he was saying, "is educating the Palestinian population that all Israel is Palestine and to hate all Israelis. They remind us of our worst enemies. What *hate* they have against us. Why? Because people need an enemy to excuse their own problems, the problems they have at home. We are weak. No one paid the price for extermination. You know, Air Marshal Harris said it was 'not in our priorities to bomb the crematoria' and yet he managed to bomb installations four kilometers away."

He didn't want me to comment, only to know. He went back to the Palestinians. "We're dealing with sponsored state terror. But we are not committing atrocities. In fact we have many teams dealing with the humanitarian side."

"On the humanitarian side, General, what about Closure?"* I wanted to hear his views on the realities of life in the Occupied Territories, described increasingly often as jails by those who worked and lived there. "What about these big prisons?"

"Ah yes. The fence." He gave me a short tutorial on tactical, strategic, and operational considerations. "The fence is the tactical and operational solution to the Palestinian problem."

"And the checkpoints?"

"I don't like them. I was flooded with complaints from the EU and *all* the others." His arms swept round an imaginary roomful of unhappy diplomats. "We have a special team improving the humanitarian situation, as I said, and we've removed half of the roadblocks. We'll need even fewer roadblocks with the fence. The fence will decrease the need for internal closure. There'll be less of a siege on their cities."

* Closure is the Israeli policy of controlling Palestinian movement within and at the limits of the Occupied Territories by physical (e.g., checkpoints, earth-mounds, barriers, ditches, gates) and administrative (e.g., permits) means.

"But the cities will be stuck inside the fence. What will happen when the prisoners can't stand being captive any longer?"

He paused. "I'm not sure I have the answer to that," the general said. "But, what I can say is that with this barrier we are saving lives, Palestinian and Israeli. When Palestinians kill Israelis, we have to take measures in retaliation: they get killed. So we save their lives this way."[1]

At that moment, I found out later, a retaliatory measure was about to start in Rafah at the southern end of the Gaza Strip. But our talk had come to an end, and we stood up. I put out my hand to shake his, and he grasped me, pulling me toward him for a kiss.

As I left I felt mildly like a bought woman, walking through the outer office with the eyes of the uniformed girls on my back. I had wondered if we would meet again, as he had said he hoped. And then he'd grabbed me. His smile as he pulled me, that hunter-smile, the same everywhere: no harm in trying, the smile said.

I drove away, forgetting the slow leak in the tire, thinking again about Peter's questions. Where was it that we had gotten to? How had we gotten here? Amos Gilad had given his answer, in part, but he had not offered much hope for getting out of "the situation." Here was a general in one of the world's most powerful, well-equipped armies, and even he was fearful. Thinking about his wife and daughter missing a suicide bombing by minutes. Just as we had—the memory kept resurfacing—missing a suicide bombing by minutes. Me and my children.

We had arrived in Israel, eventually, just before the second Intifada began. When the bombing of civilians started in Israel one month after that, we began to feel the fear. How many times since then had we been in the wrong place but not at the wrong time and therefore still alive and whole?—Café Moment, Ha'Nevim, the narrow streets of Mea Sharim where the Orthodox live, Pizza Sbarro, Ben Yehuda Street a dozen times over. My favorite café on Emek Rephaim, where the casualty surgeon died when he had broken his unbreakable rule not to go to cafés and restaurants—but his daughter was getting married the following day so why not? He and she had both been killed. No bride, no wedding. The staff in casualty knew he must be dead because he was always first there after a bomb and this time he wasn't.

The fear the general had talked about was a shackle for every Israeli, hanging round their future. It put a block on life. Life continued, but with the drag of anxiety. And then there'd be a heart-stopping boom across the valleys and the fear flooded back and took over as you tallied where everyone was. Family first: kids, husband. Then friends. Colleagues. After that you give yourself the all-clear and push back the fear and out into the normal again. You feel bad being callous, but you have to carry on, as normal. Everyone does.

How different everything had been when we'd arrived in Israel: the hope, the landscape, and the future. I had been changed by living here, stuck between the two communities, Israeli and Palestinian, moving from one to the other, hearing from each side about fear and hate and rage, facing the same things but as an outsider, and finding myself torn between the two.

The day before seeing General Gilad I was in the Occupied Territories.* Perhaps that was where the tire had acquired its puncture, not as I drove eastward on the new broad settler roads on the long detour around the new Security Barrier, but on the rough roads for Palestinian traffic as I looped back again to reach al-Quds University in Abu Dis, a suburb on the edge of Jerusalem. I was there to meet a German friend, Daniel, and wait for him to finish giving his lecture on graphic design before we headed off to Hebron. To the east of al-Quds lies the Judean desert, to the north and west the city of Jerusalem. Not far south, along the line of hills, is Bethlehem, with the city of Hebron beyond.

One of Daniel's Palestinian university friends, also waiting to see him, came up and said hello. Ghassan and I sat on a low stone wall

---

* *Occupied Territories: commonly used term for the West Bank and Gaza Strip, the "Occupied Palestinian Territory" under international law. Most Israelis call them the "territories." Some call the West Bank "Judea and Samaria."*

in the spring sun under the olive trees of the campus grounds. Beyond us, on the sports fields, construction workers and cranes were slotting together towering slabs of concrete to form another wall, *the* wall. The rest of Abu Dis, and Jerusalem, lay on the other side.

We looked across the valley at the winding wall, and at the new Israeli settlements going up amid the remaining Palestinian areas, and at the roads linking the settlements that are not for use by Palestinians. "We must go the long way round," said Ghassan, "if we are allowed to move at all."

Ghassan was born in Jerusalem, not far from where we were sitting, at the hospital where I had worked, but the Israeli authorities classify him as a Palestinian from the territories, a "West Banker," and therefore a Palestinian not entitled to live in Jerusalem. His wife, who is also Palestinian, and who, like Ghassan, works at al-Quds University, is defined as a Jerusalem resident. "The Israeli law does not allow us to live together," Ghassan explained.* They used to live as a couple, breaking Israel's rules, in their home in the Jerusalem suburb of Ras al-Amud, but now there is the Wall physically dividing them. Ghassan has to live with relatives on the West Bank side of the Wall, in Abu Dis.

"It's the control that's the worst. Israel controls every aspect of my life: where I can and cannot go, when, whether or not I can get to work, what roads I can use, even whether or not I can leave my house. They will not let me build on the land that remains to me—the settlers have taken the rest. With their wall and their permits they want to cut me off from my family, my friends, and my city. And my wife."

"Can you go to Jerusalem to visit her?"

He frowned at the question but said very slowly: "They won't let any Palestinians into the Holy City without a permit." Ghassan was formal, somber. Part of his voice had anger in it, but he held it in a dark

---

* *The nullification of family reunification by the Nationality and Entry into Israel Law of July 2003.*

place and what I heard was sorrow. "And you can only have a permit, in theory, if you are over 29 and are married and have children."

"And you're not?" He didn't look very old. His black hair was cut short and square, his clothes were pressed and neat, his shoes polished, with a tidemark of today's dust about the toes.

"Yes, I'm 33. And we have a child, a baby boy. But my son is not listed on my ID and even when I take his birth certificate they won't allow me a permit."

"But surely..."

"In any case, even if I had a permit it wouldn't make any difference. For weeks the Israelis have not let anyone through at all, even with a permit."

Ghassan was telling me this quietly and calmly. "All I want," he said, "is to be with my wife and child, to be able to live together as a family. I now see my wife for five minutes every now and then at work if we're lucky. My son is one year and three months old. He will forget me. My wife sometimes manages to get here to see me on the weekend, but it is a risk and she has to go on a long, long detour because of the Wall, even though our homes are only two minutes apart."

"And if she moves in with you in Abu Dis?"

"Then she loses her right to live in Jerusalem forever."

"And Jerusalem..."

"Jerusalem is Palestine," he said. "I used to go to the Old City of Jerusalem every day—look how close it is, we're much closer to the Old City than the majority of West Jerusalem areas are. I would buy groceries, visit the dentist, pray at the mosque, whatever. It is, Jerusalem is—how can I put it?—the center of our lives.

"My brother is in the same position. But his wife has decided to let go of her birthright to Jerusalem. She will never be allowed to return. They are miserable about this, but they are together." He slows down, thinking.

"And the *injustice*... people are 'returning' from all over the world to claim the right to live in Jerusalem, a place they may never have seen, but it's *their* 'right'—because they're Jewish, while we're being forced out." He pointed to the snake of concrete wall along the ridge, stamping its course between houses, through people's gardens and over their land.

"I can't understand the Israelis. They took the last part of Palestine in the war of '67. They want to control our land, our water, our history, our freedom. They want to drive us away, perhaps, but why do they want to break apart our families? To keep children from their parents, to keep me from my son and have him grow up in anger—what good does that do?"

He was asking me questions he didn't expect me to answer.

"My father is a retired teacher. He is so affected by the situation that he just sits at home not saying anything. Me, I see nothing beyond tomorrow.

"And my wife, my poor wife. It's very hard for her, not just raising our son without me but being harassed by the insurance."

The "insurance," he explained, is a department of the Israeli Ministry of the Interior. "They come to your house to check up on your residency status, and if you're not there or your clothes are too few they say you're not a resident and you lose your status. They raid our house in Ras al-Amud to make sure my wife's not 'lying.' Everything you do, they begin with the position that you're *lying*. They come at any time, usually very early in the morning, hoping to catch you out. They go into the kitchen, open the fridge, ask you why you have a dishwasher like this, or food like that. They go in the bedroom, they are very rude, very offensive, and open all your drawers and look at your most personal things and make comments."

Ghassan was a computer engineer. "I used to supply computers to the settlement of Ma'ale Edumim.* I had many friends there, among the settlers. They are very sympathetic but they can do nothing. They're not like the settlers in Hebron or some other places:

---

* *Settlements refer to Jewish-only communities built in the Occupied Territories, the 22 percent of Palestine that was not controlled by Israel until its capture in 1967. See Glossary.*

they're civilized. Some of the soldiers, too. My brother speaks Russian and sometimes, if the soldiers are Russian, they sympathize and let us in so we can see our friends in Ma'ale Edumim.

"You know, the Israelis, they even make us apply for a permit to move from one place to another in the West Bank. I cannot go anywhere, not even Bethlehem, without one. It's there, Bethlehem, just over the hill, you can almost see it. There is nothing we can do. What is the point of anything, even demonstrating? It does no good at all."

Daniel walked over to the wall where we were sitting. "How are things?" he asked, and we talked for a while about the students' problems getting to class. Daniel and I climbed into the car and drove away, toward the road to Hebron that Ghassan cannot travel because he is Palestinian.

To get to Hebron we had to pass through Bethlehem, and Daniel knew a back way eastward across the dry country. We wound through narrow streets, passing children and donkeys and little green tractors pulling miniature trailers. A path led off to the right down a wadi. I could see the valley below, patches of rebellious green against the sand, but I couldn't see where the path went or why there were so many Palestinians, old, young, suited, robed, making their way down the hillside.

Daniel and I kept going. There was a checkpoint ahead. A burly soldier told us that the checkpoint, separating two Palestinian areas just as Ghassan had described, was closed and no exceptions: "Security." Daniel knew the checkpoint had been open that morning and asked politely if the soldier was sure. Yes, he was sure, and now he was angry. He thought we were trouble, and started to shout, but then another man in uniform appeared. Slight, polite, and apologetic, he spoke in Hebrew to the burly man and told us: "Wait here." We waited. It didn't matter, waiting, we were used to it. Then the slight soldier motioned us to go through. The burly one had disappeared.

We passed through and curved down the hill on a hairpin bend. Now I could see where the footpath led: it was the checkpoint bypass. The Palestinians knew they would not be allowed through the checkpoint so they were walking around it to one of the yellow taxis waiting on the other side. The old, bent and leaning on sticks, found the rocky steepness difficult. The young helped them.

We drove on, through the biblical landscape toward Bethlehem, into the village of Beit Sahour, now a suburb with squares of olive orchard and blocks of concrete houses, past the Shepherds' Field and Manger Square, doubling back where the roads were blocked by earth-mounds or trenches dug by the army. But there was no traffic, the place was still. We drove across the middle of Bethlehem, past the hospital where I had given birth, and out again through another suburb-village, Beit Jala, up the hill and past the church and the well and out to coils of barbed wire: another checkpoint. Again, it was a checkpoint between two Palestinian areas, well inside the West Bank.

"You can't pass. And all of Bethlehem is under curfew." This explained the midday quiet of the town. The soldier was very young indeed. He had his orders not to let anyone through his checkpoint. But he checked to make sure, at a concrete pillbox just behind, with more soldiers away to the left watching from under the drapes of camouflage.

"You cannot pass," he came back to say. "You have to go back."

"You're sending us back during curfew? People get shot for breaking the curfew."

"No, we never shoot people for breaking the curfew. The army doesn't do that." We said nothing. It is always better to say nothing. Anyway, it wasn't his fault.

We doubled back. Now that we knew about the curfew the quietness was frightening. Rather than go back into the curfew we tried the road by the monastery of Cremisan. After the dry earth west of Bethlehem, Cremisan was green, damp, and fertile. Vines and terraces fell away below us and rose upward from the narrow road. Round the curve between stone walls the monastery facade appeared amid pointing cypress trees. The presence of water seeped through the green. But this road was blocked as well, three monks from Europe told us.

We had no choice but to go back through the curfew, through Bethlehem and out through yet another checkpoint.

Living in Jerusalem and working in the Occupied Territories means that you see a great many soldiers. One afternoon the young officer son of some Israeli friends sat down on the leather sofa in his parents' house and talked to me about working in the territories. He was intelligent and thoughtful, sensitive and expressive, speaking slowly with long pauses while he searched his mind. Every word he said was weighed, not because he was afraid of saying the wrong thing to me—an outsider, a goy—but because he was working out what it meant to him. He was working out how it was that he had ended up doing the things he didn't want to tell me about.

He was not the sort of soldier who would swing open the door of his jeep and rake bullets into a house under curfew, killing a woman on her porch in the process (the mother of one of our friends died in this way). But he had had to do things that he found unacceptable and had ended up asking for a transfer. Perhaps he was seeking control over his actions; perhaps he just wanted to escape. It wasn't his fault that he'd had to do terrible things to defend his country. But that was the nub of what he was trying to sort out in his head.

He talked of the need to sustain military order—"if that goes, then you're really in trouble"—and his understanding of "what the reality means," the reality of why they were there in the first place.

"All that the Palestinians wanted was to get to their fields or to the house to see Grandma, but we were trained to think of them as the enemy. That everyone is a potential saboteur." Some of the officers were more aggressive and let the troops have their head. "Oh, they all emphasize the need to be polite," he said. "But many of them are looking for a fight. It's boring. They're soldiers. The same Palestinians come back again and again, saying they want to get to their fields—or to Grandma's house—and you've sent them back an hour ago, and yesterday, twice, and you have to send them back again—but our orders are to keep them away from the settlers. That's our job, you see."

Soldiers contend with villagers sitting in front of army bulldozers, begging them not to demolish their houses or their orchards; with Palestinian farmers who want to harvest the olives from their trees; and with Jewish settlers who tell the soldiers this land was given to them by God 3,000 years ago and who are you to stand in our way when we drive off the Palestinians and take the olives? They are *our* olives: God gave them to us. And the Palestinians are pleading—our grandfathers planted these trees, please, protect us from the settlers. Then the Israeli peace activists try to intervene and say that the law we follow is man's law and if we follow God's law we'll be stoning each other for our transgressions, for God's sake. And the children come back from school and are trying to get to the village to do their homework and the settlers attack them with dogs and chains because this is *our* land, God gave it to us, and the Israeli peace activists say again, what kind of Israel do you want? And there they are, the soldiers, stuck in the middle, trapped.

And they know that anyone approaching them might be strapped with explosives and ready to die.

Some deal with their fears by thinking they no longer care about anything, wearing apathy like a shield. In Hebron a soldier shot the legs off two kids but, he said, nothing bad happened to him, it didn't affect him. Another said shooting was the "IDF soldier's way of meditating. It's like shooting is your way of letting go of all your anger when you're in the army." There's also "punitive shooting"—opening fire on whatever you like: on windows with washing hanging up to dry, knowing there were people who would be hit.[2] But the shield confuses the soldiers when they get home because the violence must not follow them; they must leave it somewhere, and that isn't always easy. There's no room in Israeli life for firing on children, for example: that couldn't be real, could it? Surely that doesn't happen. Israelis talk about the bubble—the place where what goes on in the Occupied Territories can't touch them. It is a place to hide.

Driving back to Jerusalem, I wondered about Ghassan. About him seeing the concrete wall towering between him and the short distance to his wife and toddling son, about him applying for a permit to be allowed to see the two of them, about his ordeal of waiting and humiliation. General Gilad had been in earnest when he said that half the checkpoints had been removed and that the Barrier would make life better for Palestinians inside it because there would be fewer checkpoints. Inside. And did he know the number of internal checkpoints had not decreased, nor leveled off, but had actually increased?

The bubble again, hiding from hearing the prejudices: people saying the word "Palestinian" and meaning terrorist, the word "Jew" and being full of hate. People who hadn't seen, or didn't want to know, or if they had been here, seeing out of one eye. And in a way I envied them their one-eyed view; simple, straightforward, knowing where you stand, stark in black and white, all sorted out, not torn. But one-eyed views didn't fix: I had stood at a party abroad holding a glass of wine and listened to foreign male certainty brush aside the things I'd seen, imposing their distant diagnoses, and I had hurried back to Jerusalem to listen to old hands who had watched for years, decades, and who admitted they had no answers and were still able to see the humanity of both sides.

I thought of trenches I had seen dug and closures tightened even as the IDF announced that closures were being eased; of conversations with foreign military observers who said time and again that the upper tiers of the army didn't know what the unit commanders and ranks were doing; of Israeli friends' shock at the finding that, even in the first few days of the Intifada, unit commanders made decisions without asking senior officers who would have said no, and then there were riots, and people—their own citizens, Palestinian Israelis—were killed.

I remembered the face of an Israeli friend, drained into anguish waiting for her soldier son to come home, then silently putting him to sleep in his boyhood bed—only he still is a boy, just eighteen—and she's wondering if she should look in his pockets to try to understand what it is that he's been doing on duty and won't talk about, just clams up. And the teacher, a settler, at my boys' school who wept in class for her baby niece shot dead by a Palestinian gunman; and the other teachers telling her class of mostly Palestinian children that she was weeping because she had a headache.

I thought of the children shot dead by army snipers as they played soccer or sat at their desks in school, their friends splattered with their blood. Of the maze of lies, and the voices pushing from abroad, the one dictating the "reality," the other interpreting it for their own use. And the voices on the ground, from both sides, crying out for reason and moderation and understanding, and for dialogue. The gags on those voices, the extremism, the blind convictions and the willful misunderstanding. And of the many Israeli peace activists, explaining to us whenever we saw them: "People don't know 'the situation,' because they are sold a version and because of the 'bubble.'"

I thought of the black-haired firebrand journalist, beating the table at the smart East Jerusalem restaurant with her fists, her bracelets crashing, saying, "The army and the settlers hit us again and again and again and here and here and here and take our land and break our trees and kill our kids day after day after day and then 'BOOM' and everyone is *surprised*?"

I thought of the hundreds of dead whose lives are cut short, and the maimed whose lives are ruined, and all Israelis and Palestinians living in fear, even the general at the top. Everyone trapped, wondering how to get out of the *situation*. The reality for so many: that, as the journalist said, 'it's easier to reach heaven than the end of the street."

And the why? The layers of complication and interpretation, and the flow of hate and love in this land, and a vengeful God sitting somewhere in the middle, and Peter's question, how to get out, unanswered, and the block on doing anything to sort it out because—well, just because.

But it doesn't help to get angry.

1

A Forest of Peace

When we finally uprooted from New York to Jerusalem in the summer of 2000 the situation was very different; there were negotiations and hope, and I had not seen checkpoints or settlements or suicide bombs or laws that kept children from living with their parents. I had been different too. I had not been someone who interviewed generals or wrote articles about places where we had lived. That began later, as a result of "the situation."

Our previous move—to New York in 1992—had been easy. We were then working in Pakistan and Afghanistan, newly married, and I was a junior surgeon in the main hospital in Islamabad. When Andrew was posted to UN headquarters in New York, we packed our few suitcases and went. Transferring from New York to Jerusalem was more complicated: we now had three children. Swept along by the HIV/AIDS crisis, my career had morphed from surgeon to public health researcher: I had examined the role of the uterine cervix in transmission of the virus, worked in South Africa testing HIV-prevention methods and evaluating condom availability and then, back in New York, helped update doctors and nurses caring for people living with HIV.

With his new posting to the Middle East, Andrew had left New York ahead of me and the children, starting his new job as I finished mine (wondering what I would do next) and the children wrapped up their school year. While I sat on benches in New York parks or sofas in Upper East Side drawing rooms listening to New York friends who knew Jerusalem, Andrew talked to our French-Israeli friend, Ofer, who found us the house in East Jerusalem.

One of Ofer's Palestinian friends had moved to Geneva with his Dutch wife, leaving their Jerusalem home empty: they needed a tenant and we wanted a house with a view. We took it and moved our life from New York to a village in Jerusalem, home to two families, one extended Palestinian and one Jewish. The New Yorkers who insisted that, even if living in Arab East Jerusalem were feasible, such a thing as a village in Jerusalem could not exist, turned out to be wrong. There are surprising patches of rural life left in the Holy City. The largest is the "Forest of Peace" to the south of the Old City, and it remains undeveloped partly because it was No Man's Land, patrolled by the UN, between 1948 and 1967. In and around the pines and dusty patches of forest are a number of Palestinian hamlets. "Hamlet" is a lush word; these places are dry for most of the year. The houses' bare walls with odd-placed windows sham lushness thanks to small gardens of powdery vines and spots of watered green: olive trees, figs, a rose or two.

Our house, in a garden of well-watered green, was near the top of the Forest of Peace on a hill called the Hill of Evil Counsel. Angled and concrete, veneered in limestone, with marble floors and bathroom walls, it looked out over the valleys of Kidron and Hinnom. Like the other houses, ours grew out of the slope of the "mountain," as the villagers called it, with most of its windows to the front. Unlike the other houses, ours was not originally built out from a cave in the hillside. Inside, it was simple, white and modern, as I saw at 3 AM when we first arrived from the airport. We filed through the living room, an expanded corridor pierced by a spiral staircase leading to a room below, filled the three bedrooms, and fell asleep trying to make out the Dome of the Rock in the darkness.

Four generations of one Palestinian family lived in our hamlet. We understood that the Jewish family, who were Orthodox and private, preferred to keep to themselves and did not want to get to know the bounding British children from New York. We rarely saw them. The Palestinians, on the other hand, were happy to know us. Our landlord, uncle to most of them, had told Andrew that if we needed help, all we had to do was stand in the garden and shout for one of his nephews—"Ahmed!"—and sixteen-year-old Ahmed would appear to carry out whatever service we needed, like running off to pay utility bills. Such imperiousness was uncomfortable and from another era; Ahmed became a friend. I could pay the bills myself.

In the sharp Jerusalem light of our first morning, a few hours after we had landed, a young woman peered round the green metal garden gate to say hello, followed by three dark-eyed daughters. Maha introduced herself, promising to tell us everything we needed to know: the shops, the supermarkets, and the secrets of the Old City. Then she and her daughters—the children eyeing each other like the cats that seemed to be everywhere—showed us the fruit trees in our garden, the figs ripening by the garden wall, the peach, grapefruit, and lemon trees. They walked us across the yard to the little farm and introduced us to the rest of the family.

Our children, fresh from a New York Chelsea childhood of asphalt playgrounds and trees with their lower branches sawn off to prevent climbing accidents, looked about them in wonder: there were not only trees to scale, fields and forest to explore, but horses to ride, dogs to roam with, and goats to herd.

The head of the family, a small man in his eighties with a bad cough, welcomed us formally. "I understand English ways," he said. He had worked for the British during the Mandate. Palestine was governed by the British after the First World War until 1948, when partition (passed by the UN in November 1947) was intended to create two states with an economic union. The UN plan allocated 44 percent of the land for the majority Palestinian population and 56 percent of the land for the minority Jewish population (who owned 7 percent of the land). In the resulting war of 1948, the new Jewish state ended up with 78 percent of Palestine; the Palestinian state remains unfounded.

"You gave Palestine away—not that it was yours to give," said Maha's husband Mohammed later, "—but we forgive you." They laughed, and we laughed. The old man, Abu Anis, and his wife Fawziya were preparing a feast, the traditional way to mark the arrival of guests: piled platters of *musakhan* (chicken with onions), *falafel, hummus, ruz falastini* (rice with pine nuts and saffron), *tabouleh* and *labaneh* (salty cream cheese), *kubbeh* (patties of ground meat encased in cracked wheat) and *za'atar* (thyme). There were olives and pita bread, vegetables hollowed out and stuffed again, fruits and nuts, and Palestinian sweets: whipped pastries of honey, dates, pistachios, and almonds. And coffee: thick, sugared coffee in tiny china cups.

We sat in their small living room with a huge TV screen against one end showing the news, and one picture on the bare walls, a relief of the Dome of the Rock. The old man sat and watched us, talking of the Mandate, while his plump wife busied in and out, bearing dish after dish, which we didn't dare refuse but could hardly dent. The children, in their fussiness, were no help, except with the conversation, filling in the gaps with requests for more Coke or less chicken and, too loud, "Do I have to eat this?"

The following morning Abu Anis was in the garden watering the flowers. A few minutes later he knocked on the door, bearing a plate of figs he had just picked from one of the trees. For a while our mornings were marked by his offerings and my return offer of coffee. Later we began to find the sight of his bobble-hatted head outside the kitchen window at breakfast-time too predictable—six days a week—and he found that my coffee was never quite right—the cup too big or the sugar too short—so his wife would be summoned down with coffee made correctly. Over the weeks he adjusted the timing of his watering and we breakfasted alone.

One of the hillside's tiny terraces that formed our garden was just big enough for a tray-sized table under a fir tree that creaked in the breeze. From the terrace I would look out over the valley, listening to the noise of goat bells and church bells, muezzins, and children. My nostalgia for New York remained strong, jostling with the excitement at all the newness. Later on Jerusalem would thread its enchantment and I would fall to its allure, but at first all I saw—despite the forest—was a dusty, ungreen, and unwatered land, the dry Judean hills stretching away toward the Dead Sea, whose dark dullness we could glimpse from viewpoints in the neighborhood.

The color green, the wet English green that I had grown up with, was missing. Trying to anchor myself in this new place, I would sit under the fir tree, reading the English-language Israeli papers and gazing over the valley at the Dome of the Rock, gleaming small but supreme in the early light, the al-Aqsa Mosque, the Western Wailing Wall, and the walls of the Old City. On the hill above us were promenades from which to take in Jerusalem, and, beyond them, at the summit of the Hill of Evil Counsel, Government House, built by the British, an austere monument to imperial control with Hindu swastika motifs embedded in its pre-war, limestone walls.

Andrew would hurry back from work, glad to be with the family again after months without us. We would talk, sit, drink, and he would play with the children. I would have done my playing with the children by the time he came home. Most evenings we would walk in the Forest of Peace. On that first evening we had met a family of French Orthodox Jews, like us enjoying the cool of the evening in one of the playgrounds. Our children were due to start at the French lycée; perhaps these children went there too? We talked, the children played together, and then as the family made to leave the parents told us to be careful not to stay beyond dusk.

"There's an Arab village nearby," they explained.

We had just set down the bones of an exchange. Was I now going to tell them that the village they were afraid of was our home, and that the Arabs who lived there were just then preparing a welcoming dinner for us? One minute we were two families in a playground, then, with a sentence of goodwill, of kind advice, we were about to step over a drawn line and take sides. I was back to the drawing rooms of the Upper East Side and the park in Union Square, hearing assumptions I was expected to share. Since the assumptions didn't fit with the little I had seen so far, I said nothing.

I was at sea, not knowing how to find the comfort of the familiar. Apart from Maha, whose world was so unknown to me, I didn't know whom to call, even what to do with the children when they weren't playing with the children next door. I had put my work aside for the moment, to give the children the time and attention they needed to settle in, and I had never been good at domesticity. No doubt everything would fall into place in a few weeks, but for the moment even the basics were baffling: reading ingredient labels in the grocery store and signs over the shop doors—everything was written in Hebrew and not always translated. Were they grocery stores? Newly illiterate, I was never sure until I was inside, pressing the avocados. Once home, I would put the groceries by my laptop on the kitchen table, examine what I had bought, set something to cook and the children to play, and then write it all down, emailing friends abroad for companionship. And of course, the children, being children, were now teaching me.

To give me mobility and not to leave me stranded when he was at work, Andrew took me out to hire a vehicle. Driving the just rented car, I gingerly followed him out of the garage. I lost him immediately in the banter of traffic and found myself in a line for a checkpoint, with no map, no idea of what to say to the soldiers and no idea how to get home.

My first checkpoint, and I was clueless. All the vehicles were funneled into one lane that chicaned through a row of concrete cubes a meter high. Pedestrians were channeled through another chicane. I would soon learn that the crux of the checkpoint is the Israeli soldier, armed, bored, and powerful. He decides if you pass or not. Only the speed varies: permission can be instantaneous— the soldier's nod—not for hours, or not at all. Faces in the line show resignation, irritation, humiliation. There were few discernible security measures, no searches, little screening of ID. Hang on, did I have the right ID? I swallowed panic. The soldier glanced at my car and waved me through. Andrew was waiting for me on the other side, patient as I threw my angry fear at him.

Now that I had a car, like many Israelis I took to driving to Bethlehem to buy supplies. A few minutes from Jerusalem,

Bethlehem belies the carol sheets. It is large and sprawling, with refugee camps* sewn into the fabric of the city, story piled on story, alleys widening into main roads and narrowing, without warning, into nothing. Manger Square is one of many places where the threads of a Christian education lead you to expect one thing and you find another: a huge concourse flanked by modern buildings and the ancient fortress church built by Constantine's mother over the caves where Christ was born. Whatever I had expected, I grew used to the town as it stood, and went frequently.

I needed help in the house if I was to get back to work in public health research, as well as to regain some control and independence. I wanted all three, but I was hesitant, telling myself I must see the children settled properly before I worked too hard. Two women in the village, Delal and Naimi, were keen to help, but were forbidden to take the job. Maha explained. It was not acceptable to work in a man's house unless he was a husband or relative. She dismissed this as "bullshit," old-fashioned and irrelevant—"if a woman wants to have a job, why not?" asked Maha. But she couldn't impose her views: Naimi was her mother-in-law, Delal her aunt.

Instead, Maha found me a helper who could overcome the cultural constraints to work in our house. One of her acquaintances from Beit Sahour needed a job. Maha arranged the interview and asked her to bring me some meat from a Bethlehem butcher she recommended. Dina arrived with chicken and beef. The chicken still had its head on; I didn't look at the beef. She changed her shoes, started preparing the food, and we talked. Christian, well educated and lively, she spoke English very well, like almost everyone I had met so far, except Abu Anis and his wife. The problems, as I then

---

* *With the war of 1948–9 resulting in hundreds of thousands of people fleeing their homes in Palestine, refugees (more fled in the war of 1967) were housed in refugee camps in Jordan, Lebanon, Syria, the West Bank, and the Gaza Strip. Many of these refugees and their descendants remain there still, partly because they have not been allowed back to their homes or compensated, and partly because their Arab hosts (with the exception of Jordan) have refused to integrate them.[1]*

saw it, were her reluctance to work long hours—she wanted to be home by 2PM for the traditional family meal—and transportation. She had her own car but was not permitted to use it beyond the West Bank. As I drove her back that day I could see that I was going to wind up ferrying her much of the time and that didn't make any sense, but it would do for the moment, and we made a temporary arrangement.

On the short journey between Jerusalem and Bethlehem, Dina pointed out two built-up areas, one well-established and one under construction. "You should notice these places: they are illegal settlements," she said. The first was Gilo. The second had two names. Dina called it Jebel Abu Gneim; "the Isra-eelis," she said, using the Palestinian inflection, "call it Har Homa." Over the weeks and months, I watched the two-named settlement grow as I traveled between Jerusalem and Bethlehem. Dina's village was in its lee. "We see it all the time," she said. "We watch our land being taken from us by force or under different 'legal' ruses and then we watch these things being built on our land, but we can do nothing." I dropped her off in Bethlehem, and headed back to Jerusalem.

At home I sat in front of the laptop I had been given before I left New York and wrote. Every detail went down on the screen: my illiteracy, the frustrations of Jerusalem traffic, the children's first days at school, and Jebel Abu Gneim/Har Homa. Some of the details ended up in emails, and I saw that I was screening the details I sent according to the sensibilities of each friend. I was choosing details I thought each one would accept, but the touchstone was not interest or hobby or like-stage in career. It was politics—the situation—and one of the criteria was to avoid being judged.

The rhythm of school was beginning to give me grounding. The children were making friends; Xan in particular with a French boy called Balthazar. Some of the parents—Hazel, Libby, Mike, and Steve—had become "co-parents" and were helping me navigate the unknown. I was slowly—for the moment—getting used to being dependent on Andrew, and thanks to Naimi being able to babysit unofficially, we were seeing something of Jerusalem and Tel Aviv by night. The buzz of our new life was beginning to trump the frustrations.

In order to keep up, I would buy either the *Jerusalem Post* or the *International Herald Tribune*, which came folded inside the English edition of *Ha'aretz*. In the *Jerusalem Post* I read the story of a Jewish family who almost drowned in the Sea of Galilee; a young Palestinian Israeli swam out and rescued them but died in the process, and the newspaper led a campaign to raise money for his widow and their two toddlers. One morning the newsagent said: "Sorry, no English papers today." The man behind me smiled, chiding: "You should be practicing your Hebrew." He assumed I was making *aliya*. I looked confused, so he explained: if I were Jewish, under the Law of Return I could settle in Israel and take Israeli citizenship. I would be encouraged to learn Hebrew as quickly as possible, and would enroll in intensive language classes.*

One Saturday Andrew and I drove the children to Jaffa for lunch with Ofer, the friend who had found us our house. Jaffa, an ancient port abandoned overnight by many of its inhabitants fleeing the advancing Israeli forces in 1948, is now mixed, with rich beachside houses and poor broken-down homes abutting each other: villas with columns and balconies next to wire-bound shanties with pecking chickens. Ofer and his wife Halley lived with their three children in a shady ochre house filled with New York furniture. Halley emerged from the bedroom and beamed at us. We sat for a while, reminiscing about New York and mutual friends.

---

* *The revival of Hebrew is impressive. An ancient Semitic language, it was given life by the efforts of Eliezer Ben Yehuda, a revolutionary in Tsarist Russia who emigrated to Palestine in the wave of aliya during the 1880s. Recognizing the need for a common language among the new immigrants, he set about forming one from biblical Hebrew and a range of other languages including Yiddish. The result of his work is now the native language of Israelis.*

Halley's youngest, Max, was older than Catriona's sixteen months, and I told myself this justified Halley's working and my not. And I'd just arrived. It had nothing to do with inertia, fear, or lack of self-esteem, nothing at all. Halley's success as a photographer put her in a different frame; since arriving I had sat in a box labeled "wife," and had done nothing to change that, so far. New life was one thing, becoming a part of it was another, and I was listening, watching, taking it all in, as a passenger. This place was full of options and I would wait, I told myself. In a few weeks, things would look more settled; no need to rush.

Ofer and Halley took us to a restaurant overlooking the beach, blown by the breeze and safe enough for the six children to roam about while we drank arak and white wine.

Catriona sat in a plastic highchair, playing with bread and calamari. Archie and Xan, six and three, followed eleven-year-old Elamar, who had a Discman and a problem at school. Halley told us about it.

His class had been set an assignment: make up a board game. Being a fan of MTV, Elamar applied lessons learned there to his homework. His mother found herself summoned to a conference with the teacher and the headmistress. The two women lambasted her in Hebrew, which she didn't speak well, so she responded in English. Her son's project, they told her, had been entitled "Monopoly of Sex." The first square had been "buy a condom," the second, "book a hotel room" (he'd named the one his grandparents stayed in during their visit), the third was "meet Madonna," the fourth "kiss," and so on. They demanded to know what he was seeing, reading, listening to, and being subjected to at home. She battled her way out of the interview.

A couple of days later the teacher said, "I've been having sleepless nights about you and your son. But I've worked out what the problem is."

"Oh yes," said Halley, "and what is that?"

"He's been spending time in America."

We laughed and headed for the beach.

Back in Jerusalem I was beginning to feel the "situation" weave itself into the days. Ofer had talked about his work bringing Palestinian and Israeli youth together and the web of problems he faced. Halley worried about the effects of living in a militarized society: both of them dreaded their children's conscription. Dina, who most days was managing to get to work without a lift from me, brought daily details of encounters with the occupation—she was not complaining but I had to ask why she was late so often and I couldn't blame her for the checkpoint delays that thwarted her attempts to leave extra time, or for her mornings standing in line at the Israeli Ministry of the Interior for her permit. Twice she stood in the heat all morning only to be told when she reached the front that the office had just been closed and she must start again another day.

I was finding that the situation was like the stone and the light of Jerusalem: mesmerizing. Everyone talks about it, but it is hard to put a finger on. The light and the stone only go so far in explaining Jerusalem's appeal; the fear and the terror that General Gilad later described and we experienced only go so far in explaining the situation. And fear was an option that very few resisted. Something happens to everyone in Jerusalem. Not in the ordinary way that things happen, but in a specific, Jerusalem way. After all, we lived just across the valley from Hell. Hell, according to biblical lore, was the Hinnom Valley, where children were burned alive as sacrifices to the god Moloch, and where Isaiah and Jeremiah prophesied that the fires of punishment would burn, an abyss of damnation. It now houses a movie theater.

I soon found that when you arrive in Jerusalem you land not so much in hell as in a maelstrom that has swallowed thousands before you and will swallow thousands more. Eventually you are spat out, land in a heap, and shake down the reality and drama of the place. People say the place has bad vibes. It is Jerusalem Syndrome, but not as it was described to me by a French psychiatrist, a psychosis where visitors wrap themselves in hotel sheets and believe themselves characters from the Bible: I was never Mary Magdalene. Instead personal dramas echo and mirror and fester within the wider human tragedy. Our life, like so many others, was subsumed by the political. The personal became inextricably wound into it, enmeshed, and left us longing for light—quiet, expunging light. So much for my few weeks of settling in: there was just time to touch down before everything went up.

Soon after we arrived, the stones and the light and the legend lured me to the Old City. I would head there before driving to school to pick up the children. Within its walled square mile you can round a corner and be in 17th-century Poland, turn down an alley and be biblical. Costume is transporting: striped coats belted at the waist with cummerbunds, immaculate fur-trimmed hats, stockinged male calves and polished shoes; long robes, unbelted, keffiyehs draped; white robes sweeping, water-pipes coiled among their folds, their owners sitting in the smoke under ceilings of vaulted stone; women in veils, women in hats; hair shaven, heads bewigged, hair hidden, wrapped in secret; sideburns—*peyot*—long and curled with care, beards stark; faces, eyes, mysteries. Stories—a whirl of histories in which every one of us is wrapped. And then back into the isolation of the schoolyard: mothers too harried to be friendly, fathers businesslike, children being much as children anywhere—noisy, running, breathless, the older ones disdainful, testing, flaunting, laden with books, hormones, and expectations.

On a brilliant September Sunday we took the children to the Old City. We began with a walk along the ramparts, the majestic walls of the Old City that have come to signify Jerusalem and were built in the 16th century by the Ottoman sultan, Suleiman the Magnificent. We started from the Damascus Gate, abuzz with Palestinian vendors, hawkers, veiled old women squatting on the floor beside pyramids of figs, melons, and sheaves of fig leaves. It's a fine place to enter the Old City, right bang into the bustle of it. At the Jaffa Gate we toiled up twisting flights of steps and caught our breath at the top of the

ramparts. There was the whole city, laid out, rigid in the upright
shadows, meeting all expectations. The Sunday School image of
Jerusalem has squat square buildings topped with domes, with shady
palms and corrals of sand sheltering animals for stars to shine on. Now
there is no sand and there are few animals, but much of the Old City
bears out the image, and throws in minarets and bell towers, Mamluk
and Byzantine, Christian domes and Arab domes in metal, silver, gold,
and stone, flights of alam and crucifix, bustling blocks of old and new,
arches and buttresses, all pale stone, emerald tile and shaded green,
clustered within the great thick walls we stood on.

As we circled the Old City the boys played crusaders between
battlements, and then we descended back into the bustle. A film
crew blocked our way down, and we had to watch actor Jean-
Claude Van Damme perform before we were allowed by. We paid
a short visit to the Church of the Holy Sepulcher in the Christian
Quarter, where the English friend who had come with us was
moved to tears by the elderly pilgrims kneeling to kiss the stone on
which Jesus was laid out. It is called the Stone of Unction and dates
from 1810.

It is not unreasonable to look for spiritual tranquility in the city
of monotheism, but there is none in the relations between the different churches controlling Christendom's most holy place; perhaps
this is not surprising. The Greek, the Armenian, and the Syrian
Orthodox churches, the Latins, the Ethiopians, and the Copts have
fought savagely over portions of the Church of the Holy Sepulcher
for centuries. In a land choked by territorial wars, the church at the
center of the Christian faith is no exception. Stories of priests wran-
gling over space and jostling over rights echo British Mandate
records that tell of officials wrestling with the claims of the various
Christian sects—infighting so intense and full of loathing that for
several hundred years the key to the Holy Sepulcher has been held
for safekeeping by a Muslim family, the Nusseibehs.

Our final visit was to the place that to Jews is Temple Mount and
to Arabs is al-Haram al-Sharif, the "Noble Sanctuary." It would be my

last chance: a few days later the Intifada would close the site to all non-Muslims. Despite its extraordinary serenity, the place is fraught with religious significance, legend, and history. It is a manmade table mountain, shored up by massive walls whose vast dimensions were created 2,000 years ago by Herod the Great. On top, where the First and Second Temples once stood, are a number of separate buildings, not only the Dome of the Rock and al-Aqsa Mosque, but also colonnaded gates and lesser domes, madrasas, covered arcades, and a Mamluk fountain offering pilgrims sweet water.

The Umayyad Dome of the Rock, which adorns the Temple Mount/al-Haram al-Sharif, and the al-Aqsa Mosque 150 yards away, form the third holiest site in the Islamic world. The whole area serves as a mosque, the acres of open space filled with praying Muslim worshippers every Friday. I was happy to loiter about, not yet over-aware of the place's heavy political weight. There had been many attacks on the Temple Mount and plots to destroy the Dome: an Australian Christian, an American convert to Judaism, a Jewish sect of moon-worshippers, a gang of yeshiva students, and a group of West Bank settlers have all had a go at the site, burning, shooting, and killing, or plotting to dynamite the Dome of the Rock and thereby hurry along the Messiah. Some were deranged, others were politically and religiously motivated. A few were ranking army officers and confessed to a string of terrorist acts. Whatever the mental state of the attackers, no one doubted where conflict over the Temple Mount could lead.

Belief and commitment aside, the Dome of the Rock makes you stand, shoeless, and gaze. It has inspired Christians not only to wonder at its spirituality and beauty but also to bemoan the failure of the nearby Church of the Holy Sepulcher to come anywhere close. It gleams golden across the valleys: a marriage of sublime architectural harmony and mathematical perfection, the experts say. In the middle of the building there is a rock. It sits, bald, unworked, and misshapen, at the center of so much exquisite mosaic and green and blue tile; it is, variously, the place of Adam's birth and burial, the resting place of David's Ark, the scene of Abraham's readiness to sacrifice Isaac, and the site of Mohammed's ascent to heaven. The rock, it is said, tried to show how much it revered the Prophet by following him heavenward, but was held down by the archangel, whose handprint remains on its rough surface.

You can believe what you like of the legends and whispers and mysteries, but you cannot underestimate the significance of the Temple Mount/al-Haram al-Sharif for millions of Jews and hundreds of millions of Muslims. And this is where, on September 28, 2000, Ariel Sharon came marching in.

2

"All Changed, Changed Utterly"

After thanking Abu Anis and his wife for dinner on our first night in Jerusalem, Andrew and I stood outside our new home in the balmy evening air and looked across the Kidron Valley to the Old City beyond. Andrew, a political officer for the UN office dealing with the Middle East peace process, had warned me on the journey from the airport the night before: "I don't want to alarm you, but tensions are so high among the Palestinians over what they didn't get at Camp David that they could explode at any moment. The fuse could be lit by any little thing."

I was not alarmed. I didn't believe him. Breathing in the jasmine, we talked about the enchantment of our new life in Jerusalem, and then we talked about the situation: Israel had just withdrawn its troops and ended its occupation of Southern Lebanon. This, carried out in conjunction with the UN, was a success and Prime Minister Ehud Barak was exultant at pulling off such a political coup. Many saw it as a brave and important step that might lead to a wider peace.

Negotiations with Syria to end another occupation—that of the Golan Heights—failed. Barak turned instead to the issue of Israel's occupation of the West Bank and the Gaza Strip. When those negotiations—at Camp David in July 2000—ended in failure, with Arafat blamed by Barak and Clinton, Israel and the Palestinians went back to the table. Negotiations continued, but now in an atmosphere of desperation—despite the seven-year peace process, the occupation had worsened for the Palestinians—spiced with some hope, since Barak appeared to be serious about reaching a solution.

For us, four weeks in, everything changed. One minute we were seeing two peoples make a reasonable effort to get along in very difficult circumstances. The next minute there was unrepressed violence and mutual distrust, with no sign at all of a terrible beauty being born. Hate and fear had been unleashed and would spread unrestrained.

On Thursday, September 28, 2000, opposition Member of the Knesset (MK) Ariel Sharon took a walk on Temple Mount. Sharon knew—everyone knew—that this was a supremely provocative act: provocative to the Palestinians and provocative to Israel's Labor government and Prime Minister. Sharon read the situation masterfully. It was not just Palestinians' loathing toward him, based on his past treatment of them,* that made his walk incendiary. It was also timing. The negotiations at Camp David had been supposed to complete the Oslo peace process, which many had believed would end Israel's occupation of the West Bank and Gaza Strip. Instead, Camp David showed how far the occupation had deepened and how distant real peace remained. For Sharon, his walk was a winner either way: if he was allowed through he could guarantee Palestinian outrage and out-hardline his rival for the right-wing Likud party, the former prime minister Binyamin Netanyahu. If he was not allowed through, Sharon could claim that Barak had lost Jewish sovereignty over the Temple Mount. On top of preying on Israelis' fear of losing Judaism's most sacred site, Sharon could prick their horror at the division of Jerusalem (East for the Palestinians, and West for the

---

* For example, Qibya, a West Bank village, 1953: in a reprisal raid, Sharon's Unit 101 blew up 45 houses with the occupants inside, killing 67 people. The twelve-month "Pacification of Gaza," 1971: a harsh policy of repression, blowing up houses, bulldozing large tracts of refugee camps, severe collective punishments, imprisoning hundreds of young Palestinians, with numerous civilians killed or imprisoned, and many others transported into the Sinai desert, Jordan, or Lebanon. Sabra and Shatila, refugee camps in Lebanon, 1982: during Israel's invasion of Lebanon, the IDF allowed far-right Christian Phalangists to enter the camps and hundreds of Palestinian civilians were massacred. The ensuing Kahan commission recommended the removal of Sharon as Minister of Defense.

Israelis). He sensed Barak's vulnerability and, at over 70 years old, he was in a hurry to have the premiership for himself.*

Meanwhile, I had parked on Ethiopia Street and walked off through the bone-dry heat to pick up the boys from school. On our way back, the boss of the car-rental company appeared. One of his employees had passed my car, seen its livery and noticed that the rear window had been smashed. He had called his boss. Boss and I now approached the car and the group of men surrounding it. Their postures spoke aggression: stiff and animal, more rooster than pitbull, but unmistakable.

The men surrounding the car saw me, a foreign woman, approaching. "Is this your car?" they said. "Do you know this man?" pointing to someone in the driver's seat, the car company employee.

I said "No," as I couldn't really see him and didn't immediately recognize what I could see.

For them this was confirmation. "He's trying to steal your car." They were sure. "We've been watching him for an hour." The men had been working in a building next to the car and had dropped a piece of masonry from the upper floor, smashing the rear window. They were fully insured and ready to give all the necessary details, but they had no idea who the man in the driving seat was, and they took him for a thief. He had tried to explain who he was, but he fit the "thief" bill, and they were sticking with it.

The truth was easily explained, and immediately, sensibly, everyone was smiles and handshakes, exchanging insurance details and no hard feelings, even friendly slaps on the back. The builders who had broken the window were Israeli, and the car-company employees were Palestinian. After the repercussions of Ariel Sharon's Temple Mount stunt that day, such a misunderstanding would no longer end with Israelis and Palestinians shaking hands and slapping each other on the back.

*Of the two main Israeli political parties, Labor was in power until 1977. Likud, which originated from several right-wing nationalist parties, has held power for much of the time since then. When Likud is in power, Labor tends to adopt a more moderate policy toward the Palestinians. Labor has served in Likud-led coalitions.

Sharon's short stroll, accompanied by more than a thousand heavily armed Israeli police, was fine footage for the world's media that night. Everyone's news carried images of the portly Sharon jostled in the throng of protective police power, and of the inevitable scuffles with resentful Palestinians that ensued. The following day was Friday, the Muslim holy day, when believers must pray at the mosque. The headlines in the *Jerusalem Post* that morning were of stone-throwing Palestinians, duly provoked by Sharon's visit. More anger was likely. Even so, there was no notion of what was to come. I had no idea at all.

During Friday's midday prayers an army of Israeli police waited just outside the Maghrabi Gate, the route for non-Muslims on to Temple Mount/al-Haram al-Sharif. Goaded by the words of the imam and by Sharon's affront to Palestinian pride, worshippers came out of the mosque and began throwing stones. The police charged and, within minutes, began to shoot the Palestinians with rubber-covered bullets. I soon learned that these are not the rarely lethal "rubber bullets": they are steel bullets with a veneer of rubber and frequently fatal. The details of the day began to spin about, and be spun, my first taste of the importance of "version." The Israeli police fired on the Palestinians to protect Jewish worshippers at the Western Wall; yet the Jewish worshippers had been evacuated within minutes of the first stone being thrown.[1]

The first I knew of the rioting was seeing ambulances, sirens blaring, speeding around the walls of the Old City to pick up the wounded. Phalanxes of heavily protected professional police had used gunfire against rioters throwing stones. And then I heard that people were being killed. Not trampled underfoot or crushed against a barrier, but shot by police snipers.

People were muttering that this could only be bad, even ominous, for everyone. There was immediately an argument between waiting parents in the schoolyard. "How typical," one parent said, "of the Palestinians to be violent. Force is the only way to deal with them." Another was even angrier: "Force?" he was

saying, "in any normal country of course riots mean *force*, yes—
police in riot gear, tear gas, water cannon, baton charges. But what
kind of control is this? Who controls a riot with snipers?"

I gathered the children and hurried home to wait. The electronic news was telling us that hundreds had been injured and that
four people were dead. My neighbors' televisions were alive.
Conversations huddled around them, and newcomers gathered.
They saw me and let me in. "So now you see," said one. "They
know that there are no armed people on al-Haram al-Sharif, but
they are shooting us with their guns."

"This is not the first time," said another, grimly. 'Only four
years ago they killed three Palestinians for throwing stones on al-
Haram al-Sharif. They do whatever they want."

"But snipers? Shooting rioters?"

"Yes, even snipers. Welcome to Jerusalem. What we can do?"
said his wife.

Seventy policemen had been lightly injured by stones; one was
moderately injured. Many of the dead and wounded Muslim
worshippers had been shot in the upper body and head. Journalists
had also been shot, others were beaten up by police; some were
beaten up and shot.[2] Medical crews were fired on and onlookers
hit.[3] Many of the ambulances I had seen heading for the Old City
were held up by Israeli forces not allowing them to pick up the
dead and wounded. Some policemen helped medics to move the
injured. Other policemen not only made it difficult for anyone to
help the wounded, they fired on them while the wounded were
being evacuated.

Friday: disbelief at the killings. Saturday: eruption. Since there
was no school we stayed at home. With unarmed stone-throwers
gunned down the day before, and apparently only hopelessness to
look forward to, the Occupied Territories exploded. Ordinary
Palestinians, bitter with their leadership, bitter with the occupiers,
rioted everywhere—Jerusalem, Ramallah, Bethlehem, Gaza—and
more stone-throwers were killed, shot dead by Israeli forces.

There were riots in our street. It's a very long street, winding through the forest, so the rioters and the police were a long way from us, but we heard gunshots and explosions and I went out on to the terrace, leaving the children inside. In the distance, mirroring the TV screen, were crowds of people running down the road on the hill opposite, away from plumes of smoke and the soldiers, their jeeps, and their weapons. The herd of goats in the valley between us and the turmoil carried on grazing, their bells jangling.

Then news came through that during fighting between IDF soldiers and Palestinians near an illegal settlement in Gaza, a Palestinian boy had been shot dead by the IDF. If we didn't believe it we could watch it on television, again and again: the terrified boy scrabbling to shelter under his father's arm, a jerk of the camera and dust swirling, then clearing to show the boy slumped on the ground, the father's head sagging, bouncing inhumanly, both shot. And the ambulance driver who tried to help them also shot: dead.

Death on TV, caught by a France 2 camera crew. The death of Mohammed al-Dura mobilized an outcry on every Arab street, including the "Israeli Arab" street. It mobilized friends around the world—Jewish, Zionist, American, European—calling to ask what the hell was going on. Boris Johnson rang from his office at the *Spectator*: "Terrible things going on, terrible. Can't believe what I'm seeing—is it really that bad your end? We could do with a piece—what it's like to be there—working-mother stuff, kids and all that. Have you thought of writing? Could you? 1,200 words? By Monday? Terrific." And with that I began writing, every now and then, about the situation.

Spurred on by the rolling scene of the Palestinian boy dying, outrage spilled over the Occupied Territories and into Israel itself. Israel's Palestinian community, one fifth of the Israeli population, rolled out on the streets, demonstrating against their country's brutal treatment of the Palestinians of the Occupied Territories. Journalists came back from covering the boy's death and talked at length about the details they had witnessed, the examination of the bullet holes in the wall behind the boy that showed the trajectories pointing straight back to an Israeli position.

On Sunday the church bells murmured across our valley, familiar sounds of England and childhood and long walks to church on chilly mornings. There was an unfamiliar murmur mingled with the bells: songs of mourning for the Palestinian dead. Sixteen killed the day before, and hundreds injured. People were counting, wondering: stones and bullets. I couldn't, didn't, say that I was happy to see pale-blue UN flak jackets in the back of Andrew's vehicle as he went out for meeting after meeting, to Gaza and Ramallah, Tel Aviv and Jerusalem, phone to ear, like everyone else, all agencies, diplomats, players, angling for some impact on the chaos of events. Journalists were sleepless, dusty. Flak jackets meant proximity to danger as much as protection from it.

Dina called to say that she was very sorry but she was confined to her house by the IDF and therefore could not get to work. In the village conversations were about the rising numbers of dead and about events: a journalist beaten up by the Israeli police in Jebel Mukaber, our area; a secretary working at al-Makassed Hospital who had come out of her office on the first day and seen Palestinians shot in the eyes. The days' violence, deaths, and mourning had taken on a rhythm: shooting, killing, funerals, demonstrations, more shooting, killing... The sequence scarcely varied. The intensity grew.

A New Zealander from the UN saw me walking in the Forest of Peace and stopped his car. He stuck his head out of the window and grinned, saying our shipment from New York had finally docked—we'd been waiting over a month—and was through customs. "But," he added, "do you really want to unpack it—why not send it straight back to where it came from?"

"Of course I want to unpack it. This can't go on."

But the anger wasn't tailing off and control was not about to be restored. I didn't get it at all: the hate. After dropping off the boys inside the well-protected walled compound of the lycée, I stopped to buy groceries. The kindly storekeeper who had patiently helped me tell yogurt from cream cheese was different. We talked as normal but when I asked him to translate the headlines in the Hebrew press he pointed to the picture of the (dead) boy and said, "He threw stones; he gets shot. So?"

Despite Dina's incarceration, her sister, Muna, had somehow managed to get to our house. Israeli soldiers had stormed her home to take up positions on the roof, from where they shot at boys throwing stones. She had been terrified by the soldiers, her elderly mother even more so, they cowered together as the soldiers rushed in, but Muna was strangely unsurprised by the soldiers firing on boys throwing stones.

Since she had made it to work, I was able to go to the Old City by way of the Dung Gate, the exit for centuries of Jerusalem's garbage. The sudden open space of the Wailing Wall Plaza was a massing military parade: armored vehicles over the flagstones, troops in all directions. The Israeli soldier who screened me asked, "Do you have any weapons?"

"No."

"Any knives?"

"No."

"No? Guns, slings, grenades... bombs?" He was smiling. "Why not?" he added.

Perhaps the level of the escalation, and its implications, had escaped him. Perhaps I didn't understand survival humor. I walked through the Jewish Quarter; everything was open, as though all was well. Signs alerted passersby to a "Pre-Third Temple Sale—buy now before the Third Temple is built and the prices go up." The Cardo, the Roman thoroughfare that is hard to visualize now—cut up, chunks buried, renovated, patched over the years—was trading. Groups of tourists listened to their guide recommending a museum of Jewish life in 19th-century Jerusalem.

The Muslim Quarter was closed by a general strike to protest the killings at the al-Aqsa Mosque. A few people milled about but the ancient covered market, the cotton souk, was almost abandoned. A week ago I had ordered mint tea and watched the sun slide in through Mamluk windows in the vaulted roof. Leaving the Temple Mount/al-Haram al-Sharif I had ventured down the 14th-century steps, under the pink and black interlocking stones of the entrance, into a 300-foot corridor of ancient shops and hammam—baths— busy with 21st-century life and colors. Now it was closed and silent, the dust playing unstirred in the shafts of light.

I picked up the boys, trying not to hear the schoolyard discussions of the situation. People I had begun to know were starting both to lose control and to be strangely accepting. Israelis were not horrified by their forces' killings or by the likelihood of this provoking more bloodshed; they were horrified by the stone-throwing Palestinians. Palestinians were not surprised by Israeli actions, but no Palestinian voices called for the street to quiet down—neither to save the rioters' lives, nor to save the political situation. Everyone was reacting to each event as it occurred, soaking up the version of events given by their own side.

I had avoided it at school, but the situation returned once I reached the house. Muna's husband had called her to say, "Come home, the fighting is very bad," and her anxiety showed. We arranged to meet her husband at the new checkpoint on a back route to Bethlehem to avoid the worst of the fighting. The Israeli checkpoint soldiers saw us approach and moved toward us. They waved their weapons and made throat-slitting gestures to encourage me to stop. Tire-slashers were ranged across the road between the barricades, armored vehicles stood about, and a camouflaged lookout hid more soldiers, their helmets moving. Muna muttered, "Please, don't go yet. If you could wait until I reach the other side. My husband is waiting there. See?" I switched the engine off. Her hand shook as it moved slowly to unlatch the handle of the car door. She got out, still slowly, her head low, walking with careful steps toward the troops. I watched as the soldiers circled and interrogated her, guns at hip. After a long few minutes, they let her through. Her husband also watched, from his distance, unable to help her. Her walk over, she sank into his car and they turned around and left.

Maha was standing in the compound yard when I drove home up the little hill. "Strange people have been walking around here," she said. "We don't know them." Unlike mine, her children had not been able to get to school, and none of the adults had been able to get to work. The children were not playing in the fields and trees; they stayed hidden inside the houses. Maha was afraid, full of unease, unsure of who would protect them if trouble came. Palestinian fears were replacing their rage, but many were still angry at the accusation that it was their own fault they were being killed. One friend had been asked why the Palestinians had overreacted to Sharon's visit. "Surely," it was put to her, "you'd have been wiser to let Sharon's visit go—without the effect he was looking for?"

"They don't understand the significance of Sharon," she told me. "Any other politician would have been different, but this man has the blood of thousands of Palestinians on his hands. Qibya, Gaza, the massacres of Sabra and Shatila—we could *not* ignore his provocation. So we're provoked, and we react by throwing stones, and they shoot people dead...?"

There was a need for someone to blame. Shlomo Ben Ami, said some—blame him, he's the Minister for Public Security, and he's the one who gave permission for Sharon's visit. He said he'd had no choice. The government had been warned not to let Sharon parade on the Temple Mount by its own security forces and by Yasser Arafat.* Later on, the international commission looking into the causes of the al-Aqsa Intifada, led by former US Senator George Mitchell,[5]

---

* *The Israeli security forces had predicted that a visit by Ariel Sharon, "with all he represents to the inhabitants of the territories, would ignite the Palestinian street. Arafat and the security forces called on Barak not to permit the visit, but he closed his ears." Arafat had contacted Prime Minister Barak the evening before to plead with him not to allow the visit, asking "Why would Sharon visit the Holy Mosque now when he did not do so when Begin... was his prime minister or even when he was the triumphant general of war?" Palestinian feelings, warned Arafat, were boiling with discontent.*[4]

concluded that Sharon's visit was a mistake, but "more significant were the events that followed: the decision of the Israeli police on September 29 to use lethal force against the Palestinian demonstrators."[6]

I thought the situation would simmer down; it never did. The *Jerusalem Post* fundraiser for the widow of the Palestinian Israeli hero of the Sea of Galilee continued, despite some letters calling for it to be stopped. Regardless of the recent events, the public's overwhelming opinion was that the campaign should continue. But the IDF were rolling military hardware into Jerusalem, and helicopter gunships fired missiles at apartment blocks in Gaza. Pleas for sense and calm were being ignored. "Can you beat this?" asked one of the long-time observers, "Arafat's appealing to the IDF to use restraint against the stone-throwers, and Israel's appealing to the Palestinians to use restraint against the snipers, tanks, and helicopter gunships!"

In Jerusalem we had helicopters spinning over us to monitor what was happening on the ground, but in Gaza helicopters were shooting missiles, not pictures. Andrew called me as he left Gaza by car.

"I should be home in an hour and a half, but if there's trouble at Erez I may have to turn back."

I said nothing.

"Don't worry," he added, "most of the fighting is supposed to be in the other direction."

I sat in front of the computer, writing my worry into a Word document. It seemed better that way, better than waiting dumbly to hear whether or not he was through Erez. People hated Erez, the main checkpoint in the fence enclosing the Gaza Strip. Not just because of the waiting and checking and interminable delays, nor because of the cattle lines to one side where thousands of Palestinians crushed each morning before dawn, waiting to be let through to their jobs in Israel. Erez was frightening: a gauntlet, hundreds of meters long, walled in concrete, with IDF soldiers sitting in bunkers but no cover for travelers if the shooting started. It was a frequent shooting gallery. Andrew turned back and tried again the next morning.

The Palestinian street was mobilizing. By the third day the Palestinians had added rifles to their stones. "This is the Intifada with guns," said one Palestinian in the village. "First we had only stones, but if they keep killing our children, of course we'll use our guns. What do you expect?" The protests were full of young men and boys throwing stones and Molotov cocktails. After the death of Mohammed al-Dura the protests grew into a civil revolt, attacking the most detested IDF military bases in the Occupied Territories, at Netzarim, which split the Gaza Strip north from south, and at Joseph's Tomb in the middle of Nablus. After nine days, with six Palestinians and one Israeli soldier dead, the IDF withdrew from the post that had turned Joseph's Tomb into a military stronghold, and the Palestinians took over, burning and pillaging.* After forcing the IDF to withdraw here, the Palestinians attacked other settlements, wanting to push out the army elsewhere and jolt awake their leaders, the Palestinian Authority (PA), telling them no more selling out in negotiations. In doing so the Palestinians were painting themselves into their TV stereotype: looting holy sites, giving way to uncontrolled rage.

I kept waiting for someone to calm things down. On the eighth day the Israeli Prime Minister gave the Palestinians an ultimatum: stop demonstrating or the IDF will clamp down for real. Hate was taking over. In the village and beyond, Palestinians' hatred of being occupied, controlled, and repressed was written on so many faces. A surge of Arab hatred of Israel was vivid on the streets of cities across the Arab world. And there was the hatred Israelis had for the Palestinians, not just against the demonstrators, but within Israel, against their own Arab citizens. Israelis knew that, thanks to television, the world was seeing the brutality meted out by their forces on the demonstrating Palestinians. This stoked increasingly bitter claims

---

* The site was later restored by the Palestinian Authority.

that they were acting only in self-defense.

I was also witnessing an urge to punish. The rioters shot down daily was one thing, but there was also the Israeli policy of Closure. I had been aware that life in the West Bank was hobbled by checkpoints: even going to Bethlehem and within Jerusalem, at a-Ram where we had rented the car. But now closures were clamped down like leg irons on the entire populace. It was a medieval siege and could only add to the anger: days of total, 24-hour curfew, a physical blockade to cripple the Palestinian economy, and the IDF smashing olive groves, fruit orchards, businesses, and buildings.

Half our new friends were stuck, immobilized, and humiliated in the Occupied Territories. The scene that I had begun to tap into was suddenly frozen; Palestinians were being killed in significant numbers. And the rest had lost any freedom of movement. Fellow parents at the lycée had to move to relatives' houses on the right side of the checkpoints or their children would go without schooling. Getting to work was fraught and socializing was out of the question.

While the army used tanks and helicopter gunships, mobs went after Palestinian communities inside Israel and in Jerusalem. Palestinian friends living near the seam of East and West Jerusalem were terrorized by crowds chanting "death to the Arabs." One of them called Andrew in tears, asking for his help. "Israeli settlers are attacking us Palestinians," she said. He could hear shouting in the background. "What can I do?" he asked me. Call the police? That was no good; in some places violent settlers were not only ignored but even aided by the security forces, especially in Hebron.[7] It wasn't just that the Israeli government couldn't stop the Palestinian uprising; it appeared to be unable to control their own settlers.

For Israeli friends, what was most shocking was not that the Palestinians of the West Bank and Gaza Strip were rising up against the occupation, but that the Palestinian citizens of Israel were in revolt too. Their own police force was opening fire with live ammunition on Israeli citizens. On October 1, in the Israeli town of Umm al-Fahm the police had killed three Israeli Palestinians and wounded many others. Putting down riots with live gunfire continued across Israel wherever there were Palestinian communities. When President Moshe Katsav announced that he was pleased that the "riots have brought Israelis closer,"[8] he did not have Palestinian Israelis in mind. Thirteen of them were shot dead by the police.

Ten days into the Intifada 95 people were dead: 5 Jewish Israelis killed by Palestinians and 90 Palestinians killed by Israelis. Eighteen of the dead Palestinians were children. About 2,500 Palestinians had been injured, over a third of them children.[9] Like everyone else, I wanted to disbelieve the figures, but there they were. And yet there were voices—in the playground, in the papers—telling us that the high casualty rate was the Palestinians' own fault: Arafat planned the Intifada, and worse, the Palestinians push their children to the front line, they deliberately send their children to their deaths.

When I worked in a hospital in Afghanistan some years back, there was often hard-hearted talk among expats about life for "these people" being cheap, and how they didn't give a damn about their daughters: "You know, they don't even count the girls if you ask how many children they have—they just count the sons." Then one day I was in the casualty unit when a girl of about eight was brought in. She had been hit by a car and she was dead. Her father, his head wrapped in a turban that fit our image of the mujahedin, cradled her small broken form. He was rocking back and forth, tears slipping down his darkened face, muffled animal cries of pain escaping from deep inside his body. He didn't fit the image. And now here there was more hard-hearted talk about Palestinian parents.

Journalists—foreign, Israeli, Palestinian—were all over the claim: "This story of Palestinians deliberately pushing their kids to the front line is fantastic," said one journalist as he grabbed a moment to walk his dog on the promenade one evening. "Can you *imagine* a scoop like that? We've all looked for these parents. They don't exist."

Image was all-important. This was the TV Intifada: recorded, propagated. Palestinians, locked inside their homes, watched all day every day. Each house in the village centered more than ever on the television. I watched with Mohammed and Maha; Mohammed was angry and silent. For all of us the news spewed out from media and mouth, but most bloodily from the television. The new Arabic satellite channels were beaming the full color of the repression.

After the funeral of one victim in Ramallah, on October 12, Palestinian anger boiled over. Two Israeli soldiers seen in the town were captured by Palestinians, bundled out of their car and taken to the central police station. A mob of youths followed, storming their way into the police station, and up the stairs to kick, club, and beat the soldiers to death: thirteen Palestinian policemen were hospitalized trying to protect them. The world recoiled at the sight of the two Israeli soldiers' lynched bodies tipped out of the upper window, and Palestinian hands held aloft, stained with the dead soldiers' blood.

Too late, my boys had seen it. I turned round to find them standing behind me. Normally they ignored the news, or could be deflected; this time I was too slow and they saw. They wanted me to explain this. The IDF said the soldiers were reservists who had lost their way; the Palestinians said they were members of the hated undercover *mistaravim* units of the IDF, notorious for their brutal methods. Whichever, their killing was horrifying, as was the lawlessness, the Palestinian police outmanned and injured in their efforts to hold back the vengeful crowd.

Israeli anger was blind, white anger, like that of the Ramallah Palestinians. But with the Israeli rage was also something less defin-able, something delicate, fragile. Even as the nine waves of Apache helicopters set off to destroy the police station, the PA's TV and radio stations, Arafat's Force 17 headquarters, his residence and PA installations in Nablus, Hebron, and Jericho, there was the sense that something had been broken. Possibilities shattered.

Andrew was at work; I was alone with the children, horrified by the lynching, horrified that they had seen it. And then the telephone rang: Andrew in Gaza.

"I'm stuck. There are helicopter gunships hovering just out at sea, and they're going to strike. We just got a call from Barak's office saying get out of the Territories *now*."

"And?"

Brushed aside. "You've seen what happened in Ramallah. The IDF are wild. They want revenge. They want the UN out of the way."

"Isn't your office next to Arafat's?"

"Yes. Not far. Some of the team here want to get out. But we can't leave, we can't just abandon all the Gaza staff. We should go to see Arafat. That's where we *should* go, to try to talk some sense into the man. I'll call again soon."

The TV news soon showed the attacks: Ramallah, Hebron, Jericho, Nablus. And Gaza. Awesome military supremacy was raining down in waves of bitter anger.

Another call.

"Where are you?"

"We're on the way to Arafat's office, and for some reason I can't get through to the IDF to tell them we're going there—I'll call you back. Don't worry." Steady voice.

Ten minutes later: "We're in Arafat's office."

"But..."

"The helicopters are still hovering out there, but the IDF know we're here. I got through to them. They won't bomb us."

Had to take his word for it and suspend time, waiting by the phone, writing.

They did bomb: the next-door building, not the one containing Arafat. Andrew came home. Calm was imposed momentarily—

Clinton, Mubarak, Annan, Solana, King Abdullah all pressurizing. There were promises of a conference, one in Sharm el-Sheikh and another in Paris. Arab leaders were organizing their own, caught between their angry street, the fear of regional war, and American pressure. The US was in the final countdown to the presidential election, its leaders caught up in domestic politics.*

Arafat appeared on TV visiting the wounded lying in Gaza hospitals—a sickening sight, knowing that whatever he felt for their suffering, he also found it useful. Both sides manipulated their suffering; victimhood was at a premium. While Palestinian mothers and fathers were trying to stop their children going to demonstrations, the PA was not doing what it could to keep children away from confrontations, even when it was obvious that children were being killed. I met one mother who had sent her teenage sons abroad to keep them off the barricades, and alive. Few Palestinian families had that option.

"Of course the Palestinians will try to manipulate the propaganda stakes," said one foreign journalist who left soon afterward. We were sitting at the bar of the American Colony Hotel. He went on, "Their gunmen know full well that the IDF are going to fire back with everything they've got. They know it looks bad for Israel to be seen using live ammunition against stone-throwing kids."

"Not every funeral is real, and not every 'martyr' is civilian," said another journalist. "They're happy to parade dead gunmen as dead civilians for the propaganda benefit."

"But this isn't the point." Another interruption.

The point, said the new speaker, an American writer who had watched the situation for many years, was that all the accusations and counter-accusations, all the hatred and manipulations, were

---

* Bill Clinton had been deeply involved in trying to settle the conflict and had famously detailed knowledge of it. When George W. Bush succeeded him as President, US policy on the Israel-Palestine issue became more disengaged. This had the effect, officials admitted, of allowing a freer hand to the stronger party.

silencing the real debate.

"Let's not forget that the Palestinians are resisting a military occupation. You'll hear every excuse under the sun to prove it isn't one. But they've had more than 30 years of oppression—and they're in revolt." He went on: Palestinians had been forced to live under two separate systems of law—one for them and one for the settlers. Many had been driven off their land and made to live in camps. They'd had to watch their land given away to settlers, and their freedoms shrink. They've been granted a pretense of self-rule but seen their leaders lose out—sell out—and cream off millions in corruption while they "ran" their lives in brutal fashion, leaving the occupiers to say "look, they can't govern themselves." They live with expropriations, closures, curfews, and having their homes demolished, with humiliation that we, he said, could not begin to imagine. "And all of that was during the *peace process*. It's not surprising they're resisting, using whatever means they can. Vile, vicious, yes, all of that."

He rolled the base of his bottle of beer around the rings of water on the tile-topped table. "And if you were the average Israeli you wouldn't be doubting the IDF right now. Israelis are afraid, and so would you be.

"They've no idea if the IDF's actions make sense, to them it's self-defense, and the world condemns them for it. They've been told over and over that the occupation is not the issue—that anyway the territories are essential for Israel's security—and that the 'Arabs' attack out of hate and Islamic zeal, nothing more. So of course they're terrified. They don't think this is a war to hold on to an occupation—they're fighting for Israel's security. To most of them, Arafat is out to destroy Israel."

Palestinians heard only hate and rebellion, Israelis only fear and terrorism. In 1993 Rabin had told Israelis that Arafat was Israel's "partner for peace"; now Barak told Israelis Rabin was wrong: that there was "no partner for peace." Claims about the Palestinians—like the claim that their uprising had been planned—took on the status of received truth, undeniable, irrefutable. In Shonka Restaurant one evening with a group of Israelis and foreign journalists, an Israeli diplomat about to take up a distant posting became very angry, saying his government had absolute proof, there was not the *slightest* doubt that "Arafat started the violence; it was all planned. The man does not want peace." Anyone who questioned that theory was silenced by an outpouring of resentment and accusation.*

While I had the occasional worry about Andrew at Erez or under fire in Arafat's Gaza compound, journalists' wives and husbands were living out their individual "spouse under fire" stories every day. Flak jackets had become de rigueur. Cars were covered—back, sides, and windshield—with tape spelling "TV" and "press": more important to be identified as journalists than to be able to see out properly. Some media agencies had armored vehicles: ITN was one. The correspondent's toddler son had a plastic pedal car emblazoned with the same letters as his father's Land Rover, unaware that the letters meant Daddy had a better chance of coming home each night. Journalists were moving in pairs and groups in case something should go wrong.

And things were going wrong. Journalists were not complaining, but they were worried. Their spouses waiting at home were especially worried. By early November, thirteen journalists had been shot while covering the West Bank and the Gaza Strip, ten by the IDF and three not proven. A number had been harassed by Palestinian demonstrators and local authorities: at least three journalists were attacked by Palestinians in Ramallah after the lynching of the two soldiers. Three others had been badly beaten up by

* *In June 2004 this view was revised when Military Intelligence (MI) director Major General Amos Malka and other senior intelligence officials asserted that General Amos Gilad, head of MI research division at the start of the Intifada, had persuaded the cabinet to accept an "erroneous" view of the cause of the violence, and hence the "mistaken conclusion" that there was no Palestinian partner for peace. Malka and other senior intelligence officials disputed Gilad's analysis because it was not supported by a single document produced by any of Israel's intelligence agencies.[10]*

Israeli forces, and two had been arrested on the basis of their coverage. Palestinian police detained the publisher of a local Hebron newspaper because it had carried commentary criticizing the Palestinian Authority. CNN's Cairo bureau chief, Ben Wedeman, was shot in the back and badly wounded by Israeli forces at the Karni border crossing between Gaza and Israel. An official at CNN said there was "no reason to believe whoever fired upon Wedeman knew he was a journalist."[11] Wedeman was dismantling his tripod at the time.

The casualty rate was high but journalists did not say they were being targeted systematically. Nevertheless, the Committee to Protect Journalists was alarmed for their safety and for their freedom to work. Journalists did complain when the Israeli Ministry of Defense ordered a ban on issuing press credentials to Palestinians working with Western news organizations. The reason given was that they were said to be biased. Without press cards, getting through Israeli checkpoints would be much harder. The Israeli authorities also cancelled the travel permits that Palestinian journalists needed to enter Israeli-controlled areas.

Dina was suffering. Usually she couldn't get to work at all, and when she did she was fearful, nervous. Her nights were filled with the sounds of gunfire, and when they were not, she waited for the gunfire—or the raids. Before long, she gave up trying to think her life could be normal, stopped work, and concentrated on trying to emigrate. She was joining the trail of silent transfer. The situation had its own vocabulary: a word like "transfer" disguised the reality—ethnic cleansing, itself another euphemism. What pushed Dina was a sudden cranking up of military firepower, from a level already high enough to shock, to the use of aerial and sea attacks on Gaza and the West Bank. Her friends in Deheisha, one of Bethlehem's refugee camps, talked of wanting to put an end to their misery, even if that meant an IDF bomb landing on their camp. Bethlehem was almost entirely sealed off, and there was no electric power to see or cook by because the IDF had bombed the electricity substation and shot at the firemen who tried to put out the resulting blaze.

Palestinian gunmen would fire at the settlement of Gilo across the valley from Bethlehem. A single bullet would bring down half an hour of IDF tank-fire on the Palestinians. Night after night there was shooting and bombing, no sleep, no respite from the terror the locals all felt. Dina had tried to soothe one friend who was pregnant and whose little child sobbed desperately, asking to run away, terrified that his mother was going to die when she had the baby. "What can I say that will help here?" asked Dina. "None of the children can sleep because of the shooting and explosions, and if they do sleep their nightmares wake them. And in the morning there's no school to give them something to do. They have to stay at home, waiting for the next shooting."

Our neighbors were getting on with their lives as best they could. Those with jobs in the West Bank could either no longer work or rely on getting through checkpoints to reach work. Those who had jobs in Israel were lucky: their salaries kept the families going. Their children were also stuck without school, bored and frightened at the same time. The women donned working veils, wrapped tight under the chin rather than draped decorously over their heads, and leaned ladders up against the trees to harvest the olives. It was a family affair. Sheets were spread out under the trees, and the boys competed in daring to go higher along the thinning branches. During harvests as a child in England I would take sandwiches and lemon barley water to my father and brothers in the fields, the combine harvester and corn-carting would stop and we would sit on bales and talk. Here the talk was of another reality: the farmers attacked by settlers. One, picking olives near Nablus, was shot dead by two settlers from Itamar in full view of the rest of his village. The Palestinian police gathered the forensic evidence and eyewitness reports, and gave these to the Israeli police. But the Israeli police set free the two settlers—who had confessed to the killing, claiming they had killed the farmer in self-defense—on the basis that there was "insufficient evidence" to prove that a murder had taken place. My neighbors were bitter, but not surprised.

There was brutality everywhere. There was the brutality of the Ramallah lynchings and Palestinian attacks on settlers. There was the slow brutality of the occupation—houses demolished, land seized, orchards razed, the closures, the curfews and the death, from a ruptured appendix, of a little girl held up at a checkpoint. There was the brutality of the settlers, killing Palestinians, stealing their harvests and land, poisoning wells, and the Palestinians with no recourse to law. And on top of the daily death toll there was the enhanced brutality of the new repression. One Tel Aviv University professor who studied the issue described the method some IDF sharpshooters used to harm children: "A common practice is shooting a rubber-coated metal bullet straight in the eye—a little game of well-trained soldiers, which requires maximum precision."[12]

On October 19, 2000, Archie, our oldest child, turned seven. We had gathered presents and cake and tried to organize a birthday party, but his new school friends said they could not come. Their parents were uncomfortable with the location of our home. Only two months before, the Forest of Peace had been a quiet patch of Jerusalem with an incomparable view. Now we found we lived on the "seam." The dividing line was between "us" and "them," between the safety of West Jerusalem, where there were norms and predictability, policemen who directed traffic and pedestrians who worried about what to cook for dinner that night, and the otherness of East Jerusalem, where there were not only policemen who directed traffic and pedestrians who worried about what to cook for dinner that night, but also Palestinians battling Israeli forces in the streets and at barricades. Many of the parents were journalists, whose professional lives took them across the seam but whose family duty was to keep their children this side of the seam, out of danger. One explained: "You just happen to live on the wrong side of the reality."

On the day of Archie's party two of the parents changed their minds and let their children come to play. That day there was a firefight near Nablus between Israeli settlers and Fatah activists; each side lost one man. Archie had started to ask how many people died each day, and how old they were. That weekend another twenty Palestinians were killed; seven of them less than sixteen years old.

Many Israelis were telling me to watch out for Palestinian retaliation to all the deaths. One month after the Intifada began, on October 27, a cyclist with a satchel on his back blew himself up at an army post in Gaza. He was a secretary in a nursery school, and in killing himself he wounded an Israeli soldier. Islamic Jihad, a small Iranian-backed group, said it was responsible for the attack, adding: "This suicide bomber is not the first and will not be the last. The oppressors of today will get their punishment."

Soon enough, as the Israelis had predicted, the attacks crossed over the seam into Israel. On November 2, two Israelis were killed and ten injured by a car bomb near Mahane Yehuda market in West Jerusalem. Islamic Jihad again claimed responsibility. This, the first attack of the Intifada in West Jerusalem, came two days after an attack in East Jerusalem, which had left one Israeli guard dead and another wounded. The PA, holding that attacks in occupied territory were legitimate resistance, condemned the attack in the Israeli West but not the one in the occupied East. Two weeks later, a roadside bomb exploded beside a bus taking children to school from a Gaza settlement. Two adult settlers were killed and nine others, five of them children, were injured. Three of the children lost a leg or an arm or both. Two days later, two more Israelis were killed and sixty wounded by a car bomb blown up alongside a bus in Hadera, an Israeli town. The area was packed with shoppers and commuters driving home from work.

Israelis in Jerusalem suddenly felt an old fear alongside their anger: the fear of civilians inside Israel being killed. For two years there had been no bombs at all. Now, after a month of death for those in the Occupied Territories, the fear of attacks in Israel itself returned. It distilled in every Israeli: radical, moderate, secular, religious, military, civilian. And we felt it too: the unpredictability, the senselessness, and the impotence that made the fear all the worse. With no way of knowing where a bomb might strike, no power to prevent and no chance to appeal, the only defense was to stay at home, out of danger. But that was no life.

Seeing the dramatic images of the Intifada, people abroad called about our safety. One American friend wondered, "Are you getting the hell out any time soon or are you going to be all British about being under attack?" I found myself saying that Andrew was sometimes in danger of being caught in the crossfire, but that we were not—"Wait a minute—what do you mean *under attack?*"

"Look, Israel is under attack," the friend replied. "That could mean you too, you know, the terrorists don't know any different." We had a long exchange, in which he patiently explained the situation to me. He was aware that there were by now scores of Palestinian dead, and he understood that the IDF was one of the world's most powerful armies pitted against stone-throwers, civilians, and poorly armed insurgents. Yet he believed the Palestinians were the aggressors, their dead were all "terrorists," the two forces were equally matched, "and what's more they're agents of Islam, out to destroy the West, and they're starting with Israel."

The war my friend was reading about was not the war we were seeing. "But I've read it right here in *Time*," he said—all about the Palestinian violence on Temple Mount, how Israeli "troops faced widespread gunfire from Palestinian police and militia," and how the Palestinian casualties that day were "sustained in riots." Nothing would convince him that the Palestinians on the Temple Mount were not armed: *Time* had said they were armed, so it must be true. Nor did he find it strange to shoot unarmed demonstrators dead. Nothing would convince him that there could be any motive for Palestinian violence other than an overpowering hatred of Jews and Israel. For him Palestinians were not living under a repressive military occupation—that was "a red herring," he said. It was all about Palestinian "bestiality" and Israeli "victimhood." "And these people—mothers even—push their kids out into the front line. What kind of animal does that?" We became accustomed to the dehumanization, and the Orwellian switch— occupier as victim.

"They're all terrorists," was the view my American friend clung to. A smokescreen hid the realities of the occupation, and it would be made thicker and blacker by Palestinian suicide bombings. We were to see this smokescreen thicken so much that Palestinians' rights could be ignored and the retaliation to their resistance justified as "self-inflicted." The denial of reality was brought home by news of Hillary Clinton, a one-time advocate for Palestinian rights, making her bid to become senator from our old home, New York. A local community leader pointed out that international law supported the right to resist an occupation: Mrs. Clinton said this statement was "offensive and outrageous."[13]

How much more fair and frank, I was finding, were many Israeli commentators. Difficult as it was, they confronted the reality and declared the need to see events in context. "Since 1967," wrote Israeli professor Baruch Kimmerling, "millions of Palestinians have been under a military occupation, without any civil rights, and most lacking even the most basic human rights. The continuing circumstances of occupation and repression give them, by any measure, the right to resist that occupation with any means at their disposal and to rise up against that occupation. This is a moral right inherent to natural law and international law."[14]

3

"The Only Real Option"

It's not surprising you feel torn by this place, look at the history of it." This was Ofer: instructive, sympathetic. He was being sunk by the conflict that had so plainly come to a head and he would soon leave. But he was right about the history. For Palestinians, Israel's very birth, the moment of success for Jewish nationalism was the *Nakba*—their "catastrophe"—the moment of failure for Palestinian nationalism, the moment of total loss. The event that gave the Jewish people a national home deprived three-quarters of a million Palestinians of theirs.

That's about as far as you can go without becoming controversial, and some will take issue even so far. I had heard how each side has its own myths and interpretations of 1948 and the years since. What was surprising was how many people were ready to put aside the myths, accept the present and make the best of moving forward. For others, however, the events surrounding Israel's birth in 1948 are to this day unfinished; Ariel Sharon himself declared that 1948 is not yet over.[1] As many Palestinians see it, they were expelled, not allowed back, and the real aim of Israel—by making their lives as difficult as possible—is to "encourage" those remaining to quit. On the other hand, Israelis hold that Palestinians' insistence on the Right of Return for the descendants of those refugees shows that they want to destroy the state of Israel, to "throw the Jews into the sea," or at the very least set up a single binational state for Jews and Palestinians on the whole Land of Israel (or pre-1948 Palestine), which, owing to the higher demographic growth rate of the Palestinians, would ultimately negate the concept of a Jewish state.

For Scott, a Brazilian Israeli yoga teacher I met at the open-air pool in the German Colony soon after we arrived, this desire to destroy Israel was the key to many Israelis' views; if Palestinians were determined to destroy Israel, then all Israeli actions were in self-defense. I was sitting on my own in the crowd, trying to watch the children swimming, but the pool was large and part of it was in the shadow cast by an awning put up to protect swimmers from the sun. A fence separated the sitting area and the pool: if I managed to keep Catriona with me, Xan would go off, and Archie was permanently out of sight. It was too hot not to swim, the children were irritable and I was worse. Scott could see my difficulties fielding the children and offered to help. He bought the children ice creams which they ate while we talked. He was uncomfortable when I told him why I was in Israel—"My husband works for the UN." I was uncomfortable in return and wished I had not admitted that we lived in a Palestinian village.

"You're crazy," he said in response, but I didn't want to talk about the situation, not just then, and changed the subject. We were newly arrived; I wanted to break through the shell of the place and listen. Since I was avoiding work, even when people offered to make introductions and get me started, I had spare time and I could meet people in the hours when the boys were at school. Catriona, aged sixteen months, stayed on my hip the while. The German Colony, an area of West Jerusalem not far from our home, was filled with small shops selling wine, hand-milled soap, and health foods, interspersed with cafés and pizza bars. Israelis are industrious, but they still like to sit in coffee shops and bars, reading papers, thinking, talking, and when I bumped into Scott a few days later while paying for what I thought was plain yogurt but turned out to be sour cream, he invited me to join him for coffee. I hoisted Catriona on to my hip and accepted.

It was then, and when we met again later, that we did talk, slowly, around the situation, and about the history of the conflict. Israel's birth was a great and glorious event but at the same time, because of what happened to the Palestinians, it was shameful. It was the Jewish people's salvation, but the expulsion of hundreds of thousands of people from their homes and land needed to be hidden, rewritten, and expunged from memory. Scott wanted me to read historians like Benny Morris to see how Israelis were now unraveling the events that had occurred. But don't, he said, presume that "lifting the cover-up on the massacres and expulsions of 1948—and after—means that most Israelis will *know* about it. We're no different from many settler societies: Israel was built on another people's homes and fields and hillsides. We hid that, and we have to get on with our lives as they are now.

"Being Jewish sets you very high standards," he went on. "It isn't easy to confront the fact that we did these things, behaved like that, however justifiable it was at the time." For a people who had just endured the Holocaust, it felt like a necessary price. For the Palestinians, who had nothing to do with the crimes of the Europeans against the Jewish people, it felt like suffering someone else's punishment.

I remembered my grandfather talking of Israel's war of 1967: the Six Day War.* Like much of the West and almost all Israelis, he saw the conquests of those days in June as a great victory against an enemy who wanted Israel obliterated. The victory brought territory, the remainder of historic Palestine, including lands that had been ruled by Israelite kings more than 2,000 years ago. Under international law, territories acquired by force are occupied and must be returned. For some Israelis these lands were bargaining tools to broker peace with the Arab world: give us full recognition and accept us as your legitimate neighbor, and we will return the territories. But for other Israelis, taking the remaining land of Palestine was the fulfillment of a dream, that of creating Greater

---

*The occupation began after the Six Day War, June 5–10, 1967, fought between Israel and Egypt, Syria, and Jordan, after months of increasingly tense border incidents and diplomatic crises. Following Egypt's announcement that the Straits of Tiran would be closed to Israeli shipping, its demand that the UN peace-keeping force (UNEP) withdraw, and its deployment of troops near the Israeli border, the war began when Israel launched a strike against Egypt. Within six days, Israel had won control of the Gaza Strip and the Sinai Peninsula from Egypt, the West Bank from Jordan, and the Golan Heights from Syria.

Israel. Some went further, saying Greater Israel stretches beyond the east bank of the River Jordan. There were even those who said that the two blue stripes on either side of the Star of David on Israel's flag represented the rivers Nile and Euphrates. I asked a senior Israeli diplomat in the Foreign Ministry if this were true. We were on our way to a party in Tel Aviv. "No," he said, mildly irked for once. "That's one of the many myths woven into the debate. Of course it's not true. The stripes come from the prayer shawl."

To Palestinians the war of 1967 meant the loss of the last of their land. More than three-quarters had been lost in 1948 with the founding of the State of Israel, and now Israel established a military occupation of the remaining 22 percent. For the majority of Palestinians of the West Bank and Gaza Strip, many of them refugees who had lost their homes when Israel was founded, the Israeli occupation was hateful from the first and they showed it within a month by demonstrations. A general strike was put down as early as September 1967.

I took Scott's advice and read Benny Morris, one of the many Israeli historians examining Israel's history from newly available primary sources. He wrote, "Israelis liked to believe, and tell the world, that they were running an 'enlightened' or 'benign' occupation, qualitatively different from other military occupations the world had seen. The truth was radically different. Like all occupations, Israel's was founded on brute force, repression and fear, collaboration and treachery, beatings and torture chambers, and daily intimidation, humiliation and manipulation." In his view, the message was unmistakable: Israel intended to stay, and would not be persuaded to leave through civil resistance or disobedience. Professor Morris concludes that for the Palestinians, "the only real option was armed struggle."[2]

Over the weeks our children grew accustomed to seeing the armed struggle, and elements of war and its context. We grew accustomed to explaining the situation to them, even in unexpected places. Making the most of Israel's tourist sites, we once visited Ayalon Park, near the Green Line—the 1949 armistice line between Israel and the remainder of Mandate Palestine. The park had all the features of a well-organized recreational area: picnic benches, gravel paths, and public toilets under the trees. The children ran about among the Roman, Byzantine, and Crusader remains, crawling inside the Hasmonean tombs, all well-marked and fascinating. And yet there was another, unmarked, story that Archie unearthed when he told his school friends where he had played: one Palestinian boy shouted at him that this was his grandfather's land. Archie came home full of questions.

What the tourist information boards had not said was that until the summer of 1967 there were three Palestinian villages in Ayalon Park, home to 10,000 Palestinians. Israeli journalist Amos Kenan took part in the destruction as a soldier, and wrote about how these villages were cleared of their inhabitants and their "magnificent" stone houses—every one "surrounded by an orchard, olive tree, apricots, vines and presses"—bulldozed. He described how the IDF soldiers were told to deal with the people: there were "no orders in writing, simply that they were to be driven out." The expelled villagers were left to wander "like lost cattle. The weak die."[3]

Every Palestinian family had their own encounter with dispossession, loss, and humiliation. The *Nakba* was only the beginning of a sequence of dispossessions. There were the refugees of '48, then those of '67, and soon Palestinians would be talking of the refugees of 2000.

I once went to a Jerusalem cinema with an Israeli friend, Natalie. The film, which was in Mandarin, turned out to be screened with Hebrew subtitles, so for my sake we dropped the idea and had dinner instead. I mentioned this the following morning to a Palestinian friend, Nihad. He knew the cinema well; the building had belonged to his family until it was expropriated. Nihad told me about his terrors during the '67 war as an eight-year-old boy: being fired on by Israeli warplanes as he played with his cousins; seeing his heroes, the Jordanians, running away from the advancing Israeli forces; fleeing across the desert to Amman with his family, believing his father, at work in East Jerusalem, must be dead; and the Israeli officer, Shlomo, who had worked for his father during the Mandate, who helped his old boss find his family again. Nihad's story came out softly and without emotion until he described his mother's efforts to bring her children home—this meant crossing the Jordan to return to the West Bank. Many Palestinians were being expelled and those who tried to return were discouraged.* Nihad's composure evaporated as he remembered one little girl whose mother was shot dead on the banks of the Jordan: "I can see her now," he said, weeping. "They put her on a truck—she was crying for her mother—and sent her back to Amman."

The '67 war had also come up in the previous night's conversation. Natalie had talked about the Wailing Wall and its profound significance—the last remnant of the perimeter wall of the Temple—for the Jewish people. The saying "next year in Jerusalem" had sustained the diaspora for generations. "But after the state was formed we couldn't pray there." Between 1948 and 1967 the Jordanian authorities had denied Israelis access to East Jerusalem and, therefore, the Wailing Wall. The IDF's conquest of the West Bank, Natalie explained, "not only ended our fear—we all thought we were going to be destroyed by the Arabs—but also gave back our most holy place. Our *only* holy place. The IDF saved us and reunited Jerusalem."

From 1967 the Palestinians of the Occupied Territories lived under Israeli military rule. Military governors—Israeli army officers—used a system of Military Orders[5] to control the population, its economy and its resources, especially water, to which Palestinians were given only limited access. These resources were adapted to

---

* *Israel's President Haim Herzog later admitted that hundreds of buses were used for the mass expulsion of 200,000 people.*[4]

Israeli needs. Palestinian political organizations were suppressed and all signs of Palestinian nationalism banned. (In order to counter the continuing Palestinian national movement in the early 1980s, Ariel Sharon, then minister of defense, devised a system of civil administration and village leagues run by Palestinians with no PLO connection; seen as traitors by the Palestinian population, these failed.) Universities were frequently closed, and censorship, collective punishment, curfew, and widespread demolition of homes imposed. Meanwhile, Israeli "facts on the ground" were being laid down: Palestinian land confiscated, settlements built for incoming Israelis, and other measures put in place to link the Occupied Territories' economic and administrative infrastructure to that of Israel.

And in 1987 the Palestinians rose up to "shake off" the occupation that controlled their lives in what became known as the first Intifada. Despite Israeli efforts to contain it (a policy of "force, might and beatings" that included instructions to "break their bones" and the use of live ammunition and a range of collective punishments) the uprising continued through 1988, 1989, and most of 1990. Across the Occupied Territories the Palestinian population was united in, and by, rebellion.

Keeping the momentum going fell to new political, home-grown organizations and leaders, and to the local Intifada committees emphasizing self-reliance. At the same time, the first Intifada saw the rise of Islamic movements that, like the local committees, now provided a wide range of basic services to the population. One of these, the Islamic resistance movement, "Hamas" (its acronym, which means "zeal" in Arabic), formed in 1987, was initially encouraged by the Israeli authorities in the hope that this group would undermine the influence of the PLO and its secular nationalism.[6]

The 1987 Intifada, with its costs in Palestinian and Israeli lives and injuries (160 Israelis and 1,162 Palestinians were killed),[7] shook Israelis' belief that the occupation was sustainable. It wiped away the impression put across in some right-wing Israeli quarters that Palestinians were content to live under Israeli rule. This, and the failure of the IDF to contain the revolt, led some Israelis, among them Yitzhak Rabin, whose initial reaction had been to break the revolt by force, to conclude that force was not the solution to their conflict with the Palestinians. The Madrid Conference was convened after the defeat of Iraq in the 1991 Gulf War to discuss a diplomatic end to the Israeli-Palestinian conflict. More talks followed in Moscow and Washington, but without agreement. Then two years later, in Oslo under the guardianship of Norway's Foreign Minister, Israel entered into secret negotiations with the PLO leadership in exile, instead of with the leading figures from the Occupied Territories who were the Palestinians' representatives in Madrid.

The Declaration of Principles agreed at Oslo was signed on the White House lawn in September 1993. The "Oslo peace process," welcomed by most Israelis, most Palestinians, and most of the outside world, outlined Israeli redeployment from parts of the Occupied Territories, granted limited Palestinian self-rule, and agreed mutual recognition of the state of Israel and the PLO. A series of agreements were to follow up on these arrangements, and to sort out the "final status issues" that remained unsolved.*

While we sat in New York thinking peace was being created, the reality of the Oslo process was very different, as we were to see. The expectations attached to Oslo were paramount: both sides were disappointed. Israelis expected security. As victims of Palestinian attacks over the years, many Israelis had been afraid that if the IDF withdrew from the Occupied Territories, Israel would be still more exposed to Palestinian attacks. Oslo tried to counter these fears by establishing a Palestinian Authority (PA) that would see organizations like Hamas and Islamic Jihad as a

---

* Final status issues included the borders between the Palestinian entity and Israel; Palestinian refugees; Jewish settlements in the Occupied Territories; the question of Palestinian statehood; and the status of Jerusalem.

threat to its own status, and would therefore control them on Israel's behalf. Palestinian expectations were also high: they expected Israeli settlement building to stop and Israeli forces to withdraw from the West Bank and Gaza Strip on a fixed timetable, giving the PA control over more than 90 percent of the Occupied Territories. Ultimately, they believed, Israel would withdraw to the Green Line demarcating Israel from the West Bank, thus fulfilling Israel's obligations under international law, and that they would achieve an independent Palestinian state.

Although the process began well, with Israeli withdrawal from limited areas, joint Israeli-PA security patrols, and the establishment of the PA and the installation of Yasser Arafat as President, both sides began to accuse each other of violating the agreements. The "real" intentions behind the signing of the agreements began to be reevaluated in the light of each side's violations, perceived or otherwise, and in the light of the interpretations offered by their respective leaderships.

The West Bank is tiny and the autonomy given to the PA was highly curtailed. Before Oslo, the occupation was relatively distant, with Israel controlling the external borders but with limited internal restrictions. After Oslo, the occupation moved right in, and Palestinians had to contend with internal checkpoints, watchtowers, roadblocks, and a system of permits and paperwork that constrained their movement. One of the myths that irritated Palestinians was the Israeli belief that Oslo had allowed the Palestinians to run their own lives. I heard a range of figures quoted by Israelis: the "Palestinians have control of more than 90 percent of their territory," "78 percent of it," "at least 65 percent." In fact, the PA had security control over 18 percent of the West Bank. Seven years after Oslo was signed, Israel maintained full control of 60 to 70 percent of the West Bank and virtual control over the remainder. In Gaza, until 2005, less than 1 percent of the population (the 8,500 Israeli settlers) occupied, with the IDF, nearly 40 percent of the land; the million-plus Palestinians of the Gaza Strip made do with the remainder. One frequent Palestinian worry was water: Israel had kept control of the aquifers, often by positioning settlements on top of them. Israeli settlers had four times more water per head than Palestinians—in the Gaza Strip before the settlements there were withdrawn, almost seven times more.[8]

Equally important in Palestinian eyes was the impact of division. Oslo divided the territories into dislocated areas (e.g., A, B, and C in the West Bank); on top of this, the IDF imposed military roadblocks between Palestinian areas, using security concerns as their justification. The combination of this division and control came to be seen as a means to prevent the future Palestinian state from being one unified land while ostensibly pursuing "peace," a development many observers interpreted as evidence that Israel had never intended to give up control of the land.

The expansion of settlements on the only land remaining to the Palestinians only added to these fears. Throughout the Oslo years, settlement building not only continued, but increased. Settlements were being built all over the West Bank at an astonishing rate, faster than they could be filled. These houses, towns, and cities, built in the Palestinian Occupied Territories, were for Israelis.

Two of our friends tested the water of settlement life. A good-looking couple, American upbringing and education, degrees from Harvard, Yale, and Stanford, careers in a highly profitable profession—the law—they attended a settler-recruitment drive at one of the big Jerusalem hotels. They went through the interview procedures necessary before signing on, listening to recommendations about the choices available: "You'll be much happier in Pisgat Ze'ev than in Har Homa. In Pisgat Ze'ev you can completely forget about the 'neighbors,'" the recruiter said with a wink, meaning the Palestinians. He carried on, explaining: "In Har Homa you have to look across the valley at them all day."

They moved on to the financial stages. You will qualify for these discounts, those benefits, and so on. At the point of signing the deal, the couple said, "There is one thing we think we should mention. We're Palestinian." The smiles of welcome, the admiration at the chain of degrees, the eagerness to have them along, melted away.

"Oh no, you can't come."

"Why not?"

"You wouldn't like it. You're not suitable—it's impossible... Quite impossible. Forget it."

While construction for Israelis boomed in Palestinian areas, for the Palestinians under Israeli control the opposite was true: new building was actively prevented, and existing houses were demolished. An Italian friend witnessed a house demolition. He was almost in tears. "You had to be there, to see the people—you know, one minute they're like us, they have their home, their belongings, the chicken boiling in the oven. Then the next minute they have the bulldozers plowing over their house, and they are suddenly refugees, penniless refugees with nothing but bags they have thrown together in minutes. They become another number for the international community to shelter. What had they done wrong?—nothing. What could they do?—nothing. There were children there—trying to collect their toys..." He turned away. "I can't tell you about the children. I just can't believe people do this."

Sometimes there was no demolition to see—instead Palestinian houses were taken over by settler groups using spurious legal means to throw out the Palestinian families, usually in the middle of the night, immediately moving settler families into their place. This happened under the eyes of the Israeli forces, sometimes with their assistance, the Palestinian owners waving the title deeds—and documentation of the Israeli courts' rulings on their rightful ownership—at the police to no avail.

During the Oslo years, close to 100 square miles of farmland, pastures, and groves were expropriated from their Palestinian owners. Tens of thousands of Palestinian olive, orange, almond, pear, and apple trees were uprooted. A network of roads, over 300 miles of them, was built to service the colonies and control the land—a blaze of development that many Israelis heralded as progressive, bringing modernity to a "backward godforsaken part of the world."

I once visited a spring in the Wadi Qelt in the West Bank and met a young Israeli historian with a group of students. He had a machine gun hanging from a strap over his shoulder, and was wandering happily about the wadi. When he saw me, he came over, concerned that I was alone and unarmed.

He, Yigal, offered me his protection, and a guide to the local flora. "It is something else, this place," he said, full of enthusiasm. "We bring young Israelis out here on weekends to show them the Land of Israel—some of them have never been out of the cities." He was very bright, with an eager love of the land and keen that others should share it. "We're opening this place up so that all Israelis can enjoy the Promised Land. I want to see streams of Israeli cars coming out here at weekends, like they do to the beach." To him the road network was a means to an end, and essential for progress. Other Israelis saw it as insensitive as well as politically destructive. "It's a pity," a public health worker said to me as he looked out over one settlement and the swathe of roads sweeping up to it, "that the planners seem to have had no sense of proportion, no sensitivity to the landscape. This is the Holy Land after all, not the Midwest. Why do we have to treat it with such violence?"

Apart from the settlement building, dispossession, and demolitions of the Oslo years, Palestinians also lived with "Closure." By the time we arrived in Jerusalem the control of movement of people and goods was a well-established circumscription of Palestinian life. I asked Maha about the closures. "Oh, they're not new," she said, "they started around the time of Oslo. They just got much worse, that's all."

Maha explained that once they reach their sixteenth birthday, every Palestinian has to apply for a permit from the Israeli military authorities. She went through the process, describing to me how acquiring a permit is an endurance test of waiting and submission to the occupier, a test that must be repeated monthly. A permit allows Palestinians to approach the Israeli military at the checkpoint to ask permission to leave their towns and villages. If allowed through, they can then travel within the West Bank, until they get to another checkpoint. Jerusalem requires a different permit, one limited to Jerusalem residents: West Bankers are excluded.

Maha noted wryly that the settlers' mobility was not restricted. "They can move freely—in fact Palestinians are held up and made to wait to let settlers pass sometimes. Of course," she added, "the settlers say they feel restricted—because they are attacked by the trapped Palestinians. Maybe if they thought about what it was like to be trapped..."

It was not just personal freedom of movement that was controlled: the economy too. Goods, produce, imports, food, oil, raw materials, finished goods—nothing could move in or out without Israeli soldiers' permission. The Palestinian economy was buttoned into that of Israel. Israel also controlled the labor market, the electrical grids, the road network, and the urban infrastructure.

One morning I took Maha to Bethlehem because she was desperate to get to work. What stopped her was the ring of Israeli army checkpoints, and the Palestinian license plates on her car. Green license plates are confined; yellow Israeli license plates are not. My foreign passport and the UN plates on my car gave me a status different from that of the Palestinians. As we approached the soldiers Maha looked down at my passport lying by the gear lever ready for inspection. She, stateless, had no passport. We could see from the soldiers' posture, guns slung with apprehension, that they were uneasy. Their unease made them aggressive.

"What are you doing, why are you going to Bethlehem?" they demanded.

I was going to give way to my irritation, but Maha's fear caught my eye; not so much the taut knuckles as the look of helplessness.

The look spoke full submission; she had accepted that the soldiers had a raw and unlimited power over her, and she wanted nothing more than to pass through their process and get out the other side. Any antagonism from me would only prolong her humiliation. In every other situation Maha was a friend, a mother, an honors student, and an equal. Here, in front of me, she was a number.

I answered the soldier's questions; he looked long and hard at Maha, but was eventually satisfied that she was only going to work, and we carried on. Later that day, when the children and I went to her daughter Denia's third birthday party, Maha and I became equals again. Trays of sweets and raw vegetables were handed round, music played and some of the older girls danced. The children sat about eating chocolates, breathing cigarettes, and drinking Coke. Some were playing with the new toys, or with the paper, and the adults discussed the "situation."

I at least could avoid it by sticking to West Jerusalem and pretending there was no problem. This was the option most Israelis chose to take up—but not all. One such Israeli was Rabbi Arik Ascherman, executive director of Rabbis for Human Rights. During the post-Oslo period, he said, "Israel committed human rights violations in the Occupied Territories, destroying homes and cropland, expropriating land and treating ordinary Palestinians like criminals. With every violation, more Palestinians lost faith in the peace process until frustration spilled over into uprising. American Jews and Israelis don't realize what is going on because they have not seen what we have seen."[9]

What they did see was Palestinian violence. Oslo had promised Israelis security; we heard time and again how far they were disappointed. "It wasn't long before we were under attack again after Oslo," Scott told me. The first suicide bombing came in response to Baruch Goldstein, a settler from Brooklyn, killing twenty-nine Muslims at prayer in Hebron in 1994.*

---

* Goldstein, who was himself killed in the massacre, is revered as a hero by some Israeli extremists.

Many Israelis felt vindicated for criticizing the Oslo agreement: it had granted their enemy not only political recognition, but also the weapons and space to attack Israeli civilians. Israeli observers pointed out that the types of weapons being brought in by the PA, and the number of Palestinians in arms in PA territory, went far beyond the agreed limits. Under the Oslo process the PA was required to prevent attacks on Israelis both by combating the organizations responsible, and by arresting and prosecuting the individuals. "The Palestinians violated the Oslo accords," Israelis often said. One explained: "We thought they'd police their extremists, we thought they'd do it better than the IDF and that it would be better for the Palestinians that way. We gave them the arms to do it and instead of living up to the agreements they turned those arms on *us*."

Despite some real attempts and real successes by the PA in reining in militias—later the US and Israeli secret service pronounced that the Palestinian security apparatus had worked with determination to prevent terrorism during the last years of the Oslo process[10]—many Israelis retreated to their old beliefs about Palestinian intentions, seeing, above all, Palestinian determination to destroy Israel. The overwhelming impression was that, far from disarming or even holding back Hamas and the Islamic Jihad, the PA allowed them to operate and refused to arrest terrorists. And when the PA's forces did make arrests, Israelis saw what they called the "revolving door" policy—detainees returning to freedom instead of being kept locked up. Many were convinced that it wasn't merely a case of "doing nothing" to prevent terrorist attacks, but that the PA actually sponsored the terrorist organizations.

As proof of the PA's real intentions and another violation of the Oslo agreement, Israelis cited Arafat's failure to drop his call for the destruction of Israel. This belief persisted despite all evidence and witnessings to the contrary.[11] A further Israeli complaint was that Arafat refused to wear civilian clothes: this was seen as verification of his continuing military campaign and destructive intentions.

But far more important than Arafat's military wardrobe or the clauses of the Palestinian National Charter were the attacks on Israeli civilians. The assassinations by the IDF of Hani Abed of Islamic Jihad in Gaza in November 1994 and then its founder, Fathi Shikaki, in October 1995 were followed by a spate of suicide bombings against Israelis. In 1996 came the assassination of the Hamas bomb "Engineer," Yehiya Ayash, who had organized the bombings in response to the Goldstein massacre. More than 60 Israelis died in the suicide bombings triggered by this assassination, a campaign often cited as one of the reasons behind Netanyahu's victory. The memory of the horrific killings in 1995 and 1996 would not be dislodged from Israeli minds. There were three more suicide bombings in 1997 and one in 1998. Between September 13, 1993 and April 30, 1999, 258 Israelis (and 364 Palestinians) were killed.[12] It was little wonder Israelis felt that the Oslo years were full of death.

Despite Palestinian anger at the deepening occupation, and despite the failure to achieve even interim agreements, in July 2000 both sides were summoned by the Clinton administration to negotiate the final status issues: refugees, borders, statehood, and Jerusalem. The PA warned the Americans that neither side was ready to leap this far ahead without having achieved the preliminary steps, like Israeli withdrawal. Arafat was reluctant to attend until President Clinton, in front of others, personally assured him that there would be no blame assigned if the talks failed. When the time came, and the talks did fail, and any hopes for Nobel Peace Prizes evaporated, he excoriated Yasser Arafat before the world's press.*

---

* There are two schools of thought on Camp David: the Clinton-Barak school, blaming Arafat entirely, and a more nuanced position, put forward most notably by Clinton's own special assistant for the Middle East, Rob Malley, and the UN envoy, Terje Roed-Larsen, which holds that all three parties at Camp David made major mistakes and contributed to its breakdown.[13]

At the Camp David talks, Israel's position meant keeping most of the settlements, annexing 9 percent of the Occupied Palestinian Territories, and offering 1 percent in exchange. In addition, Israel kept control over another 10 percent of the Occupied Territories, including the entire Green Line area between the West Bank and Israel, as well as the border with Jordan. As a result Palestine would have been separated into four largely disconnected wards: the Northern, Central, and Southern West Bank areas and Gaza. For Palestinians to move between these areas would have meant crossing Israeli sovereign territory with Israeli control over both people and goods, and therefore the economy. Israel would also have continued to control all Palestinian borders (and airspace and water), thereby allowing Israel to control not only internal movement but international movement as well. To Palestinian eyes, Israel's Camp David proposal was the military occupation repackaged, confirming their fears that Israel had had no intention of giving up control of the land.

Later, Shlomo Ben Ami, who was minister for internal security at the time, was direct: "Barak showed me a map that included the Jordan Rift Valley and was a kind of beefed-up Allon Plan.[14] He was proud of the fact that his map would leave Israel with about a third of the territory. If I remember correctly, he gave the Palestinians only 66 percent of the land. Ehud [Barak] was convinced that the map was extremely logical. He had a kind of patronizing, wishful-thinking, naïve approach, telling me enthusiastically, 'Look, this is a state; to all intents and purposes it looks like a state.'"[15]

Now, seven years after Oslo—just as we arrived—its realities had come to a head. For Israelis, the Palestinians had thrown away Barak's "generous" offer and proved they were not serious about peace, returning instead to the violence Israelis had endured during the Oslo years. For Palestinians, the conditions of the occupation had worsened throughout the Oslo years, Israel had doubled the number of Israeli-only settlements built on the future Palestinian state, and then confirmed their unwillingness to end the occupation by "repackaging" it at Camp David. Even as the Israeli government improved its offers after Camp David* and the negotiations became more acceptable to the Palestinians, the impression prevailed that the Palestinians were not "partners for peace."

Despite the worsening situation, people were doing their best to keep up a semblance of normality. The end of 2000 in Jerusalem was cool, and the rains came to fill the aquifers. Basil, Ahmed, and their father led the Arab mare, Nur, on to the terraces of our garden, hitched her to a rudimentary plough, and tilled the soil. It was hard work, the mare throwing herself into the harness to pull it through the hard earth, and Mahmoud jogging to keep up. A pretense of normal life was possible, up to a point.

One morning, two months into the Intifada, the phone rang. It was a friend, Hazel, with children at the same school and a husband in the UN.

"Are your bags packed?" she began.

"Packed? What are you talking about?"

"You're being evacuated—we all are. Every UN family is out of here. There's a flight tonight."

We were to be dumped out of a military plane somewhere in middle Europe, and given a wad of cash to find our way home. Home? To stay with relatives in England, with no schools and no freedom, splitting up the family.

"Andrew, they're trying to evacuate us. I'm not going, it's madness."

"I don't believe it. What are they thinking—you don't *want* to go do you...?"

"Of course we don't want to. This is home now."

According to the Clinton Parameters issued in December 2000, Israel would annex 4–6 percent of the West Bank, and Palestinians would receive a 1–3 percent swap of land in Israel, and sovereignty over all of Palestinian East Jerusalem.

It is discomfiting when something alien to you makes decisions about your life, your family, your choices, and imposes its own will without allowing you a voice. Someone, somewhere, had determined what was to happen to us, and we were not being consulted. Powerlessness is very provocative. The UN was being protective, and generously so, but the children and I had come independently so I decided that we fell outside the UN umbrella. We stayed.

We arrived at school the following morning to find gaps in the classes where the UN children had sat.

"You still here?" asked a journalist.

"Where've they gone?" my children asked. All the children wanted to know why some of their friends had left in the middle of the night without saying goodbye.

"What danger? Mum, what's it all about?"

"The UN has evacuated some families because they think there *might* be danger."

"Hey, when are they coming back?" I didn't know.

They came back two months later.

We went to England for Christmas. Andrew was glad to get away, out of "the madness," as he called it. As we reached Ben Gurion airport for the early flight out I looked at him and saw someone changed, someone strange to me. Beside us in the line for the security check, a British journalist and his family wore the same expressions: the grimness of what we were living in and seeing, and the lightness in anticipation of a break from it. The security check was mild, just a few questions—each of us separately. My questioner, a slight young girl, reminded me of a patient I had once tended to in a London emergency room. She asked if I knew any natives.

"Natives? Er, do you mean Palestinians?"

"Yes. Do you know any Palestinians?"

"Yes."

"What are their names?"

I started going through an alphabetical list. When I reached Chantal Malouf, the girl stopped me, frowned, and waved me through.

As we flew back to London, I could see Andrew lighten and smile. "I'd no idea it would be so good to get away," he said. And away from the conflict, away from all the misery that he had to deal with because of his work, he began to be himself again. With the endless meetings and interviews, cables and proposals, he had begun to shrink into a self that was mechanical, not him, just functional. He needed time to be with the children, without the endless phone calls that left him moody with irritation. We needed time to be together without the constant feed of bad news and interruption.

We put the conflict and Jerusalem out of our heads and talked about negotiations for our new house in Scotland. It was a long-held dream for the two of us, an idea that was now beginning to look real. We could walk around the blueprints in our head, building bookcases, hanging pictures in the future. Andrew's humor, uninterrupted, came back, and his whole demeanor lifted. "It's good to feel free again—I hate all those distractions, they keep us apart," he said. "The job is great, but living in Jerusalem makes me wonder if we even begin to appreciate our freedom."

4

A Sense of Closure

The situation changed when Ariel Sharon came to power. On February 6, 2001, he was elected by a landslide, with a margin of twenty percentage points over Barak. There was no school that day so I took a large group of children, aided by a Christian evangelical nanny loaned by other parents, to the Jerusalem Biblical Zoo. There we wandered happily through the display of animals: zebra, gazelle, various forms of sheep, more gazelle. A long elevated walkway made of wood swept us over the animals toward the ark at the end of the trail. The animals roamed in huge enclosures; it was we humans who were penned in. At the ark the children sat riveted by an animation screened for them in English; delivered by Noah, it was a call to environmental sensitivity.

Other families were taking advantage of the holiday. A group of Orthodox families walked by as we stared at a group of chimpanzees. The chimps were putting on an enthusiastic display of copulation, coprophagia, and masturbation. The children demanded explanations. But behind us the Orthodox party suddenly panicked: one of their toddlers had stopped breathing. There were screams and shouts, someone ran for help. I stepped forward and offered mine. The child, lying limp in a man's arms, was turning blue. "I'm a doctor, I can help," I said. One of the women looked grateful and urged me on, but the others, the men mainly, ignored me. I just wasn't there. I tried again: the child needed resuscitation urgently. No reaction from the adults. And then the child came round, turned pink, and they moved away, leaving me wondering what had happened.

Back in the reality of the elections, there was bleak resignation among Israelis and Palestinians we knew. Some Palestinians claimed to be positive about Sharon being elected; they could deal with him because there was no pretending—they said they knew what he was and where he stood and all about his intentions. Most, however, were full of foreboding. Those Israelis who detested Sharon and everything he represented were angrily blaming the Palestinians and their violence for bringing him in.

"Oh right, like we'd vote in the National Front because of an IRA bombing campaign," said a British journalist to some Israeli liberals. We were having a drink in a Russian bar near the school and the vodka was loosening opinions. "You Israelis voted in the bastard," he went on, "it's your own fault you've got him."

One of the Israelis, with years as a peacenik behind him, had taken Sharon's victory especially hard. "He betrayed us," he said bitterly.

"Who?" asked another, "Sharon?"

"No. Arafat, of course. He betrayed us. We told our people to trust him, and look what he did. He's made us a laughing stock. He's lost us our credibility, the left. It's gone."

Many Israelis were bitter about their new government, and even found Sharon's accession to power alarming. Some did their best to persuade themselves that the man who had spent much of his career trying to erase Palestinian claims and building more settlements would become a man of peace, real peace, overnight. One Jewish friend, René, on the phone from Paris, tried to explain to me and perhaps convince himself, that there would now be a new Sharon, not the old Sharon, he said—just as Maha had said—of Qibya, Gaza in 1971, Sabra and Shatila, the godfather of the settlements. This would be Sharon the strong, not just Sharon the hard.

"He evacuated the settlers in the Sinai, he can do the same in the Gaza Strip and in the West Bank. You will see," said René, "I am not wrong." Sharon, he insisted, and as many others claimed, was "the only man who could evacuate the settlements and bring peace."* "As to that," an Israeli commentator told me derisively, "there is only one Sharon, and that's the old Sharon."

---

* *René apologized two years later for the apparent error of his prediction. Then, in August 2005, hundreds of lives later, Sharon pulled all the Israeli settlers out of the Gaza Strip, and from four settlements in the northern West Bank.*

Old or new, Sharon had been elected to deliver security to the Israeli people. The Intifada had run for four months and Israelis were full of fear. The occupation was not sustainable after all: far from running it for them, the PA had joined in the revolt. Arafat had broken the deal; he was not their partner for peace. But for those who saw ending the occupation as the key to peace, the question remained: how to get out of here? The occupied land had been colonized, and those settlers who didn't want to leave were vocal, powerful, and determined. Israeli commentators were confronting the issue of the settlements, pointing out the irony of Sharon, who had been partly responsible for the colonization campaign (for example, as Agriculture Minister in the Likud government), arriving in the premiership at the moment when it had all come to a head. "Sort it out," they challenged him.[1] Whereas Labor's settlement program had been to install security areas, Sharon's enduring aim had been to forge a situation in the Occupied Territories that was totally irreversible, so that no Israeli government would ever be able to withdraw.[2]

First to feel the effects of Sharon's premiership were the ongoing negotiations at Taba in Egypt, on the border with Israel, that were bringing the two sides to the brink of a workable peace. Sharon put a stop to them. The new Prime Minister declared that he would not divide Jerusalem, give up any settlements, or offer as much land as Barak had offered. I sat listening to the despair of an American who had worked at Taba. Like many others, he was glum about the prospects for peace under Sharon, mourning the wasted opportunity Taba had presented. "With Sharon in power, Israel stopped cooperating with George Mitchell.* But Taba was a real chance. It was the first decent negotiation the parties had. There could have been an agreement."

"Wasn't it all too last minute?"

* Former US Senator George Mitchell arrived in Israel in December 2000 as a result of the meeting at Sharm el-Sheikh in October.

"No. For once it was for real. It may have been like two lovers on a sinking ship who throw away the condoms, but, oh yes, it was serious. Dead serious. And of course there was time. The discussions began in Washington last September [2000], there were more in December, and finally at Taba just now."

"But it was too late to wind them up, no?"

"Of course they could have concluded. Sharon has just shut them down and made a demand for seven days of quiet before *any* negotiations will take place. He wanted to pull the rug out from all negotiations that were not on his terms."

When Sharon was sworn in, he brought with him a huge cabinet, a unity government that included Shimon Peres, with eight seats each for Labor and Likud, five for Shas, and a few others (Likud had only nineteen seats in the Knesset).

Mohammed's comment, when he came to wire in the video, echoed many others: "There is no opposition."

"And Natan Sharansky," added Mohammed, "is one of the worst." Sharansky was given the portfolio of building and construction. "An immigrant from Russia who thinks there's nothing wrong with telling Palestinians we can't build anything on our land, anywhere, and that in any case the land isn't ours and the Israelis are going to build on it instead." For Mohammed and many like him, Sharansky embodied the discrimination that had led many to accuse Israel of "racism": the 1950 Law of Return giving anyone with a Jewish grandparent the right to "return" and settle on land in Israel, and yet any Palestinian, Muslim, or Christian, was forbidden that right even though they owned the land in question.

Mohammed was saying, "Andrew told me he used to write to the Soviet authorities asking for the release of Natan Sharansky."

"Yes," I replied. Andrew headed an Amnesty group while at school in the eighties, and he and his colleagues had adopted the cause of a number of political prisoners.

"I bet he was surprised at what Sharansky did next, the minute he was freed," said Mohammed. "Refusing another people's rights and calling for them to be even more oppressed than they were already."

"Er, just a little."

It was not long before Palestinian violence began again: two days after the election, to be exact.[3] Their violence, which many thought Arafat had been encouraging in the belief that it would persuade Israel to offer more at Taba, was instead to lose Palestinians much sympathy. On February 8, 2001, driving back from a music lesson in East Talpiot, a Jerusalem suburb, we heard a thudding boom over Jerusalem. We were well aware that just before Christmas three IDF soldiers had been injured in a suicide-bomb attack at a roadside café in the northern Jordan Valley, and that on New Year's Day a car bomb had exploded in the center of Netanya, injuring 60 people. Now was this another bomb? We drove on, wanting to get home.

Andrew was in Gaza, and within minutes he rang to say he had been having trouble getting hold of me. We soon grew accustomed to the authorities shutting down the mobile phone networks immediately after a bomb; it became one of the signs that a bang had been a bomb. I turned on the car radio and heard the BBC World Service reporting a bomb in Jerusalem only minutes before. A correspondent had happened to be there. What we had heard driving along was the powerful car bomb exploding in the ultra-Orthodox neighborhood of Beit Yisrael: a frightening noise for us, a disaster for those involved. Four people were injured.

While waiting for the inevitable retaliation, we would pretend things were normal. The children carried on with their homework and games and I carried on with plans to go to Aida refugee camp.

Maha, a social worker by training, wanted to show me the camps. As I drove her through the Forest of Peace, she told me her children were still unable to sleep. After the outbreak of the Intifada the three girls, who shared one room, had woken throughout the night with nightmares, shouting and crying for their parents and grandmother. There had been one night when a group of armed settlers had made their way to the village in an ugly mood and the children had picked up the defenselessness their parents felt. This was nothing, she said, to what those families in the West Bank and Gaza Strip were suffering.

She also said, "It can't be easy for those settlements in the line of Palestinian fire, like Gilo." She explained that although she saw the settlements as legitimate targets, she didn't like the thought of the Israeli children suffering any more than the Palestinians.

We made it through the checkpoint in our by now customary silence and headed for the center of town. Once again, the IDF had rearranged the internal roadblocks that turned towns into a daily-changing maze. The main road runs past Rachel's Tomb. Rachel, co-wife of Jacob with her sister Leah, and mother of Joseph and Benjamin, is a matriarch of the Jewish faith and revered by Muslims. Her tomb, once a pillar raised by her bereaved husband, is now a fortress. Inside, behind the slab-gray concrete defenses, there is a tiny synagogue, a veiled tomb, and a small army to guard it. The tomb, holy to Muslims but out of bounds to them, was a flashpoint. Demonstrations in Bethlehem frequently began at Rachel's Tomb, and it was becoming impossible to drive anywhere near it. The main road had long been blocked to traffic, but now the IDF were moving the blockades further and further away, diverting vehicles through small residential streets before they, too, were blocked off.

As we wound our way through the latest variation of roadblocks within the city, I realized I had begun to dislike going to Bethlehem, and to dislike the anger I felt every time I went through the checkpoint. Confronting the checkpoints and the barriers to normal life for every Palestinian made it impossible to be in denial about the closures. And yet it seemed that many Israelis must either be in denial or ignorance: to them the siege of whole towns a few miles away was a non-subject.

We drove on, through the gloomy city, its shop fronts shuttered and their courtyards emptied. Inside Aida refugee camp, in the middle of Bethlehem, people were miserable. The silent shooting, bombing, sniping—silent because others rarely heard about it—had gone on and on since the early days of the Intifada, adding another stratum of unhappiness to refugee life.

The camps are so well integrated into Bethlehem that their presence is barely noticeable. There is no perimeter fence or other demarcation, you just arrive there, all of a sudden, across a narrow road or down a small street. On either side the buildings had grown, unplanned, built on, and up, and over. The sense of spacelessness was sharpened by their look of instability. Maha explained to me that often families had to build on top of existing buildings, or hard against another, with a resulting clash of structures.

There were now holes in many of the structures, signs of bombardment. We entered one building and picked our way through the debris up the stairs. A family living there was assembled on a landing, the cold wind coming through the blown-out windows, sliced by the hanging shards of glass. They shook hands and smiled in greeting before showing us the remnants of their apartment. "This is where we were sitting when the rocket came in last night," explained one of the sons, pointing around the edges of the room. "My mother was just here. My nephew—that's him— was sitting on her knee. We were watching the news when the rocket came in. Thanks God"—always *thanks* God—"no one was killed." "*Al-Hamdil'allah*,"* said Maha, nodding. The room was not just bombed; it was blackened. The blackness was everywhere. A thread of lamp wire hung down from the charred ceiling, swinging. My shoes crunched glass as I avoided the wire.

One of the sons ushered me away from the glass toward the open window. "There is the IDF tower. That's where it came from. But we have this so many nights. They shoot, so of course our time would come." I looked across the dance of roofs, and saw a tattered fortress-tower. And another, further round. They had all the angles

---

* *Praise be to God.*

on the camp, which was in Area A, part of the 18 percent of the West Bank where the PA had been granted "full" authority.

We retreated. Maha explained that the family had wanted to "welcome" us—to give us coffee—but had no means of heating the water, and were ashamed by their failure to be hospitable. I asked her how many had been made homeless. Four families in that building, "But they will cope," said Maha.

As we left she pointed toward Gilo. "Over there are the children on the edge of Gilo I was telling you about. They aren't getting any sleep either." Maha was wry: "The Gilo settlement was built on land belonging to Beit Jala. Beit Jala fires on Gilo, and what does the world see?—only 'terrorism.'" She went on: "And of course, when you fire bullets at Gilo, you get fired on by tanks and helicopter missiles in return."

We went on to another bombed building. On the ground floor were two airless rooms piled with thin foam mattresses, patched with color and shabby. This building had been bombed some nights before, so gas canisters with cooking rings had already been installed in one corner. The air carried wafts of staleness, old rice and gas. We climbed upstairs again, following a tired man who had started to show us the damage. He was an engineer, unemployed and too demoralized to care that he couldn't be hospitable. His corduroy trousers had the hang of having been owned before. At the top of the stairs he led us over the fallen beams toward the gash in the side of the building, a flap of roof hanging down precariously over the missing wall. There were three families—sixteen children—sleeping in these two rooms, to ride out the repeated attacks and their damage. Two missiles had hit the building that night, showering the refugee families with glass, four of the children ending up in hospital. "How do you explain to your children?" he asked. "What do I say to them when they ask me why the Israelis try to kill them? There is nothing I can say."

The engineer said, wearily, in anticipation of the usual question put to Palestinian refugees, "Yes, we have the keys to our house—it's in Beit Jibril," a village in what was now Israel. He also had the deeds to the house, he said, given to him by his grandfather who in turn had been given them by the Turks during Ottoman rule. He brightened a little: "My grandfather used to tell us Balfour* was a bloody fool. Always, until he died, and we would laugh every time he said it." He turned around, and interrupted himself—he had made this speech once too often.

"You know, there were journalists here this morning, and other people will come later. None of them do anything—none of you. What you can do? You all say this is terrible, and how can it be happening, and I believe you all believe what you say. But you listen, and then you go. Still nothing changes. I showed them my father who still talks of his village and how he ran away in 1948 from the Israeli army. He told them his story then, and he tells them his story now, his grandchildren also tell the story, but we are still here, we are still refugees. What we can do, *ya'ani*? It's cold. I have to keep my children warm. I have to feed them. How I can do this? How?"

And he trailed off, sensing the futility. Maha said afterward that perhaps he felt that, compared to those refugees stuck in Lebanese and Syrian camps, where Palestinians were treated—by their Arab "brothers"—like lepers, denied all rights, all jobs, citizenship, help, hope, or future, he was lucky.

We emerged from the cold building into the street. A couple of children were playing with one of the chunks of ragged glass that had dropped from the top floor where we had stood looking down.

* *The Balfour Declaration, 1917: in a letter to Lord Rothschild, Foreign Secretary Arthur Balfour wrote: "His Majesty's Government view with favour the establishment in Palestine of a national home for the Jewish people, and will use their best endeavours to facilitate the achievement of this object, it being understood that nothing shall be done which may prejudice the civil and religious rights of the existing non-Jewish communities in Palestine, or the rights and political status enjoyed by Jews in any other country." The document, hailed by the Zionist movement, has been criticized for failing to clarify how it is possible to provide a national home for one people without prejudicing the rights of the majority people—95 percent of the population—already there.*

It bent pleasingly because of the lamination. Their uncle took the shard from them and threw it away with a shrug of despair.

Maha and I went home later and each settled into the usual round of preparing food and sweeping plastic toys off the floor. The phone rang. It was the young Canadian I had taken on to replace Dina and help out with the slough of domesticity. When we had met she'd come across as an enviably independent world-traveling 24-year-old, but now her voice had changed: "I've spoken to my mother and she wants me to come home and she's going to pay for my ticket and my college fees and so does my dad and I don't think it's fair on you if you want a commitment if I can't deliver on that and I'm really confused." She was already halfway gone. I wished her luck.

Small leaves in brilliant green unfurled on the fig trees. The little farm was full of birth: a batch of puppies sprawled and tussled. The long-eared goats had kids, silken-coated and skittish, in the paddock. There were always kittens, most of them with thin, hungry mothers. Maha liked the cats; they killed snakes. And now there was a foal. We arrived home just as Basil was scooping the placenta and membranes into a bucket, and the damp foal was lurching from skinny leg to skinny leg, nudging his mother's belly rudely, impatiently, to persuade the milk to let down.

Normality: we learned to avoid the danger zones, the shopping areas favored by bombers, the movies, theaters, and malls—all out of bounds. Parking by the school in Mea Sharim was always a risk—there had been attacks in the area—but we had no choice. Parking in a safer place would have meant a longer walk through a high-risk area; it was more dangerous to walk than to drive and run. The Anglican school along the street was less exposed, and British consulate children arrived there in an armored vehicle every morning. The Anglican school also offered a large sweep of off-road parking so that no one need park outside. The French school had no such safety area, but it was protected within the compound it shared with a convent of nuns, so once inside school the children were safe. Each set of parents developed a route, and a parking area, which they hoped lowered the likelihood of being bombed. None of the ruses made much sense—one father favored a U-turn across three lanes of oncoming commuter traffic in order to avoid a road vulnerable to bombers—but taking some control of safety, making decisions about security, however faulty, helped.

Early on the morning of February 13, 2001, Israeli helicopter gunships took out a vehicle in Gaza, killing the occupant. It was an airborne death-squad. There was no debate about the legality, logic, or likely effects of extrajudicial killing. Instead people asked only whether or not the dead man qualified as a terrorist. The PA denied that he was involved in any militant organization, the Israelis claimed that he certainly was. Andrew called just afterward to say that rockets had been fired uncomfortably near the UN compound, at least they weren't sure if they were rockets or bombs—in fact there were endless conflicting reports—but he was fine, so not to worry. Of course not. As he spoke I thought back to the refugees in Bethlehem and wondered what I would do if we were forced into evacuation, how it would feel to hear him describe how close the bombs had been in Gaza if I were sitting in London. I could hear a helicopter above the noise of the dishwasher. It was on its way to bomb Beit Jala, just over the hill.

The following morning Maha asked her husband, Mohammed, to take me to Talpiot, a semi-industrial Israeli shopping zone in southern Jerusalem, to help me with my application for a better satellite connection. He had worked with the company in the past, and was close to the other employees, his former colleagues, who were all Israeli. They made a big fuss of him when we arrived: "Mohammed, where've you been? It's been a long time!"

They were more natural chatting away in Hebrew, rather than in English for my benefit—I was the alien—so I sat while the young Israeli girl behind the desk filled in the forms. I watched two of them, Mohammed and his particular friend, and found myself counting off the similarities as they talked: the deep dark color and the short blunt cut of their hair, the shape and texture of their clothes, the blue sweaters with close-fitting T-shirts, the depth of the brown in their eyes, the pigment in their skin. How fraternal they seemed. As I watched, I became aware that people were taking an interest in the TV monitor over our heads: the news in Hebrew. I could see scenes of Israeli police milling about and that people had been killed. There were body bags on the ground. I asked Mohammed what was going on. He muttered into the space between us, and waited until there was a buzz of Hebrew conversation to drown ours. "A Palestinian has driven into a crowd of soldiers waiting for a bus." The man, a regular bus employee, had decided to use the bus he drove as a fatal weapon, killing eight people and injuring twenty-five. Many of the victims were young soldiers heading for Tel Aviv to report for duty.

I waited for an outcry, for some reaction to the killings. Mohammed was the only Palestinian present, and much as he might look similar, the divisions were up there, vivid on the screen. But there was no reaction, no rancor, just a quiet sorrow clinging to them all. If anything, it was me who was the excluded outsider, staring dumbly at the Hebrew literature in their office, listening deafly to their questions about me. Mohammed filled in the details of where I lived and how to get there to install the satellite receiver. No one said anything about the killings.

Later that day, outside the boys' school, I talked to a Palestinian parent, Robert. He had promised to give me a bar of olive oil soap from his estate near Nablus, and now he handed me a small parcel. As everyone always did, we talked about the day's events. Catriona was taking a nap in the back of the Land Rover, and Robert, in his expensive tweed coat and shirt and tie, was leaning in through the window. At one point he looked at the approaching cars and said, "I keep thinking they're going to run me down in revenge." I changed the subject. The soap was rich and yellow, wrapped in tissue paper and smelling of ripe oily fruit. He explained how best to use it, how to work up a good lather, how it is hard at first, and also about the farm where the soap was made. "I'm still hoping that one day we'll get back the house my family built in West Jerusalem; it was expropriated in 1948 and now it's valued at $3 million."

On the way to Talpiot, Mohammed had told me he wanted to build a sitting room to improve their home. It was windowless and "underground" because our house had been built in front of it, and when his uncle had decided to expand he had simply built on top of Mohammed's house. Now Mohammed and Maha, their three daughters, and Mohammed's mother, Naimi, lived in two dark bedrooms with a third room that served as their living room. Mohammed's brother-in-law had started building a small house on their land, a terrace below the village. The Israeli authorities, whose policy was almost always to deny permits for new Palestinian housing, were bound to object. All these families were expanding, Mohammed said; growing sons take on young wives, and they can't keep squeezing yet more families into the same buildings. Meanwhile there were new houses and incentives for Israelis; I remembered seeing in the paper that week news of a Knesset bill giving financial rewards to Jewish families who bought houses in Jerusalem.

When Israel annexed East Jerusalem in 1967, it redefined "Jerusalem" (see map, x). The newly demarcated terrain was not only the ancient city, but also a tract of land swallowing a third of the West Bank. Until 1967, East Jerusalem had covered only 6.5 square kilometers. Most of the land annexed by Israel as "East Jerusalem" belonged to 28 Palestinian villages in the West Bank which, all of a sudden, found themselves part of an "indivisible" Jewish city. Maha and her family—and we—lived in one of the many Palestinian areas where planning restrictions and expanding concentric bands of colonies built to encircle the new Jerusalem had prevented any Palestinian growth.[4]

But Jerusalem is not simply a religious site of unquestionable importance to Jews, Christians, and Muslims alike; it is the center of Palestinian life and the focus of 40 percent of the Palestinian economy. It had been so for generations, and now they were being walled out. It was, one Palestinian said, "like walling the English out of London, the French out of Paris, or the Spanish out of Madrid." Many Israelis have described the Palestinians' strong attachment to their land.[5] Some of those who worked in the Occupied Territories said this was self-evident: only a profound connection to the soil and color and contours of a place, let alone its history and memories and meaning, would keep a people from quitting under such pressure. There were other Israelis, however, who held that this connection was fabricated, even part of a conspiracy to thwart Israeli dreams. What was more surprising was another question I heard more than once: "Why do the Arab refugees keep their keys, why do they hold on to them year after year? What does it mean to them?" An expatriate nurse, listening in disbelief to one of these conversations, blurted out, "But surely the Jewish people, of all people, understand the strength of connection to a place?" That, she was told, was different.

One morning when Amer, a neighbor from the next village, had dropped by on his way to work to bring us warm bread baked with thyme he had picked from his hillside, and was standing at the door, Maha telephoned to ask if I would come have coffee. Naimi let me in, and I found Maha in her kitchen, the oldest part of their house. We were underground. There were no windows, and there was no door, just an opening in the wall, its hewn mouth painted in shining white emulsion. It was a cave, albeit white-washed and with all the electric appliances and worktops of a kitchen: nevertheless, a cave. Maha smiled as I looked at the rough-ness of the walls that she had turned into a feature: "I told you it was a cave," she said.

We sat with our cups of coffee in the living room. She wanted to tell me that the planning department had, as feared, visited her brother to tell him he was building illegally and must apply for a permit. "They want him to wait for one of those permits that are never granted, so people end up building anyway, and then either watch the building pulled down or pay a huge fine to the ministry." Maha's brother also faced a fine for employing a Palestinian from the West Bank. "The West Bank and East Jerusalem are like the body and the heart that beats inside it," said Maha, "but the Israeli administration wants to amputate them, cut the one off from the other."

I listened: listening with frustration and injustice sitting like a block, as they did so often in conversations with both sides, all sides. My frustration was making me intolerant of the victims. There's nothing I can do. I'm sorry. There's nothing anyone can do. I wanted to hide away, pretend none of it was happening, that it would all turn out okay, somehow. So I went to work. Having more or less settled the children, war permitting, I wanted more regular work than just writing occasional articles.

I had been given an introduction to a doctor on the faculty of al-Quds University, and through her I began research work in the university's school of public health at al-Bireh near Ramallah. On some days I went to the main campus in Abu Dis, driving the short distance from home to the Old City, around the Mount of Olives and through the checkpoint: the route that would later be cut in half by the Security Barrier. The minute you leave West Jerusalem the roads become dilapidated and tangled; there are few signs, not much in the way of road markings, and an air of imminent road anarchy. I would go past the gatehouse and into the university, to where olive groves and fields, part of the agriculture department's water-treatment trials, edged the campus. The campus breathed a rural space, with views across the valleys and down toward the Dead Sea. On the other side of the road were blanks in the fields, marked out for sports stadiums, but stalled as large half-finished squares of sand.

The Abu Dis campus was lively with groups of male and female medical students, who would become the first homegrown Palestinian doctors. One day, as I was heading off to a meeting, the students were homing in on the large auditorium to hear a panel discuss depleted uranium, focusing heavily on its chemistry rather than its politics (Arafat had recently lashed out, accusing the IDF of using depleted uranium against Palestinians).* Since the discussion was in Arabic, I was given a brief translation. One of the students, bearded, tall and disarming, grinned down at me and apologized that he could not, on account of his religion, shake my hand. I withdrew it and changed to the "hand on heart" gesture I had learned in Pakistan.

My meeting was with a group of researchers from the school of public health. We sat in a small conference room and talked about the department's projects. The researchers were cheerful and full of plans despite the situation and its effects on their lives. Each of them had, that morning, as every morning, faced the humiliation and irritation of the checkpoints. One had been ordered to stand aside for questioning, and challenged by an eighteen-year-old soldier to prove her credentials. She had told him about her undergraduate and post-graduate degrees, and the universities where she had studied, and he had let her go. "He was just a kid," she said, "I think he'd have liked to go to London University too."

I had found my morning's checkpoint experience infuriating, and commented on their resilience. "It's been getting steadily worse for years," said one. "We know what we are facing, and we know we just have to keep going whatever happens." Education, she explained, was their most important weapon. She said that, as occupiers, the Israelis had gone to some lengths to promote Palestinian educational institutions, and yet they threatened them in so many other ways—physically closing them down, censorship, confiscating documents, and arresting participants. "But we refuse to be deprived of our education and our academic freedoms." She told me about the research she was already doing, and other proj-

---

* *Depleted uranium: a radioactive heavy metal used in armor-piercing munitions and in enhanced armor protection for some tanks. Taken into the body via metal fragments or dust-like particles, depleted uranium can pose a long-term health hazard. No evidence was produced to back up Arafat's accusation.*

ects that she was planning, and said, "Come on, come as much as you can, we have too much to do."

To be free to do this I needed more domestic help. Once Dina had quit, Delal and Naimi had started helping me out with the cleaning on an ad hoc basis, in return for groceries rather than cash so as to bypass the social veto on working in another man's house. One morning they had been reduced to ducking below the windowsill to avoid Abu Anis and his disapproval, when he had come to the house to return some coffee cups and a tray. An arrangement with Delal and Naimi would have suited everyone involved, but it was impossible. Knowing I needed more help, a Palestinian friend at the lycée reintroduced me to Samia, a Christian Palestinian I had met before the Intifada began; she suggested we meet at the boys' school.

I didn't recognize Samia; she was a changed woman. We said hello inside the walled compound of the schoolyard, but Samia's eyes were elsewhere, everywhere, scanning, arcs of white under her black lashes. Children ran with the excitement of release from class, and picked on her as cats pick on people who fear them. They jostled, bumping her and spinning her until she lost her thinly held control and whirled about. I led her out of the throng and drove her to the quiet of our house where we could talk. She asked repeatedly if where we lived was safe: "Are we *safe* here?" I tried to tell her that we were quite safe, insulated even, but she wouldn't be convinced. It wasn't only people she feared; it was noise, movement, anything sudden.

She let go of her hesitation and spewed out that she no longer had a house, it had been bombed, and she was living in a church, eating food handed out by charities, and that "Every night the shooting starts, so my people shut up their houses and wait, wait for the retaliation that they know will come," from the IDF, "from their tanks and missiles," she said, "and they hit us and destroy, destroy, destroy." She had a strange numbness: everyone had become an enemy, bar the Christian inhabitants of Beit Jala. In her eyes the

Israelis were a greater enemy than "the Muslims," but the Muslims were their enemy too: "Nothing will stop them from shooting at Gilo, nothing we can do, even when we die." She had stopped thinking about anything beyond the grind of day into night and out again: "It gets dark, they start to shoot, they come closer and shoot again, we move out to escape, and then the tanks and helicopters start. We have no work, we have no food, we have no sleep." Nothing mattered except being able to see the next day begin.

I had installed Catriona in a preschool in Jerusalem and the boys were happy enough at the lycée. Taking on Samia would give me more freedom, and I thought a live-in job might give Samia a break from her fear, and allow her to wind down from her state of constant vigilance. We agreed to try one another, and I showed her the ropes. As we walked down the hill to drop off the garbage in the community dumpster (there is minimal garbage collection in East Jerusalem) we met Amer, on his way home to the lower village. I introduced them and he welcomed her with his usual grin. But she stiffened, accusing him of not being Palestinian because he didn't roll his Rs properly.

"She thinks I'm Israeli," he laughed. "That's okay." He thought it funny, perhaps a little irritating. His mind was full of his daughter's problems. The little girl had been born with a shortened left arm and only two digits on her left hand, and was being treated at the Israeli hospital next to the French school. Her next surgical step in the long schedule of operations had been delayed yet again because she had a chest infection, and he was unhappy that she was losing time in the program to rebuild her arm. While we talked, Samia jumped, and I rewound the sounds in our ears. Something large had dropped in the valley below, which must have sounded to her like a gunshot.

I hoped she would feel more secure once she started work. There were times when I found her sitting silent in the house, staring at nothing, but in general she seemed to be calmer. It wasn't because she slept well at night: she insisted on going home to Beit

Jala every afternoon. "Home" was where her nephew was, somewhere in Beit Jala, perhaps in the church, but she didn't say; she simply said she had to be with him at night. Then one day she admitted that they had applied for visas to get out: "We are leaving Palestine. It is finished," she said.

When she made her announcement, Mohammed was connecting a new phone line for the satellite installation. He looked at her but said nothing. He turned instead to a lithograph of a castle built by Saladin on an island in the Red Sea just beyond the southern tip of Israel, and began examining it closely. Samia finished talking about Palestine's doom, and Mohammed said: 'I want to take Maha and the girls away for a couple of days." Then looking closer at the lithograph, he said, "That isn't there any more, right?" pointing to the castle. I admitted that it was, and that we had taken our children there during a recent long weekend.

Without passports, Mohammed and his family had few opportunities to travel. We now viewed our freedom of movement, which we had always taken for granted, differently. We were also keen to explore Israel and went north during the next long weekend, overcoming our war-induced apathy and our disgruntlement at the wetness of the weather. Green again: the Galilee was lush and verdant, brimmingly fertile and lovely to look on. We visited Armageddon on the way north, a benign, ruin-strewn hillock with a heavy name. Capernaum, where Jesus picked his fishers of men, fed 5,000 with five loaves and two fishes and preached the Sermon on the Mount, hovered on the edge of the Sea of Galilee, a pale expanse of quiet water. Up in the foothills of Mount Hermon rises the spring—at Banias—where the Romans had worshipped Bacchus and contemplated fertility in temples whose scattered columns remain, tumbled about. We could escape, the strains of Jerusalem falling away during our tour of Israel's northern attractions.

Back in Jerusalem again, work was a struggle. On many days even attempting to get to the school of public health in al-Bireh was out of the question, either because of the intensified IDF closures, or because of overnight or threatened bombings. When I did try, I could spend so much time held up at the checkpoints that when I finally made it to work I had to turn around and start for home again.

The process was wearying: beginning the day in the dark to get everything ready and on the road for the boys' school, Catriona's preschool, and then my work, the pressure of rush-hour traffic through Jerusalem, where roads were white-lined and orderly, but aggression was not. Then through the Palestinian areas of Shuafat and Beit Hanina, with signs to the settlements on both sides, construction everywhere for the new roads to serve those settlements and the Palestinian roads disintegrating. Toward Ramallah, beyond a-Ram checkpoint, which could strangle the traffic for any length of time, and into an area without white lines, where roads were gravel, dust prevailed, and traffic lights had lost their colors, so you look for red with your foot on the brake and see only white and hear people hooting from behind. Then you realize the white light dangling on a wire that swings into view when the wind permits is the green-for-go sign but it's missing its colored filter. Through the lights, the traffic forms itself into lanes across the road in the dust, or mud if it's raining, according to speed and the drivers' daring. Yellow taxis race by, 4x4s get the upper hand in the mud, trucks grind remorselessly, and everyone slams on the brakes before the sleeping policemen—huge hillocks in the road laid by locals—throw the unsuspecting into the air.

Then all drivers are funneled into one arena—Qalandia. The Palestinians' simple, now-bombed, airport lies to the left. Ahead are the soldiers, unseen because of the thronging mass of cars and jostling trucks. There is usually an unspoken "in-the-same-boat" mentality that dampens argument. Frequently the edging forward creates a logjam, in which case people appear from the sidelines to direct the mess into flow again. Boys squeeze between vehicles carrying decorative jugs of drinks, hawkers sell oddments, tea-merchants pour long spouts of hot liquid from jugs. But the hours spent lined up in a funnel—this is not a border checkpoint—are still angry ones. In one direction your work is waiting, colleagues looking at watches, understanding. In the other direction your children are waiting, alone in the schoolyard, thinking of arrests and shootings because they hear about them every day. Your friends will step in for the children, but maybe they've been held up too. The situation is organizing you: it wants you to give up work and retreat.

I was often angry: it was not only the difficulty of getting to work. Amer had been making a little sleigh-bed for Catriona and had had to go to Ramallah to find a mattress to fit. He admitted later that he had been forced to pull down his trousers at the check-point on the way back. I felt responsible for his humiliation, and for such a trivial cause—a mattress. He brushed it off, saying he understood why the soldiers did these things and didn't hold it against them, but nor would he let the humiliation get to him. He smiled broadly, "You just have to keep smiling and not minding whatever they do—that really pisses them off."

One day, Karen, a Jewish-American friend from New York came to stay, bringing luminous stars for the children. They lay in their beds with their glowing stars stuck to the walls beside them. Karen and I talked about the next day's plans for a "day of rage" in protest at the total closure of the villages around Ramallah. People were saying it would be *real* rage this time, the frustrations beyond controllable. Only that morning a colleague, bleary-eyed and now bitter, had told me of her daughters' fears the night before, lying on the bathroom floor yet again as the gunfire rained down from the settlement above, strafing their home, and nothing they could do about it. The settlers complained about the same problem; Palestinian gunmen firing up at them so that they were unsafe in their homes too, their children too terrified to sleep. Everyone living in fear.

We joined friends for dinner in West Jerusalem. The situation dominated: there was worried talk about the brutality and where it might lead. The group was upset by recent reports in the papers: for example, that soldiers had shot unarmed, handcuffed Palestinians. One talked about a letter from an ex-IDF officer who had been shocked at the sight of soldiers dragging a bleeding young Palestinian through the streets of Hebron.[6] We talked about what life must be like under Closure, and about all the dead children and the mentality of suicide bombers and of snipers picking children out. "What goes on inside a bomber's head as he looks at the people he's about to kill?" and "What makes a sniper target children and children's *eyes*?"

"There is massive denial among Israelis," said one friend, Joni, "about the existence of the brutality, never mind where it's taking us." He assigned this denial partly to Israelis' understandable fears, and partly to manipulation. "If you want to hold on to the territories, you can't have people understanding the link between the violence and the occupation. You have to manipulate and break that link. So you push two basic lines: Arabs are intrinsically violent, and the territories are vital for Israel's security."

"And where are we heading—where are the negotiations?" Karen asked. "How can we get peace without negotiating?" Many people bemoaned the blocks on getting back to the table since the Taba talks; there was the now-familiar grumble, that the Palestinians weren't serious about peace so what was the point in trying to negotiate. But one said there was an old pattern of stonewalling.

This pattern, said another, was typical. By prompting Palestinian attacks, either steadily by closures and collective punishment, or more dramatically by assassinating their leaders, it was easy to maintain that it was all Arafat's fault. Never Israel's fault: "Israel wants only peace,"—he was hamming up the delivery—then added, "on Israel's terms."

The denial Joni talked about was pervasive. One afternoon I took my two younger children to a playground while Archie had a cello lesson. I was just aware of strange construction noises, I thought, or could it be thunder—the weather had grown very hazy through the day and the dust hung heavy in the air. Then it sank in that the noises were tank shells landing on Beit Jala. I began to listen properly, realizing that the thuds were shells because the shelling was interspersed with machine-gun fire. They grew louder as the wind changed. There I was in a playground— some would point out on expropriated land—with my two children, while just across the valley other children were cowering in a theater of war.

There were other parents with children playing, but the parents were ignoring the noises. I had seen a couple of the mothers before; one was a friendly American with a hairy dog. We had talked over the children and done the playground exchange in the past, but as we lined up for an *'afurch* at the tiny coffee shop on the corner I broke the situation taboo and said: "You hear the bombing? It must be terrifying for them." She looked at me. "No, I don't hear anything. Nothing." And turned away.

I saw and heard denial everywhere. I applied it myself. My mother visited against the advice of her husband: I said he was being too cautious. She had a list of Holy Land sites she wanted to see but gave up after Bethlehem, in disbelief. I tried to say that the closures weren't so bad; she said, "Fine, let's try some other places." She wanted to go to Hebron, Nablus, Jericho, and the monastery of Mar Saba. Blocked at every one of them, we went to the Old City and bought lithographs of these places instead. David Roberts lithographs, from Yasser Barakat.

"Don't you *see* the guns anymore?" she asked as we walked through the alleyways of the Old City, passed more Israeli soldiers, all hung about with weapons.

"Of course..."

"Doesn't it make you want to scream when they stop you at the checkpoints every time?"

"But there's nothing you can do. The soldiers at the checkpoint have absolute power, there's no *point* to getting angry. And are you going to scream every day, twice a day?"

Later we were at another checkpoint, and a middle-aged man in a suit was being pulled out of a taxi on the other side of the road. "No, no, that can't happen," she said, as the police began to rough him up.

I drove her away, saying, again, there's nothing you can do. No point. When I did get angry I'd had soldiers shouting at me: "I am the *law* here, you obey *me*," and it was true. They were the law, even if they were breaking international laws in the process, and I did have to obey. "This happens all over the world, not just in Israel."

"That doesn't mean it's right," she said.

"And you can go back to London and forget how angry you feel now. It's a good thing you have to leave," I said, looking at the disgust written on her face.

Before she left, Maha and Naimi laid out a special feast for my mother and gave her presents of ceramics and embroidery from the Old City. They knew where to buy from local artisans, rather than the ubiquitous Chinese tourist products and sparkly Indian fabrics. My mother was touched by their thoughtfulness. At the airport she was interrogated: who had she seen, who had she met, why had she come, what were the names of the Palestinians she had seen and why had she met them. All reasonable questions given the circumstances; Israel had to control the Palestinian uprising after all, she said. But it was the attitude that was so painful. A few hours before she had sat as a guest in Maha's house, then at the airport this friendship had been criminalized, and she had felt obliged to deny it existed. When she returned to London and told the story she was asked why she had associated with *Palestinians*. The word was used as a pejorative, like *barbarian* or *savage*, in a menu of ignorance. My mother turned away.

5

It Can't Get Worse

The night my mother left there was a savage act by a Palestinian: a baby girl was killed by a sniper in Hebron, shot dead as she lay in her father's arms. Her name was Shalhevet Pass.

Since Sharon's accession, town after Palestinian town had been invaded by the IDF, terrifying the inhabitants; Palestinians had attacked Israelis, terrifying them in their turn. By the end of March 2001, 68 Israelis and 409 Palestinians had died in the new Intifada. Since the killing of eight Israelis by a Palestinian bus driver on February 14, one Israeli had been killed and nine injured by a bomb in a taxi in Wadi Ara, and three days later three people were killed and at least 60 injured in the Israeli town of Netanya—the first Israelis killed in a suicide bombing since the start of the Intifada. Two car bombs were defused, including one in Mea Sharim near the boys' school. Now, nearly two months after Sharon's victory, evacuation hung over us again. And yet at home in the Forest of Peace we felt safe; the bells around the necks of the goats rang out against the quietness of the valley, and there were meowing kittens and fat puppies. One of these, the furriest, was going to be ours, promised to the children by Maha's niece, Rasha. The foal was growing well. Flowers abounded, crimson poppies, yellow mustard, blue rosemary, and countless tiny flowers I couldn't identify, almond blossom painting the trees palest white-pink.

On March 27, 2001, there were two bombs in Jerusalem: the first, in the morning, was a car bomb in Talpiot injuring seven people. Andrew called me on my cell phone to say be careful, and also that this might trigger the beginning of a widely predicted Israeli onslaught.[1] The second, that afternoon, was a suicide bomb aimed at a bus in French Hill. Twenty-eight people were injured, two seriously. Traffic all over central Jerusalem was knotted up, and

I was forced to go deeper into Mea Sharim where we were held stationary. I was not happy about being made to drive through this area: my control over risk was taken away from me. The streets were narrow and contorted, and jammed up very quickly, leaving you pinioned in a dangerous place, unable to escape. People walking by became threats, backpacks became explosives, costumes disguises.

The next day there was a bomb in Qalqilya, a Palestinian town, and another was defused in Netanya. The IDF shelled again: Gaza, Ramallah, and Hebron. Sharon's efforts to convince President Bush that using military force would bring peace had been successful, and there was little hope, moderates on both sides complained, of the intervention they needed from the US.

Samia hadn't turned up on a number of mornings, and it was difficult to know whether it was because of the soldiers at the checkpoint or her efforts to emigrate. When she did come, she was as jumpy as ever. One morning she found a giant centipede three inches long writhing in the sink, and screamed.

"If they bite you, you die," she cried. I was at home trying to write a report; I dealt with the "forty-four," as the insects were called, and tried to calm Samia. There were fresh almonds on the table, picked from the trees, with their strange greenness and sharp taste; we had no idea what they were until the evening, when Maha came around to tell us she was having a baby. After three girls, she was hoping for a boy. She showed us how to eat the almonds, and we watched the foal canter awkwardly up and down the little drive. The foal had been left alone while Basil took its mother out for a ride; later Basil came back for his little brother, Hamoud, and led him quietly along the dusty road by the house. The mare sensed that her new rider was a beginner, so she was gentle, not the spirited ride she had been with Basil, who had raced by, tassels flying. Rasha came to the house to tell us that we could take the new puppy. The children ran about chattering and we settled the fluffy fat thing into her new basket, but the puppy was mournful and howled for her brothers and sisters all night.

The ten-month-old murdered Israeli baby, Shalhevet Pass, was finally laid to rest in April. (Her Hebron settler family had initially refused to bury her until the IDF took over Abu Sneim, from where the shots that killed her were fired.) The talk since her death had been about the mentality of a gunman who could fix his sights on, and kill, a child. Now Hebron, where there was always incipient trouble even at the best of times, was boiling.

Even those who had become inured to the daily tests of the occupation had trouble believing the reality of Hebron. Four hundred Jewish settlers and 140,000 Palestinians live in the city of the Patriarchs: Abraham, Isaac, and Jacob are believed to be buried there with their wives. Forty thousand of these Palestinians live under Israeli rule and, for much of the six months since the start of the Intifada, had been kept under complete 24-hour curfew. This allowed the 400 settlers to move about freely.*

Even when there was no curfew, it was sobering to visit Hebron and see its slow strangulation. You drive in through Palestinian bustle, streets crammed with life, the sharp new buildings against the softer stone of the old. Suddenly the wide main road becomes a market—instantly, from street into souk without taking a breath. The market had to be here now: the original souk was closed up. Gargantuan cabbages on every side, wooden trolleys speeding through impossible gaps, boys running, old men slow in white djellabahs and dark keffiyehs, mounds of purple garlic, broad beans in wide piles, towers of flat-smoothed vine leaves, pyramids of spice, cages of pigeon, duck, and geese, and noise.

The noise dulls steadily into quiet as you make your way through the concrete cubes blocking the narrowing streets, walking along the double-storied buildings, shops below, homes above, the

---

* After Baruch Goldstein gunned down 29 Muslims praying in the mosque at Hebron in February 1994, the Israeli government nearly withdrew the settlement, but Rabin hesitated. Israel accepted the presence of unarmed international monitors in the town. Known as the "Temporary International Presence in Hebron" (TIPH), the group was restricted to the role of making notes on attacks they were powerless to stop.

shutters green metal and mournful. The closer you get to the Jewish settlement, the heavier the quiet. The dead center, the site of the old market with its now boarded shop fronts, often marked black with fire and violence, is sepulchral. There may be a few settlers standing at the checkpoints—they wear their weapons and their religion with equal ease. Green army vehicles patrol, eyeing us, checking us out. A white TIPH car, its two unarmed occupants looking uncomfortable, edges by in silence.

There are ancient stone houses in the center of the city, many of them abandoned: "encouraging" the Palestinian inhabitants to leave has been going on for years. Inside, the houses are filled with absences: vaulted ceilings; ovens for baking; stairs now winding up into nothing; delicate colors lingering on the peeling plaster; vines and weeds taking over. The views from the rooftops over the city toward the great Herodian edifice—the Tomb of the Patriarchs—are punctured by watch-posts, whose camouflaged eyes are all-seeing.

An American journalist, Joe, the father of one of Archie's school friends, came back from Hebron aghast at the violence and virulence he had encountered. Knowing he was going to be late, he had asked me to pick up his daughter from school. He came to collect her and accepted a drink before they left. He sat, stunned, under the tree overlooking the valley, and talked.

The night before, he said, the settlers had set off a bomb in a row of Hebron shops, injuring their own soldiers. Joe had watched them marauding, flaunting their freedom to the shuttered doors and the Palestinians locked in behind them, unable to move, or work, or go to school, day after day. It was the settlers who attacked Joe, who happens to be Jewish, and were verbally aggressive when he tried to interview them, then physically aggressive when he admitted that he had interviewed Palestinians as well. "Get out of my face!" they spat at him as they beat him away. "God gave us this land!—God gave us this land!" they said repeatedly and with a loathing he said he had never seen in all his time as a journalist, and hoped never to see again.

"I never said a word about their right to be there. I hardly got anything out at all—they didn't give me a chance."

"This is not living," one Palestinian had told Joe as he hurried past to find food for his family when the curfew was lifted for an hour, as happened every few days. "This is not life."

Curfews were not new to Palestinian Hebronites; nor was conflict. The original Jewish community in Hebron had been massacred by Palestinians in the riots of 1929. Since 1968, when Moshe Levinger installed the first Israeli colony, settlers and Palestinians had lived alongside each other angrily, with frequent violence. The Palestinians attacked the settlers and the settlers attacked the Palestinians. The law, however, was weighted against the Palestinians: Israeli government commissions and human rights organizations repeatedly found their forces failed to protect Palestinians from settler attacks, sometimes even joining in.[2] Under the protective might of the IDF, settlers had virtual immunity to bully, beat, and mob Palestinians who could only watch as their market and livelihoods were bulldozed.* Many had given in to the terror and left.

One Norwegian observer stationed in Hebron told me of the frustration of working there, of the number of times they were themselves attacked by settlers, and of the ironies. He once witnessed a fight between two American Israelis. They were standing on a road in Hebron built with American government money. One was a peace activist; the other was a settler. One said to the other, "You have no right to be here. Go back to America," to which the other replied: "No, *you* have no right to be here, *you* go back to America."

More visitors came to stay with us in Jerusalem, ignoring warnings from people in London and New York. During my parents-in-law's visit the IDF bombed Beit Jala again. I left my

---

* *In January 2001 there had been outrage among Israeli moderates when a settler found guilty of clubbing a Palestinian child to death with a rifle butt was sentenced to six months' community service.*

mother-in-law at home while I took the boys to play soccer, but when we returned she was distressed. Sitting in the garden among the unpruned roses, listening to the rumbling explosions of the IDF barrage on Beit Jala, she could not know how close the bombing might edge.

"I'm not really enjoying this," she said. Realizing how immune I had become to the noise of the IDF, I assured her that our village had never been bombed. I had to leave her again to go with my father-in-law to visit one of his old friends, Israel Shahak. Amid the chaos of books and papers in his tiny apartment in Rehavia, the sadness was bleak and heavy. A survivor of the Warsaw Ghetto and of Bergen-Belsen, after a lifetime of standing up for justice and common sense in Israel, even Professor Shahak had been pushed too far by Palestinian attacks.

"How things have changed since we last met, Ian."

My father-in-law murmured, "Indeed, Israel, and not for the better."

He meant not only the terrible violence, but also anti-Semitism. "As an Israeli Jew," said Shahak, "I've been shocked by the levels of hatred in Arab countries." He mentioned a vitriolic song—"I hate Israel, I love Amr Moussa"*—playing to huge approval in Egypt. "And President Assad's vicious comments to the Pope when he visited Syria..."[3]

Ian agreed. They talked about anti-Semitism and the danger that the Intifada would lead to more. Neither man, both long-time observers of the politics of the Middle East, held out much hope, especially with the US not taking on the role of impartial arbiter.

"But the State Department has at least *protested* that more than a billion shekels are to be used for settlements," said Ian.

Shahak brushed this off—Sharon had apologized to the US, saying the money was for security, not expansion, and would be spread over several years.

---

* Egypt's then Foreign Minister.

"What nonsense," he said, "Sharon does not change."

Ian mentioned the possibility of Shimon Peres using his cabinet post to restrain Sharon. Again Shahak was dismissive. "Oh, Peres and Sharon," he said, despairing. "They're just like each other."

"In what way?"

"The two of them are the biggest liars in Israeli history."

For Ian, the saddest moment was when his friend, who for years had stood up for dialogue, coexistence, and genuine peace declared his new position: "Separation is the only option." Shahak explained: "We cannot talk peace with them, only a ceasefire behind an iron wall." This was the majority Israeli view, he said, and now, sadly, it was his view too. Others, pointing to the fence around Gaza, insisted that separation was not a solution: Condemning hundreds of thousands of people to a life of dependency inside a big prison does not bring genuine peace. And therefore it would not bring security either. But Palestinian bombings were pushing Israelis, even long-standing and vocal peace advocates like Israel Shahak, into a position they had thought they would never hold.

"The Palestinians have lost all sympathy," he explained. "Arafat united all Israelis by first demanding the Palestinian right of return." There was a peace camp joke, he said: "We thought we were struggling for two states for two nations, now we see the Palestinians want two states for one nation." The implication being that the Palestinians would have not only their own state in the West Bank and Gaza Strip but would also, by returning hundreds of thousands of refugees, secure a demographic majority in Israel as well. (This, many held, was Arafat's chosen method to destroy Israel.)

Shahak's second reason was Palestinians' insistence on attacking Israelis inside Israel, instead of attacking only settlements inside the Occupied Territories. "Attacks against settlements in the territories shock few Israelis," he said. "I don't call those terrorist acts—except in a few cases. Most are acts of legitimate resistance to the occupation, but not all. The killing of two young boys in the cave, and the two men in the Tulkarem restaurant when they spared the Israeli Arab—these are different—and not legitimate resistance by any definition." The murder (May 8, 2001) of the two fourteen-year-old boys had been horrifying: Koby Mandell and Yosef Ishran had been beaten to death by Palestinians in a cave near their settlement, Tekoa.

"Where is the situation heading?" I asked him. "People are talking about 'transfer.'"

The professor looked pained, and shook his head slowly. "The transfer idea was alive until the 1980s," he said. "But it was killed by Oslo and the first Intifada." He talked about Zionism's aims, the plan to conquer the land, leaving as few Arabs on it as possible, and how this had been pursued in various ways: forceful expulsions, the destruction of villages, churches, mosques, historical sites, homes, and businesses, the expropriation of land by a number of legalistic ploys, the expropriation of water, and other measures including massacre and rape. And with varying success: 1948 saw the territory of the new state of Israel cleared of 75 percent of its Palestinian inhabitants. Yet in that respect the war of 1967 failed: the population of the newly occupied territories fell by only a fraction; the majority of Palestinians, having learned the lesson of '48, stayed. "And now," he said, "transfer is dead."

"But the problem of the settlements," he continued quietly. "The two worst are Itzar and Tapuach. These," he added, "are even worse than Hebron." His thoughts ran on. "Likud shouts, Labor builds: it's always been this way..." he said, explaining that while Likud made a big drama about building settlements, Labor quietly went ahead and built them. "The Sharon government will last as long as the war," he said finally. I was unsure which he meant was driving which. We left and never saw him again. Professor Shahak died a few weeks later. A great man, he was widely mourned.

If Israel Shahak, a long-standing pillar of the left, had been pushed too far by Palestinian violence, it was not surprising that many Israeli moderates had moved into the fear camp. It, the fear—and the situation—kept nagging at our daily routines. Andrew rang from Gaza one morning while I was in a meeting with colleagues at work. He wanted me to know that despite the IDF destroying a building 100 meters from the UN compound, he was fine. But he didn't much like the whistling in and then boom of the missiles, he said.

There were Palestinian attacks and reprisals, Israeli attacks and reprisals. Shalhevet Pass was no longer the youngest victim of the Intifada; another baby girl, Iman Hijjo, was killed by Israeli tank-fire in a Gaza refugee camp. She was four months old. The IDF shelled in retaliation for a Palestinian mortar attack on an Israeli settlement in the Gaza Strip. The mortar attack caused no injuries. Ten Palestinian children in a primary school were among those injured in the retaliation.[4] All the while there was the constant backdrop to most of our days: the steady thud, thud of IDF actions in the territories, too continuous to be news.

May 15, 2001 was newsworthy. The anniversary of the *Nakba*, the Palestinians' catastrophe and Israelis' triumph at the founding of the state of Israel, it stood in direct contradiction to the refrain of Israelis as victims. There was widespread Israeli anger about Palestinians marking the event by street protests and riots. Continuing Palestinian incitement against Israel was one of the main Israeli complaints against the PA.

During the day we heard that a friend had been shot. At first we had no idea how bad his injuries were, but the shooting had been caught on film by one of the many international film crews, so we found out soon enough as it was widely broadcast. One of France's main TV journalists in the Middle East, Bertrand had been covering the *Nakba* Day demonstrations at the Ayosh junction in Ramallah, when, as the video recording showed, an Israeli border patrolman got out of his jeep and made his preparations. The soldier, a cigarette dangling from his mouth, lifted his M-16 rifle, which was fitted with a telescopic sight, took aim at the journalist, who was standing amid a group of reporters and their cameras, and fired a single shot. If it hadn't been for his flak jacket, Israelis read in their paper, he "might have been mortally wounded."[5] As it was, the force of the shot left Bertrand lying injured on the ground, the shreds of metal bullet embedded in his flak jacket.

I saw him a few days later when our families were swimming at a friend's house. The bruise on his chest was over his sternum, just to the left over the fifth intercostal space.

"He was a good shot," I said. "One inch more and he'd have been right over your heart."

"No, he was a *very* good shot," came the reply. "I was at a slight angle to him," said Bertrand, indicating that the shot had come in from the left and would, without his flak jacket, have penetrated his heart. "But let's not talk about it," he said, making a quieting sign with his finger to his lips. "The boys," who were in the pool with mine, "don't know what happened, and we don't want them to."

His wife, Charlotte, a designer, blonde, English, and very attractive, talked about an encounter with an Israeli she had come to know. She told him, when he asked how she was and how things were in his friendly way, what had happened.

"No, it couldn't have been," he said. "I was in the army. Our security forces don't do that kind of thing."

"But I'm telling you," said Charlotte, "it was filmed, recorded, it's right there on the screen."

He would not be moved: "It didn't happen," he said.

Three days after Bertrand was shot, a Hamas suicide bomber detonated himself outside a shopping mall in Netanya. Five Israelis were killed and over a hundred were wounded. This attack, like each one before it, ruined hundreds of lives. Israel retaliated immediately, this time sending in war planes—F-16s—to bomb Gaza and the West Bank for the first time since 1967, killing sixteen Palestinians and causing widespread damage.

I managed to take Catriona to preschool. "Managed" because new checkpoints had sprung up one immediately after another in crazed fashion. The traffic in Beit Hanina was gridlocked, and those parents who had been forced to move in order to avoid the checkpoints were maddened: "What do we do, move *again* so we can get the children to school?" Andrew called to say that perhaps our boys shouldn't swim that day, as tensions were running very high in Gaza, Ramallah, Nablus, and Jerusalem. Just after we hung up there were two loud blasts over the city, different from the normal construction blasts, but I heard nothing on the news. I was anticipating bombs.

We were beginning to see signs of the strain even in our little village. One morning, while I turned the car around, the boys went ahead down the hill as usual to put the rubbish in the dumpster. I could hear voices and a tone I didn't like. When I reached the boys they jumped into the car and said, "Let's get out of here," so I drove away. "What happened?"

They told me that a gang of boys from the lower village had bristled up to them, saying "What's your name" in the loud and uncomprehending way that happened from time to time. I should have been more alert. The bigger boys, three of them, about twelve years old, had slapped my two (now aged seven and four) on the cheek, kicked Archie in the back, and surrounded Xan and pushed him around. My boys said they hadn't liked it but they didn't want me to go back and sort it out, nor would they run up the hill to find me if it happened again, because they said they would look scared. So much for absorbing local lessons: they had learned that not losing face was more important than finding a solution. I called our landlord to find out the telephone number of the *mukhtar* (village elder) so that I could speak to him about it. All the landlord could offer was to ask why I hadn't called his father, saying he *was* the *mukhtar*. I said I would sort it out myself.

The landlord passed the word to his father regardless. To Abu Anis I was a woman who needed protecting when Andrew was in Gaza or traveling abroad and probably an irritatingly disrespectful one at that. Besides, he felt that administering local justice was his territory. He appeared at my door that evening saying he was going to get Basil to bring the boys to us, and if we identified them as the right boys Basil would hit them.

"No—no hitting," I said.

So Abu Anis told me the culprits were afraid of his boys, who would show them the dogs and tell them that they would feed them to the dogs if they did wrong. I glanced at Basil, standing beside his grandfather looking uncomfortable. I knew him as an Androcles, always looking after and finding food for his menagerie, shy with me but very kind to the children. He was here out of duty.

"No hitting," I repeated. Abu Anis insisted; I blocked again. This went on with no ground given on either side, until he decided it was a translation problem, and gave up.

I should have been more grateful for his concern. I had appeared disdainful to him and his system of justice, but I was feeling belligerent, especially when he said "I am your father." In other words: you can't look after yourself. The language and culture of victimhood was everywhere, debilitating. "Don't you see how like each other they are?" asked one of the more jaded commentators that night at the journalists' favorite haunt, the American Colony bar. "Both sides convinced they're the victims, both adamant that the other must give way, both obsessively determined not to look beaten even if it means continuing the bloodshed instead."

That day I had been dependent enough to ask for Amer's help in fixing our phones. I didn't know that his 90-year-old father had had a stroke and was being taken to the hospital. Amer helped me and then rushed off to see to the Israeli ambulance that had arrived. I watched it leave, under armed escort, a police jeep with machine-gun-wielding soldiers inside.

Ambulances, and their sirens in particular, had become a warning system. They were sometimes the first indication of a bomb; two would raise the alert, three would make journalists sit up and stop talking, more than four had them heading for the door. One night we woke to the ominous sound of ambulances

speeding down the Hebron Road in the direction of Talpiot. Those
journalists who were not in bed were on their way. The sleeping ones
caught up later. The ambulances were arriving in droves. What they
found when they reached the scene was, for once, not a bomb.
Everyone had assumed a suicide bomber. The victims were Israelis,
but this time the villains were not Palestinian terrorists but corner-
cutting Israeli businessmen, who had skimped on building materials
and constructed a death trap of a banqueting hall. The TV news
played a sequence shot by a guest at the wedding being celebrated:
the bride and groom dancing among their happy guests and then,
calamity. The floor of the hall gave way, collapsing under the feet of
the dancers, dropping them through space and crushing them under
masonry and falling columns.

It was a further tragedy for Israelis to swallow. Another
followed shortly, when Palestinian gunmen murdered three settlers.
Former US Senator George Mitchell called for an immediate ceasefire to allow confidence-building measures and a renewal of peace
negotiations, and a freeze on expansion of Jewish settlements in
the Occupied Territories. Sharon rejected the freeze, saying the
settlements were a vital national enterprise. It was a stalemate,
budged by acts of aggression from each side. Correspondents were
struggling to keep their coverage acceptable to their editors back
home—so many of the day-to-day Occupied Territories stories
were "the same," they'd heard it all before. "How many times can
you report that a few Palestinians were killed during an IDF incur-
sion?" asked one, morosely.

Catriona was thriving at preschool; I was frustrated at work. I
had little enough time there as it was and could not be very
productive. Besides, there was always talk. One morning my
colleagues decided to take me to the best patisserie in Ramallah so
that I could try the famous sweet cheese confection, *knafeh*, that
they had often talked about. They drove me through the streets to
show me their town. Ramallah had been under attack and repaired
so often that it almost seemed to be enjoying a construction

boom—if you ignored the reason for the piles of rubble and scales of scaffolding.

While we sat at fake-marble formica tables in the bakery—the confection was indeed very sweet, layers of soft white cheese and melting sugar—one colleague, a Harvard-educated PhD, her head tightly veiled and face beautiful in her sadness, described being an alien everywhere she went and the pain of never finding a home. She had been born and brought up in Kuwait, where her parents had worked. They returned to Palestine in 1990 when Kuwait expelled its Palestinian community—400,000 people—because of Arafat's support for Saddam Hussein. "Being dispossessed," she said, "is only the beginning of the misery." She had not been accepted in Kuwait because she was Palestinian, and then she was not accepted in Palestine because she was from Kuwait. And it had not been easy to assimilate as a student in the US.

Back at work later that morning we were discussing research issues and efforts to build up the school of public health when a stranger hurried in and announced that Faisal Husseini had died. Everyone was quiet. "This is a great loss for us," my colleagues explained: Faisal Husseini had been a voice of authority and common sense. The head of one of Palestine's leading political families, Husseini had been a key player in negotiations with Israel since the first Intifada and was a notable moderate.

Diplomats and politicians drove to Ramallah to pay their respects at the PLO headquarters, standing about in the hot sun observing Palestinian grief at Husseini's death. Andrew stood in line with the newly arrived British Consul General who had been at the same school as him. It was a school where boys could choose, if they wished, to be drilled in military formation. "Bit like the corps, this," the diplomat quipped.

The dignitaries and representatives reassembled later at Orient House to join the funeral procession. Orient House had been the Husseini family home, built in the 19th century when Jerusalem expanded beyond the Old City, and the scene of famously lavish parties. Under Faisal Husseini, Orient House became an intellectual and political focus in East Jerusalem. Diplomats and dignitaries were received there, though this irritated Israeli authorities who resented displays of Palestinian officialdom in East Jerusalem. Now, for Husseini's burial, they were to await the arrival of the funeral procession, before joining it on its way to the al-Aqsa Mosque, next to which he would be buried. Settler groups, incensed that he should be buried on Temple Mount like generations of his ancestors, threatened to cause trouble.

For Palestinians the day was a short-lived liberation of East Jerusalem, or at least a taste of it. The Israeli police stayed out of the eastern side of the city completely, allowing the tens of thousands of mourners to drape Palestinian flags over the Damascus Gate and the city walls, as they peacefully marked out their sorrow along the twisting route through the Old City to al-Haram al-Sharif, where they buried him unconfronted by settler groups.

And then the following night the phone rang at 1AM. We were lying in bed unable to sleep; it was hot, there was no breeze. What was up this time? A senior IDF general had a tendency to call between midnight and 1AM on Saturday nights to update Andrew on Hizbollah movements on the border with Lebanon, and to berate him for the UN's inaction.

But this was different. Andrew was saying, "I can't hear you—what? It's a terrible line—what's happened?"

And then, "Oh God."

A suicide bomber had detonated himself at a Tel Aviv nightclub, the Dolphinarium, killing sixteen young Israelis, and injuring scores of others. So now, Sharon had said, the gloves were off, and a security cabinet meeting at 8AM would determine Israel's response. There was immediate talk of UN evacuation: the UN's Gaza staff were told to take three days' rations and assemble at the meeting point. The death toll rose over the hours, and in the end was twenty-one. Twenty-one young people murdered.

Our friends Ofer and Halley in Jaffa, on the verge of leaving Israel for ever, lived a nightmare that night. Their son Elamar had gone out for the evening. They had often deliberated the choice between tying him down or taking the risk that there might be a bomber out there. And that night he had gone out—they knew only approximately where—and they heard the blast. They lived the hell of their imaginations, driving through the emptying streets until at last they found him, safe.

Diplomats and UN officials, Andrew included, rushed off to Ramallah again to see if they couldn't talk sense into Arafat, who had condemned the bombing, but not forcefully enough. As ever, diplomacy was only a background hum to events, with no one able to break through the block on negotiations. Joschka Fischer, the German foreign minister, happened to be in Tel Aviv at the moment of the bombing and had already visited the site. We had learned the pattern: attack, retaliation, revenge, with no starting point; it was circular. And we kept asking: would Arafat do whatever it took to prevent more F-16s or whatever the "gloves-off" policy was to be? European and American diplomats had long complained about Arafat's promises and assurances, and many had lost patience with his inability to effect a ceasefire. And now, even if he did pull off a ceasefire, would that stop the momentum?

The waiting was grim. Palestinians who had nothing to do with suicide bombers, martyrs, or political activity of any kind waited, knowing that they were sitting ducks for whatever actions in revenge the Israeli cabinet decided to take. And the cabinet had to do something, not least to satisfy public opinion. Knowing retaliation would come, Andrew's father called to make sure Andrew was not in Gaza. He was not happy to hear that he was in Ramallah instead.

Arafat was persuaded to declare an unconditional ceasefire. Precarious as it was, it held off the immediate attack that everyone was expecting. Rumors continued to circulate that the government was planning a major offensive.

"I'm sorry to say it, but I have to," said my friend Scott, when I met him that afternoon, "Arabs are animals, they're not human." In his view, Palestinian bombings—in the two months before this latest bombing there had been three suicide bombs and five car bombs, killing eight Israelis*—had proved the government right. He didn't want to be reasonable any more—what was the point?

At dinner Andrew said, "This tragedy, this single bombing, the killing of those Israeli teenagers, will efface all the killings and tragedies the Palestinians have suffered, every one of them, and silence even more of the Israeli moderates." The occupation would no longer be visible to the outside world. "Both peoples are in for far, far worse now."

I sought out an Israeli friend, Shoshana Halper, wanting to hear her say the situation wasn't so bad after all. I drove to her home in the Yemeni quarter of Jerusalem, walked up to the house and rang the doorbell. As the door opened a dog rushed through.

"Hey, look what the dog brought in," said Jeff, her husband, welcoming me. "Hello, I'm just off to get the paper." Shoshana made coffee, gave me marbled cake, and from time to time tended the washing on the line.

Shoshana talked about her fear as a child in the fifties living near the border with Jordan, afraid of Palestinians who would come and steal their cattle. Her parents—Orthodox, right-wing—felt that the Arabs were trying to destroy them, just as the Nazis had. Her parents came from a large village in the Carpathian Mountains, and when Hungary handed over its Jewish population to the Nazis in 1944, her mother and aunts were sent to Auschwitz. They endured the ordeal of Mengele's selection. "My grandparents were sent off to one line." Her mother and three sisters were sent to another, bound for Bergen-Belsen.

*March 28, April 22, 23, and 29, and May 18, 25, 27, and 30, 2001. In this period 23 Israelis and 97 Palestinians were killed.[6]

In Bergen-Belsen Shoshana's mother and aunts were forced to work at a range of different tasks, including some for the German manufacturer Krups. "I avoid their products." She sat tucked into a large armchair as she told this story, a smile of kindness and understanding on her face. Understanding, that is, of my discomfort at her family's ordeal, of the unspoken.

"There was an epidemic of typhoid in Bergen-Belsen. One of my aunts died 48 hours before the British liberated the camp. I'm named after her—Reizel means 'rose'—and I was renamed Shoshana by my kindergarten teacher in Israel. She thought we should all have Israeli names. Actually," she added, "Shoshana is more a lily than a rose.

"Anyway, when the war ended, my parents married almost immediately. There was a strong urge to create families quickly, and my brother was born the year they were married, 1946. They lived in a big German house with a piano, in the Sudetenland. The Germans had been evicted."

In 1949, after the communists had come to power, "my parents decided to move to Israel. They had considered it before, of course, but the communists gave them the impetus they needed. In Israel they were given a great big Arab house, in Tira, an Arab village near where Ben Gurion airport is now. This was survival struggle; they didn't think about who had lived there before, or what had happened to them." Soon, in the drive to erase signs of the Palestinian past, the rest of the old Arab village was razed but their house was left for another four years because it was on the edge of the village. Eventually they moved to an Israeli house in the new village.

Shoshana grew up in a community with no grandparents and few children born before 1948. Her parents would not talk about the Holocaust, but everyone of Shoshana's generation "knew their parents had a big hump on their back, a taboo." Her first real exposure to that evil was the Eichmann trial in 1961. "Everything stopped in school, we all stopped, listened to the radio. It was a huge thing in Israel, it was, to face the issue of the Holocaust."

At that moment the door opened and Jeff came in carrying the papers and a bag of groceries. He wore a long-suffering grin that belied an incident: an angry fellow Israeli had accosted him at the mini-market.

"Some woman jumped on me yelling, 'Arab lover! My kids are in the army and you love the Arabs!' She attacked me."

"What did you do?"

"Yelled right back." Jeff, a well-known campaigner and peace activist, was used to being attacked, verbally and physically, by Israeli individuals as well as by Israeli forces, especially in his role as head of the Israeli Campaign against House Demolition (ICAHD). From time to time we would see him with cuts and bruises, and ask what had happened. He would explain that the security forces hadn't liked his campaign, which usually meant that he had been sitting in protest in front of Israeli bulldozers and had been arrested, often beaten up in the process. But he would always laugh it off and carry on.

Shoshana too was a campaigner—as part of the women's protest movement "Women in Black," but yelling was not her style. "I tell Jeff it's futile arguing, that talking is the only way: find some common ground, then try to persuade."

Both personally and professionally—she is a professor of medieval and Jewish history—Shoshana feels how important it is not to minimize the legacy of Jewish history, "which the left often tends to do. After everything the Jews have been through? No, no one should try to minimize that. But it doesn't excuse what we're doing now.

"Now," she said, "where we've got to, I'm feeling despair for the first time. Once things were very clear: two states, end the occupation. But now, with so much brutality and division? Now I fear for Israel."

I joined a demonstration and saw Shoshana in action. "Women in Black" was in its second decade of campaigning for withdrawal from the Occupied Territories. The message was short:

"End the occupation"; the image was stark: dress in black. The rhythm was simple too: every Friday, in Zion Square, at 1PM for one hour. This time, the week after the Dolphinarium bombing, it was a big international event, with black-clad women from all over the world and an international line-up of speakers, all of them against the occupation and all against the violence. While the women's voices called for negotiations and an end to brutality, extremist settlers hurled abuse. The settlers, shouting furiously in Hebrew, clashed against the calm dignity of the Women in Black. In some cases the calm came from not knowing what the settlers were saying as they spat at us because we didn't speak Hebrew.

An Israeli woman in front of me did speak Hebrew. She was responding, occasionally and quietly, to the lashings of abuse from the mouth of a settler woman in front of her. The settler's long clothes were, for once, colorful against the black of all our clothes. Her enraged voice, hoarse by now, was suddenly silenced when her adversary gently pulled her out of the path of the oncoming traffic, some of it honking in protest, all of it speeding. The settler woman had been so transported by her hate that she had stepped out into the road; she had found herself saved by someone she despised.

Shoshana was standing on a wall next to a potter whose work I'd seen displayed in the Yemeni quarter. The young settler men yelling at her were on her eye-level. As they yelled, she stayed calm. The louder they screamed, the calmer she appeared. This incensed them. They screamed louder. She smiled, not superciliously, and began to counter their shrieks with a few softly spoken words. Quietly and clearly she answered their accusations, and after a while, one or two of them began to listen. I didn't know what the words meant, but I could see her soothing their fury and bringing them to reason again.

"It won't do much good," she said later. "They'll fill up with hate again back in the outposts."

Shoshana and other moderates were waiting for Israelis to see sense while the extremist settlers and their supporters were urging on Israeli opinion with their zeal, their unshakable belief, and their determination to hold on to the land, whatever the cost. And Palestinian suicide bombers and their crimes were telling Israeli moderates that they were crazy to think the Palestinian people would ever live in peace alongside Israel. On the one hand, Shoshana and many like her were trying to counter the rigidity and inhumanity that can come from fear and fundamentalism. On the other, diverse strains of fanaticism and fundamentalism— Christian, Islamic, Jewish—were feeding off each other, intensifying each other everywhere.

Early one morning as I made the children's packed lunches for school, I heard the Voice of Israel news declare that it was "essential for the Palestinians to stop the killing and bring an end to the violence." There was a pause. Then the presenter went on briskly: "A Palestinian was killed last night"—by an Israeli settler organization. The press said it was possibly a Palestinian killing—a case of mistaken identity—even though the settler group (called "Shalhevet Pass") had claimed responsibility. And, the announcer added, three Bedouin women had been killed by Israeli tank-fire while they sat in their tent near Netzarim in Gaza.

George Tenet, head of the CIA, arrived in Israel to pressure both sides into a more robust ceasefire.* The suicide bombings had presented Palestinians as barbarians, giving credence to those who insisted the only way to deal with them was to put down their rebellion with military force. As I took Maha to her parents' home in Silwan by the walls of the Old City, she said, "Palestinian blood is cheap. And the IDF know how much they can get away with."

There was no withdrawal from Palestinian cities and no easing of the siege. The IDF would not pull back from the reinvaded Palestinian areas unless there was a complete cessation of violence. "So as usual," said Maha, "Hamas and Islamic Jihad will be thanking the

---

* Under the terms of this ceasefire, Yasser Arafat was to clamp down on militants, and Israel was to withdraw from territory seized during the Intifada.

Israeli government for the invitation to ruin the ceasefire. And then Sharon will be thanking them when they do." Though the ceasefire was holding, just, the underlying situation, and the fears, were worse than ever.

Meanwhile, I discovered that I was pregnant, proving that malaise can be attributed to elements other than the political situation, and that modern contraception is as fallible as the books admit.

6

The Head in the Yard

Unlike many Israelis and virtually all Palestinians, we were able to take a break during the summer, flying away from sirens and bombings to a place where the news was not filled with daily killings. In a wet green valley in southwest Scotland we submerged ourselves in plans for our new home, working out the roots we wanted to set into the earth, laying down our own place, and retrieving a semblance of control.

Control felt good. While the children explored their new and forever home, Andrew and I walked through our small towerhouse, which sits in the crook of a tumbling burn looking out across the fields to an ancient wood. We were with Nick, the architect, and his Icelandic wife, Limma. Nick wielded a large crowbar and, for good measure, a sledgehammer.

"Let's see what's hiding behind these layers of plasterboard," he said, slugging the sledgehammer into the wall. Plaster and dust spun away from his blows, and he stopped to shake down and examine the damage. "Look, here's the old fireplace—I think it's *almost* intact." Attacking the ceiling, bringing down debris on himself, he shouted, "Not much to be said for these oak beams, I'm afraid. You'll need new ones." And later, covered in centuries of dust, surfacing with a satisfied smile: "You've got a spiral staircase behind this wall."

After all the destruction we sat down to work out how we wanted everything laid out. "Kitchen? How about here—we could make a new window there, cantilever a new floor here..."

"Oh, and Limma," added Andrew. "You know we said we needed three children's beds... Can you make that four?"

Four children: we were both taken aback. Three had seemed manageable. Then again, said Andrew, Catriona will have a playmate. She may be two now but the boys pair off together and leave her out of their war games—all their games. I was seeing laundry and diapers and the long months and scent of breastfeeding, not to mention labor. "Another child is going to be wonderful," he smiled, "you'll see. They'll fill this house and it will be perfect."

We returned from Scotland restored, but almost immediately the bombing began again and the noises and the fears swept in, closer than ever.

On the last day of July we heard that an IDF missile strike had assassinated Sheikh Jamal Mansour, a senior Hamas political leader. With that, Hamas's nearly two-month-old ceasefire on attacks against Israeli civilians came to an end. The next day angry Israeli commentators warned readers that since Israel had violated the ceasefire they should expect Hamas to retaliate.[1] On August 9, Hamas duly dispatched a suicide bomber who detonated himself on the corner of Jaffa Road and St George Street, 200 yards from the boys' school. When there's a bomb, one of the things you take to doing in an attempt to deal with the horror is to monitor the casualty count. It kept rising through the day: by 6PM we heard that nineteen people were dead, with constant news footage on all the networks. Then the toll came down. It was finally given as fifteen dead. Seven of the dead were children.

The bomber had picked out a pizza parlor, Sbarro, as his target. We had been there a few weeks earlier, pizza being a staple of normal life. I had walked past it the day before. That very pavement was now covered with blood and death. We knew we would have to drive past it twice a day on the school run once the autumn term began. On the day and time the bomber chose, lunchtime, Sbarro was full of people and their children going about their daily business, living—or so it seemed—normal lives.

A Palestinian neighbor, who had asked me for a lift to Damascus Gate that morning, sat sullen in the evening, insisting that Israel deserved it. She had been changed as much as anyone by nearly a year of being ground down and sniped at, her and her family's lives besieged, made unlivable. There still seemed no hope of any progress, the leaders incapable and unwilling. The IDF had tightened the repression again and again and ratcheted up the number of "extrajudicial killings," including an attempt to kill Marwan Barghouti, the Palestinian leader one notch down from Arafat. Even so, it was alarming to hear how far her reason had stiffened into inhumanity, and to know that there were many Palestinians who felt the same.

Israelis' security concerns were growing. Suicide bombs were claiming many victims. Horrifyingly many. Peace Now, the Israeli campaign organization, had an encampment on the pavement near the Prime Minister's residence; one of their placards monitored the death toll. In September 2001 this was 168 Israelis and 693 Palestinians. We passed it every day on the way back from school, watching the number rise as we turned the corner. Yet the death toll measured only a fraction of the suffering and grief, only a small part of the fear and freezing of normal life. Perhaps those maimed in the Intifada were the ultimate among the silenced; their lives ruined, turned dependent, in a second. It was not until I visited a clinic for the disabled victims of the war that it really sank in: finding myself looking at a bank of shelves filled with rows of different-sized prosthetic legs, their stiff feet unbending toward the sky.

That evening I sat at home thinking about the clinic. The staff had been professional and positive about their work; rehabilitation was their job. They had talked about helping victims of attacks come to terms with living with a disability, and how it was possible not to be filled with hate for the people who were responsible. One rehab nurse admitted that it was sometimes difficult to wake up in the morning and go about your life as an able-bodied person, working with people who had once been like you, able-bodied and independent, until, at the command of some distant shadowy figure, their life was blown apart.

Andrew came back from Gaza with his own grim story of a *New York Times* reporter witnessing snipers shooting children "for sport."[2] Andrew told me the story quietly, then sat down and reread favorite stories to our three children before we headed for the Old City, to a dinner given by a Palestinian philanthropist and businessman called Zahi. His house was perhaps the most beautiful in the Old City, with its winding limestone staircases leading through cool atria dressed in simple elegance up to the roof. The broad views of the Old City and al-Haram al-Sharif/Temple Mount laid out around and below us were lit by points of yellow light and bars of fluorescent green on the mosques. As we sat at the stone table on the roof the conversation was of Zahi's patient campaign to persuade the Israeli authorities to release his phone company's new equipment from the port where it had docked months before. None of the officials or ministers Zahi approached could explain why the equipment, which would have delivered a state-of-the-art phone service to Palestinians, was denied clearance. "This is not unusual," Zahi said. "It seems that commercially and economically, the Israelis don't want us to succeed independently."

Palestinians continued to bomb and kill Israelis inside Israel. A British friend emailed from London to see if we had survived the latest bombings, and I emailed back our domestic news: a baby on the way. He wanted full details, and I hid from the reality of each day by replying at length about childbirth choices rather than about the risks of ending up as collateral damage.

Andrew had gone to Ramallah for a meeting with Marwan Barghouti. Part of Andrew's job was to monitor the political pulse on all sides, to see influential actors and assess their readiness (or not) to negotiate or compromise. On his way to the meeting he called to say he would be back in time for dinner. He did consider, but didn't mention, that we both knew the IDF might make another attempt to execute Barghouti by missile. I put away imagining the technicalities of how—whether by missile or bomb in his office or at home, and the probabilities of when—perhaps while Andrew was with him. What I didn't know was that earlier in the day over lunch in Tel Aviv with his friend Moshe

Kochanovsky, deputy director-general of Israel's Ministry of Defense, Andrew had let it be known that he would be seeing Barghouti later. Andrew called at 8PM to say he would be back in an hour. An hour or more later, he called again, saying they were in a line at the Qalandia checkpoint that was worse than ever, even so late at night. I could hear the murmur of engines, the angry honking, and raised voices of other trapped drivers. The wait was five hours: he called me intermittently with updates, irritation, resignation, disbelief, and more irritation.

I lay in bed that night, as on many nights, unable to sleep, glad when Andrew finally returned from checkpoint dementia. The following morning brought back control, for a while, then unnerved me again. Maha had wanted me to take her to Bethlehem. I rang to say "Let's go," but she replied that she wasn't going any more, and to take a look at the news. The IDF had bombed—with F-16s again—a number of Palestinian towns. They were targeting Palestinian security forces in retaliation for a militant attack on an IDF post in Gaza in which three IDF soldiers had been killed on August 24. Family in Britain saw the bombing on the news and called me because both Andrew's phones were out. They would watch the news, see an attack or a bombing, try to get hold of him and think the worst when he was out of reach.

Assured that Andrew was safe, they wanted to know if I had made a decision about where to have the baby. I said not yet, but probably in Jerusalem or Bethlehem. "Is that a good idea?" they asked.

I had to admit that London looked safer: London was not, then, vulnerable to suicide bombings, or to broken ceasefires, repetitive military "lessons," and patterns of revenge and retaliation. My case for staying in Jerusalem and keeping the family together soon hit another problem. On the first day of the autumn term at the lycée, Andrew headed for the office in Gaza, dropping the boys at school on his way. A few seconds after he left the house

I heard the door open: he came back saying that he hadn't said goodbye properly. Twenty minutes later there was a massive boom across the valley and a choir of sirens struck up. A bomb? I looked at the kitchen clock: ten to eight, the time when Andrew and the boys would be driving along Ha'Nevim Street. I called his mobile—they were fine—it had not been a bomb after all, not this time. The following morning, September 4, 2001, Andrew was still in Gaza so the school run was mine. We woke early because the dog, who was normally too scared to bark even at the tomcats stealing her food, had joined the birds' dawn chorus. Thanks to her barking, we were in good time, and our mood was unusually upbeat for the beginning of a school day. But then the boys' dressing slowed up and stalled: favorite items were missing, socks needed help, shoes wouldn't tie, and we ended up being late.

We drove along to the Khaled tape that had become the boys' obsession. The music was hammering and sinuous; the children were squabbling in the back of the car. Catriona, strapped into an itchy carseat, pulled at the parts of her brothers within reach. Vexed by the kids and frustrated by the traffic, I cursed into the wind. Suddenly, on the last stretch before school, our road was blocked. A frantic policewoman was redirecting traffic, gesticulating wildly, herding us in the opposite direction from the one we wanted. I dithered for a moment, knowing that it must be a bomb, but I didn't want it to be true.

She yelled at me: "No English, no Hebrew—GO!" and I broke off, a rabbit in the headlights.

I turned into a small street. We stopped, parked, to think and take a call. Steve, a Canadian journalist and fellow parent, confirmed that it was a bomb, and very close to the school. His children were distraught, school was closed, talk later. We headed home in a daze, and a round of phone calls began. Mine to Andrew: "There's been a bomb, we're okay, we're all okay." He was calm: we were talking to him so we were alive. Then other calls, to me—were we all right? Everyone with a story, an escape: how bizarre it was that this morning the alarm clock had failed to go off, that their mother had called from home with a crisis, that the cat was sick. All to make each family late. And miss the bomb. I still didn't get it, how close we had been.

When we drove into the yard at home, Amer was waiting for us. Maha appeared immediately.

"Thanks God," they both said. "You are safe."

Amer had heard on Palestinian radio that a bomb had gone off at Yad Sarah—not just near the school but right outside the gate—right there, on the two-foot-wide pavement we should have been treading had we not been those few minutes late. Amer knew what I still hadn't understood: we could have been dead.

Piecing together the news through the day, we learned that the suicide bomber had disguised himself as an Orthodox Jew, but with a backpack—not characteristic of Orthodox Jews—and he had been challenged by two border policemen before he could penetrate further into West Jerusalem. There and then he had reached into his bag and detonated himself, the explosion sending his severed head flying over the wall and into the schoolyard, dropping with a thud in the dust at the feet of the Palestinian nursery teacher. Other bits followed; an eye on someone's shoe. The new headmaster, one week in, laid a cloth over the head and shreds of body to shield the children from the sight and horror.

No one could believe that, despite the location and timing, only one pupil had been injured, and not too badly. One of the two policemen was critically injured, twenty other people mildly wounded. The when and the where should have left many children injured or killed. Still, the damage to the children was enormous. And to the staff: the doorman's wife was hysterical because when she saw the rolling head she thought it was her husband's. He was always stationed right there, by the gate. Quickly the headmaster summoned parents and counselors, all rallied round, children were shepherded home, and the clearing up began. Someone scraped the blood and flesh off the wall, which would be bleached white in a tell-tale arc my mother never noticed when she came back to stay a few weeks later and visited the school.

"Where was the bomb?"

"Oh, some way down there."

The children talked of course, pondering every detail. Archie, at seven, felt it important to tell me a few days later that it had not been the bomber's body that flew over the wall, "just his head." Xan's Palestinian teacher was distressed: as the severed head rolled to a halt "it touched my leg," she whispered. The other teachers and parents tried to comfort her, but it wasn't easy: in the past year her home had been shelled by IDF tanks, her sister's house had been demolished by IDF bulldozers, and her family had twice been fired on by settlers as they drove home.

Andrew hurried back, without the guest who had been coming for dinner. I was unprepared in any case and the fridge was empty. What with bombings and the children home all day I hadn't made it to the shops. Shops—maybe a bomber there too. Andrew ran into the house and found me and held me. We stood, silent, breathing each other. The children coursed in, broke us up, claiming their own hugs. All safe, together. We slowed down and read stories but the stories and Catriona's quiet questions at bath-time only brought home the nearness and the risk, so we put the children to bed and sat down to a meager supper and drank and laughed with relief.

Turning our backs on Jerusalem as soon as possible, we spent the weekend in Tel Aviv. Among the sun-happy crowd on the beach we put reality aside, as Israelis were doing. Bikinis, buckets, and beach restaurants transported us instantly. But the sea was big that day, and I found myself standing knee-deep in the breaking waves, arms akimbo, telling the children to come in from the surf—it looked too dangerous, and minutes after that three ambulances pitched up on the beach to deal with the drownings. The waves, despite the breakwater, swelled and surged and the swimmers tried to kick their way back but it was hard, fighting the current, and by the time Andrew, who was swimming further out, made it back to the beach the first ambulance parked on the sand was busy. Two bodies were pulled in, unconscious. One swimmer was beyond saving, drowned, and the children saw the body bag lying white on the sand with a watching crowd surrounding, and wanted more explanations.

Back in Jerusalem, back at school, walking past the arc of bleached wall, seeing the dent in the metal gates and the patches of lingering sand for mopping up. Now there were more police and soldiers on the street and a new checkpoint for glancing at documents, in an Israeli part of town for once. But everything carried on. Four-year-old Xan said he wanted to learn to read, but he hated school now because his teacher kept twisting his arm. Andrew had to go to Cairo; I was hating him being away. On September 9, 2001 two suicide bombers exploded, one of them a Palestinian Israeli—a first. The bomber waited until the Tel Aviv train had arrived and people were leaving the station before detonating himself, killing three and injuring scores. Then a drive-by shooting, killing two settlers, and Israeli reprisal helicopter attacks in Ramallah. And so it went on, endlessly. We went out for a walk in the evening light through the winding paths of the Forest of Peace, and as the children played they picked up interesting bits of burned pipe and syringes, things they couldn't explain—"Mummy, what are these?" Drug paraphernalia.

September 10, and Catriona was starting at a new school in the German Colony, West Jerusalem. There were too many checkpoints between our home and Beit Hanina, and since I had now admitted defeat in the struggle to get to work I couldn't hack checkpoint frustration any longer just to get a two-year-old to nursery school. Standing in line with dozens of people who knew that this was not about security. Even the IDF said checkpoints didn't work.[3]

Checkpoints did not stop suicide bombings but they did close down lives: waiting, each car, long enough to be searched and then not searched, just made to wait, to gnaw with frustration day after day, twice a day. And I was now more than six months pregnant, discovering what it was like to be forced to wait for minutes and hours when you hurt for want of a pee with the baby pressing down inside you. So I'd given in and stopped work and changed Catriona's school in order not to have to wait at checkpoints or worry about being caught in crossfire. Then again, the new school was in an area where bombs were likely: Palestinians chose to target Israeli civilians, so they might choose this place. These were the choices: for Palestinians it was either put up with checkpoints and curfew and occupation or quit Palestine, if they could; for Israelis it was put up with suicide bombs and gunmen or quit Israel. Rather than face the locals' choices, and confronting their own and their children's night-mares, more expat parents were leaving, some for a few weeks, some for good. All unnerved by that bomb, a mere six days ago.

Amer came by to talk, badly timed—I was trying to feed Catriona. He talked and talked, about the bombs, the daily IDF actions, about what had gone on in Durban where the UN had held a conference on racism. Israel was being accused of racism. "What good does that do?" he asked. "The situation has rotted something inside all of us," he said, "our friends included." He had taken his kids for a walk on the promenade and saw a policeman: an Israeli policeman, of course. He said to his son, "Don't be afraid, go up to him and say hello." "Why did you tell him that?" asked his Palestinian neighbor. "You should teach him to piss on them."

That afternoon on the way to school I fell down at the corner of the street opposite the hospital, Bikur Cholim, where Amer's daughter was being treated. Fell in a heap of pregnancy and toddler, Catriona in my arms, my ankle twisted. "Please don't cry, Mummy," she said. No one stopped to help or asked if I was okay. I got up, dusted down my clothes, picked up my child, and limped off to school.

The day was 9/11. Sitting lame in the warm sun after school by the Crowne Plaza pool with three other parents, I was watching the children have their first swimming lesson of the season. Yitzhak, the teacher, was another friend about to quit Israel for good. Then Steve, perched on the edge of the sun-chair next to me, took a call from his wife. She was the correspondent for ABC: two airplanes had flown into the World Trade Center. Another call to another parent: ITN's correspondent telling his wife Libby the same news. Another call from ABC: the Pentagon hit. Thousands, she said, were dead in New York and Washington.

In the car on the way home the radio began to reveal the scale: the television took over once we were inside the house. Andrew finally reached me by phone. He was in Beirut, sitting with Walid Jumblatt, the Druze leader, watching aghast the collapse of the Twin Towers on the guard's television. The enormity and mortality were only just beginning to dawn, and the immediate reactions, some competent, others not, added to the obvious, the only certainty: nothing would be the same again. Governments were on high alert. Israeli embassies all over the world were evacuated, as was the White House, UN headquarters, most of the US federal government. The children full of questions; they saw the Twin Towers they remembered so well, and watched them go down. How could I explain anything? Waking during the night, seeing over and over the Twin Towers disintegrating with all those people inside and underneath. Family called twice, or was it three times, to say they were really worried about us and didn't I think it was time to come "home"?

Interviewed the following day, one-time Prime Minister Binyamin Netanyahu was asked how the attack would affect relations between Israel and the US. "It's very good," he replied. "Well, not very good, but it will generate immediate sympathy... and strengthen the bond between our two peoples, because we've experienced terror over so many decades."[4]

The IDF had invaded Jenin and Jericho, killing more than seven Palestinians, including a little girl, in Jenin; the deaths were not mentioned on Israel's morning news. I talked to friends in New

York, our old home. Firefighters from our street, West 19th—
generous, patient men who had always made a fuss of the children
as we walked by, and hooted when they drove past us in their fire
engine—had been killed. Friends all said the same thing: we get
up, we go to school, we go to work, we don't know what will
happen next, but we get on with life. CNN and the BBC were
saying that New York was in chaos, no one sleeps, ordinary life
over. Both simultaneously true.

Andrew came back from Beirut via Egypt, wondering at the lack
of security at Tel Aviv airport, and exasperated by senior Arab officials trying to claim the attack was not the work of Arabs but of
Japanese terrorists. Much of the world behind the US, mourning.

Days went by with dozens of emails from New York friends.
My stepbrother turned up there, not dead amidst the rubble. My
sister-in-law rang again: why the hell weren't we coming back
immediately? Suddenly everyone was feeling daily risk and
bystander's impotence and telling us to do something about it,
perhaps because they couldn't. For them, on their behalf: come
over here, be with us, join our risk. People were full of panic; some
were asking what I thought about full-length chemical warfare suits
for the entire family—in *New York*? And why ask me? Because of
where we lived.

Israelis were not panicking. Now perhaps they would be
understood, whereas Palestinians, said Edward Said, were sure to
lose either way, as always. There was chaos abroad, yet calm in
Jerusalem. The smallest details set the big picture: acceptance,
understanding, camaraderie. I bought ice creams for the children
after school and the man behind the counter was blithe and
friendly: "Tell me how you do it, make such happy children?" The
newspaper vendor saved me a copy of the *International Herald
Tribune* the day after the NYC/Washington attacks. The pet-shop
man refused to let me carry any of the sacks of dog food that I had
just bought. A woman stopped me in the street, wanting to say
hello to my little girl, talking gently and kindly, saying "Stay well,

my dear" as we parted. The violin-maker, deep-voiced and slowly smiling, was happy to laugh with me at something daft the children said.

The routine of daily life returned. ABC journalist and writer Charlie Glass, finishing a book, was coming to stay. Trips to the beach—as long as there were no drownings—helped us to feel normal, just by leaving Jerusalem for a few hours. But there were always reminders.

I gave an Israeli friend, Sara, a lift home one afternoon. Normally she took three buses to get home, so she knew, she said, that her day would come. She also said she'd heard that I'd joined the peace group, Women in Black. I hadn't. "Funny," she said, "I heard you were a signed-up, paid-up, full-on member." I was going to say that I had only been to some demonstrations when she told me that she had been a member from 1990 to 1993. After Oslo she felt she could retire.

"Now," she said, "I can't go back to them even though I'm still as opposed as ever to the occupation. It's simply that my people, my family, are hurting too much, and you can't kick a man when he's down." She described how isolated she felt as a religious Jew, with religious friends all of whom seemed to be very right-wing, she said. During Rosh Hashanah she had dinner with some of them. One turned out to have been involved in a plot to blow up al-Aqsa Mosque.

Another had questioned her about the Anglican school, where she taught, next door to the lycée: "Don't a lot of UN kids go there?"

She was cautious, non-committal.

"Yeah, well, we should bomb the hell out of them," he had said.

"I'm 100 percent sure," she told me, "that this particular guy would not actually bomb a school full of children." But she was worried that he "might have that conversation with someone who might."

"What did you say?" I asked.

"I lied my head off about the level of security, the number of CIA agents there, the armored cars, the impossibility of getting in without special permits, passes, status, etc., etc."

On Yom Kippur I arranged to meet our new guest and give him a ride home. Tolerance is inconsistent: I drove. No Israeli is supposed to drive on Yom Kippur, the Day of Atonement. Earlier, on the phone, I had pointed out to Charlie that it was Yom Kippur but he said, in his suave way, "Oh, that won't be a problem," so out I went into the evening. The roads were abandoned. Even the traffic lights were switched off. It was the smoothest, darkest of drives, sweeping effortlessly through the middle of the city.

There was Charlie sitting at a table in the leafy courtyard of the American Colony Hotel, by the fountain that reflected lights in the dark evening. As I arrived, he looked up at me, smiled hello, surprised. "You know, someone said you wouldn't be coming."

"Really, why?"

"Because it's Yom Kippur and your car will get stoned."

"Who was it?"

"A Palestinian woman. She seemed afraid."

We had dinner and I drove Charlie back to our place. Where East and West Jerusalem meet on the broad lanes of the Nablus Road, Israeli "Route 1," we saw a small crowd of people on the far side of the road.

Charlie was suddenly worried: "Hey, what are we doing? It's Yom Kippur!"

"Yes, Charlie."

"Well, hey—you see those big stones over there, lying on the road? Those are rocks. And you see those guys in Orthodox kit standing by them?"

"Yes."

"Yeah? Well, those guys're going to pick up those rocks and then they're going to throw them at us. Let's get out of here!" The rocks flew as we swung by, but their aim was off.

"Charlie, you said it would be okay."

"Well, even ABC gets it wrong every now and then."

The following day was September 28, 2001, the anniversary of the beginning of the Intifada: exactly a year since Sharon's visit to al-Haram al-Sharif/Temple Mount. During the day, six Palestinians were killed, including a ten-year-old child. Charlie received a call from the nervous Palestinian who told him there was no way he could get to where he wanted to go—the IDF had added another layer of checkpoint at Qalandia: a pedestrian one, which would take at least an hour to pass and, if you didn't live in Ramallah, you could not, she assured him, pass through.

He shrugged off her caution, saying only, "So now there are three open-air prisons: Northern West Bank, Southern West Bank, and Gaza. Welcome to the only democracy in the Middle East," and headed out.

7

In Bethlehem?

In the dead of night, woken by nightmares of being chased by stone-throwers, I lay awake thinking with dread about childbirth. But I had to confront the growing reality. As far as obstetrics was concerned, the choice was between two philosophies: European or American. The European model was practiced by Palestinians; the American was favored by Israelis. I had trained in the former, given birth in the latter, saw the options and made my choice.

My three experiences of giving birth in New York had been perfectly safe, but I was a vehicle in a system geared to thinking litigiously. I had had to battle the staff not to be tied to a CTG* continuously, to keep my babies beside me, to prevent the nursery staff giving my babies a bottle rather than letting me breastfeed them, and to keep some control over what was happening to me and my babies. And it is no fun fighting when you are in pain, and against people who are good, kind, and only doing their job, but who are looking after too many mothers and too constrained by "medicalization" to allow that birth is not just another surgical procedure but a normal physiological process, one that can, of course, go wrong—in which case medicine is very welcome. Then—but only then—please step in and intervene, thank you very much.

This time there would be a different battle: to get to the hospital. Less importantly, I also had to defend my choice. I was never questioned on my choice of dentist, pediatrician, optician, or vet, but I was berated for my choice of obstetrician. The former were Israeli; the obstetrician was Palestinian.

Having trained as a doctor in Britain, and seen British midwives' genius for helping women to experience labor as something positive, I longed to have a home birth under their care and

---

* Cardiotocograph, monitoring contractions of the uterus and fetal heartbeat.

direction. "Hell," exclaimed some friends, "how dangerous is that!" Statistically, less dangerous than a hospital birth for a low-risk case like mine. But home-births were hard to come by. So, if not a home birth, I would have to have the baby in hospital. And yet I was frightened by the thought of a birth in Israel or Palestine. The stone-throwing dream rolled into a waking nightmare: I was lying on a bed bleeding after the delivery, saying to a gray shape trying to push me away: "Tell them I'm bleeding," but no one was coming to help me; they were letting me bleed, unheard, alone.

In reality I was under attack for being irresponsible—fairly, for not finding prenatal care as early as I should have, and unfairly, for choosing a Palestinian hospital. How could Palestinian obstetrics compete with Israeli obstetrics? Some Palestinians asked the same thing. On the way to Bethlehem in labor the year before, my pregnant American friend Julie had been stopped at the Israeli checkpoint: "What are you doing going to a Palestinian hospital? There are great hospitals back there in Israel," the soldiers demanded. She and her husband insisted. Further on they were stopped by Palestinian security: "Hey, what are you doing going to a Palestinian hospital? There are great hospitals back there in Israel."

I had visited a number of hospitals in the area; seeing obstetric departments was making the pregnancy real, the denial harder—something about the sight of stirrups. Even chintzed-up "delivery suites" were still dark cells with huge stirrups on the "beds." They might be the discreet, pop-up-when-you-need-them variety, but you know they're there, the drill by the dentist's chair. I phoned the Israeli midwife everyone recommended in one last attempt to arrange a home birth but she refused on account of my address. She wouldn't, she said, put herself in any danger.

The Holy Family Hospital in Bethlehem offered everything I was looking for: a progressive approach, mother-centered care, excellent credentials,* and good facilities in a glorious setting.

---

* Accredited by the Royal College of Obstetricians and Gynaecologists.

Admittedly it was in the middle of a war zone but as long as the town was quiet when I went into labor, the Holy Family was the place. I talked to Julie about giving birth there the previous Christmas. Her verdict was that the hospital had been excellent, and that although the bombardment of the town during her labor had been "a little off-putting," she had been sure the IDF would not target a hospital.

Architecturally the Holy Family was not so much hospital as monastery: wide airy corridors of limestone arches and a cloistered courtyard of orange and grapefruit trees which the lab technician, who was on site to do any test the doctors ordered without delay, tended with particular care. I watched him one morning, walking about the cloisters in the sun, scattering his coffee grounds about the trees' roots to nurture them. The hospital was ideal, both philosophically and technically, assuming supplies were allowed through the checkpoints. The rooms were spotless, comfortable, and unpretentious, the staff kind and accommodating. And Dr. Salsa was a calm, sympathetic doctor, a considerate teacher to the medical students who followed her about, and we laughed together as we reminisced about our experiences of working in British hospitals.

As soon as I'd decided on Bethlehem it became a war zone again. This happened every now and then. At the end of August 2001 the IDF assassinated Abu Ali Mustapha, head of the Popular Front for the Liberation of Palestine (PFLP), and occupied the Bethlehem suburb of Beit Jala. In retaliation the Palestinians fired on Gilo, the settlement on the opposite hill. A British intelligence officer working for the EU brokered a local ceasefire. This lasted for more than six weeks, giving citizens a much-needed break and the chance to sleep at night. But the ceasefire ended when the IDF assassinated three Fatah officials (one of whom the PA was supposed to have arrested) and predictably the Palestinians fired on Gilo again. The IDF then reoccupied Bethlehem in response to the Palestinian "breach of ceasefire."

That was Bethlehem. The war-zone factor intruded again when

on October 17, by way of further retaliation for the killing of Abu Ali Mustapha, the PFLP assassinated an Israeli cabinet minister, Rehavam Ze'evi. By now we were used to the news of assassinations by the Israeli army—the IDF had executed more than 35 people in the past few months—but this was the first by Palestinians.[1]

Bethlehem, my increasingly unlikely location for giving birth—and I was now in my seventh month—was invaded. Israel gave the PA an ultimatum to hand over Ze'evi's killers within a week. The PA did not comply. One of the assassins was known to be in Bethlehem, but Bethlehem was under total curfew, making it difficult for PA forces to move around and arrest him without being shot for breaking the curfew. While I worried about the effects on Bethlehem, others were worrying that the more the IDF attacked the PA's security services—arresting and killing their personnel, bombing their offices, destroying their vehicles—the more Sharon demanded that these same forces perform security miracles. Even those Palestinians who berated Arafat said it was unreasonable to blame the PA chairman if someone wasn't arrested when he himself was under house arrest.

When the invasion of Bethlehem began, five people were killed within a few minutes and the IDF cut off the town's water and electricity. None of this boded well for a quiet delivery. After a fortnight, an Israeli editorial concluded that the invasion had paralyzed civilian life as never before, intensified Palestinian hatred, and increased support for the resistance.[2] I let myself believe that editorials like this were a sign that a change in policy was possible.

I was overly optimistic. Bethlehem for childbirth now? Bombed and blitzed and under curfew, with no water or power? Andrew wanted to know if I'd changed my mind. "A mother and her baby died at the checkpoint. Do you know that?" he asked. Yes, I knew that. Rihab Nufal had been trying to get to the Bethlehem hospital to give birth. The soldiers would not let her through and she died: died in childbirth, blocked from getting to the hospital. Her unborn child had no chance.

I was supposed to go to the hospital for a routine check-up. That was out of the question while the army continued storming the city. Bethlehem had shut down, its inhabitants terrified, unsafe even in their homes, the streets full of rubble and tanks. Then came news of another woman in labor stopped at the checkpoint on her way to the Holy Family Hospital. Her baby died. Unlike me, these two women had nowhere else to go for medical help. Unlike me, this woman had no children. The mother, Rawida, pregnant after five and a half years of waiting and IVF, went into labor early. Her husband Nasser drove her to the checkpoint and pleaded to be allowed through, explaining that his wife was in labor and how critical it was to reach the hospital. The soldiers were adamant: "No." The couple hurried home, picked up Nasser's mother in the hope that she might have more influence, and tried again. Again the border guards said "no." In desperation the family drove around the checkpoint, across fields and along dirt tracks to get to the hospital. It took them an hour and a half and the baby was born on the way. The Israeli organization, Physicians for Human Rights (PHR-Israel), reported that the baby weighed 1,416 grams—a birth-weight with a good chance of survival given proper care. But the baby arrived in serious condition, too late for proper care. The doctors' attempts to save him were futile. He died an hour later.[3]

PHR-Israel had managed to slip into Bethlehem when the tanks were pulled back from the two main hospitals for a few hours to allow a solidarity visit by Muslim and Christian leaders. PHR-Israel came out saying: "Today, not only do patients find it almost impossible to access medical aid, and doctors cannot reach their work—now even patients within medical institutions are exposed to gunfire and danger of injury and death."[4]

IDF tanks had shelled the Holy Family Hospital. The PHR-Israel team were told that anyone who moved within the hospital courtyard was fired on, including a woman who had just been discharged. She hurried back for cover. The neonatal department had to be rapidly evacuated: all the newborns were trundled off to a part of the hospital that was out of range of the IDF. The children of the hospital's orphanage were paralyzed with fear, the few staff doing their best to hold them, to soothe them. In Beit Jala an anesthetic technician and the doorman were shot and a man next to them killed outright; they were standing at the door of a hospital when they were picked off by a sniper in the settlement of Gilo opposite.

Tomer Feffer, director of PHR-Israel, received reports that the army was firing on the hospitals and went to see first-hand: "With my own eyes, I saw the bloodstains, the places where the building had been hit and the bullet holes..." But, said Feffer, "the IDF spokesman claimed that nothing of the kind had happened and that the IDF is a humanitarian army that tries not to harm civilians."[5]

Julie had been sure that the IDF wouldn't fire on a hospital; I had thought the only risk of having a baby in Bethlehem would be the checkpoints, and if the soldiers wouldn't let me through then all I had to do was turn around and retreat to my back-up hospital in Jerusalem. The other criticism leveled at me, that a Palestinian hospital was by definition a bad one, was racist and groundless. But the IDF did fire on hospitals, and had shelled the Holy Family itself. Why not give in and opt for second-best?

Not yet. Things couldn't get any worse. Andrew and I decided to be flexible; before attempting any visit to the hospital we would make a decision based on the level of IDF activity in the area and the political situation. Revenge attacks with tanks and F-16s had so far been launched some time after the provocation. Where once I had thought that waiting for IDF retaliation was painful, I now found it useful; the waiting would give me time to get out of Bethlehem. If there were any risk of an IDF attack, we would go for second-best. I knew I was lucky to have that option.

I went to Bethlehem as soon as it was safe. The IDF had trashed the city. Tanks had made a point of crushing everything they could find: there were zigzag tracks from the tank treads snaking from one side of the road to the other—every traffic light, road lamp, car, and pylon had been pulped. Buildings were bombed and the town strewn with debris, flattened vehicles, the detritus of the military operation. Hotels were gutted: the new Intercontinental in pink and white stone that had so impressed us when we first arrived had been commandeered by the IDF and was sordid. In the streets Bethlehemites were getting on with life, glad to be free from curfew at least, to be allowed out of their houses, and had started to clear the debris. They would rebuild, make repairs and patch up their city—until the next round of invasion.

As my pregnancy progressed the days shortened and the nights grew cold. Our house felt jerry-built, with power outages every other day and every time I used the toaster. The children came back from school talking about schoolyard superheroes. When I tuned into their talk, I learned that their Palestinian friends' heroes were not Digimon or Zorro but martyrs and sharpshooters. There was sudden and unusual rain and the house flooded, adding a dampness and moldy smell to the general feeling of gloom. The pregnancy was making me heavy and tired, my pelvis ached from the hormone relaxin, and anemia sapped my energy. The rules were broken this time: taking vitamins, eating properly, being serene and happy, seeing the doctor regularly for prenatal care. At least I had the option of good medical care, whatever happened. Dr. Salsa said how glad she was that I had a back-up in Jerusalem. She, like the other medical staff, would not complain or be drawn on the situation.

"We could never allow the situation to stop us from providing proper medical care to our patients," she said. For three seconds the doctor in me felt envious of her: head down, sorting out people in need, dealing with their problems whatever the obstacles. Then the obstacles became real for me: how trapped and angry and hopeless Dr. Salsa must feel. I was being doctor-woman-mother-wife, but I had choices. As a pregnant woman I might be under siege and occupation, swanning in and out of the city where Dr. Salsa was captive, sampling their ordeal, but I could always escape back through the checkpoints. In the Israeli world I lived with terror, not daring to go to malls and restaurants and public places, but I could escape this too, heading into East Jerusalem or away, abroad.

I also existed inside the Israeli bubble, the place where some of them hid. Every time I passed Pizza Sbarro my body clenched with a small but acid fear. Every time I parked in Mea Sharim I wondered, what if...? I hated going to Ben Yehuda Street and admired the buskers I sometimes saw there, playing their defiance. I was convinced that the German Colony would be targeted, but I had to go there too. And on that September morning I had driven the children away from the school bomb, knowing afterward that if we had not been late they might have been killed—killed by a Palestinian suicide bomber fitted out with explosives and sent by Palestinian dispatchers who had every intention of destroying as many lives as possible. And for what? To block any remaining peace process and so condemn all Palestinians to collective punishment and the wrath of the IDF, and all moderate Israelis to the power of their extremists. I talked to Andrew, wondering if he should be more afraid of the suicide bombings or of those other, daily, bombings and crossfire incidents.

He took me to the Jerusalem Theater to hear Schoenberg: *Verklärte Nacht*. By chance we ran into Israeli friends as we were having our bodies and belongings checked for bombs at the entrance. "Let's have a drink in the interval," they said to us from the other side of the security guards. Later we sat waiting for the concert to begin. The director of music took the stage and made an announcement. "I want to thank you all for showing such support. I want to thank you all for coming here, for being here in spite of all the dangers."

During the interval Andrew talked to the husband about the music, I talked to the wife about the announcement. She had not been surprised that the director wanted to make such a statement. "He just wanted to be frank. That's what he really feels. We all feel. People accuse Israelis of manipulating the role of victim, but you can't expect us to be rational in the face of terror."

"That's what terror does," she said. "It imposes rule *by* fear: we're watching our kids and our families being blown up by people who may have miserable lives, okay, but to murder civilians like that? Is that going to get them anywhere? And then when we defend ourselves the world gets upset? I know we have the most powerful army in the region, by far—thank God—but do you think that we don't feel afraid, terrified? That we're not still dying? And if we don't protect ourselves, who will?"

Maha gave birth early. She had been struggling by taxi, *servees* (minibus), another taxi, on foot, and then yet more taxis to Ramallah every week for lectures in pursuit of her master's degree in social work. It had become increasingly hard for her. Finally, there were flare-ups and rain and shooting across Qalandia, and Maha was running in the mud and the fear and the mayhem, and her contractions came on that night. Mohammed drove her to the Red Crescent Hospital and she delivered an hour later. It was a boy, named Feris after Mohammed's father, who had died in the 1967 war trying to defend East Jerusalem.

The situation in Bethlehem eased. My check-ups at the Holy Family became frequent, almost weekly, and to make the check-point waits less worthless I combined the trip with shopping for groceries in Bethlehem. Storekeepers were having a hard time after the invasion, but they kept trying to pretend that life was normal. There was one greengrocer whose pyramids of oranges, apples, avocados, and peaches were always especially architectural. He also built mounds of luscious dates and soft piles of figs, and ranked jars of date syrup thick as black treacle, and honey by the gallon. Next door was a butcher who ground freshly cut, trimmed lamb or beef and threw handfuls of clean green herbs and maybe an onion into the big metal grinding machine. The butcher kept mounds of eggs that he would secure in cardboard trays, wound in wide ribbons of cellophane to stop them breaking on the journey home. And while I waited a boy would be sent for coffee.

Once there was no wait at all at the checkpoint. I was so inured to being made to wait that it felt odd when it didn't happen. It was more like being in the hospital itself, where there were no queues, no waits, and no hanging around for blood tests or being sent miles to another clinic. Nor was there the "no service until you pay up front" system. The administrative quagmire of "advanced" medicine had not yet reached Bethlehem.

In the broader picture, however, the situation was worse than ever, and I knew that Bethlehem's quiet was still precarious. In Khan Yunis, Gaza, an IDF explosive device had killed five little boys from one extended family. Senior Israeli officials expressed regret for the deaths. This regret was published in Palestinian papers, but the Palestinian public reacted in same way as the Israeli public when Arafat expressed regret for Israeli deaths. Israeli commentators noted that the boys' deaths were closely followed by the "liquidation" of a Hamas leader and other IDF "provocations" intended to raise the temperature before the arrival of the latest US negotiator, General Anthony Zinni, to pull off a cease-fire.[6] The holy month of Ramadan was barely a week old, and twenty Palestinians had died since it began.

Israelis who knew the daily goings-on in the Occupied Territories were exasperated. In an attempt to show his readership what was happening, and how Palestinians felt when the PA demanded a ceasefire, veteran Israeli journalist Danny Rubinstein listed a sample of seven days of IDF actions (on top of the twenty Palestinian dead that week): the IDF had "withdrawn" from Tulkarem—except they didn't, it was "only symbolic"; destroyed more swathes of the agricultural areas in northern Gaza, wiping out families' incomes and decades of work as well as their futures; and confiscated 200 dunams of land from its owners in Dir al-Balah, in the middle of the Gaza Strip, handing it over to the Jewish inhabitants of the adjacent illegal settlement. One of the main roads out of Ramallah was completely blocked. In another town a closure had been imposed that stopped pupils getting to school. Family visits to Megiddo Prison were suspended. Birzeit University had been raided by IDF troops. Jewish settlers had invaded a village near Nablus, cutting electric wires and polluting the water system. And the Israeli authorities were preparing to seize more Arab houses in East Jerusalem. This, Rubinstein said, was a typical week of occupation reality. He added that as well as all this, on TV and in the papers every day there were pictures of the dead and the funerals, and of IDF tanks ranged against children and IDF soldiers stopping worshippers from praying at al-Aqsa—during Ramadan. He concluded that given all this, when Israelis hailed American Secretary of State Colin Powell's speech demanding that Arafat stop the violence, it was hardly surprising that Palestinians asked in astonishment: "*We* are the ones who have to stop the violence?" Despite the constant diet of IDF aggression, Rubinstein reported, Palestinian officers and commanders had received explicit instructions not only to prevent terror attacks at any price but also not to respond even if Israelis opened fire on them.[7]

Israeli friends were as worried as some Israeli commentators about the sincerity of their government's intentions to make peace—particularly now that Arafat seemed to be making a real effort: not only was there the directive to the security forces, but Arafat had finally risked the wrath of his public and forced Hamas to agree not to attack Israelis inside Israel.[8] Our friends' worry turned into open dread when the IDF assassinated Mahmoud Abu Hanoud, the commander of Hamas's military wing in the West Bank, on November 23, 2001.[9]

Sure enough, there was a salvo of suicide bombings in retaliation: twenty-nine Israelis were killed and hundreds wounded in the week after the assassination. On November 26, two border policemen were wounded at the Erez crossing in the Gaza Strip; November 29, three Israelis were killed and nine wounded in a suicide bombing on a bus en route from Nazareth to Tel Aviv. And on the first of December, late on Saturday night, two suicide bombers killed eleven Israelis and injured nearly 200. The bombers chose Ben Yehuda Street at a time when it would be full of young Israelis enjoying the end of Shabbat. Then a car bomb exploded nearby twenty minutes later, to pick off those trying to help the victims of the first two attacks.

The situation was worse than ever. The children and I joined an English couple in their garden the next day. The children played, the adults sat in despair. As we sat, news came through that yet another bomb had gone off: fifteen Israelis had been killed and forty wounded, several critically, in a suicide bombing on a bus in Haifa.

Andrew called: he had been instructed to go to see Arafat in Ramallah. And just then—boom! Another explosion—and I wanted to call back and say "please don't go to Ramallah tonight, not tonight, I've seen what F-16s do to cars, maybe it's the wrong night for you," but I held back and it turned out that the noise that had set me askew had been the Iftar gun, the signal to break the Ramadan fast. He did go to Ramallah and in the end it was not the West Bank's turn that night; the IDF attacked Gaza instead.

A few days later I went to the music store on Ben Yehuda Street. I knew of no other store to find the music the children needed, so I had no choice but to go. I told myself that this would not be a problem. While there I met a French Israeli woman I knew, and we stopped to talk, but neither of us wanted to stay in the danger zone for long. Instead, she came to see me at home, not scared by the area, and we discussed other things determinedly for a while.

Then: "You know," she said, "two of my friends were killed in Saturday night's bombings." I didn't know. She wanted to tell me about them, and why they had died, and how near she had been to losing her children. She had to talk. We talked, I listened. Two of her children, she told me, had wanted to go out that night, and with those same friends who had been killed. But her children hadn't gone, and now they were still alive because she had said one word: "No."

"What if I hadn't said it? What if I'd stuck to what I normally do, letting them go out when they want to go out because you can't lock young people up inside their homes and tell them they can't go out. Not—'just in case'—can you? Not night after night. That's no life for them, they'd go crazy. And so they do go out, and I go crazy, until they get back. Except I did say no this time, but I nearly didn't."

I kept listening. She wanted to talk about "them"—trying to understand, somehow. What was it that made them do this? Why do they hate us so much? Why do they have to destroy? "What more could we have offered than at Camp David?"

It was not the moment to reply, as so often it was not. I silenced myself because she was caught in the middle, just as most people were caught. It began to rain, and she hurried away.

The rain was pouring down outside. Outside the bubble there were more deaths, no negotiations and little hope. And why, Israelis were asking in disbelief, was Washington so wholeheartedly behind Sharon when so many *Israelis* were saying "Stop?" Not just liberals, peaceniks, and journalists, but the foreign minister, Shimon Peres. He was reported to be standing up to the prime minister, saying the government's policy was wrong and that he would resign from the coalition if the destructive repression continued. But with no backing from the US, and Europe powerless to make anything except statements, Peres lost the argument and failed to resign. Furious at the role of Labor in Sharon's government, Avraham Burg, former speaker of the Knesset, said later, "We have become the fig leaves of the radical right wing... a fig leaf to a government bent on destroying the Palestinian Authority in order to avoid giving up settlements."[10]

The baby—what a time to be delivering—was technically full term. Going into labor now, or in the next few days, was not a good idea. Officially no one was allowed even to visit Bethlehem, and the UN had evacuated many of the Gaza staff to Amman. Our old friend Michael was stuck in Gaza, his wife Kim and their daughters waiting for him in Jerusalem. And the weather: relentless, washing rain. Yet again the cycle of vengeance: in revenge for the bombing that was now devastating Gaza and the West Bank, a young man turned himself into a bomb, exploding outside a King David Street hotel at 7:30 in the morning on his way to another West Jerusalem destination. The bomb claimed no victims, but brought the area to a standstill, so it was nearly impossible to get to school. But the violent were still determined to carry on attacking until the other side gave in. An Israeli government spokesman, Arye Mekel, blamed the incarcerated Arafat, saying: "So far, he has not heard our message, and we may have to send some more."[11]

Another few days and the cycle calmed again. It was my due date, December 12, 2001, and I was to go back to the Holy Family for yet another check-up. The wait at the checkpoint was so long that I parked the car by the side of the road and walked across. The air was clear and warm, the views across the valleys sharp. I wove my way through the concrete maze channeling pedestrians and joined the end of the line. I could see the fan of cars a few meters away, pushing but unmoving. The pedestrian line was long, but at least it was moving, and I could get a taxi on the other side to make my appointment. In front of me shuffled a somber collection of women, children, and old men. A similar line approached us from the other direction. The children were inexplicably tolerant, quiet and uncomplaining.

Ahead of me was a wizened, bent man, his face furrowed with sun lines. He looked like Abu Anis setting off to pray at the al-Aqsa Mosque when he would dress himself up, swapping his baggy tracksuit and gardening sweater for a suit, and his bobble hat for a white keffiyeh. Now in the queue, this old man stood in his best clothes, a clean white buttoned-up shirt, a dark suit too wide and long for his shrinking body, a crisp keffiyeh. He presented his papers to the two soldiers standing in their private shade. One soldier looked out from under his metal helmet, eyeing the old man, and then down at the papers in his hand. He turned them over, and muttered something. The old man protested, but the first soldier was decided and the second made no move. Other supplicants joined in, and I asked what was going on.

"He wants to go to the mosque to pray," said one man.

"And they won't let him through?"

"No, they won't, but we don't know why. The soldier says there's something wrong with his papers, but he won't say what."

The old Palestinian gave up trying to persuade the young soldier to let him through. He turned slowly, repositioning his walking stick homeward, and then walked away.

"He's been going to the mosque to pray for decades before that Russian soldier immigrated to this country, and now the Russian can decide the old man will not go today."

The line was silent as people watched the old man's defeated tread. The next person up presented her papers. Some were allowed through, but within three minutes three people seeking health care were denied passage. Two were trying to get to appointments with their doctor, but the soldiers, who swapped from time to time, declared variously that something was wrong. Dennis—I asked him his name when my turn came—the young Russian immigrant who had stood between the old man and his prayers, became more specific, perhaps aware of the mutterings, declaring that one woman had the "wrong insurance."

The third was a woman with a belly like mine. The curve of her pregnant uterus began just under the arc of her ribs, and rounded outward and downward, stretching her clothes smoothly. We mirrored each other. She offered her papers and her appointment card, as the two others had done in front of her. Dennis was unmoved, and motioned with one circling finger for her to turn around. She complied, wordless. An American woman in the line muttered to me that there was no logic to the soldiers' decisions, and that even her US passport was of little use in easing the checkpoint ordeal. Her husband, she said, was not permitted to leave

Bethlehem. Her problems had begun at the airport—because she was married to a Palestinian.

My turn came. I held the red of my British passport in my hand but did not immediately offer it. Dennis and I had no common language beyond, "What is your name?" The other soldier lurked. I asked him why they had refused to let the other pregnant woman through, adding, "She can't get to her prenatal appointment now."

Challenged, he looked mildly embarrassed.

"How do I know she's pregnant?" he said, bolstering himself. "Everyone's fat round here." Pleased with his assertiveness, he waved me through, passport unchecked.

I found a taxi, attended my check-up, and headed home again.

That night we had dinner with a group of friends and Andrew's work colleagues at a large, empty restaurant inside the Jaffa Gate—much of the Old City was empty these days. We had planned to go to Ramallah for a Mexican Christmas party, but in the early evening the news came through that Palestinian gunmen had ambushed and killed ten settlers in the Gaza Strip, and that two suicide bombers had detonated themselves at another settlement. During dinner a call came from a colleague in Gaza to say that they were being bombed by F-16s. Around the table people sat in silence. We wondered where else the IDF would attack: maybe Bethlehem. The Braxton-Hicks contractions that plagued me most of the time strengthened and became intense. Andrew, watching me, was mouthing "Please, not tonight."

Bethlehem was spared that night, and I did not go into labor, but the next evening Andrew's Gazan colleague called again while we sat at home. For the second night running he and his family were under heavy bombardment, over and above the routine. His children were hysterical, he said, and he had lost the wherewithal to calm them. What could he tell them? Across the table I could hear the blasts reverberating out of the phone. The bombing continued. Another call came through in the morning to tell us Andrew's office in the UN compound in Gaza had just been hit, the explosion shuddering through the building, throwing people out of their chairs and off their feet, showering them with glass. The window of his office had been blown in, his chair sprayed with splinters. I said I was glad that my still-pregnant state had kept him from that. He, hearing the fear of his colleagues, was not comforted.

The character of several IDF operations and the trail of destruction that the IDF was now leaving through the West Bank and Gaza Strip challenged the security myth: it appeared that the prime minister's aim was, still, to destroy the Palestinian national movement whatever the price.[12] And Palestinian attacks were helping achieve this goal. Virtually no foreign diplomats were in touch with the militants, the majority talked only to the PA. Andrew was almost the only international official who sought out Hamas and Islamic Jihad in an attempt to persuade them to stop their attacks. Questioned on this by diplomats with similar briefs who either chose not to or were not allowed to see Palestinian extremists, he would respond, "What's the point in the UN going yet again to see Palestinian ministers with no influence? We want to stop the violence—the people we need to persuade are the ones who are doing the bombings."

Israelis and Palestinians were dying in the streets and the extremists were dictating events. Israeli journalists were not holding back from the obvious conclusion.[13] Ze'ev Schiff, Israel's leading military correspondent and rarely critical of IDF actions, was blunt: "It is impossible to shake off the impression that the Sharon government is more fearful of the quiet that will follow a cessation of Palestinian violence than it is of the attacks perpetrated by the Palestinians."[14]

Arafat delivered a major speech to the Palestinian people calling for an end to all hostilities, including suicide bombings. The following morning Sari Nusseibeh, an urbane, tweed-jacketed Oxford philosopher, scion of one of the oldest families in Palestine, was arrested for holding an Eid reception. His guests included the

British consul general who described it as a sober affair. Likud minister Uzi Landau insisted the reception was "terrorist activity." Some Israelis openly admitted that Palestinian moderation was a risk to their agenda, which relied on projecting all Palestinians as extremists. Ze'ev Boim, parliamentary leader of Likud, said of Professor Nusseibeh: "If he is a moderate, he is dangerous."[15] Indeed, along with ex-Shin Bet* chief Ami Ayalon, the professor had produced a joint peace plan, confounding again the claim that there was "no partner for peace."

Arafat's speech had launched yet another ceasefire: this one lasted three weeks and opened the way for progress at last. And for me it meant that I could give birth in my hospital of choice. At the pre-Christmas parties I turned up to, still pregnant, I was gently teased for holding out for a Christmas baby born in Bethlehem. "Maybe it's the checkpoints putting the baby off—which I presume is going to be a boy?" said one. Cindy, an American friend, mother, and health professional, reminded me to stick up for myself in the delivery room and not be bullied into whatever the hospital staff determined was convenient. Steve, who was more concerned that I should get to the hospital in the first place, offered: "We'll give you a convoy of journalists loaded with cameras and recording gear. That'll get you through, no problem."

When labor started, Andrew checked with his IDF contacts that the ceasefire was still on, that Bethlehem was quiet and, most important, unlikely to be targeted. No one could vouch for Palestinian militants not breaking the ceasefire, but it had held so far. Our friend Libby arrived in her dented Toyota and took the three children to her house. Andrew and I left for the hospital. The ceasefire was holding; Bethlehem was peaceful. The checkpoint was abandoned apart from a crowd of soldiers. A contraction came on just as we came to a halt at the barricade.

---

* The Israeli counter-intelligence and internal security service.

"Why do you want to go to Bethlehem?" He looked at the two of us, from one to the other. I was clutching the armrests.

Andrew looked across at my pregnant posture and said the obvious: "We're going to the hospital." No reaction. The soldier looked at my belly. Andrew pulled out our foreign passports and I put on a smile as the contraction ended, hoping it hadn't made me appear aggressive.

The passports pleased the soldier once he had had a good look. He handed them back and turned away to talk to his friends.

Bethlehem was quieter than ever, but I wasn't thinking about sieges or retaliation or shells landing on hospitals—I was thinking about labor. Two nights before we had sat with friends in a favorite restaurant, Askadinia. I had stared at the bare high wall in front of me, block after block of limestone right up to the roof, picking at an arugula and pomegranate salad, picturing the other wall in front of me: labor. Now here it was, and I wished I'd opted for an elective C-section.

I felt combative when we reached the hospital, but the doorman was expecting me, said "hello" and welcomed me by my first name. This gave me pause: for Catriona's birth the welcome had been simply: "Do you have a number?"—this from a nurse whose eyes remained stuck in the paperwork on her desk. I softened. The midwives also said "hello," and showed me to my room, bustling about. I tried to make the most of the contractions being moderate, but I couldn't rest—right outside my window was a huge truck, red and yellow, bearing a crane. I couldn't read, my mind was island-hopping. A concrete mixer was mating with the crane, its drum spinning deafeningly, spewing concrete. I gazed out at a poinsettia tree among the roses and across the path to the hospital building, which had been pierced by an IDF tank shell a few weeks before, sending shrapnel into all these rooms. The crane and the concrete mixer were making repairs.

I was trying to finish an article I had been writing, but was slowly turning into a patient. Dr. Salsa came by and assured me I would have the baby today. Then paused, smiling, "or tomorrow." Wanting to keep moving, I visited neonatal intensive care, where a newborn set of triplets, huge, were doing well, lying in their little incubators. And Andrew and I walked about the cloistered courtyard in the sun, detaching ourselves from the outside world. A statue of the Virgin Mary looked down at us from the top of the courtyard wall. We went inside again and walked along the limestone corridors. The midwives had urged me to walk, walk, walk, squat, gyrate, rotate, and let warm water pour over me in the shower. Andrew stayed with me the while, sitting, reading, trying to talk between contractions, not looking at me when each one came on, just rubbing my back, helping.

With labor moving along, Dr. Salsa came in to see me again and said, in her matter-of-fact way, "What about pain relief?"

"What are you offering?"

"Well, there's pethidine, there's epidural, there's gas and air, there's..."

"Gas and air would be great, I always wanted to try that." It had not been on offer for my first three deliveries.

She started pulling at the tubing, and then said, "Oh, I'm really sorry, the mask seems to be broken." She looked around, and the midwife apologized, saying "We've been trying to get the parts, but... you know, supplies aren't getting through..."

I carried on without. The pain changed: intense, but centralized, and shorter in duration. Andrew sat on one side of me as the midwife started to run a new CTG trace (monitoring the fetal heart rate and uterine contractions). The midwife, Imam, was from Deheisha refugee camp and a village near Ramla. While Imam ran the trace she and Andrew talked across me, about the camp and the situation. Hey, I thought, for once can't we drop the situation? Sandwiched, speechless, and a tad forgotten, I tried to focus on the pain, breathing softly, eyes shut, willing it not to get on top of me. But it was getting on top of me, slowly, by the time she'd finished the trace and their conversation.

The delivery rolled me along: midwife, doctor, and Andrew supporting, encouraging, enabling. No more talk of the situation or of refugees. No more worries about checkpoints or being bombed. Hearing my own gasping screams and seeing flashing lights and losing it, and then the flood of instant, absolute relief as indescribable as the pain. The baby, a boy, born late at night in a welter of pain and power, the two of us folding into one another with his arrival.

Later, they put me in a wheelchair and took me back to my room. My pelvis creaked in disarray, bones not linked to each other. Andrew made sure I was looked after, rang family in England and went home to be with the children. The two midwives asked if I'd like anything to eat.

"No, no," I said, "don't worry." It was midnight.

"Yes," they insisted. "Tell us what you'd like and we'll bring it for you."

"Well... I don't suppose there's any soup?"

"Anything you like." And they brought hot brothy soup a little while later, with bread and fruit and good things to get me to eat. Sated, exhausted, I fell asleep instantly. The baby, all nine-and-a-half pounds of him, lay swaddled in nylon wool knitted by some kind person with great care in fluorescent yellow and green. Then I woke and had a strangely sleepless night. Having been emptied out in the delivery room I slowly felt myself filled again, and the situation faded well away. Little noises kept breaking my thoughts: the baby.

With his limbs curled back into the shape he had formed fattening inside me, he was content to sleep off the efforts of being born while I took in the contours of his face, wondering who he might be. I pushed back the swaddling green from his brow to kiss the softness of his head, remembering the same kiss for each of his siblings. Tomorrow the three of them would launch themselves at their new brother, exuberant but wary, watching him take his place in the family.

The following day Sister Sophie, in charge of the hospital's orphanage, visited me and peeped at my wrapped-up baby. We talked about children. She said the orphans in her care were much better now that the invasion was over, and she prayed that it stayed that way. Bethlehem radio, Reuters, local TV, and *al-Quds* newspaper came to interview me, the expat who had chosen a Bethlehem hospital in the city attacked so frequently. The obstetrician had ordered an X-ray, and the radiologist came for me just as the first camera crew arrived. The midwife and radiologist argued while I was being lined up for the X-ray, lying captive on the slab, fretting to get back to my new baby. The radiologist looked down, adjusted me for the shot, and launched in: "To understand things, we have to go back in history," he intoned.

"To the British Mandate?" I said, weakly, hoping this would be brief.

"No—to the Canaanites," and I knew I was in for a long one, as he listed every power that ever flexed in the Holy Land. Reaching the Mamluks, he broke off, a sudden thought he must enlighten me with: "You know, 2,000 years ago there were no Jews here."

I don't know the Arabic for "Don't be bloody ridiculous," but that was clearly what the midwife blurted. Leaving them to a noisy historical row, I hurried back to my room, where the TV cameras wanted me to be lying in bed, the newly delivered mother, babe in arms.

Andrew came to fetch me, cross after being held up for an hour and a half at the checkpoint. My bones were coming together again; pelvis feeling more steady. We wrapped up our baby boy and said our goodbyes to the midwives, me lingering; I had become a patient and liked being able to call for analgesia. Andrew bustled me out of my dependency, hurrying to get me home and back to the children. Having patiently respected my professional judgment and personal choice, he wanted to bring my childbirth-in-Bethlehem experience to an end. As we drove out of the hospital and through the town, Bethlehem was hushed and black-dark, with no streetlights left upright. We went slowly through the darkness, past piles of rubble still lying here and there. As we approached the soldiers at the now-empty checkpoint, they seemed to be dancing in the middle of the road. We came closer. They really *were* dancing, cheerily singing a version of "YMCA." They saluted jovially as they waved us straight through, unhindered and unchecked. We waved back and went home.

Our friends called and visited, bringing presents and saying "*mazel tov*," "*mabruk*," "congratulations." The family and I adjusted to our new sizes over the days, opening stockings, singing carols in the nearly empty St. George's cathedral, and eating turkey at the American Colony Hotel. The children swung from the walnut tree, hurtled down the hill on their Christmas bikes, and ran back periodically to look at their new, still nameless, brother.

On New Year's Eve I gathered up my baby and returned to Bethlehem. There was to be a second attempt at a peace march organized by a group of Christians and Muslims, led by the Latin Patriarch. The first attempt had been blocked: a well-publicized peace march was more worrying than a violent rally. IDF officers sometimes confided[16] that they dreaded a well-coordinated mass campaign of non-violence above any other form of resistance: Palestinians were not supposed to look moderate, reasonable.

The plan was to walk from Bethlehem to Jerusalem, encircle the Old City in an "embrace of peace," and pray at the al-Aqsa Mosque and the Church of the Holy Sepulcher. Many of our friends were going, and I joined one, who brought along her baby and her mother-in-law. We parked before we reached the checkpoint and walked. Palestinians were lined up for inspection, but instead of following the makeshift signs painted on the concrete blocks pointing us through the enclosure, my older companion, Lady Adams, made straight for the soldiers. She had been the British ambassadress in Jordan and Egypt some years before, and carried an air of unquestionable authority despite her 79 years and not being very tall. None of the soldiers made any attempt to stop her. They seemed bemused by our intention to visit the place they were guarding, our babies in our arms, their arms at their hips. They warned my friend and I not to go through with children, explaining frankly that they thought it better because there were "a lot of our soldiers in there."

But on we went, following the indomitable Lady Adams past the checkpoint toward the many, massing soldiers in full combat gear, lined up across the road, backed up by new, heavily armored riot-control vehicles and jeeps, and snipers positioned in the trees. The peaceful, church-led procession approached from the opposite direction. The soldiers were looking uncomfortable: they were not going to allow a peaceful demonstration beyond the limits of Bethlehem, let alone to reach Jerusalem.

There was Charlie Glass among the clerics coming toward us. Debonair as ever, he leaned over the linked arms of the soldier-barricade to kiss me hello. The mood was light, and friendly, beaming messages of peace, balloons bobbing, banners flying, all in cheery contrast to the dark drama of the military. The IDF had let the marchers through the first roadblock only on condition that they wouldn't ask to go beyond the outer Bethlehem checkpoint. Instead the march leaders said prayers at the checkpoint. The Latin Patriarch called for an end to the violence and the occupation. Sari Nusseibeh, president of al-Quds University, stated the unequivocal: that Jerusalem should be a city open to everyone, including Palestinians.[17] With no choice, and up against the power of the Israeli army, the march dissolved obediently.

I had written a piece for the *Christian Science Monitor* about the problems checkpoints were posing for pregnant women. Its publication provoked a gentle, impassioned letter from an Israeli doctor. He reminded readers that the pain for Israelis and Palestinians alike had made understanding each other's suffering almost impossible. But, he said, he avoided blaming either side.

"The historic and emotional patchwork here is multilayered. In the pain and emotion of these miserable times it is tempting to seek myopic solutions. Indeed, this seems to be the pattern of the day. The solutions of the Islamic Jihad and Hamas who are dismissive of any Israeli claims of justice, as well as those of the Israeli right, who are equally insensitive to Palestinian rights and aspirations, leave us to wallow in this quagmire... For now I yearn for a time without checkpoints, when I can return to my calling without the justifiable fear of being shot or lynched by hate-filled people for whom I am just another 'enemy.'"

The Israeli doctor longed for "great leadership," but there was none. The ceasefire still held and the deadline passed but the promised return to negotiations had not materialized. Soon after the New Year the Israeli navy seized a cargo ship, the *Karine-A*. Captained by an officer from the Palestinian navy, and with Iranian support, it was carrying arms including rocket launchers, anti-tank weapons, mines, and explosives destined for the Palestinian Authority in Gaza. Had these weapons reached their intended destination the Palestinians would have been equipped to fight tanks and, with rocket launchers with a range of about 12 miles, would have been able to threaten communities inside Israel. Caught, the PA lied about having had anything to do with the shipment, and thus looked stupid as well as deceitful. For many Israelis the sight of the shipment's weaponry displayed on their TV screens and newspapers showed that Arafat was indeed bent on destroying Israel, lying to everyone as he pursued his aim. Other Israelis, after pointing out how small, even pitiful, a cache it was when compared to the weaponry being used against the Palestinians, asked why the PA didn't just admit they were bringing in weapons—after all, *someone* had to defend the Palestinian people against the Israeli army, air force, and navy.[18]

Despite Israeli officials' fury over the weapons shipment, the US envoy General Zinni returned: he declared that he was pleased with progress by both sides, and that Palestinian violence against

Israelis had effectively stopped since Arafat's December 16 cease-fire. Yet the American administration was hesitating and, instead of engaging the two sides in negotiation, echoed Sharon's demands for "seven days of total quiet": that seven-day deadline had passed, ignored, on Christmas Eve. For once we were waiting not for revenge or retaliation, but for talks; this was a real moment for progress, and moderates on both sides were calling loudly for action. But action required the backing of the US administration. "What are they waiting for?—Arafat has finally done it, now is the time to capitalize, to go for peace..." groaned a US diplomat over dinner. The Americans had only to push for implementation of the Mitchell Committee recommendations.* The Palestinians had repeatedly been promised progress on these issues if they could bring about a reduction in violence against Israelis. Stopping violence had been pulled off, at significant domestic expense. Afterward, the former US national security advisor Zbigniew Brzezinksi concluded that the US was unintentionally perpetuating the conflict.[19]

Instead, the Palestinians reeled under a wave of IDF bulldozers in Rafah, destroying more than fifty houses, leaving hundreds homeless in the bitter cold. On top of that there was another assassination. The IDF killed a local Palestinian commander, Raed Karmi, and the conflict flipped straight back into the cycle of revenge. Israeli commentators vented their rage about the effects of and motivation behind this policy.**

* A settlement freeze, the lifting of the closures, and the resumption of permanent status negotiations.

** Ma'ariv said the policy could be seen as "a deliberate provocation intended to cause the collapse of the ceasefire,"[20] and Uzi Benziman concluded that it was "impossible to shake off the suspicion that this method of operation serves Sharon's unwillingness to take advantage of the truce periods in order to renew the political dialogue." He noted "a pattern of Israeli behavior that has recurred since Sharon began running the country: When a period of calm prevails in the confrontation with the Palestinians, circumstances are created that induce Israel to carry out military operation in a manner that renews, or accelerates, the cycle of violence."[21]

The al-Aqsa Martyrs Brigades responded to the assassination with an inevitable, bitter, statement: "The hoax of the so-called ceasefire is cancelled, cancelled, cancelled."[22] Shortly afterward, Palestinian gunmen shot an Israeli dead near a West Bank settlement, and now many were concluding that Israel's assassinations generated far more damage than the benefits they were supposed to bring.[23] For a moment it had looked as though leaders were going to set the agenda. Now the conflict was back in the grip of the extremists.

Not long after Sholto—we settled on a name at last—was born I had to return to the hospital to be given the postnatal all-clear. The baby was feeding, sleeping, and growing well, monitored by an Israeli pediatrician, but I was still under the care of Dr. Salsa in Bethlehem. I heard that a friend had driven into Bethlehem one morning and decided to grab the chance to go there for my check-up while things were quiet.

As I entered the quiet courtyard of the hospital, a battle-scarred Virgin Mary, blackened and full of bullet holes, looked down at me from the high point of the cloister. A passing pediatrician explained: "She was machine-gunned last night by a tank. I don't know why the IDF went to the trouble of aiming up there." The statue had been erected 120 years ago and had withstood all previous occupations. The hospital's legend, the doctor told me, held that a Turkish officer tried to have her removed but as he waited for his men to take her down, he was kicked by his horse and died. The statue had remained ever since, but now had to be taken down; too many holes to be mendable.

The hospital director, whom I had met many times, came across the courtyard.

"Bombed again," he said gamely. "How's the baby?" He showed me some of the damage from the previous night's attack. Doctors and midwives had hurried from room to room carrying mattresses and shepherding the mothers and their babies into a ward facing away from the line of fire. He took me to one blitzed room: "The lab tech left his bed here to do a test one minute before the bomb hit." Now the staff were complaining that there was nowhere in the hospital without windows, no basement and no safe place to shield patients from incoming fire and rockets.

"It's not the sort of complaint I'd expected to be fielding as hospital director," he said, in his mild way. "Some of the staff are suffering from PTSD (post-traumatic stress disorder), and they're all permanently on call at the hospital these days, leaving their families in order to look after the patients."

He had tried to mobilize support wherever he could. "One of our board members lives next to Colin Powell and has contacted him about the hospital being bombed. We're waiting for a response. The Order [of Malta] has contacts in Ireland, Britain, France, all over, as well as the States. They're all trying, but it's hard. The French military attaché in Tel Aviv, for example—he contacted the Israeli authorities about the last time we were hit, and he received an answer. There was, apparently, 'no tank activity' here in October."

We visited some of the mothers in the maternity ward. One of them, Abeer, had arrived in the night by ambulance, petrified by the sound of bullets and bombs as they drove her and the other passenger, a dialysis patient, through the curfew. The Red Cross had negotiated with the IDF their safe passage through the town, and when they were stopped at the checkpoint the soldiers had seen that Abeer was having contractions and let them through. The ambulance men sang songs and laughed as they drove through the dark in an effort to keep up the spirits of their charges.

Abeer, nursing her newborn son, began to cry at the thought of previous night. She rocked little baby Ahmed against her breast. "Having a baby is meant to be something we celebrate, something to make us happy, but we have nothing to be happy about now. We have only fear."

I headed for the registry to register Sholto's birth—late. I was fined seven Jordanian dinars. It seemed odd to hold me to their deadline when there were curfews and IDF bombing campaigns, but I didn't argue the point. While I went through the paperwork the registrar talked. He was Christian, he told me almost immediately. "Do you know how long we have been here?" he asked. "Always. We were the first Christians."

He went on, wanting to know my data. "How many children do you have? Where were they born? In America? Oh, those Christians in America are so strange. I don't understand why they have no feeling for us fellow Christians. Where is their humanity?"

I explained that it wasn't all Christians in America, only some Christian fundamentalists who seemed oblivious to the rights of Palestinian Christians.

As I finished the forms, Andrew phoned me.

"Where are you by the way?" he asked as we were saying goodbye. "—in *Bethlehem*? What the hell are you doing there? *Please*, get out right now. And call me the minute you're out." He had heard that there was about to be heavy military escalation that day. Foolishly, I hadn't checked with him.

I hurried through the paperwork and was back home when the escalation started.

8

"When We Are Destroyed"

Sholto's arrival changed our sleeping habits but blew out the black hopelessness of the situation. Out of all the disintegration now there was a baby to brighten and distract: I hid myself away, tending to the somnolent dictator. My life had been changed in another way, by the arrival of Julita Arsenio who came to help us, all the way from Manila. Instantly adored by Catriona and the boys, Julita gently took charge, smoothed out our chaos, and became my close friend.

There were other distractions, including our new house in Scotland. Thick brown packages of plans and architects' drawings arrived periodically for us to linger over. The children fussed over the baby and were happy in school, busy at home with their bikes and toy soldiers, and doing well. Jerusalem had us enthralled, with its irresistible light and beauty, the heady concentration of brilliant people, and the many good friends we had made.

We were all happy. It was just the situation, living alongside two extraordinary peoples who were bent on killing each other. Except they weren't all. The killing was driven by the few. The baby had been born at a key moment, after a surge in violence and death and during a three-week ceasefire that gave a real chance for peace but which was rocked by the capture of the *Karine-A* weapons ship, then killed off by the IDF's assassination of Raed Karmi.

We spent time with other friends, trying to keep the situation a taboo but it only worked so far. On our first outing without the baby we went to Ein Kerem with my friend Alison and her husband, Avi, who told me wicked tales of conferences in the Mediterranean and the passage-creeping antics of the Israeli and Palestinian attendees. Alison was explaining to Andrew that whereas many of the Jewish diaspora were understanding and reasonable, some Jews abroad pushed Israelis to make the Palestinians submit totally, "to hit them harder and harder 'until they learn.' 'You must do this,' they rant from far away, 'whatever the costs.'" The costs, she said, "are the lives of *my* children—not theirs—it's our children who have to serve as soldiers," and also Israel's future security. "Look what happens every time we assassinate one of their leaders—more violence, more suicide bombings."

Avi broke off listing indiscretions and brought up a recent row when the French ambassador had called Israel "a shitty little country" at a private dinner in London. "You know," said Avi with his mischievous smile and eyes full of humor, "I called Peres, and said to him, 'Shimon, what's this ridiculous story, how can we object to that?' Peres said, 'Of course, when it comes to the Palestinians, shitty is exactly how we behave.' And he's right. I don't have a problem with that."

Val Vester, the much-loved matriarch and owner of the American Colony Hotel, would often take us out of the conflict. On New Year's Day, 2002, we had headed for her house in Jericho, sitting on the scarp beneath Mount Temptation, overlooking the ancient city. She and her late husband, Horatio, had been going there since long before the occupation began. Now, more often than not, the soldiers refused to let her pass through the Israeli checkpoint that controlled the city; the other roads to Jericho were blocked by concrete cubes and by the trench. This time a UN friend, French and unbreakably cheerful, persuaded the IDF blockade to let us in, with Val in our convoy of three families in three UN cars. The troopers on duty made an effort to question her, but not for long, and we spent a happy day in the golden Jericho light under the male and female mulberry trees of Val's garden, preparing pitchers of Bloody Mary, eating smoked salmon sandwiches and talking about anything but the situation. While our children, with the two other families, one of four boys and another of four girls, ran round the famous archaeological digs of Kathleen Kenyon—the Walls of Jericho—Val told us about her life as an undergraduate at Somerville College, Oxford, in the 1930s, her aunt Gertrude Bell who had helped map Iraq, and her own drive from London to Jerusalem in a Mini in the 1950s.

Now, in February, we celebrated Val's 90th birthday: even then the situation broke in. The party was held at her hotel, the American Colony Hotel, described increasingly often in the Israeli press as a haven for foreign journalists who closed their eyes to the Israeli side. The reality was more prosaic. It was a remarkably fine hotel, unique, unpretentious, informal, and people liked to gather there: Israelis, Palestinians, and expatriates. On balmy nights there was an outdoor bar under the hushing palm trees, and when it grew chilly in the autumn, the bar went underground into dark, cushioned alcoves where the tall banged their heads on the low limestone arches and red wine was served in vast glasses to the unsuspecting. And because it was just inside East Jerusalem, many Palestinians felt more comfortable there, and less likely to be harassed for being Palestinian.

Many of the guests at Val's birthday party were journalists who had stayed at the hotel over the years while covering the conflict, and now watched from afar. These incomers, one of whom had just then been two minutes away from a suicide bombing, were festive enough, but having returned, inevitably they wanted to talk about the situation. They were shocked by the escalation in attacks on Israelis, and how much the Israeli people were having to endure in the post-ceasefire storm of revenge.

They told us that watching from abroad left them vividly aware of the terrible violence inflicted on Israelis. That endured by the Palestinians, on the other hand, was too grinding, too chronic to be covered equally. I had heard this before, and would again.[1] Almost without exception, they were saying, an Israeli death at the hands of Palestinians would be reported in the US media, whereas it might take up to ten dead Palestinians to warrant a report of their killing. And then an official Israeli line—"caught in the crossfire," or "suspected terrorist cell'—would appear in the report, leaving the listener with the impression that every death was "justified." Even describing the pattern as a "cycle of violence" implied that the sides were equally matched—an impression that helped deflect criticism for disproportionate military actions, and conceal that one side was resisting occupation. The context, they said, was hidden.

Despite my hiding from the situation, I could not avoid seeing that the violence was growing. On the ground the "kill-rate" increased. In two weeks (February 28–March 14, 2002) 2 foreigners, 58 Israelis, and 168 Palestinians, almost all of them civilians, were killed. More suicide bombings and more large-scale military onslaught followed: ground forces, tanks, attack helicopters, naval gunships, F-16s, missiles, and bombs of heavy tonnage used across the West Bank and Gaza, with a number of attacks on humanitarian agencies.

A female suicide bomber struck on February 28 at a checkpoint outside Nablus. Her story was unearthed soon enough: 21 years old, she was a refugee living in Balata camp. One month before she blew herself up, her brother had been killed by the IDF. A week before, the IDF had killed her fiancé.

The IDF struck back in return. Tanks and troops invaded Balata and Jenin camps, home to Palestinians who had lost their lands and houses in 1948 and 1967. I talked to a French friend who had returned from covering the situation in Balata in time to attend the bar mitzvah of the son of a mutual friend. In the marbled rooms of the best West Jerusalem hotel, the King David, a crowd of guests pressed and kissed, seemingly unaware of what was going on just a few miles away. The French journalist was swirled uncomfortably into the warmth and elegance, surrounded by platters of delicious foods, lulled by an orchestra playing South American music. She was at sea. And yet, as she said, the hosts resisted the occupation in their own way, in their own time, and were just trying to be normal for their son's sake on his big day.

Trying to be normal was one reaction to the powerlessness that many Israelis felt in the face of extremism. Israeli papers were full of foreboding, some warning that Israelis must understand the causes of terror, and that terror came from despair, and of the consequences of the right wing's agenda.*

Andrew and I went to a Peace Now rally outside the prime minister's residence. Earlier that evening another Palestinian bomber had exploded himself, this time in Mea Sharim, near a synagogue just as the faithful were leaving after the last Shabbat prayers. Ten Israelis died, including a twelve-month-old baby. In many ways this bombing was even more appalling than the others: picking on worshippers, so many of them children, and the ultra-Orthodox, some of whom for theological reasons were not even supporters of the State of Israel.

I don't know why we felt it was a good idea to go to the rally—there could so easily have been another bomber out there. We met American, French, and Israeli friends for a drink in a West Jerusalem wine bar, and then went on to join the thousands of Israelis calling for the occupation to end. Once through the police security checks, we milled about, bumping into other friends. At one point there was another loud explosion and a tremor went through the crowd. But it was not a bomb this time, we heard later on that night. Just something that sounded like a bomb.

Andrew said aloud, "How typical of the Palestinians to bomb now—what a sense of timing, with Israeli moderates demonstrating against the occupation."

* *Nahum Barnea, chief commentator for* Yediot Ahronoth, *Israel's most widely read newspaper, advised his readers not to regard terror as a "blight of nature." "The current escalation in terror began with the government's decision to ignore the arrest of Minister Ze'evi's assassins, and to continue to keep Arafat under house arrest in Ramallah," which he defined as part of the right wing's intention to humiliate Arafat in front of the Palestinian people. He urged Israelis to recognize that "the terrorism of suicide bombings was born of despair, and there is no military solution to despair," and that the only one who could radically change the situation was Ariel Sharon. The right wing, he warned, "is pushing him to an all-out war, at the end of which, so hopes the Right, the door will open to the expulsion of millions of Palestinians."[2]*

"It's not surprising if it is a bomb," came the firm response from Simone, art expert and wife of an Israeli government spokesman, "after what they did in Balata refugee camp."

"Who—" asked Andrew, a little surprised, "the Palestinians?"

"No," replied Simone, looking at him hard. "The IDF."

The mood was bewildered, dispirited, funereal. Everyone knew about the bomb that evening, and that there might be another. Everyone felt the hopelessness. Placards waved in the darkness, numbering the dead Israelis and the dead Palestinians. The quietness was almost apologetic. One Israeli woman wandered among the crowd asking for donations of blood. Confused, a French journalist asked her: "Is that for those injured tonight in Mea Sharim?"

"No, there's enough for them," came the reply. "This is for the Palestinians injured in the attack on Balata."

But all the talk of ceasefires, diplomatic initiatives, and imminent envoys—let alone a few demonstrations—was now an irrelevant whisper against the clamor for destruction and revenge. Both peoples were being driven to new levels of vengeance and rage: while Israelis lined up their dead, killed by suicide bombers, Palestinians lined up their own dead, killed by the IDF, and coped with the relentless demolitions, bombings, curfew, closures, raids, settler attacks and shootings.

By March 9, 2002 Israelis and Palestinians were being killed almost every day. Refugee camps were ravaged, Israeli tanks were deep inside Palestinian towns, destroying, shooting, crushing cars, and soldiers were running amok through Palestinian homes and lives. That week the Israeli prime minister had stated: "We must cause them losses, casualties!" shocking many, including commentator Ze'ev Schiff, who feared Sharon's war-cry would be interpreted "as a call for indiscriminate casualties." Schiff warned that "if we follow the course now suggested by Sharon, it will guarantee the most possible chaos and perhaps also some massacres."[3]

On the night of Schiff's warning an enormous explosion tore

apart a popular Jerusalem bar, Café Moment, hard on the heels of another suicide bombing, in Netanya. In the heart of Jerusalem, Café Moment was feet from the prime ministerial residence where we had demonstrated with Peace Now. We had been to the restaurant from time to time and passed it at least twice each day. Now it was a killing-zone. Twelve people died, the bomber making thirteen. A few days later 39 Palestinians were killed during IDF raids into Jabalya camp in Gaza and Deheisha camp in Bethlehem.

Efrat Ravid was twenty years old when Café Moment was bombed. Human Rights Watch, which condemned suicide bombings as war crimes, reported that her thigh was shattered and she suffered a serious brain hemorrhage. She couldn't speak for a week, walked only with crutches months afterward and never smiled. In the interview she described her reactions: "My biggest fear was that they would amputate my leg—there were so many people in that hospital with missing limbs. They told me not to worry—they did an artery transplant, and said that even if it got infected later, there'd be enough time to do surgery. I've had ten operations since the attack. I also had a nail just a few millimeters from my heart... The friend I had been with was also injured—her intestines spilled right out. We don't talk any more. It brings up too many bad memories. The girl sitting on the other side of me—I didn't know her—she was killed. My friends don't go out any more. They realized when this happened to me, it could have been them."[4]

By March 25, IDF military incursions were daily events, leaving 23 Palestinians dead in that week alone, and many more wounded. As Maha and I nursed our babies together in her house one afternoon, the television on as always, she leveled curses at the images we were seeing from the refugee camps. "For the refugees," she said, "invasions are terrifying events," in lives already full of terror; families never knew whether the invasion meant they would lose their homes (again) or perhaps their lives. Each time the tanks invaded they demolished yet more homes and even fired into houses and makeshift shelters put up for the newly homeless. The

IDF spokesman announced that "one Palestinian was reportedly killed during Israeli army activity in Rafah": he was describing the death of a four-year-old girl, shot in the head as she sat inside her home.

One Israeli friend told me later how Israeli TV audiences were shocked to see footage of one of the many IDF raids. On their screens a Palestinian mother was hit by shrapnel as the soldiers blasted their way into her home. She bled to death in front of her children—and the Israeli public. Sharon was maddened, accusing the TV station of "serving the interests of our enemy." Knesset member Ran Cohen defended the media, pointing out that they were only doing their job, and it was the soldiers who were doing these things to Palestinian civilians. Israeli television crews found themselves banned from accompanying the IDF into Palestinian areas.

Then, in the last week of March, the Arab League offered Israel a peace plan. A military solution would not bring peace, the authors said. The Saudi Peace Plan called on Israel to withdraw from the territories occupied since June 1967, achieve a "just solution" to the Palestinian refugee problem, and accept the establishment of a sovereign Palestinian state in the West Bank and Gaza, with East Jerusalem as its capital. In return, the Arab League would end the Arab-Israeli conflict and establish normal relations with Israel.

Andrew phoned from Beirut. Beirut is closer to Jerusalem than New York is to Boston, but because of the state of Lebanese-Israeli relations he had to loop through complicated telephonic hoops to speak to me. Through a New York connection that was put through to the UN office in Gaza, and then to me in Jerusalem, he talked about the plan's great significance. Recognition and normalization: the very things most Israelis longed for. All those debilitating and understandable fears of being surrounded by a sea of Arab aggression—and here was the Arab world offering peace, after decades of war and insecurity. Not only that, but the effective abandonment of the Palestinian refugees' right of return. "It could be a breakthrough. The question is, which lot of hardliners will screw it up for everyone else first."

Instead of welcoming the Saudi plan and jumping at the peace Israelis longed for, the government would roll tanks into Ramallah a few hours after the summit ended. The day before, on March 27, 29 Israelis had died at the hands of a suicide bomber sent by Hamas, giving justification for the invasion. The infamous Passover bomb was one of the most atrocious inflicted on Israel. The victims were mostly elderly people sitting in a hotel in Netanya, celebrating the holy feast of Passover. It was a repulsive crime. And it came on the brink of the long-expected military offensive.

Hamas admitted using terror to control events: "Our operation coincided with the Arab summit in Beirut... (It) is a clear message to our Arab rulers that our struggling people have chosen their road and know how to regain lands and rights in full, depending only on God."[5] Likewise Islamic Jihad had aimed to spike General Zinni's latest mission to establish a ceasefire, admitting, "The Zinni mission [which included the disarmament of groups like Hamas and the arrest of their leaders] was bad for us."[6]

One of the hundreds injured in the bombing was Clara Rosenberger. Seventy-six years old, she had survived three and a half years as a prisoner in Auschwitz. She had chosen to celebrate Passover at the Park Hotel because she was afraid of bombings and thought the hotel would be safe, and had gone to the seder with one of her friends. The bomb killed her friend. Shrapnel severed Clara's spinal cord, leaving her paralyzed. Her daughter told Human Rights Watch that Clara withdrew into her own world: "She was involved in all kinds of senior citizens' activities... Now she is very dependent. She has no strength to deal with it—it was punishment enough that her life, with its tragedies, was as it was. She can't sit up because she is paralyzed from the underarms down, so she has no chest muscles. From the first moment we spoke after the attack, she said, 'What happened to me was the very thing I did not want to happen to me, to be a burden on others.' She won't ever be able to return home."[7]

Andrew came back from the Arab League summit. I picked him up in Herzliya and we drove back to Jerusalem through the quiet. It was dark when we reached the monastery of Latrun, the last of the plains before the hills rose to Jerusalem. Up the winding Route 1 snaked a convoy of long, low military trailers. Each trailer bore a tank, heavy, vast, impregnable. We passed them silently, our vehicle thin-shelled and feeble. IDF officials were telling diplomats: "We've had enough. What we're about to launch in the territories is something you can't imagine." Final preparations were in overdrive, confirmed by the long columns of tanks and armory filling the wide Israeli highway toward the West Bank. Now it felt like war. Ramallah was invaded, and the offensive launched.

Sharon addressed the Israeli nation: "The State of Israel is in a war, a war against terror." He went on, "Ever since I was elected, the State of Israel has made every effort to reach a ceasefire. Amidst the wave of Palestinian *terror*, we set before us the goal of doing our utmost to achieve calm and make progress toward political agreements... All we received in return for our efforts was *terror, terror* and *more terror*.

"We must," he said, "wage an uncompromising fight against this *terror*, uproot these weeds. It is impossible to compromise with someone who is prepared—like the suicide bombers on the streets of Israel's cities and at the World Trade Center in the US—to die in order to kill innocent civilians, children, women, and infants."

And, he said, this terror was operated, directed, and initiated by one man—Yasser Arafat. The PA chairman was "an enemy of Israel in particular and the world in general."[8]

Thousands of reservists had been called up. It is strange to watch people you see and talk to every day suddenly dragged out of their civilian lives, reclad in uniform, and sent off to war. Sometimes people just disappeared, without warning, like the newsagent from whom I bought *Ha'aretz* each day. Others had received their orders in advance, like the man in the dry-cleaner's. He said very little about going, only that he "had to." There the conversation ended; both of us knew the unspoken—the risk that he might be killed, the reality that he might have to kill—but neither of us wanted to start that debate and find out just what the other thought. Not at this point.

Israelis wanted to hit back, such was their great anguish, magnified so starkly by the Passover bombing. It was not the urgent need to respond but the nature of the response that so many people took issue with.[9]

We tried to escape again. We left the gathering madness to head for Luxor and the quiet of the Nile for a few days during the school spring break, mainly out of duty to the children. Having planned the trip weeks before, we went despite knowing what was coming—there had been too many, too horrific, Palestinian attacks on Israelis—and now the major offensive, so long on the drawing board,[10] was rolling. Getting away usually gave us a break from the constant wearying confrontation, but not this time: sitting on a felucca pretending to be on holiday was a party trick played for the children, who didn't enjoy it either. It didn't feel good to be admiring Nefertiti's newly renovated tomb and the achievements of the builders of Karnak when half a dozen CNN bulletins a day showed the siege and bombardment that friends were suffering. We were glad to get back.

Having watched the onslaught from afar—as town after Palestinian town was invaded—we returned to a wet and somber Jerusalem. Rain and mist blurred the city and the greening hills around us, and the checkpoints became a slurry of mud. News and stories were filtering through from those trapped in the territories: friends, work colleagues, and journalists of all description. One UN friend shook as he told us how the IDF had grabbed his (Palestinian) colleagues, arrested them, and led them off—they wouldn't tell him where. Jerusalem throbbed with the sound of helicopters and jets overhead, but no information was forthcoming—officially—from the battlefields: the IDF were, alarmingly, determined to do their work unseen.

A colleague from Ramallah, a lecturer in public health at al-Quds University called Raghda, met me in Jerusalem. Wrapped in winter clothes, we sipped mint tea in a café near the Damascus Gate in the Old City. A forthright woman, more at home discussing iodine deficiency than military strategy, Raghda now appeared almost subdued. She and her children had managed to get out of Ramallah on the day the IDF came in, but she had had to leave her husband and extended family behind. "Even when the curfew is lifted," she said, "the IDF still shoot. There is no burial of the dead. Houses are being demolished. We won't recognize Ramallah when we get back. When the children and I left there were 700 people trying to get out through Qalandia. Qalandia— a checkpoint between two Palestinian areas! The soldiers were shooting at us and swearing. We tried to explain to the children why they did this, but it is difficult to find a reason."

It became clear enough, soon enough, that "Operation Defensive Shield" was on a bigger scale than anything in the West Bank since 1967. The media were full of Arafat's compound being laid to waste during the recapture of Ramallah. The TV images of buildings toppled and crushed, homing in on the one where Arafat was holed up, were like a child's game: how many buildings can you destroy before the whole thing collapses?

All over the West Bank cities were under total curfew, massive bombardment, and persistent sniper fire. From afar, it looked like war. On site, it must have been infernal.

And yet, close as the two peoples were, there had never been more separation. In our lives there were distant war noises and anguished phone calls from the besieged, but the supermarkets were spilling over with food and policemen were concerned with directing traffic and parking offenses. Unless we listened, we would not hear the destructive misery just over the hill. And it seemed most Israelis were not listening, or were hearing something different. Where we heard descriptions of families cowering in one room, their homes blasted into by squads of combat troops bursting through the walls of one house into the next,* searching, arresting, looting, beating, and blasting out again to do the same to the next family, Israelis heard that "terrorist nests" were being rooted out. Where we heard friends in Ramallah or Nablus tell of their dread of the nightly pounding from aircraft, tanks, and helicopters, a behemoth hauled out and wielded against a civilian population, Israelis heard that the IDF were "fighting a tough and hardened enemy," bringing security to the Israeli people by crushing other people, something malevolent. It wasn't that our Israeli friends had never had contact with Palestinians—not at all, many had a number of close friends who were Palestinian. Now, though, they no longer saw them: literally and figuratively.

On the other side, the invisible needed to hear from the outside world. They needed to talk to friends who were not living under curfew, running out of water, food, and medicines, and whose streets were not patrolled by army vehicles manned by soldiers who would shoot them if they went out to look for food. A Christian friend in Ramallah told me that for once the bombardment had not been too severe, but that she had nevertheless been up all night calling the hospital. Her mother had a long history of cardiac problems, and her symptoms had started again: shortness of breath, pain down her arm, the usual. Except that the "usual," in another world, would have been dealt with by calling an ambulance and getting her to the hospital. Instead, she had to make do with a treatment program cobbled together out of the bathroom cabinet directed by a doctor on the end of the phone. The IDF were not allowing ambulances to move. The sick and wounded were scattered around the city without access to medical care.

---

* A military practice known as "mouseholing": using explosives to punch holes between houses to avoid exposing troops to the street.

Ambulances were not even allowed to help mothers in labor or kidney patients in need of dialysis. Shots were fired at ambulances that did try to evacuate patients.[11]

When you say baldly, "Curfew means not getting the sick to the hospital," you can avoid feeling the fear, the grinding frustration, and the injustice; words, however accurate, are inadequate. It is easier to hear "On Friday, April 5th, tanks moved in to encircle Jenin camp and the hospital" than to imagine just how that feels. Tanks are monsters: heartless, omnipotent, petrifying. They crawl, rumbling ominously, crushing metal and concrete like scraps of waste paper. When one turns its massive gun slowly toward you, you know what impotence is; your quiet flesh against awesome firepower that can pulverize whatever it pleases. From the tanks' insides, voices over loudspeakers ordered Jenin's hospital staff and patients to evacuate the top floor, which had views south over the refugee camp. One patient, too slow to obey, was shot in the throat as he looked out of the window.[12]

Within four days of the invasion of Jenin, the hospital's mortuary was overwhelmed and the staff had to dig graves in the hospital grounds to bury the dead, including a thirteen-year-old boy shot by an IDF sniper on the first day, a newborn baby, and an old woman who had died for lack of oxygen—the oxygen bottles had been damaged by gunfire two days before. While the hospital staff dug into the earth to create the graves and bury the dead, IDF helicopters circled overhead, firing warning shots.

An Israeli peace activist, Neta Golan, added her voice to the hundreds of Palestinian academics, human rights workers, aid workers, and individuals all begging the international community to do *something*. One of a group of volunteers providing a human shield inside Arafat's compound, she wrote: "Inside the pockmarked building surrounded by Israeli tanks and snipers there is one question on everyone's mind: how many international laws does Israel need to break before the United Nations demands a full and immediate Israeli withdrawal from the West Bank?... Israel has now escalated from interrupting food shipments to shutting off water to the Palestinian city of Ramallah, endangering the lives of 120,000 people. The shelling of Palestinian civilian structures such as power plants, schools and sewage facilities is occurring at an alarming rate. Unarmed civilians are being killed daily."[13]

Israelis had just had enough—enough death, enough fear—and now they felt that "at last" they were hitting back. On March 11, right-wing demonstrators in Tel Aviv had chanted, "We want war," and waved banners that shouted "Arafat is part of the axis of evil," and "Peres and Beilin are more dangerous than Arafat," presumably because of their efforts to arrive at a peace. Now they had their war. Sharon's approval rating rose from 45 percent to 62 percent between March and April.[14]

Sharon addressed the Knesset on April 8. He spoke of the many victims of the latest suicide bombings in Netanya and Haifa, and of individual acts of great nobility even at moments of the greatest suffering—a bereaved wife, Zahava Wieder, had agreed to donate her husband's organs to a Palestinian. He spoke of entire families being destroyed in the heat of murderous insanity, and he scorned Arafat's assumption that he would be able to defeat Israel and break its spirit. In an admission that ran counter to the widely touted claim that Arafat's plan was still a Palestinian state on the whole of Israel rather than just the Occupied Territories, Sharon declared: "In our sensitivity to the sanctity of human life and in our openness for political debate, he sees basic weakness. By way of blood and horror he wants to force Israel into a unilateral withdrawal to its 1967 borders."[15]

I lingered in Salahadin Street, in East Jerusalem. This road was a long curve of stores selling almost everything you could want, including good bread. The baker, who held a degree in economics, always liked to discuss the latest development, military and political. He still did, in contrast to some Israeli friends' uncharacteristic silence. He said he had been amazed at the ironies of Sharon's speech—"Thinking he can convince a people to renounce violence by beating them senseless, for a start"—as well as by his condemnation of killing civilians. And, he added, Palestinians didn't care if the withdrawal was unilateral or not—the '67 borders would do just fine.

Sharon's speech was published on April 9, Holocaust Day. On the same day I read that Peres was worried about the international reaction when the world learned "the details of the tough battle in the Jenin refugee camps, where more than 100 Palestinians have already been killed fighting with IDF forces. In private," the report said, "Peres is referring to the battle as 'a massacre.'"[16] IDF officers told the reporters that they too were worried by the operation in Jenin. "When the world sees the pictures of what we have done there, it will do us immense damage. However many wanted men we kill in the refugee camp, and however much of the terror infrastructure we expose and destroy there, there is still no justification for causing such great destruction."[17]

That day thirteen IDF soldiers were killed in an ambush in Jenin refugee camp, lured into a trap by Palestinian fighters, the terrorists who were being "flushed out." Israelis were mad with anger at the soldiers' deaths. The radio, TV, the papers, the conversations on both sides were stiff with fury and the desire for revenge. "No one understands," one Israeli told me, "what we've been through—129 Israelis were killed in terrorist attacks in March alone." Outraged that the world could not see how "moderate" the IDF was being, some said, "If we were a third world country we would have surrounded the camps with artillery and opened fire." A reservist put it more bluntly: "What are they [the world] talking about... If these were Americans, they would tell everyone to get out, and then they would bomb the place with jets, and whoever didn't leave, it's his own problem."[18]

Equal wrath was unleashed from the Palestinian side. "They use all those high-tech American weapons to slaughter Palestinians and they're outraged that we *fight back*? What are we supposed to do—lie down and *let* them kill us?" was the greeting that hailed me as I met one woman in the schoolyard. She was normally sanguine, even long-suffering, but this had pushed her over the edge.

On April 10, shortly after Sharon announced that IDF operations had stopped the terrorists in their tracks and had them on the run, there was a suicide bombing near Haifa. Eight people were killed and fourteen injured. The dead included Noa Shlomo. Eighteen years old and a talented ballet dancer, she was the niece of Israel's ambassador to the UN, Yehuda Lancry. Another suicide bomb followed two days later; six people were killed and 104 wounded by a woman suicide bomber at a bus stop on Jaffa Road at the entrance to Mahane Yehuda market, not far from the school.

In Jenin the fighting, which had paused after the thirteen IDF soldiers were killed, began again. Now the Palestinian fighters—and civilians—were contending with yet more hardware raining down on the camp. Fewer troops coursed through its narrow alleys, searching from house to house, but there were more giant bulldozers and bombardment with tanks and missiles. Israeli media reported estimates of the number of Palestinians killed in Jenin: 150.* The IDF were pounding the Palestinian infrastructure. The Palestinian Preventative Security offices in Ramallah and Hebron had been totally destroyed. And there had been break-ins at the offices of the Palestinian Legislative Council, with reams of files and documents stolen.

Why destroy children's exam records? people asked. Where does destroying driving license records get the Israelis? And *dental* records? Even the archaeological center's incomparable collections were taken. "This is what Sharon did in Lebanon too," said my colleague Ayesha over the phone. "He's trying to rob Palestine of its past as well as its future. But he cannot remove our past."

---

*The final figures were 54 in Jenin. More than 80 were killed in Nablus. In that city on April 6 the IDF bulldozed a house on top of 10 members of the al-Shu'bi family, killing 8 of them. The dead included three children, their pregnant mother, and their 85-year-old grandfather. Two elderly relatives were found—alive—under the rubble a week later.

The IDF had cut off electricity and water days before. The curfew throughout the West Bank and the intensity of the Closure were making a bad situation impossible. Frantic phone calls came through from friends and colleagues in the West Bank: even if people ventured out of their houses when the curfew was lifted for a couple of hours, supplies of food and medicines were not getting through to stock up the shops, and these were being looted by IDF troops. If they could reach the shops and if the supplies had got through and were not looted, then people hadn't the money to pay for them. On top of this were the fears of being picked off by snipers and of being "visited" by an IDF unit: at any time of the day or night the door would be beaten in, the place ransacked, belongings stolen, televisions smashed, clothes pulled out and ripped up, food supplies that weren't stolen emptied on to the floor and trodden underfoot, and soldiers shitting on their possessions. And then, after all the destruction, there could be arrest and detention—hundreds held without trial, no one knew where.

Meanwhile the outside world still appeared, to those inside, to be doing nothing about it. This reinforced the Palestinian belief that they did not qualify as human beings in the eyes of foreigners. Ayesha, on the phone again, was distraught at having to watch an old man lying dead in the street outside their house, his daughter bleeding to death beside him, and no one able to help because of the curfew and the likelihood of being shot. "When two statues in Afghanistan are destroyed," she said, "there is outrage.* When we are destroyed—there is nothing."

The remaining 29 fighters in Jenin ran out of ammunition and surrendered on April 11. A convoy of international agencies left Jerusalem with humanitarian aid for the besieged town, Andrew included. Many of those in the convoy had met the night before, having congregated at the American Colony bar after a

---

* In September 1999, the ruling Taliban regime blew up two giant Buddhas that had been carved into the mountain walls of Bamyan Province 1,700 years before.

reception given by the British Consul General. The bar had been full, as so often when there was a "big story," and there was talk among expatriates and Israeli journalists about what was going on, what was going to happen, and what should be done. Soon they would bump into each other again in the field, an altogether different meeting ground.

Andrew phoned to say they were about to enter Jenin camp, but called back a few minutes later to say they had been stopped. Having told the international delegation they would be given access to the camp, within an hour the IDF had changed their mind. The camp, they said, was "full of booby traps" but specialist IDF units would clear the camp of these traps by the following morning. Then the convoy could go in.

In Jerusalem we watched and listened. Journalists were doing what they could to file stories despite the army's restrictions. Consulates were doing what they could to help employees and nationals stuck under curfew without supplies. I was hearing details of people's plight elsewhere in the Occupied Territories— one was stuck alone in Ramallah with two very young children and no food left. But after the death of the thirteen Israeli soldiers, Jenin was dominating everything. The international delegation was trying to persuade the IDF to allow humanitarian aid through to where it was needed. The PA was shouting about massacres: their spokesman Saeb Erekat was interviewed, claiming hundreds were dead, from his Jericho base. The IDF announced that two companies of IDF infantry were about to be dispatched to collect bodies, and that terrorists would be buried in the Jordan Valley.[19]

The delegation split up: Andrew and an ICRC* official went to the Jenin hospital. Andrew talked to the hospital staff while the ICRC official went upstairs to meet the head of the hospital. As the official and the hospital director stood talking three bullets were

---

* *International Committee of the Red Cross. The Red Crescent is the Islamic branch of the Red Cross.*

fired between the two men, who were feet apart, hitting the wall behind them. A retired British colonel, the ICRC official had no doubt about the source of the shots: the building was flying Red Crescent flags (showing that it was a hospital), and the window through which the shots had been fired overlooked the town, which was under full Israeli control. He went downstairs and told Andrew what had happened, looking jaunty enough but saying that he had never been nearer to death in his life. His comment, after the sniper had missed him, on the IDF's explanation for not allowing relief organizations into the camp—the threat of booby traps—was that this was "spurious crap."

The ICRC delegation members' anger at not being allowed to start work mounted. That a government would prevent their relief work—this *never* happened, however dangerous the setting. Not in Afghanistan, Somalia, Kosovo, nowhere. War was what they dealt with, they said, the risks were theirs to take on and no one kept them out. The ICRC is usually the first in and the last out of a crisis: when I worked in Kabul its people were busy repairing mine injuries and war injuries with consummate skill and professionalism under terrible conditions. And they do not comment on the political situation, but in this case they did comment, saying they might have expected such treatment from drugged-up kids or warlords in Sierra Leone, but not from a government or its army.

Refused entry to the camp, and thinking the IDF would allow them in early next morning, Andrew and the ICRC team spent the night at the Jenin hospital. We talked by phone at intervals, Andrew concerned that his phone batteries would fail: the power was still cut off. Every now and then he would ask, "Did you hear that?" at the sound in the distance of controlled explosions. Tractors and bulldozers had been busy that afternoon, and continued long into the night, and there were bursts of unopposed fire. The next day the delegation was, again, denied entry to the camp.

One of Andrew's team joined a ward round in Jenin hospital. When he returned to Jerusalem he told me what he had seen: an

85-year-old man shot in both legs in his home on the second day of the fighting; a 60-year-old man shot in the buttock while he prayed at home; a pregnant woman shot in the leg; an elderly woman shot in the hand as she lay asleep in her house; a 79-year-old man shot in the right hand—he had been told to leave his house at night, which he did, with his hands up, but he was shot anyway.

An IDF surgeon told the ICRC chief the next morning (April 13) that there were no more wounded in the camp. "None of the wounded are alive." There was still no access to the refugee camp. Peering in from its northern edge, those trying to get in to help could see swathes of destruction, which the IDF were clearing. Refugees were leaning out of houses inside the camp that bordered on the city's limits, calling out for water and for food. The fighters had surrendered, the negotiators said: what could be the delay? What could be stopping the IDF from allowing the distribution of water? The delegation continued to push. The IDF said they must wait another day. Humanitarian workers were passing in food and water to anyone they could reach. One was a family whose pleas were heard from just inside the camp. The Israeli soldiers on guard let the UN workers drop off supplies that the family could pick up. By morning, the soldiers had been told to stop them.

An American friend contacted me from Chicago to say he'd seen Andrew interviewed from Jenin on Peter Jennings' ABC primetime news. He looked unshaven, sunburned, angry but composed. He'd been stopped by journalists on the way out and asked for his assessment.

"There are reports of hundreds of dead in the rubble. But we can't verify this because the IDF won't let us in," he'd said.

"Why not?"

"They say it's for our security."

"And what do you think?"

There he was cut off, having declined to answer.

At last, on April 15—more than two weeks after the invasion—the ICRC and PRCS (Palestine Red Crescent Society) were allowed into the Jenin refugee camp. The ICRC came out of the camp saying it looked as if it had been hit by an earthquake, with houses destroyed and collapsing into streets filled with rubble. The people were in shock, in urgent need of water and food, and pleading for information about relatives who had disappeared.[20] An UNRWA (United Nations Relief and Works Agency) convoy was standing by, loaded with food and water for civilians inside the camp. The local IDF liaison, IDF Central Command, and a high-level general assured the UN team that the convoy had clearance and that a special liaison officer had been appointed to help them. The trucks advanced toward the camp checkpoint.

Five hours later, the convoy was still trying to persuade the checkpoint soldiers that IDF Central Command really had granted permission for the trucks to enter. Andrew called me during the farce: the cycle of phoning Central Command to reconfirm clearance, then telling the checkpoint soldiers, who refused to let them in. The cycle ended only when the UN military advisor, Mick Humphries, a no-nonsense Australian colonel with a commanding presence, handed his cell phone to the soldiers on the checkpoint so that they could hear, with him watching, the liaison officer saying: "*Let* the convoy *through*."

Then once through, and barely inside the camp, an IDF platoon stopped the convoy again. An hour later the soldiers decided the convoy could unload the supplies where they stood. But, the soldiers added, the curfew was not going to be lifted—on any account—until the following day. The convoy knew what this meant: depositing the rations inside the camp would tempt the refugees to break the curfew, leave their houses, and risk being shot to get water and food. So they turned back, trucks still laden. Along the way children, mothers, and old people leaned out of windows, begging for food. The drivers managed to give out handfuls of supplies. This was four days after the last fighters in the camp had surrendered, and after days of continuous negotiation for humanitarian access. Finally, the following morning, April 16, a couple of trucks were allowed through and were able to distribute water and food.

I was following the saga with a steady simmer of amazement. Then a friend emailed an American article: all the destruction and cruelty, which the children could see and many Israelis said would only create more terrorists, were for our own good: "It's yet another burden that Israel must carry in its courageous battle to defeat the evil menace of terrorism."[21] I mentioned the article to an Israeli friend. She was not surprised, but I was—by her reaction: "This is nothing new, it's always been the role given to Jews, to do the West's dirty work for them." Israel, she said, was playing proxy to the US administration's agenda in return for tolerance of the Israeli government's agenda. "France and Britain used us in '56 when they wanted to deal with Nasser, just as kings in medieval Europe used Jewish communities, and the result now, as then, was that the Jews ended up taking the blame and being hated. See the rise in anti-Semitism now?"

She ended with: "Look at the confusion in the US administration; they use us when they need us and condemn us if they think we go too far." First the world had seen the US President ignored: he had called for the Israelis to withdraw, and when they still hadn't obeyed three days later, Bush had menaced, "When I say withdraw, I mean it." But still Sharon did not withdraw. And then a little later, "the day after the refugees were allowed food and water, Bush called Sharon a 'man of peace.'" She was not alone in noting the inconsistency of US policy.[22]

On Thursday, April 18, the UN Special Coordinator visited the Jenin refugee camp. Standing in the rubble, a flak jacket on his torso and a smell under his nose, he looked appalled. "No military operation can justify this scale of destruction," he said. "Whatever the purpose was, the effect is collective punishment of a whole society." His observations, including that the conditions "were horrific, beyond belief," and that Israel had "lost the moral high ground," offended Israelis, and he found himself smeared on an unrelated front: a bizarre allegation of financial impropriety.*

On Israel Radio there was a live interview with a reservist, Colonel Didi Yedidya. The colonel said that the UN representative had been misinformed, that the IDF had not denied entry to rescue teams at all. He said that they had been allowed in during the entire period, subject only to the condition that they pass through an Israeli inspection point so that the Israelis could make certain that wanted terrorists were not smuggled out. Few teams, as he recalled, had accepted these conditions and furthermore, he said, the IDF had found wanted terrorists hiding in evacuation vehicles.[23]

Three days later Major Dr. David Tzengan gave a briefing on his recollections of Jenin. He described the fear we all felt so often, the panic of knowing that a bomb had gone off near the hospital where he worked in Jerusalem and of not knowing where his children were. He also described the feelings after the Passover Massacre, of wanting to volunteer for "a war for our lives and our children's lives." In Jenin, he explained, the IDF took risks to avoid harming civilians, but the camp—home to 13–15,000 people—was not civilian, he insisted, it was a center of terror. The UN accusations were baseless, he said, the hospital in Jenin was not fired on and ambulances were not stopped.[24]

The army version survived despite the evidence, despite eyewitness accounts, and despite Israelis' own attempts to hear what happened. The first Israeli eyewitness testimony was an interview with a soldier who drove a D-9 in the Jenin refugee camp, published in Israel's most widely circulated newspaper. D-9s are armored bulldozers of a scale that makes you, when you see them, feel suddenly shrunken. They are colossal, malevolent, and out of all proportion to the driver, who sits tiny inside a carapace of

---

* *Some years before, the UN representative, Terje Roed-Larsen, and his wife, Mona Juul, had received prizes from the Peres Peace Center. Though straightforward and declared at the time, the subject was brought up again now in an attempt to create a scandal, presenting the award as "evidence" of corruption.*

tonnage, encased in thick steel to withstand rock, concrete, and mines. They are used to break houses, shear orchards, crush greenhouses, crops, workshops, and to terrify.

The soldier, a reservist called Moshe Nissim, described his role in the Jenin refugee camp: "The funny bit is, I didn't even know how to operate the D-9. But I begged them to give me a chance to learn... The moment I drove the tractor into the camp, something switched in my head. I went mad... I had no problem of fatigue, because I drank whisky all the time... Anyhow I could not leave the tractor. You open the door, and get a bullet. For 75 hours I didn't think about my life at home, about all the problems... sometimes images of terror attacks in Jerusalem crossed my mind... I had no mercy for anybody. I would erase anyone with the D-9, just so that our soldiers won't expose themselves to any danger... This is why I didn't give a damn about demolishing all the houses... I wanted to destroy everything... For three days, I just destroyed and destroyed... They were warned by loudspeaker to get out of the house before I come, but I gave no one a chance; I didn't wait. I didn't give one blow, and wait for them to come out. I would just ram the house with full power, to bring it down as fast as possible... I didn't give a damn about the Palestinians, but I didn't just ruin with no reason. It was all under orders. Many people were inside houses we started to demolish. They would come out of the houses we were working on. I didn't see, with my own eyes, people dying under the blade of the D-9, and I didn't see houses falling down on live people. But if there were any, I wouldn't care at all. I am sure people died inside these houses. But it was difficult to see, there was lots of dust everywhere, and we worked a lot at night. I found joy with every house that came down, because I knew they didn't mind about dying, but they cared for their homes. If you knocked down a house, you buried forty or fifty people for generations. If I am sorry for anything, it is for not tearing the whole camp down..."[25]

9

Sumud and Corruption

When the military operation came to an end, I went back to Ramallah to try to work again. Ramallah was a different city, as I had been warned. It was a patchwork of miseries: scarred wastelands, faceless buildings, rotted roads ploughed with trenches, service pipes and cables disemboweled from their earthly guts and spewed out by IDF bulldozers. Indoors, people were picking through the layered remnants of their homes and workplaces: soldiers had made a point of ripping, smashing, stealing, and piling up mounds of detritus, all sprayed over with soldiers' shit and piss. The shit said what so many words could not—the stench of loathing, unalterable contempt: nothing—you are nothing.

Work had already been difficult because of the closures. Now it was even more difficult because of the damage to the health system. Operation Defensive Shield had set back Palestinians "quite a long way," explained Rita Giacaman, head of Birzeit University school of public health. She liked understatement. I had transferred to her unit after Sholto's arrival. Her reputation in the world of public health meant that her name came up in conversations in London, Cairo, Beirut, emails from New York, and later in Senegal, where I met an EU envoy who knew her work. I caught up with her at a pizza restaurant in Ramallah, where we sat outside at round tables and watched Palestine go by.

She said simply, "Tell me about yourself." I gave a brief summary, and she asked more questions. Within a few minutes she had understood exactly. Not that I had told her; I had consciously tried telling people from time to time, but without success. The most I ever managed was mutual grumbling with other women in the same state: career on pause, new baby, the tyranny of children, and a husband mystified by the stranger—

me—we both lived with. Now, unconsciously, I had told Rita everything or, more accurately, she had seen it. She laid out research programs she would attach me to, objectives to be decided on, goals to achieve. The subjects were childbirth, maternal health, and healthcare access and policy.

But there were obstacles. "Not the usual obstacles to healthcare," she said. "No, these are a little different." She described, with disdain and pragmatism in equal measure, the extent of IDF damage to the clinics, ambulances, equipment, records, dispatching stations, "even hospitals." And how patients had suffered: people needing dialysis, hemophiliacs, children with epilepsy, and people with cancer who ran out of medications, individual cases needing urgent surgery—"and none of them capable of lifting a finger against anyone." She had spent days and nights manning a makeshift ambulance dispatch station, trying to send help to, and calm, the hundreds of people needing doctors, midwives, transport, help of any sort. "Everybody did what he or she could. We were totally united."

Most Palestinians were shrugging even at Operation Defensive Shield, picking themselves up and starting again. "We have no choice," Rita said, adding, "That cliché makes me sound like an Israeli."

Palestinians said they knew this would not be the last IDF attack, only the biggest so far in a continuing series. They would adapt and find a way around the layers of damage and blockade. One of my new colleagues commented on the irony of the military operation: "It will take us months, years—maybe we'll never manage to get back all that the IDF have destroyed. But our extremists," she said, "it will take them no time at all to get going again—the IDF has made it so much easier for them. They've got more volunteers and recruits than ever now. The IDF is the best recruiter Hamas and Islamic Jihad could ever hope for."

Rita adapted the department to ease people's daily lives as far as she could. Many of the researchers lived in Ramallah, so she moved the main office from Birzeit, a village to the north, to Ramallah in order to cut out their hours of trudge across the grueling Surdah checkpoint that lay between the two communities. She relocated the staff, computers, data, and records in a colleague's garage: an upheaval, and not an ideal destination, but the only way to counter the IDF closures. Since I was based in Jerusalem, Rita and my co-worker Laura tailored my research into childbirth policy to center on al-Makassed Hospital on the Mount of Olives so that I had to make only occasional trips to the new office in Ramallah.

Adaptation was going on all through Palestinian society. "Whatever they think up to block us, we will find a way around. They won't make us give in," said a biostatistician after a more than usually arduous checkpoint experience one morning. Since children and students were so often barred from schools and universities by checkpoints and curfews, educators were mobilizing information technology for students to study at home using the Internet. Some Palestinians in the health industry decided to look on the destruction as a chance to create something groundbreaking. Closures permitting.

At al-Makassed Hospital Dr. Ibrahim, one of my new colleagues, listened to my reaction to the resilience of Palestinians and told me about *sumud*. *Sumud*, being steadfast in the face of all difficulty, was one of the qualities that kept Palestinians going. That, he said, and the conviction that one day the law would be upheld and their internationally recognized rights granted.

In the Occupied Territories, the sense of injustice was acute. Not only were Palestinians suffering and dying but their suffering and dying went largely unrecognized. It appeared to them that the West just didn't care about Palestinians, or if it did, it couldn't say so. Worse, some in the West blamed the Palestinians for what was happening. Another colleague, Dr. Jamal, whose Nablus estate had been taken by settlers, said during a break between a C-section and a laparoscopy, "The Palestinians' greatest misfortune is that we are the victims of history's greatest victims. If we defend ourselves or if anyone defends us—the victims of the victims—this is the same as siding with their oppressors, and being anti-Semitic. We seem unable to get around this problem."

Through the suicide bombings the Palestinians had become invisible, inhuman. Their rights could be ignored because of the actions of extremists. "Should we judge everyone by their extremists?" asked Rym, a paramedic.

Despite the steadfast approach, people needed to talk about what had happened to them. And talk meant hearing what my colleagues had been through.

Rym happened to be under curfew at home in Ramallah when she was called out to help distribute first aid and emergency food and medicines. Her family tried to stop her breaking the IDF's curfew but she went anyway. "Everything—everything—was destroyed. I've been working with the NGO for seven years. Here is our life—what was happening to me?" She was dazed.

"We were all wearing our first-aid vests. We all said over and over, 'we're *health* workers, we're here to help the injured, we're not doing anything wrong,' but the soldiers rounded us up like animals and put us into a parking garage, with families—and one mother; they wouldn't even let her get milk for her baby. One of the doctors, Dr. Mohammed, they took him and put a gun to his head and they used him as a human shield so they could search the building."

Rym was sitting in her office at a small table talking to a British nurse and me over thin plastic cups of coffee. She didn't touch hers. Her red sweater and dark hair listing over her shoulders were glamorous, but her face was a picture of fear. We were meant to be discussing the effects of Closure on childbirth policy, but Rym was in no fit state. She pressed her fingers to the corner of her eyes to stub out the tears as she told us that she had seen a man peering out of an upper floor window opposite, hesitate, then jump rather than be shelled to death. Rym and a doctor had rushed to help him. He was still alive. But the soldiers refused to let them tend him. Shooting randomly, they picked up the injured man and took him away.

Rym's unit used "walking teams" to get food and medicines to families and the old and the sick: going out under curfew, trying to talk to the soldiers, sometimes let through, sometimes not, but always afraid. "There were many lessons learned," she said, putting on a professional face. "Now we have plans in place for the next invasions." As for the shock and horror of the troops' behavior, "You get used to it. You have to help." Then her fear flooded back: "I was in an ambulance with three women helping—one was from Denmark—and it was hit by bullets. We got out and lay on the ground. And there were soldiers there in a tank who didn't know why their own snipers were firing on us from above. At an ambulance. And if *they* didn't know why their own troops were firing on an ambulance..." She let this go.

"And your family...?" I asked. Rym grimaced. "When I went back they were so afraid for me that they wouldn't let me out again."

Keeping services going was hard, Rita said. On top of all that the IDF had done, thousands of people had been arrested. Many were now in "administrative detention"—prison without charge or trial. And many were suffering from the psychological effects of the war. Counseling services coping with them were overloaded. "All the counselors," said Rita, "have the very symptoms they're asking about in support groups, focus groups, and questionnaires." Ambulance drivers were badly affected; constantly in the front line—literally, fired on, arrested, beaten up, forced to strip, and sometimes threatened with death. Three ambulance workers in the Ramallah dispatch station told me their experiences. As usual now, I took notes while they talked. They were sitting in their common-room with the TV playing quietly above us, ignoring the bustle of other teams heading out from time to time. Their trousers and shirts were prim white, the trimmings blood-red.

"People think we're not well-trained because we don't always stabilize patients in the field," said one.

His friend joined in: "They think we're unprofessional, you mean."

"They do." The first paramedic laughed. "Try stabilizing the wounded when the IDF's shooting at you."

"That guy," he said, pointing to a man snoring on the sofa next to us, "went to help an injured person—a teenager who'd been throwing stones." He had been on duty all night—a heavy night—they explained, and had fallen asleep where he had laid his head. He looked unrousable. "So, he ran to the injured man, and—boof! He gets shot in the thigh by a sniper. Hit his femoral artery. Blood pouring out of him. So now look, there are two patients," the others are laughing, "and another ambulance comes, picks both men up, and then they run for cover before anyone else in Red Crescent gear gets hit."

"The shooting's not what I find so hard," said the first paramedic, "it's the checkpoints. Every day of our lives we're stopped—how many times? No, we're never allowed through without being checked, but it always takes fifteen minutes minimum. They go through everything, every little thing. They want you to show them. They're too frightened to test things themselves, like the oxygen cylinders, or lift anything up, like the coverings on the stretchers."

"Some of them are good with us, you can see they hate having to do this work. But some are shit. They want to hurt us, to humiliate us."

The second was unwilling to tell me about the humiliation, so the first took over. "We all have these experiences, we've all been forced to strip naked, in front of other people, and kneel on the floor, and get beaten sometimes, hit, struck. I don't mind so much when they hit us. It's when these kids at the checkpoints want to humiliate us, and they can. They do."

"Why us?" said the second. "Why ambulance drivers? I had a

time—remember how cold it was when the invasions started? There was a huge IDF attack on the communications center here in Ramallah, and three ambulances were called out to deal with the wounded. Our way was stopped by tanks. We tried to turn around but another tank came up behind, blocking us in. The soldiers made us get out—it was freezing. The first thing they did was make us take the batteries out of our phones so that we couldn't call base for help. They made us take up all our clothes, and then get down in the muddy water. Then they made us kneel, we were blindfolded, and they handcuffed us. If any of us tried to talk the soldiers fired guns beside our heads. They held us for hours."

He slowed down his reliving, watching me write. He looked up at a third colleague who sat stiffly next to the sleeper. "Tell her your story."

"I don't feel like telling my story."

"Yes, you do. Tell it. You were in Nablus, go on. What happened?"

The man was scowling, unwilling to go over his encounters with the IDF. He sat; I sat. The other two cajoled him, he closed his eyes for a moment, and then he told his story.

"I was on duty, at night, in Nablus. The curfew was on, heavy. We got a call that a little girl was sick. So we asked for clearance from the IDF to go pick her up and bring her in. It wasn't far. We got clearance."

He stopped for a moment. Then—"We were blocked by a tank even though we had clearance from the IDF. This happens all the time, we're used to that. We tried another route; that's what you do when you get stopped. But there was another tank, blocking us again. You have to learn the language of the tank. It's the barrel that talks. You have to know what it means—side-to-side means 'no'—okay, that's easy, but try it for yourself when you're so scared and it's dark and they're scared too. All you are asking is to fetch the wounded, or, this time, a little girl who's sick, and they stop you, search you, fire on you, pull you out of your ambulance, strip you, handcuff you—all right, all right." The others were slowing him down, stopping him from running on with his thoughts too fast for me to write.

"This tank made us stop. The soldiers came over, made us get out. They tied our hands and blindfolded us. One of them was crazy with anger. He seemed to be in charge, and he just screamed 'Kill them!'

"That was it—the angel of death was on me. Looking at me. 'Kill them!' he shouted again. I knew I was going to die. The soldier was so angry, so out of it, completely crazed. And he was in charge. We stood there for thirty minutes, blindfold, waiting to be killed. He kept saying, 'Kill them!' I kept waiting. Then something happened and they just let us go." He stopped to think, those thoughts rolling back in his head. "I don't know if the little girl got to the hospital or not."*

Other Palestinians took *sumud* even further and turned the destruction into creativity. An artist in Ramallah created a huge installation out of cars smashed flat by IDF tanks. The artist watched, locked in under curfew, listening to the bored drinking of the soldiers stationed there. They took a look at her art. She could see their puzzlement as they wondered what were these Palestinian crazies thinking, piling up useless cars like that? One soldier unzipped his uniform and pissed an arc of urine over the twisted cars. The artist, filming his response, was delighted. And, better still, the living art was completed when an IDF tank-driver

---

* Many health workers were not so lucky. In the first two years of the Intifada (to June 2002), two PRCS personnel were killed, 129 injured, and 71 ambulances attacked and damaged. By September 2005 the attacks on ambulances numbered 341. Dr. Khalil Suleiman was killed trying to evacuate an injured girl from Jenin refugee camp, on March 4, 2002. The ambulance he was traveling in was fired on and hit by machine-gun fire and a grenade launcher, and caught fire. The paramedics in the back of the vehicle managed to jump clear, suffering severe burns. Dr. Khalil was seen screaming, trapped inside. Camp residents and a second ambulance tried to rescue him from the burning vehicle but were fired on by the army.

drove his machine over the pile of cars to flatten them anew.[1]

My colleagues—pediatricians, neonatologists, anesthetists, obstetricians, and gynecologists—talked between cases about the psychology of Operation Defensive Shield and of soldiers serving in the IDF. They were strangely detached, as though they were discussing a patient, one needing multidisciplinary medical care. At other times the professionalism wore thin. After one ward round and morning meeting, a doctor mentioned "Let the IDF win," the Israeli cry that I had heard so often during the build-up to the big offensive. "The Israeli government did let the IDF win," he said. "It let the army loose, and the army won."

"And now," said an anesthetist, "we've got an IDF with its morale sky-high. Now they really know they can do what they want."

The first doctor was weighing up Israelis' horror at two things: IDF soldiers marking Palestinian detainees' arms with numbers, and the news that an IDF officer had recommended learning Nazi tactics used in the Warsaw Ghetto.[2] "They didn't seem to mind about the bad stuff," he was saying, "not about burying people alive, using human shields, stopping patients getting to the hospital and dying as a result, or about their troops stealing and shitting and looting like thugs, but they did mind about marking prisoners' arms with numbers."

"No," said the anesthetist. "Israelis *did* mind about the looting, because it made them look bad, it went against their image."

"But marking our arms with numbers was the least of our problems," said the doctor. "There were hundreds of worse things—like shooting a nurse in uniform and killing a handicapped man in his wheelchair—but it seems that the only things they feel bad about are things that bring back what was done to them by the Nazis."

"Don't underestimate the sensitivities of the Israelis," said the anesthetist cynically. "Things like that are burned into their collective memory. Don't underestimate them."

Some doctors were also angry with the UN. The UN had tried

to send a commission of enquiry to Jenin, Nablus, and other centers affected by Operation Defensive Shield, but the Israeli government forbade the investigators access. The commission had carried immense expectations for most of our Palestinian friends as well as moderate Israelis, who saw it as a mechanism for restoring peace. Others saw it as the world beating up on Israel: where was the commission investigating those who sent out suicide bombers?

One doctor said, "Let's have the commissions investigating suicide bombings—let's ask *exactly* why it is that young people are ready to die and kill."

"And," said another doctor, "while we were being killed the West stood by and did nothing—but they say it's a war on 'terror,' not a war on a people, so that's okay. And the Arabs do nothing either."*

There was a logic, they told me, behind the IDF decimating everything, even the Palestinian police, thereby creating a security vacuum in the Occupied Territories: it drew attention away from the ongoing building program, the creation of the Israeli government's "facts on the ground." The West Bank had long been a building site but now the pace had quickened. The diggers and bulldozers cut quickly into the loam and hills of the West Bank: ribbons of ocher soil across the Palestinian valleys expanding the settler road network and linking the planned industrial sites; swinging cranes and troops of trucks building settlements; loops of new-cut earth among the stripes of rocky land becoming the concrete drives and layouts of new suburbs. All growing visibly each time I went by.

"It's all about making sure that when the final peace settlement comes, Israel will keep control of most of the West Bank land and its resources." The speaker was a Palestinian American who had been involved in negotiations and was disillusioned on many levels, not least with the role of the American government. ("My friend

---

* *Arab countries are vocal about Palestinian rights and use the issue as an excuse to maintain their current political systems, but in reality do little to help.*

understood US 'balance,'" he said, "when one senior White House official stated frankly during talks, 'We don't want to hear from the Palestinians.'") And "ironically," said the Palestinian American, these "facts on the ground" may physically prevent the two-state solution* from happening. "Ask why no one *really* tries to stop this happening beyond a little meaningless posturing by the West." The West let it happen: Arafat just provided the excuse to let Israel continue.

The small figure of Arafat lurked like a djinn in the background. The word "Arafat" came up in countless conversations: terrorist, scapegoat, leader, figurehead, proxy, betrayer. Almost everyone called him betrayer at some point; Israelis because he had not brought them security,** Palestinians because he had not brought them freedom, and internationals because they weren't sure where their donated money was going or whether, if ever, he was telling the truth.

Many Palestinians were almost as harsh about their own leaders' shortcomings as they were about IDF practices. Many regretted the presence of the "Tunis crowd," those Palestinians including Arafat who had been in exile for years, most recently in Tunis, and who had been swept back in by the Oslo agreement. There were home-grown leaders—Haider Abdel Shafi, Mustafa Barghouti, Hanan Ashrawi, Marwan Barghouti—who, some believed, would not have sold out to the Israelis, imposed authoritarian rule, or been stained with corruption. One of my workmates put it simply: "Our struggle has two stages. First we get rid of the Israeli occupation, then we get

---

* *Two-state solution: two independent and sovereign states, Israel and Palestine. The alternative some advocate is the "one-state solution": a bi-national state for Israelis and Palestinians.*

** *Whereas he had been acceptable enough to the Israeli government for the Oslo process to take place, he now fell short of Israeli requirements: to maintain Israel's security while the occupation deepened, and to sell to the Palestinian people whatever final deal the Israeli government wanted him to accept. As one Israeli journalist noted of the end of Arafat's role as Israeli proxy, Arafat "stopped doing our dirty work, now his presence is great, it's buying us time."³*

ourselves some decent leaders."

Occasionally I had to go to Gaza to work. I was permitted to cross Israel and enter Gaza; my Palestinian colleagues were not. During my work there I met Dr. Haider Abdel Shafi, who had been head of the Jordanian-Palestinian delegation to Madrid in 1991, and was described by many as the greatest man in Palestine.* He was widely admired, not least for having done his best to uphold Palestinian rights. After we talked in his office one spring morning about healthcare delivery during the Intifada, I asked him about Madrid. His descriptions of the negotiations and Oslo said much about the Palestinians' current situation. A tall and elegant man, suited in tweed, his kindly smile showed no bitterness. He was quiet and reassuring, his considerate manner, honesty, and decency unmistakable, as was his care for his people. At more than 80 (he was born in 1919) his disappointment was visible, not as anger, but as regret at the lost opportunities for peace.

At Madrid, he explained, Israel's negotiators vacillated over Resolution 242, which called for an end to the conflict based on the concept of "land for peace," withdrawal from territories occupied as a result of the war of 1967. "What are you asking?" they said. "We are settling in our *own* territory." The US tried to stop the Palestinians from pushing for Resolution 242, saying that Israel was ready to allow Palestinians some autonomy—in education, for example—so why not delay on the rest? When Dr. Haider and the other negotiators stuck to Palestinian rights under international law,[4] refusing to relinquish them even under American pressure, the PLO was wheeled in for secret negotiations in Oslo in the hope that the exiles would prove more pliable.

Dr. Haider found himself summoned suddenly to Tunis. There,

---

* *Israeli historian Avi Shlaim described Abdel Shafi's speech in Madrid as the "most eloquent and the most moderate presentation of the Palestinian case ever made by an official Palestinian spokesman since the beginning of the conflict." Avi Shlaim,* The Iron Wall: Israel and the Arab World *(London: Penguin, 2000) 488–90.*

Arafat showed him the Oslo document that had been settled in secret while he and the other Madrid negotiators held out: it was three days before it was due to be signed. "I read it. It was very bad, full of difficulties, and I explained that Mr. Arafat had to open his eyes, to see what was really going on. But he wasn't listening. He simply said, 'Of course, you're going to attend the signing.' I said, 'Mr. Arafat, you're not listening.' But it was useless."

Dr. Haider's disappointment was colored with disdain for his compatriots' failure to see the meaning of Oslo. "Everyone was euphoric. We went to Washington, and the euphoria continued. The press asked me what I thought of Oslo, and I condemned it. Nabil Sha'ath [who became the Palestinians' foreign minister] was not pleased: 'For heaven's sake, why so pessimistic all the time? Can't you see this is the beginning of the Palestinian state, that this is already a reality?'"

He paused, thinking of the repercussions of Oslo. "Abu Mazen and Abed Rabbo* wanted to know my reaction. I asked, 'Was there a legal representative with our delegation?' They answered, 'No.' I asked them simply, 'How *could* you?' They said nothing."

I went back to Ramallah and talked about my conversation with Dr. Haider. Some of my colleagues suggested that the PLO negotiators' long exile, and the fact that they had never lived under occupation, explained something of their failure. They never grasped the link between what was being negotiated at Oslo and the Israeli expansionism that was continuing on the ground. And the PLO negotiators appeared to believe that the "spirit of Oslo," plus the undertaking that "neither side shall initiate or take any step that will change the status of the West Bank and Gaza Strip pending the outcome of the permanent status negotiations,"

---

* *Two PLO officials. Yasser Abed Rabbo, whose support for Oslo was muted, became minister of culture and arts. Abu Mazen (Mahmoud Abbas) later became Palestinian prime minister, briefly, in 2004, and then president after Arafat's death in November 2004.*

would be enough to halt the expansion of the settlements.

"They were fools," said my friend Rahman, a Palestinian lawyer now working for an organization set up to remedy the PLO's earlier legal unpreparedness. Abu Ala, the chief Palestinian negotiator (he later became prime minister), had boasted to these lawyers that he had stood alone against the ranks of Israeli legal brains and skilled negotiators.

Rahman added, "Thanks to that arrogance they were taken for a complete ride at Oslo. The result was the Intifada and the miserable situation we are now in."

Over the weeks I heard more from colleagues, for example about how, once they were installed as the Palestinian Authority, the incoming exiles from Tunis were no less disappointing than they had been as PLO negotiators. About how the PA undermined its own legitimacy not only by having signed up for continued Israeli control, but also by eroding what institutions the Palestinians did possess, and replacing them with nepotistic, ineffective, and duplicative organizations, all of which fell under the ultimate control of Yasser Arafat. I met Palestinians who had worked for years in NGOs providing important "pre-state" services, but these were swept away by Arafat, who offered nothing better in their place, only a corrupt Palestinian Authority. People complained about the style of his leadership: creating a web of security forces and agencies with no clear division of labor, encouraging bickering among his team, and relying on a close inner circle cut off from the Palestinian reality.[5]

Eyad Surraj, a human rights activist and mental health doctor, joined Andrew and me for dinner in Gaza under the crimson lamps and draped hangings of the Deira Hotel. We drank red wine out of white teacups—alcohol being forbidden in the conservative Gaza Strip—and listened to Dr. Surraj's tales about life as a Gaza psychiatrist. His anecdotes said much about Arafat's leadership: authoritarian, unpredictable, and reliant on shaming and sycophancy. On one occasion Arafat summoned Dr. Surraj to his presence. At the time, he was imprisoned—at Arafat's instigation—for having spoken out against the many human rights abuses by Palestinian forces. He was brought—unwashed, unshaven, and in prison clothing—to Arafat, who set about trying to recruit him as one of his ministers. Dr. Surraj had no intention of leaving his work with the Gaza Mental Health Program, let alone of joining the PA. Politely, he declined the post. Arafat pressed him. He declined again.

This went on until eventually Dr Surraj insisted that he could not accept a post, because "*Rais*, I am not qualified."

Arafat swept his hand around the room, which was filled with his crony-ministers. "Look at all these people, you think *they're* qualified?" They all laughed obsequiously.

Before I left New York in 2000, an American acquaintance working for the UN, Rick Hooper, described the PA to me: "Seven years after Oslo and all the billions the international community has ploughed into the PA, what have the Palestinians got? Egyptian standards of bureaucracy, Syrian standards of human rights, Lebanese standards of accountability—and all to serve the interests of the Israelis." A harsh judgment perhaps, from a man who had spent ten years working to improve the lot of the Palestinians, but few would say it was entirely unfair.*

PA corruption was very evident, and very painful for those Palestinians who were doing their best to make do with less and less just to keep the children fed and clothed. People would not complain, unless I asked, about the non-payment of their salaries or about the fact that when their salaries did come through they had been cut.

An EU official came back from Gaza in a rage after seeing a

---

* *Rick, one of the best and the brightest in all the UN, was later blown up and killed with 18 others in the bombing of the UN headquarters in Baghdad in August 2003. After the bombing the UN was assailed by celebrity US law professor, Alan Dershowitz, who wrote that the "UN deserved the attack because of its protection of Palestinian rights."*

new Cadillac being delivered to a PA cabinet minister. "You know, their insensitivity is mind-blowing. Even in the good times this would have been sick enough, with so much of Gaza on less than $2 a day. But *now...* how can they not see?" Arafat's wife lounged in Paris on vast sums that were later investigated by the French authorities. Visitors to the Muqata in Ramallah would ask politely, in English, after Mrs. Arafat. Mr. Arafat would answer politely, in English, that she was well, thank you, but then, aside in Arabic to his aides: "I haven't set eyes on her in three years," showing, as his Arabic-speaking guests also noted, no regret.

Rumors accused Abu Ala, speaker of the Palestinian parliament, of supplying the cement that went to build the illegal settlements. "You can understand the Palestinian laborers," said Maha, "those who have to take construction jobs in the settlements—they're desperate. But the fat cats, why do they have to sell the concrete that steals our land?"

"Abu Ala doesn't have to worry about feeding his family," said another. "He's so rich he sends taxi drivers from Abu Dis to Ramallah to fetch a tub of his daughter's favorite ice cream—and charges it to the parliament." Hatred of officials, the PA, and Arafat was never far from the surface.

Arafat's many failures were bemoaned in private: he failed to react to continued settlement building and to ongoing Israeli strategies to deprive Palestinians of East Jerusalem, failed to offer leadership or strategy when the Intifada broke out, failed to communicate effectively with the Israeli public to counter the claims made against him, or to present the Palestinians' case internationally. He had become, many Palestinians admitted, a liability. Yet, loathed and blamed, at the same time Arafat was still revered as Palestinians' leader and father, the man who had given international recognition to their cause when the rest of the Arab world's incompetence had failed to do so.

Periodically and like repeats of a bad TV soap opera when

everyone is almost sure they know the ending, Israeli threats were aimed at Arafat. He was besieged in the Ramallah Muqata (HQ); his Gaza Muqata was destroyed and then destroyed again. There was talk of expelling him to Gaza or beyond, and sometimes, when tempers were particularly jagged, there would be talk of killing him. This would trigger protests from embassies and governments and resuscitate his flagging popularity—there would be demonstrations of support from Palestinians on the streets of the West Bank, the Gaza Strip, and among the refugees in the camps of Jordan, Syria, and Lebanon.

I was caught up in the middle of one Gaza demonstration in support of Arafat. It was larger than normal, by all accounts. A New Zealander was in the driving seat; he took one look at the big black 4x4s packed with men in dark masks, spiked with automatic weapons, and festooned with Hamas flags. "Let's not hang around these guys," he said, calmly enough, but turning the car in the opposite direction.

"I suppose a bullet-proof vehicle would be comforting," I said, missing the point.

"No," he said. "Not the guns. Helicopter missiles. They turn even the heaviest armored cars into lumps of metal." Now I saw the point. The IDF were assassinating people regularly, and it was more or less open hunting season on big black 4x4s draped with Hamas flags.

We left the scene in a hurry but half an hour later I was back in the middle of the demonstration by mistake, this time being driven by a Palestinian friend, Basem, who was taking me to the health ministry. I mentioned to him the matter of the Israeli helicopters, saying I wanted to avoid being "collateral damage." It was too late. We had turned into the thick of the march and were surrounded. On television the scene would have looked dramatic and threatening, potentially violent; but on the ground, from where I sat, it looked more like a long, sober party. The demonstrators were meandering, and where I had initially seen guns, masks, black-and-white keffiyehs, and jeepfuls of trigger-light machine-gun-laden "warriors," I began to see people. Women and children were marching with the crowds, men smiled at each other in greeting, there were songs and laughter—albeit pockmarked with "happy-fire." People waved to Basem, who seemed to know everyone. Many came over to the car and shook my hand through the window as he introduced us.

The street filled with color against the white of the Gazan sky, the clothes of the marchers outdone by the flags of Hamas, Islamic Jihad, the PA, and Palestine. Greens, gold, black, and red; sweeping trails of Arabic script across the colors; posters and declarations of support for Arafat were everywhere. And so was the humiliation: the march, an attempt to show strength, only emphasized that all Gazans were like ducks in a fairground shooting-range if an Israeli helicopter chose to liquidate one of them. Like the Palestinians' bombing attacks, their self-defensive measures, ranging from gunfire to laying anti-tank mines, not only invited more retaliation, they were also largely useless. Palestinians were incapable of protecting themselves against the massively armed Israeli forces, just as incapable as the imprisoned Arafat.

Our new Ramallah office was not far from Arafat's Muqata, so from time to time our work was interrupted. There would be clashes between stone-throwing youths and the IDF, and then gunfire. My workmates were used to hunkering down when the shooting started and the tear gas began to fly. They had a ritual: cars would be pulled off the street and into driveways so the tanks could not crush them. Tables and chairs set out for us to enjoy the sun during meetings would be abandoned, everyone rushing indoors. Volleys of phone calls began, locating and instructing family members at risk. The most urgent calls were from parents trying to make sure their children in nearby schools were safe.

The first time I was caught up in the shooting I stared at the others who swept me along, and then watched my car from a distance—I had not been quick enough to move it—hoping the tanks would not take to the idea of trying to flatten a Land Rover. As I watched, I listened to the gunshots and the fear of the other mothers checking on their children, and was glad that mine were relatively safe. I asked Rita why the children were at school at all, given the dangers. A number of children were shot by IDF snipers while inside their schools.

"With so many curfews we have to give them some normality, some routine and a pattern to their days. If we were to give in, if we stopped school... well, it's no life at all to be imprisoned at home, and they all know how important it is to go to school," came the patient reply. "And I'm sorry to say they're not safe from snipers' bullets—even at home."

Not long after Sholto was born, I was taken to meet Arafat in his prison-office. He was walled in behind layers of buildings and a coterie of flunkies, bored secretaries, and ministers. The women eyed me like slow-moving fish while we waited. They were used to visitors, and the visitor of the hour was my father-in-law, who had first met Arafat in a slit trench in Jordan decades before. We were led into a long room hung with pictures of Jerusalem, furnished with stiff chairs and low tables. Drinks and sweets were brought in, and then Arafat. He greeted us, his gray face luminous like a creature who never sees the sun; he rarely did, for fear a sniper might pick him off. He was even smaller than I had expected, dressed in his signature military green and a draped keffiyeh. Someone told him I had given birth in Bethlehem and his smile broadened. The Israeli government, he grumbled, had not allowed him to travel there from Ramallah, even to attend the Christmas Eve service at the Church of the Holy Nativity.

He wanted to talk about the increased numbers of Christian Israelis. When the million or so immigrants from the former Soviet Union had exercised their right to Israeli citizenship under the Law of Return, many people had doubted the authenticity of their Jewishness. Sharpening their sense of injustice was the knowledge that many of the new immigrants had never had any connection with the land whereas the Palestinians and their forbears had lived there for generations. The immigrants were in no ordinary sense of the word "returning" anywhere. Exiled Palestinians wanted genuinely to return—home.

"He's going to show you his filing cabinet," someone whispered. Arafat stood up and turned his backside toward us, patting his butt. Out of his back pocket he pulled a sheaf of old but neatly preserved pieces of paper.

"Here," he stuttered, finding an old cutting from *Ha'aretz.* "Seventy percent, nearly three-quarters, of the Russian immigrants are not Jewish at all, they're Christians, and my people, many of them Christian, are forced to remain in exile from their ancient homes."[6]

Arafat's function in Israeli eyes lay in giving Israel an excuse not to negotiate and at the same time in being a useful object of humiliation: it was so easy to humiliate him and through him, the entire Palestinian people, whose predicament he mirrored. There he sat, month after month, cooped up in the blitzed carcass of his compound, confined to a shrinking space, kept alive by the very forces that occasionally, when it was politically useful, rattled his cage to threaten him and stoke the anger of his people.

10

Living with Terror

There was no getting used to suicide bombings. We would hear the "boom" over Jerusalem and know when it was not sonic, but murderous. After the boom the quick tally: family, friends, colleagues? Israelis did the same. If family and friends were not involved you could breathe again and carry on with the day—you had to—until the stories of the victims hit home: the children, old people, the personal tragedies, the heroism, and the unbearable task of clearing up, of picking up the pieces of life and personality, dreams and hopes reduced to gobbets of flesh.

Operation Defensive Shield did not stop the bombings. Friends continued to email and phone from abroad, asking if we were still alive, and then, "What's it *like*, living with 'terror'?" The answer varied, depending on what had happened that day and how close the last bomb had been. Once, after being in Bethlehem, I started describing the signs of trauma in the Palestinian children I had visited in the clinic. Then I realized this was not the variety of terror my questioner was after. On June 19, 2002, I fretted for hours, convinced that one of my Israeli friends had been among the seven people killed and fifty injured in French Hill. My logic was simple: she lived there and would have been coming home from work when the suicide bomber exploded. That and a bad feeling. But I found out later she was safe. The bad feeling was panic, losing yourself to fear and to the idea that probability would get you one day.

Every day as we trod the short walk to school we saw the arc of limestone wall scrubbed clean of blood and the concavity in the metal gate: reminders of the blast that blew a man apart, "our" bomb, our terror. Every mother in the land, Israeli, Palestinian, or other, worried that her children might not come home from school alive, bombed by suicide bombers, shot by IDF snipers, or caught in the crossfire.

For Israelis there was the underlying, omnipotent fear of annihilation, and beyond that, other terrors. Taking Catriona to preschool one morning I broke in on a scene that went on all over Israel every day, as normal to Israeli families as it was poignant to me. Catriona's school was in a private house tucked away inside the German Colony, and the teacher's son, eighteen or nineteen years old, was home on leave from his three-year compulsory stint in the army. He was lying asleep in bed under a pink blanket, his mother wondering whether he would like eggs for breakfast or something else: she was a wonderful cook. She looked at the dark head cut close and I felt my own hand cupped around the smoothness of my baby's head half an hour before. I began to ask about her son, and she let out the agonies of knowing that he had chosen a dangerous unit and of seeing him set off "on exercise," somewhere, she was not to know where, or what his duties were. She had to wait until he came back—or for news.

Alison, a close friend, confided that she had picked out a photo of everyone in her family for when one of them was killed. "I know how it sounds, but it's one way of coping with the *constancy* of terror." The press would demand photos and she would be ready. Her son, a newly commissioned officer, talked about the problems of training raw recruits. I skirted around the "refusenik" issue—the refusal to serve as a soldier in the Occupied Territories—asking mildly if he had had any doubts about serving in the army. No, he said, he had always been the outdoor type.

Others skirted around the notion of risk. Some asked themselves how close "terror" came, trying to measure the likelihood of being caught next time. There would, of course, be a next time. This meant being obsessed by probability—to the point of not being able to live at all. In any case, for so many people there was no choice. I varied. We had just returned from a trip to northern Israel when, on June 5, 2002, Islamic Jihad drove a car packed with explosives into a bus at Megiddo. Seventeen people were killed and thirty-eight injured. Three days before this bombing we had driven through the junction and now I pictured us alongside that burning bus. The hill of Megiddo is Armageddon, site of the Book of Revelation's final battle between good and evil. We had wandered around ruins of a city strongly fortified 5,000 years ago: through a Canaanite gate, up a Solomonic ramp, into temples where citizens had worshipped for a thousand years, and down a stone-cut stair deep inside the hill to a 230-foot tunnel built in 900 BC to keep the city watered under siege. It was a while before I could think through my panic: in my mind I was ruling out all future trips around Israel for fear of being at a junction when Islamic Jihad rammed explosives into another bus, and all the while here we were living in Jerusalem—where there was bomb after bomb.

A few weeks later our Jerusalem shrank again when another bomber exploded by the school. This time, nine months after the last one on Ha'Nevim Street, the bomber detonated further from the school door. This time, as last time, only the bomber was killed, but five other people were injured. The bomber was no doubt on his way somewhere else: a falafel stand took the brunt of the blast. I thought of our first days in Jerusalem when the woman behind that same falafel stand had taken great trouble to explain falafel to me. I held the children while she filled warm pita with shredded lettuce, orbs of chickpea and spice, spoonfuls of salads and herbs, and a slathering of tahini. She looked down at the children's waiting faces as she handed each one a delicious pocket of the new food, and then beamed at me. Was she one of the five? How was she now? Within a day there was more killing: students at Hebrew University on Mount Scopus. Nine young people dead and eighty-five wounded by a Hamas bomb planted in the student cafeteria.

Resilience and reactions varied. Some people, by nature or experience, or a combination of the two, were more resilient than others. There were Israelis who wouldn't visit us in our house, Israelis who wouldn't visit Jerusalem at all, and Israelis who stood in protest in front of IDF bulldozers. There were Palestinians who stood square when the IDF were shooting but, when confronted by a small terrier, confessed that they were "afraid from dogs." There was Hazel from Northern Ireland who came across the bomb disposal squad worrying around her car one morning, pointing out a suspicious box of garbage left next to it. Hazel was having none of it. "There were a few wires sticking out of the top of the box," she said, "nothing to get all upset about," and insisted on moving her car before the bomb squad performed their controlled explosion. And there were those who quit Jerusalem after their first bomb.

In terms of resilience, I was somewhere in the middle. The bombing at Hebrew University disgusted people above the usual level of disgust. And then you catch yourself and ask why is the killing of so many students worse than the killing of women and children, or old people—or anyone? How was it that we were grading the value of a life?

And there was the bombing of the buses; we had a car. June 18, 2002: nineteen people were killed when a suicide bomber attacked a bus from Gilo to Jerusalem. A friend was there minutes later and called me, hysterical, unable to get the images out of her mind, the words out of her mouth, or, most distressingly, the smell out of her nostrils: each breath brought back the images. July 17: five people killed in a double suicide bombing near the old bus station in Tel Aviv. August 4: nine people killed on a bus in northern Israel. September 18: a 21-year-old policeman killed stopping a bomber boarding a bus at Umm al-Fahm. The day after that, six people killed by a bomb on a bus by the Great Synagogue in Tel Aviv. October 10: a 71-year-old killed when a bomber blew himself up trying to board a bus near Bar-Ilan University. October 21: fourteen people killed by a car bomb alongside a bus to Tel Aviv.

The suicide bombings were so horrendous, so shocking, that their impact erased all other thoughts. Everything else would block out: the starkness of killing civilians so close to us, so close that it might have been us. A darkness would fill the place voided by the horror, as I pictured the bomber walking on to the bus, or into the restaurant, and looking about at the faces of his, or her, victims. The bomber who *paid her bill* before she detonated. And I compared the other forms of killing: those from further away, or from so great a distance that the victims are unseen, and the killings that are sanctioned by our laws, or someone's laws. There was something different about killings when the killer dies too, but don't look too closely. Those who try to understand get burned. Never mind the cause: treatment only.

Flesh is something you deal with in medicine. You become accustomed to it. It is made acceptable. You dissect it in your first term, delve into it in surgery, stitch it together in casualty, and take it apart in pathology. It becomes a fascination: its design, versatility, functions, strength. In Israel there is flesh everywhere. Some of it is covered, modest, Orthodox flesh, but most is on display and beautiful. Israelis make the most of their long Mediterranean coastline, and they luxuriate in the Red Sea to the south. They don't parade excessively—they don't have to—they are a varied and attractive people. One day in Herzliya two friends talked about racial superiority: I was on the receiving end. "The British Empire," they laughed, one Sephardic and the other Palestinian Israeli, "it lost its aura of power when your people took off their clothes, and showed the vulnerability of their flesh. You never should have done that. It's *green* in our light, not warm and strong like our flesh. We are beautiful. You green Europeans, that is your weakness: you paraded in red uniforms and conquered the world, but when you took off your clothes your empire was doomed."

And then there is the other flesh: not on-the-beach glorious living flesh, tanned deep-dark and animate, but dead. Dead flesh. Dismembered, dehumanized by a human bomb, a man or woman who sets out to detonate and kill. The images of death were everywhere: the immediate devastation, the photos of the victims, the burials, and the waves of grief. One organization, Zaka, fielded volunteers who picked raw, newly dead flesh off the hot tarmac of the summer Jerusalem streets, finding tiny bits of it plastered against walls, rolled in dust behind cans and debris, placing every last shred inside a plastic sack for sacred rites of burial. Flesh splattered against children's clothes and in their hair. Resting up after soccer, standing too near a window in the house, a sniper's bullet that shredded their flesh. Hidden damp holes in flesh—the Palestinian child who died "from shrapnel injuries," except her flesh was perfect bar the sniper's hole in her brain. There was the dead gray dormant flesh of the young girl buried alive in Jenin; her eyes closed, dusted, nostrils full of powdery death. Bodies blown apart, unidentifiable, by tank shells, Apache helicopter weaponry.

Terrorism is a weapon of the weak against an enemy of superior military strength. It is also a weapon of the strong to force the weak to submit. Either way, it is repellent. One Palestinian claimed to me that a suicide bomb was the most powerful weapon in the world.

"It is far more advanced than any weapon yet designed," he said. "It walks, it talks, it thinks. It can decide when and where to detonate. It can withdraw, unexploded, if it thinks it best. It can hesitate, change its mind, go back again and then explode. And look at its effects." He drummed home his claim: "Suicide bombs give immense power to people who have no power. We are the weakest people in the world; we haven't even got a state."

I mentioned this to Andrew, who said in exasperation: "They just never get it, some Palestinians, just exactly how disastrous the suicide bombings are for them. They are *not* the most powerful weapons in the world. Their sheer awfulness brings down universal condemnation on the Palestinians and silences any debate."

Stateless or citizen, there were many parallels: where Israelis saw through different lenses depending on their level of pain and suffering, so did the Palestinians. Both saw clearly through their rational lens that ending violence made sense, but then emotions would take over, their ordeal and fear and refusal to be defeated and their humiliation all dictating the need to inflict pain in return, to take revenge. Revenge was consuming. In Israeli eyes their rage meant backing the IDF solution regardless; in Palestinian eyes it meant support for suicide bombings. Each felt justified in responding to the other's violence, regardless of the repercussions of those responses.

Both sides had parties prepared to say that the rational path was the right one. But these were not in power. After 9/11, reactions from abroad were even more submerged in the emotional response. We were not so much "living with terror," as living with its effects: the silencing, the self-silencing, the denial, with good people pretending that things like brutal repression and a fundamentalist agenda were not happening or that, if they were, it was somehow acceptable. Acceptable in the short term because "they" are the enemy; acceptable in the long term because, well, how are we supposed to get out of this?

As my Palestinian doctor colleagues pointed out, Israelis were suffering deep, indescribable fears. The fears came from believing that there were people out there who wanted you dead just because you were Jewish, wanted you wiped off the land, pushed into the sea. And everything seemed to fit. Palestinians kept bombing Israeli civilians. Therefore, said the settlers and their supporters, the settlers' fight—to keep the Occupied Territories—was all Israelis' fight. According to this line, the two wars, one against terrorist attacks and the other to keep hold of the Occupied Territories, were one and the same. The fact that there were two separate wars, only one of which had the support of the Israeli majority, must be hidden. Lose the West Bank or Gaza, said the settlers, and they'll come for you in Tel Aviv. We are your front line: force us to give up the settlements and you'll give the Arabs the green light to turn us all into victims again.

Israelis were being murdered, cruelly and randomly, as they tried to lead normal, civilized lives. Israel itself was under threat. Israel needed security and those saying the Palestinians needed security too, let alone those who said that the Palestinians had turned to terrorism because of the Israeli occupation, were drowned out, or worse, dubbed traitors. Those Israelis who pointed out that Jewish groups had also turned to terrorism because of the British occupation of Palestine, successfully as it turned out—well, they were brave.

There were, of course, many Israelis who saw things differently: people who felt the fear but refused to be dictated by it, who lived with terror but would not be bullied by those who tried to manipulate it. While some Israelis talked about driving the Palestinians out of their homes in the West Bank, other Israelis were refusing to serve their country's military occupation.

Individual Israelis spoke out time and again, in public and in private. Many Israelis joined marches and protests, wrote books, resigned commissions, put on exhibitions of photographs and gave interviews, trying to show Israelis and others what was really happening. The pianist and conductor Daniel Barenboim joined forces with the Palestinian intellectual, Edward Said, to establish a joint youth orchestra to the acclaim of many and the bitter disapproval of others. Barenboim insisted that: "Israel was not intended to be a colonialist nation, and the Jewish settlements in the territories are like a cancer in the body of the process."[1]

The former mayor of Tel Aviv took the trouble to visit a number of West Bank checkpoints to see and judge for himself, and wrote about his findings. Among other things, he saw ten trucks loaded with provisions to feed Nablus, and ten empty trucks ready to take the food from the checkpoint into Nablus, and all twenty of them made to wait at the checkpoint, denied permission to unload and reload by the arbitrariness of the local IDF commander. He found the sight of Palestinians being made to walk several kilometers between checkpoints, and in particular four mothers shepherding eight blind children of four to five years of age, hard to take. He doubted that the checkpoints served any purpose other than to make the Palestinians suffer, leaving the young Israeli troops with difficult emotional baggage for later life, and urged "for the sake of the Palestinians, but mainly for our own sake, the faster we end the occupation and leave the territories, the better for us."[2]

Some families, bereaved by the conflict, reacted to their grief by forming support and action groups.[3] A number of Israeli farmers continued to support, often financially, or with frequent phone calls—any way they could—the Palestinians who used to work for them but were now unable to, locked in behind Closure. One Israeli group, horrified by scenes on Channel 2 of the IDF pounding Gaza, raised money to help rebuild Palestinians' demolished homes.[4] Other groups responded to injustice on their doorstep, like the residents of Mevassaret Zion who joined a petition to the Israeli High Court requesting an amendment to the route of the Security Barrier in favor of the Palestinian village next door.[5]

In Jerusalem I went to a lecture given by an Israeli woman in her fifties, part of a group of women who had rallied together to try to protect Palestinians from the excesses of the checkpoints, "*machsom*" in Hebrew. The group was called Machsom-Watch, and the women monitored the most notorious checkpoints in rotation, playing on their age and being female. The lecturer explained that the women believed that the soldiers would be less likely to be cruel or violent if they knew they were being watched by Jewish women who looked like their mothers and grandmothers. They also became witnesses to crimes others claimed did not exist.[6]

I met the lecturer again later and watched out for news of the group's work. In interviews the group's members explained their motivation: to ease conditions for Palestinians and repair the damage being done to Israeli society. "What we are doing is horrible, not just for Palestinians." Soldiers' misconduct translates into misbehavior in society, "and it is ruining us."[7] But it was also, as one explained, to "reclaim the humanistic revolution of Zionism. We are calling on the world to help us reclaim our humanistic values."[8]

In doing so they confronted fear, the anguish of not being able to prevent abuse, and the truth of what soldiers sometimes do. One Israeli volunteer witnessed checkpoint soldiers shooting Palestinian children who were throwing stones. "During previous times, I had seen them shooting in the air, but that day they were shooting toward the children." She and a colleague alerted the commander. He responded that the troops were only firing in the air. One fourteen-year-old boy, Omar, was shot in the head and neck, and died.[9]

The human rights organization Ta'ayush was another joint Israeli-Palestinian organization. I met one prominent member, David Shulman, a poet and Hebrew University professor. He described Ta'ayush's efforts to defend Palestinian farmers who were victims of a long-running campaign by settlers to seize their lands near Hebron. The professor told me he had been to war and seen terrible things but he had never seen hatred like the hatred he saw in the faces of the settlers who attacked him and his fellow campaigners; the settlers' eyes wild with loathing. One woman was rifle-butted in the head for trying to protect the farmers. Israeli law had no meaning for the settlers, said David, they have their own, and since the government does almost nothing to stop them they know they can get away with anything, even murder. The IDF had assured Ta'ayush that soldiers would intervene, but when the settlers attacked they did so unopposed, beating and terrorizing the farmers. Then, instead of arresting the settlers, the IDF arrested the farmers and confiscated their tractors. Eight farmers were locked up for plowing their own land. They were kept handcuffed and blindfolded, sitting on the floor in a nearby military camp, for eight hours. From time to time, the soldiers kicked and hit them.

The names of groups that were formed told their own story: Courage to Refuse, Breaking the Silence, Checkpoint Watch. The groups were organized, and active, putting their dislike of the occupation into more than just words. The Israeli Committee Against

House Demolitions (ICAHD), Physicians for Human Rights-Israel (PHR-Israel), Rabbis for Human Rights, Ta'ayush, Peace Now, Women in Black, hundreds, thousands of Israelis. Soldiers and pilots were speaking out. Before the launch of Operation Defensive Shield fifty reserve officers and soldiers signed a protest letter announcing their refusal to serve in the West Bank and Gaza Strip because of moral difficulties with army practices. They called the fighting "the war for the peace of the settlements"—a cause they did not believe in. More soldiers and pilots, even great heroes like Yiftah Spector, followed suit.

One reservist major, Ishai Menuhin, explained the *selective* refusal to serve: he would defend his country but would "not participate in a military occupation" that had made Israel "less secure and less humane." Israelis and Palestinians alike, he said, think of their "soldiers as 'defense forces' or 'freedom fighters,'" when in truth these soldiers take part in war crimes on a daily basis." He spoke of how terror blanked out the truth: "Daily funerals and thoughts of revenge among Israelis tend to blur the fact that we are the occupiers. And as much as we live in fear of terrorism and war, it is the Palestinians who suffer more deaths hourly and live with greater fear because they are the occupied." He hoped that more Israelis would see the reality of the occupation, and that "perhaps we will be able to let go of our fear enough to find a way forward."[10]

Arik Diamant, the director-general of the Israeli refusenik group, Courage to Refuse, stated, "IDF soldiers know very well that 90 percent of the army's activities in the territories are not related, even indirectly, to preventing terror. They also know that while they protect and guard a lunatic outpost in the heart of Samaria, they are in effect doing nothing for the security of the people of Netanya, Jerusalem, and Tel Aviv... Our army, the rock of our foundation, the people's army in which we enlisted and in which we served for many years, has become a private army for the settlers."[11]

I met a former fighter pilot at a party in Tel Aviv. He was born in a kibbutz and was eloquent in his description of the kibbutz ideal, the conflict he felt between the appeal of the model and the pain he had felt at being separated from his parents. He talked about his dead mother, leaving me wondering if any of my four would be as understanding of me as he was in his affection of her. He then said he was going to be in Jerusalem the following week and could we talk again? I suggested the American Colony Hotel, but when he turned up there I was surprised by his nervousness. "This place is full of terrorists," he said. I laughed. He didn't. I thought he was joking—whom could he mean: Val? Pierre the Swiss manager? The waiters? Perhaps the two American journalists waiting for a taxi in the lobby? I tried to reassure him and, knowing that he had been a fighter pilot, I asked him about his experiences. He toyed with his coffee cup, "I bombed Damascus," he said simply. "That was in '73."

"Oh," I said.

"And I bombed Beirut in '82. That was a beautiful operation." He was proud. "Being a pilot was something technical, just a job." And he chatted away for a while about the technicalities of bombing a city, then looked at me.

"But come on, I want to hear about you."

I stalled. "I've no military background," I said. I was trying to think about my children, wanting to hurry back to them and their world, the world of homework and squabbles and wondering if Basil might let them ride the mare again soon.

But I was reminded of an interview with another fighter pilot who talked about people like himself seeing "the black flag." The black flag was the point at which you felt you had to disobey.* I looked up the interview: it was with Dr. Yigal Shochat, who called

---

* The black flag was a reference to Judge Binyamin Halevy's verdict on the IDF shooting dead 43 Palestinian civilians in 1956 for breaking curfew. Those killed were returning from the fields to their village of Kfar Qasem, unaware that curfew had been imposed.

for soldiers to refuse to serve in the Occupied Territories because it "undermines the country's security while contributing to the security of the settlers."[12] Dr. Shochat believed it illegal to bulldoze houses to clear areas for the convenience of the IDF, or to stand at checkpoints deciding whether a woman should be allowed to go to a maternity hospital, but he knew it was hard for draft-age soldiers, and sometimes career soldiers, to act on this. For one thing, refusal ruins careers. My friend had not seen the black flag, and I had failed to understand what strength it took, not only to see it, but then to act on it and refuse orders.

Israelis were stunned when, in December 2003, thirteen elite Sayeret Matkal commandos wrote to the prime minister saying that they could no longer participate in Israel's oppression of Palestinians in the Occupied Territories. They wrote "out of a deep sense of foreboding for the future of Israel as a democratic, Zionist, and Jewish state." The army responded: the soldiers should be dismissed or jailed. Israelis, horrified to see members of such a prestigious unit challenging the accepted line, sent them waves of hate mail, abuse, and even death threats. A well-known former Sayeret Matkal member, Binyamin Netanyahu, objected that refusing to serve would lead to the country falling apart. One of the commandos responded, "If a plane is going to crash, you can jump out or you can try and prevent it from crashing. That is how we feel about the state of Israel."[13]

Not long after the thirteen commandos wrote their letter, a serving IDF officer resigned after Israeli soldiers opened fire on unarmed protestors who were demonstrating against the Security Barrier. Among the injured was an Israeli civilian, Gil Naamati, who nearly bled to death. Lieutenant Colonel Eitan Ronel wrote: "A country in which the army disperses demonstrations of its citizens with live gunfire is not a democratic country... I saw this deterioration, stage after stage: the blind eye that was turned to the abuse of detainees in violation of the army's orders... to soldiers' gunfire on unarmed Palestinian civilians... to the settlers' unlawful behavior toward Palestinian civilians; the oppression of the population; the roadblocks; the curfew; the closure; the blind eye the army turned toward humiliation and abuse; the searches and arrests; the use of live fire against children and unarmed people... This is an educational, ethical, and moral failure."[14]

In November 2003, the Army Chief of Staff, Lieutenant General Moshe Ya'alon, astonished the government by contradicting the official line on checkpoints when he declared that "restrictions on the movement of Palestinians are *counterproductive*, generating greater hatred of the occupying army" and strengthening terrorist organizations.[15]

But when four ex-directors of the Shin Bet security service— Yaakov Perry, Ami Ayalon, Avraham Shalom, and Carmi Gillon—gave an interview to the major Israeli daily, *Yediot Ahronoth*, Sharon took notice. His later volte-face on withdrawal from settlements—the unilateral disengagement plan of 2005—was partially attributed to many Israelis speaking out, but particularly to these four.[16] Together, the four men, with their unparalleled knowledge and experience, decried the failure of the Israeli government to deliver on peace and urged ending the occupation by dismantling settlements in the West Bank and Gaza. Shalom said, "We must once and for all admit there is another side, that it has feelings, that it is suffering and that we are behaving disgracefully." The Israeli preoccupation with preventing terror, he said, "is not a mistake. It is an excuse. An excuse for doing nothing."[17]

My days at al-Makassed Hospital were full of the situation and the conflict. I watched the doctors struggle to get to work through two, three, or four checkpoints, struggle to stay awake having woken at 4AM to start their short but interminable journey, and struggle to deal with their patients' problems.

More and more women came in "unbooked"—without any prenatal care because they just couldn't risk the checkpoints except when labor gave them no option. The results were many-layered:

poor health maintenance, preventable problems not prevented, increasing levels of anemia, increasing numbers of undetected complications. Doctors railed at the increase in morbidity: "We have patients with eclampsia who would normally be picked up *beforehand.* We have known cases of cardiac problems who *can't get to us.* We have women coming in with post-partum hemorrhage, infection, you name it. This *should not* be happening."

Many women tried giving birth at home but got into difficulties and were a mess by the time they finally reached the hospital. After 1967, Israeli policy in the Occupied Territories had been to increase the number of births in hospitals and phase out the community midwives, the doulas. The policy had been successful, except that now, with hospitals so often out of reach because of checkpoints and barriers, women were having to deliver at home unattended. Palestinian organizations were scrambling to mobilize the doulas again—and to position more midwives on the patients' side of the checkpoints.

Jerusalem provided specialist care for the West Bank. There was St. John's Eye Hospital in East Jerusalem, for example, the only ophthalmic hospital for three million Palestinians; now, because of measures to deny Palestinians access to East Jerusalem, it was out of bounds for the majority of them. Normally hundreds of cases would be referred to al-Makassed Hospital for specialist care; these ranged across specialties, and in obstetrics even included patients from fertility clinics in cities like Nablus. Now there was Closure. Patients with complicated pregnancies struggled to be allowed through the checkpoints to the tertiary care they needed in Jerusalem. Palestinian agencies and their officials spent hours trying to work with the Israeli officials to authorize passage through checkpoints for patients, and even then it didn't always work.

I once interrupted Mustafa Barghouti, the head of UPMRC (the Union of Palestinian Medical Relief Committees) and the future presidential candidate, at the checkpoint. I was phoning about meeting him and his wife for dinner, but all I could hear beyond his frustrated voice was the hoot and growl of vehicle engines. He told me later, at dinner in Ramallah, that he had been trying to help an ambulance crew bringing a woman from Nablus to al-Makassed. Everything had been cleared in advance with the Israeli authorities, and between Nablus and Ramallah they had been allowed to pass. Then the ambulance was blocked at a-Ram checkpoint. They were told to turn around and go back. They explained that the patient, who had an occluded iliac artery, cardiac problems, and diabetes, needed specialist care at al-Makassed and that she had clearance from the IDF to pass, but the checkpoint IDF soldiers said no. The crew had to call in Dr. Barghouti who prevailed eventually, but not until after the media and PHR-Israel had been recruited to help.

"There's an Israeli woman," he said in exasperation, "—does she have medical training?—who sits at the Beit El DCO and decides which patient may or may not pass the checkpoints to reach the medical care they need. She's effectively the Minister of Health."

And, one morning at work: "Where is their humanity?" whispered one doctor in despair at the story of the day. A family driving their aged father to the hospital for urgent treatment had been arrested and their car confiscated—all because the old man had no permit to enter Jerusalem, his own city.

Years before, on wards in Islamabad and Kabul, I had seen families helping out all the time. In those places the nursing profession was undermined by the qualms of Muslim Afghans and Pakistanis, and there was a shortage of nurses, with most jobs filled by Christians who were often looked down on for being Christian and for doing "dirty" work. Every patient was attended by a mother, aunt, wife, or sister—and not just for companionship. Patients were nursed and fed, as well as comforted, by their families, who would arrange rotas and bring in stacked metal containers of rice, meat, and vegetables, and piles of naan. In Palestinian hospitals the nurses were hard-working and skillful, but the presence of family members was no less important for patients' well-being. At al-

Makassed you could immediately tell whether patients came from Jerusalem or beyond: those with gatherings of families beside them were from Jerusalem, those who were alone were from beyond. It was hard for patients, having been subjected to the checkpoints, now to be in the hospital without family visits and support.

My colleague Dr. Ibrahim and I spent unprofessional amounts of time talking. He spoke perfect English, yet he maintained that in English he could not say exactly what he meant. Arabic, he explained, was so rich in expression.

I had asked early on about the hospital's childbirth policies. He took me through their policy on the management of labor and then on to post-partum practices. "We favor rooming in, of course. Keeping mother and baby together—instead of in the nursery for the nurses' convenience—is essential for mother-infant bonding and the establishment of breastfeeding, but it's not so easy now. The mothers complain about not getting a break." While Israeli mothers at Hadassah Hospital were asking for rooming in, Palestinian mothers at al-Makassed were asking for the opposite, for the nursery nurses to take care of their babies. After all their problems getting to the hospital and coping with the situation as well as with labor, they needed a rest.

Dr. Ibrahim was late one morning because there had been a road accident near one of the checkpoints on his route. He had jumped out of his car to help, and the soldiers had tried to stop him because he was Palestinian, but he had insisted, and there he was trying to save lives and having to fight to do it even when the facts were laid out bleeding on the ground for the soldiers to see, but they had no orders, or no rules, and eventually his authority had overcome their confusion, and common sense had won. He went so far in telling me what had happened, but then gave up, saying it was impossible to explain the subtleties.

I, he noted, had been shaped by a system of justice that I took for granted and assumed would protect me, and that I rarely had to put to the test. In Jerusalem Israelis talked about the injustice of the suicide bombings that targeted innocent civilians, and about the injustice of those who criticized Israelis for defending themselves against such attacks. Palestinians talked about the injustice of being left unprotected by local or international law, and about the injustice of the two-tier system of law imposed by the occupying power. (Palestinians in the Occupied Territories had been, since 1967, subject to the system of Israeli Military Orders: these do not apply to the settlers who live there.)* Palestinians also talked about the layers of impotence and defenselessness. As a neonatologist said to me on the ward one day, "Our families can't protect us—IDF soldiers and Israeli settlers can do whatever they want to us and our children—our Authority can't protect us, and the international community refuses to act, even though it means ignoring international law or even breaking it. What are we left with?—only God."

---

* *One of which, number 898, gives Israeli settlers the right to detain any Palestinian, including children.*[18]

11

"Only God"

"God gave us the Land of Israel—that's a given," the settler spokesman told me. I was sitting on a hard-backed chair in his tiny, book-lined, Jerusalem office, feeling thirsty.

He, David, was direct: "You're not Jewish, I can see. What are you—Christian? Muslim?"

"What makes you think I'm not Jewish?"

"I can see from the color of your hair."

I thought about the debate I'd had with the colorist in the Israeli hair salon over what color to go next, and I thought again about being Jewish, but he was emphatic. "That's all there is to it. It was God's promise to Abraham that determined the land ownership. He promised the Land of Israel to Abraham and his seed for ever. No human law can stand in the way of that truth. The Arabs have just got to understand this."

"Didn't Abraham have two sons?"

"What?"

"Isaac and Ishmael."

"Well, yes, he did have two sons." He paused. "But Ishmael didn't get the Land of Israel—he got the other twenty-two countries." I had often heard that: since "the Arabs" have twenty-two countries (Jordan, Egypt, Libya, etc.) why do they need another? Palestinians would laugh: "Oh yes, that one," a psychiatrist at work had said. "It would be so convenient if 'we Arabs' felt this way too, and just packed up our bags, rolled up our history, threw away our love for this land and left. For where? Some big tent in the desert, I suppose. And what would you British do if some tribe with an ancient claim to Berkshire suddenly said the Europeans have dozens of countries, so you can all run off and live in Belgium?"

David had shifted on his chair and picked up again. "I understand the Palestinians," he was saying. "The trouble is, the Israeli left *think* they understand the Palestinians, when in fact they have no idea. This is where the problems start. I, on the other hand, know them well, very well, and I know exactly how to deal with them. The left are just badly educated. And misinformed."

I asked in what way the left were misinformed. He was giving me something of a talk; my questions were batted away, his knowledge erasing any other. I envied him his certainty.

"Don't get me wrong," he said, "the Palestinians are lovely. They're lovely sweet kind nice people—I know them well." His American accent was taking me back to our life in New York. "They're just misinformed. Yes, them too. The settlements are not the problem, the PLO is the problem, and, once Saudi Arabia is dealt with, the PLO will lose its funding and disappear. *Then* we can make peace."

"Could you explain...?"

"The PLO brainwashes the people about the land, that they *must* have it, that it is theirs *by right* and other nonsense. In fact, what the Palestinians want is very simple. All they want is two things. Nothing more."

"What do they want?"

"They want a job, and they want dignity. That's all. And not one without the other."

"And how..."

"When they stop attacking us, then they can have their areas. The Torah protects non-Jews who live in the Land of Israel, you know. Unless they fight us. If they do that, then the Torah does not protect them, that's very clear. All they have to do is agree to live in peace and stop killing us. Then we have a solution."

"And the settlements..."

"The settlements are not a problem, not at all. The PLO is the problem."

"Yes, you said that."

"Ask them. Ask any Palestinian if they want the settlements. No Palestinian wants Gush Katif or Efrat. No, they want Jaffa and Ashkelon." These are towns in Israel: he was repeating the claim that the Palestinians' real aim was to take over Israel itself. "They don't mind the settlements at all. In fact they *like* them. The settlements give them work, jobs—there you are. If they are working the land for us, we protect them."

"There are many Israelis who disagree with you."

"Those Israelis..." he sighed. "Some of them have bought in with the PLO. Others are just misinformed, badly educated." He was consistent. "It's very sad. They don't understand the Palestinians and they sit in their Arab houses in Bakaa*—*we* never turned an Arab out of his house—they sit there in their ignorance and tell us we're the problem. They don't think. We need Halachic law.** We need to re-educate the Jews."

I went to see my friend Joni, an Israeli writer who lived in one of the previously Arab areas of West Jerusalem. He made tea and we sat looking out over Jerusalem through the sandy light. "When you said you Israelis have domestic problems, you weren't joking," I said.

We talked. He talked. "This is a fight," Joni said, "over what kind of state Israel wants to be, and it will be a battle. Israel, do you

---

* *An area in southern Jerusalem captured in 1948 whose Palestinian inhabitants were expelled. This area includes the site leased by the Israeli government to the US government for a proposed US embassy: more than 70 percent of the site is owned by Palestinians.*

** *Jewish fundamentalists want to replace the State of Israel with a Jewish Kingdom that would be ruled by the Halacha, Jewish religious law. Rabbis would interpret this law and appoint a king, a Sanhedrin would replace the Knesset, religious appointees would enforce Halacha throughout the land and citizens would be required to report any wrongdoing. Men and women would be segregated in public and laws would enforce modesty in female dress and conduct. Adultery would be punishable by death. Anyone who desecrated the Sabbath, by driving a car for example, would be liable to death by stoning. The Halacha would institutionalize discrimination against goyim, non-Jews. Any crime or sin committed by a non-Jew against a Jew would be more heavily punished than the same wrong committed by a Jew against a goy.*

want to be a democratic or a theocratic state? Obey the laws of man or the laws of God?" It's very hard for those in the diaspora, he said, especially liberal and secular Jews, to understand. "We live a battle between the Orthodox and the more liberal sides of Judaism."

The previous year Israel Shahak had also talked to me about the unwillingness of some American Jews to confront the reality of Jewish fundamentalism, and what it would mean for the future of the only democracy in the Middle East. Joni was more direct: "The settler extremists are forcing on us a choice we want to avoid—the choice between democracy and Jewishness—by insisting on keeping the territories. If we keep the territories we must either give the Palestinians citizenship, allow them to stay but deny them equal rights—apartheid—or throw them out altogether. And yet most of us want more than anything to be able to coexist, to live in the Middle East without feeling threatened and threatening the whole time."

Coexist, he said. For a while during the early months of the Intifada the great walls of the Old City were decorated with banners promoting coexistence between the three monotheistic faiths. The symbols had been painted into the imperative: "Coexist." The "c" was formed by the Islamic crescent, the "x" by the Star of David and the "t" by the crucifix. The designer had been clever and the message was clear but the artistic effect was uncomfortable, the monotheistic emblems jarring.

"Why did you talk to someone like that?" Joni was asking. I had wanted to hear the views of an ideological settler. He had shown me an Israel very different from that of the great majority of Israelis I met.

"You saw a tiny slice of settler views," Joni told me. I knew that the majority of the settlers were only settlers because, like anyone else, they wanted cheap housing, tax benefits, and a big garden, and that many didn't even think of themselves as settlers. In some ways the settler movement had failed, Joni was saying: "There are 200,000 of them, sure—but it wasn't meant to be like that. It was meant to be all faith-based but the Gush* couldn't bring in enough people who wanted to live the settle-the-Land-of-Israel thing. They had to resort to importing a different type to build up the numbers: the economic settler.[1]

"And they're doing all right economically, the settlers. We're the ones in trouble. They get subsidies and assistance on everything. We don't get anything like the help they get. We voted in Sharon to make us safe, but everything has got much, much worse—unemployment, inflation, everything. But do we say anything? No, we're all silenced by the security argument.

"And yet the ideological settlers are not only a whacky, lunatic fringe. They're all of that, but they also have power." Settlers had positions throughout the body of the state, in every branch of government. And, Joni complained, Israeli governments—Labor and Likud—had encouraged the radicals. They may have claimed they were opposed to what the settlers were doing, but all the while they were quietly backing them up, putting in roads and services for them, even during the Intifada.

"We're bogged down in the occupation, and some settlers want to keep things that way."

I drove away thinking about the implications of what Joni had described. It wasn't just the Palestinians who were trapped by the occupation.

The following day I was back at work and hearing the other side again. Al-Makassed Hospital had a medical library. Like many hospital libraries it was located out of the general way of things, so that readers could find tranquility as they flipped through the latest studies in their field. Al-Makassed's library was tucked in behind a low wall in a spartan building and I would go there from time to time for research. It was full of battered texts and weary journals, with equally weary physicians reading them in carrels and at small

---

* Gush Emunim, "Bloc of the Faithful," the group that spearheaded the settlements.

tables. The librarian was a veiled woman who chain-smoked in an unaired room, and we would often talk about the situation while I made photocopies. She had described her daily ordeal of getting to work, in taxi after taxi, across checkpoints and earth-mounds; I had wondered why she went through such a grueling routine in order to sit in her airless room and pass the day with assorted medics and researchers who happened to drop by.

It was simple: getting to work was her form of defiance, her personal statement of the determination not to be deprived of a normal life. It was the same for all Palestinians, even schoolchildren—no "unwillingly to school" here. Getting to school meant having a life. Getting to class at Birzeit University for the students who lived beyond the village of Birzeit often meant a round of applause from classmates. This was non-violent resistance, the refusal to be defeated by siege and closures.

That day the librarian was not her usual soft-spoken self. She was smoking still, perhaps more than usual, but she was angry. The veil about her face was more tightly tucked around her chin, her long beige robe smoothed straighter under her agitated hands. Her thirteen-year-old nephew had been arrested. Enraged that a child could be treated in such a way, she told me what had happened.

The soldiers came in the middle of the night while the nephew's family was asleep. They were shoved awake by a battering at the door and the soldiers barged in, demanding to see the boy, searching through the small house as though it were a box of items left over at the end of a sale. "This is their home," she said. "The soldiers have no respect. If they wanted to talk to the boy why couldn't they come in the daytime and knock at the door like everyone else?" The boy was terrified and cried for his parents to do something to help him.

"What could they do?" They could only watch as he screamed.

The soldiers handcuffed the child and took him outside, threw him into an army jeep and pushed him on the floor with others they had arrested. They then drove them all away. They were on the road for what seemed to the boy to be hours. They ended up at a detention center where the boys were interrogated: "Why did you throw stones?" "Who else do you know?" "What are their names?" and other questions he had no way of answering. The librarian insisted to me that the boy would not have been throwing stones. She felt she had to prove that he hadn't deserved such treatment—because he was innocent of stone-throwing. Finally the soldiers dumped the boys in the road and told them to walk home. They didn't know where they were, and it took them hours lost in the cold night to find their way back.

"What I have to tell you is, my nephew was lucky. Another boy the same age was arrested that night, but he wasn't released, and now no one knows where he is, why he's been taken, or what's happening to him."

I never heard the end of that story. Not because I didn't go back to the library, but because it is hard to track down these children and that last story dragged on beyond my stay in Jerusalem. Parents spend days and weeks and months finding out where their children have been taken and applying for permission to visit them, or just to be able to attend their hearings. Hearings are frequently delayed and the detainees moved to different locations, often inside Israel, without their parents being informed. They wait, helpless, in a judicial limbo. The children's testimonies show a pattern: taken from home in the middle of the night, subjected to physical and psychological abuse, beatings, often denied legal counsel, denied family visits—sometimes denied even food and drink, all as a way to intimidate the population into not resisting the occupation.*

The judicial system that permitted this applied only to the Occupied Territories. It was labeled "cruel" and "injurious" by

* Children in Israel achieve adulthood at eighteen in the eyes of the law. Israeli military law says that children in the Occupied Territories—Palestinian children, that is—are adults at sixteen.

Michael Ben-Yair, Israel's Attorney General from 1993–6. He wrote: after 1967 "we enthusiastically chose to become a colonial society, ignoring international treaties, expropriating lands, transferring settlers from Israel to the Occupied Territories, engaging in theft and finding justification for all these activities. Passionately desiring to keep the Occupied Territories, we developed two judicial systems: one—progressive, liberal—in Israel; and the other—cruel, injurious—in the Occupied Territories. In effect, we established an apartheid regime in the Occupied Territories immediately following their capture."[2]

The librarian's anger at the army's violation of her family's sense of safety, and the hatred of the occupier that had been inculcated in her nephew and all the other arrested children, were now immovable. "And they accuse the PA of inciting hatred of Israel," she scoffed. "Why would we need PA incitement when we have Israeli soldiers to make us hate?"

I went back to the obstetric department and sat in the office. One of the younger doctors was trying to make a call about a patient but couldn't get through. He looked at me. "What's up?" he asked. I told him about the arrested child. "Ah yes, the children. But we've been going through this for a long, long time. We're not defeated yet."

Families were affected in so many ways. One colleague, Amina, had managed to be positive again soon enough after the ordeals of Operation Defensive Shield, and was encouraging her three teenaged children—one wanted to be a doctor—to study hard. But it was not the case for her husband, Tariq. I had first met him at the American Colony Hotel a few months after the Intifada began. He was a surgeon specializing in ear, nose, and throat diseases. We talked about the changing medical profile arising out of the conflict, and about the increase in respiratory diseases during the *hamseem*, when the wind blows sand across the mountains from the desert, and the light fills with yellow dust. He had been quiet, interesting, a moderate man, and gentle.

Now, sitting at their kitchen table with Amina and me, he was still quiet, still gentle, but there was a slow-burning, deep anger inside him.

"He's been working seven days a week since the start of the Intifada, without a break," Amina muttered.

"What else can I do? I'm a surgeon, and there are people being shot and killed and injured here every *single* day. Medical services smashed. We can't even vaccinate: immunization rates are down to 60 percent from 98 percent before the Intifada. There's no access and there's no money."

"He takes ten minutes to eat, wolfs down his food, and then he's back to the wards again."

Tariq's anger overflowed: "How are my colleagues supposed to deal with a woman who needs kidney dialysis twice a week just to stay alive but who can't get to the hospital *because of curfew*, and, even if there's no curfew, there are checkpoints and soldiers who just say 'No'? How? How does a doctor explain to a mother and father that their child with leukemia can't get the chemotherapy that might save his life? Or that a patient died because we couldn't get supplies of oxygen through?

"No more prevaricating, not any more. Only the truth will do: the will of God. All this is written about in the Koran, you know. I've seen things I thought I would never in my life see, things I can hardly bring myself to describe—a mother holding the brains of her son in her hands. He'd just been shot at point-blank range. And she sees me, she looks at me, and she looks at her hands and you know what she says to me? You know what she says? She says '*Help me.*' What could I do?"

I could say nothing. Amina said nothing. Her discomfort at his bringing up this story was not just the pain of the mother's suffering, or because it was awkward for me. It was because it was one of the moments of the conflict that had changed her husband: one of those that could wipe out all gentle reasoning and push a man into a bitter, cruel place.

"You think I sound radical? You're not meeting the religious ones, the young men. You should hear what they're saying these days." He finished his food and hurried back to work.

"He's right though, you should hear them," said Amina. "You should hear how far they've been radicalized." She talked about the desperation, saying that at some point hopelessness inevitably allies itself to religion, whatever the initial starting point. "On top of the occupation, everything else has failed them: the PA, international law, democratization. And then try talking *moderate*," she said. "People who were reasonable, ready to listen and find a common way, just won't any more. They're looking elsewhere for help. Higher up."

Amina would cope with her husband's anguish. Every family showed some effect of the situation, though in different ways. The most distressing—apart from the grief—was the radicalization. Tariq was not the only once-moderate friend who now openly quoted the Koran as irrefutable evidence, or prophecy—even the Barrier was predicted by the holy book according to one man. Opinion was slipping further and further from the hands of the moderates: it was slipping instead toward the comfort of religious extremism and all that this boded, particularly for women. There were, of course, those who had always seen Allah as the only answer, but now far more were being pushed in that direction. Some were pushed very quickly. Others, like Tariq, took longer.

As for me, I had never felt less spiritual, living in the bosom of the three great and interrelated one-god faiths. It was something to do with being confronted with dogma and the abandonment of choice. I had built for myself a self-indulgent place to try to hide from the bewilderment and frustration. I would sit at work with Palestinians in the morning, listening to them trying to fathom why the IDF left the injured to bleed to death; and in the evening I would hear Israeli friends spit with rage at Palestinians' stupidity in carrying on their campaign of suicide bombings. "What do they think that's going to make us do?—roll over and let them walk all over us? With every terrorist act, we take a step backward. Why don't they see that? They're so *dumb!*"

There was watching Andrew come home each night having struggled all day to be professional. There was me coming home from work to pick up the children, leaving behind colleagues in a shrinking prison. There was going out in the evening to meet Israeli friends and being overwhelmed by how much I liked Israelis and Jerusalem and yet Israelis were the ones imprisoning my colleagues, and purposefully shrinking their world. And there was, at the same time, finding aspects of some Palestinians that were repellent: the brutal killing of collaborators, the rough justice meted out, the corruption, the treatment of women, the sickening so-called "honor" killings, the determination to see all the West as ranged against them. And then being appalled at my even contemplating the option of closing my eyes, shrinking down into the bubble, believing the myths, pretending it was somehow okay, or not happening, that we'd all get out of this, or that all's fair in war—that this *was* a war, as if the two sides were somehow matched.

I concentrated on the family, and upholding normality. This became harder and harder. The school itself was still a sanctuary from the conflict through dogged efforts by the staff, and the headmaster in particular. The children carried on playing soccer every Sunday in Sacher Park, in the lee of the elegant Knesset building, but soccer was affected one day because of a bomb-warning on the road—it turned out to be a false alarm, and a controlled explosion by the army did away with someone's bag of shopping before we could get to the sports field. Even close to home, events would expose the fears. One evening, the children and I were on our way back from tennis lessons at Ramat Rahel, an old kibbutz in southern Jerusalem. Around the now-so-familiar bends in the road through the firs and past the blossoming Judas tree of the Forest of Peace we came across a fleet of army vehicles, with border guards and soldiers swarming. They blocked our way.

A soldier came up to the car and told us to turn around and go away. I said that we lived further along the road and that there was no other way to reach our house. He refused to let us pass. I explained that I had to get back to breastfeed my baby, but he wouldn't listen. Sometimes soldiers take on an expression that blanks out reason, and this is what he did. If there had been danger there would have been intense activity, professionalism, urgency, but there was none here.

You learn to read the different masks below the helmets, just as ambulance drivers learn the language of the tanks. Some masks are not masks at all; they show kindness, compassion, and regret. Some show anger, furious frustration. Some show real fear and real danger, like the policewoman who screamed at us when the suicide bomber exploded outside the school. Or the real fright and confusion of the boy soldiers near Ramallah that a friend almost ran over while driving too fast and not seeing the new checkpoint in the dark. "What the *fuck* are you doing standing in the middle of the road!" he, a tall Canadian, roared to the frightened troops. "Are you drunk?" they ventured. "*Drunk?* You must be drunk to be standing in the middle of the bloody road!"* Then there was the warrior-mask that Andrew had found so raw in Jenin: bloodied, grim, and baying. And some masks were just bloody-minded.

I gave up on the bloody-minded soldier and shrugged as you learn to do—*sumud* perhaps—when you see that mask. Just then I recognized a policeman as one of those who regularly patrolled our road, so I got out of the car and walked over to his vehicle. He smiled hello at me, "Shalom," we said, and I asked what the problem was.

"Someone's died," he said, not wanting to tell me any more. I asked if I could be allowed through to go home.

---

* *This incident happened at the beginning of the Intifada, before procedures at checkpoints became more concrete. Later on Andrew Kuhn, the tall Canadian, would not have got away with it.*

"Yes, sure," he said, "no problem." I thanked him and walked back to the car, past the first soldier, who watched me.

But when I climbed into the driving seat of my car the children were crying.

"What's the matter?" I asked.

Eight-year-old Archie sobbed, "We thought—we thought the soldiers were going to *shoot* you."

I had believed we had protected them from fears like this one. Their Palestinian school friends "lived" checkpoints, saw their parents humiliated, forced out of their cars at gunpoint, their all-important IDs torn up or confiscated. To many of their friends, even those who had Israeli teachers and school friends, Israelis were soldiers, no more no less, and soldiers to be feared, not idolized. Our children knew that things were different for us. They knew we weren't Palestinian and that this made a difference. They also knew that Andrew and I went to the Occupied Territories and that we were careful. They had asked about the flak jacket in the back of Andrew's vehicle, and the blue helmet he never wore, and they knew that if he were in a dangerous area he would have protection. And just then the soldiers had been reasonable, the police officer helpful.

Archie once said, as I was checking his hair for lice, "Mummy, if I was a suicide bomber—which I'm not going to be—but if I was, I'd choose a bus full of soldiers, not ordinary people." And once he said he wanted to leave the pizza place, saying that a suicide bomber might choose it, but it was a ruse rather than real fear; he'd finished his pizza, and ice cream, and played on the machines. He just wanted to leave.

By the time we reached home on this occasion the children were less unhappy and ran in to play with the hungry baby. But Maha was very distressed. She and her girls had taken a walk through the paths of the Forest of Peace, as they did most after-noons. In among the trees they saw a man they thought was praying, but when they got closer they saw that he was dead. He had hanged himself. It was his suicide that was the reason for the mass of army and police on our road.

The children had many questions about what they were seeing, and we answered without giving them more to think about than they wanted. They had other questions, too, unrelated to the situation. There were latchkey kids at the lycée, kids who were abused at home, kids who were given no lunch box and no money either. There were children with emotional problems; mine were picked on by a mixed gang of boys, saw "acting out," bad language and bullying.

It was impossible to avoid glimpses: a van pulled over from the line of traffic by border police, its occupants hauled out, the elderly veiled women gesturing for the troops to be less rough, young veiled women with hands to cheeks; a line of Palestinian men ranged against a wall near the site of the Mandelbaum Gate; a group of Palestinians being beaten up beside an army position in southern Jerusalem. A friend's children watched from their car, stuck at the checkpoint, their mother unable to drive them away from the sight. At traffic lights three armed plain-clothed men leaped out of a car in front and brought down a pedestrian as I watched. The men looked at me, paused, waved me on with ugly gestures, and turned back to him. A Briton stopped at the Bethlehem checkpoint with his ten-year-old after dropping a Palestinian school friend home—suddenly there was the muzzle of a machine gun at his daughter's head, click-click, cocked, the checkpoint soldier at the other end of the gun shouting wildly. He was angry, perhaps, or frightened.

All these needed explanations. Unexplained, they filtered into the playground banter and acquired reasons of their own, unhealthy reasons. The children's questions unsettled me; it was my recoil from the situation, not reluctance to answer them. They became more absorbed in what it meant to be soldiers. One of their young Israeli playmates told them he would go into the army in a few years' time, "because we are fighting a war." My boys, then four and seven, wanted to know about the war and whether they would be soldiers, and I had to give them answers. It was one thing to understand the impact of terror, it was quite another to understand the enduring impact of the army on society, to understand what it meant to serve in the IDF, or to be a citizen of a country in which the army plays so predominant a role.

To some people, especially those in the line of fire, the very name of the IDF was ironic: "They're not *defensive* forces, they're forces of occupation and repression." The IDF were often referred to as the "IOF"—the "Israeli Occupation Forces." To Israelis, on the other hand, 16 percent of whom may be in military service at any time, the IDF were just that: defensive forces. And they have been successful. Over a couple of Gold Star beers at a beach-side bar in Tel Aviv, an American journalist was unequivocal, "This is a country whose own territory—not including territory it was occupying—has never been invaded by the armed forces of another country since the War of Independence. Not in '56, not in '67, not in '73 or '78 and not in '82. That's some defensive force."

"Come on," I said, "give Israelis a break. They don't feel it that way. They believe the Arabs are out to get them. And they are."

"Listen. Even in '73, which was the only one of those wars these guys didn't actually start, the Arabs attacked the Israelis *only* in the Sinai and the Golan Heights—lands the Israelis had captured from them in '67. That's the Arab-Israeli conflict."

"Whatever. You can cite historical facts until you're blue in the face, but it won't change belief, or fear."

What was true was that, after centuries of discrimination and suffering, the Jewish people now had a refuge, a state of their own; the state was their fortress against a world of hostility, not only the twenty-two Arab nations whom they felt were out to drive them into the sea, but even beyond if necessary. And they had a mighty army to defend them and their country. That army was considered pure, without stain, and for many Israelis it remained so. To them it was the most moral army in the world, bound by the principle of "purity of arms." An American Israeli I met in Jerusalem talked about the importance of the IDF's morality, ending with: "I've served in the IDF *and* in the US army—and I can tell you," he said, "the Israeli army is *way* the most principled army in the world."

The purity of arms principle derived from qualities that I could see for myself in everyday Jerusalem life, but was having a hard time seeing in things the IDF and radical settlers were doing. One minute I was hearing the verdict on a dead child: "He throws stones—he gets shot. So?" and another minute reading Israel Harel, a journalist and hard-line settler, describe how "the Jewish people has a natural, inborn sensitivity for human life. And when photographs are broadcast of children who were hurt when they happened to be in—or were pushed into—combat zones, our own citizens' hearts break."[3] The genuine belief that the IDF still practiced purity of arms, that it was not just an ordinary army, persisted despite overwhelming evidence that this was not the case.[4]

"Israeli attitudes to their army are very interesting," said Dr. Ibrahim one morning. He had just finished operating on a woman who had been trying for days to get to the hospital for surgery but had been blocked at the checkpoints. "It's not just that they don't want to—or can't—accept that the philosophy of purity of arms is meaningless in practice. They also think the IDF are above political interest—yet the government and top jobs are full of soldiers." Many leading Israeli politicians had been generals: Rabin, Sharon, Dayan, Barak, Mofaz, Mitzna, Lipkin-Shahak, and Ben-Eliezer. Netanyahu had been a colonel. "Theirs is a highly militarized society."

Israelis themselves did ask questions: "How is it that the sons of Israel's liberal intelligentsia are all serving in the most elite combat units, on the front line?" was a query I heard more than once, and by Israelis from different angles. I asked the same question. The answers, which lay somewhere between their commitment and sense of duty to the state, and their incontrovertible Ashkenazi abilities, explained much about Israel and its ethos. Israeli children go through their studies knowing that when they finish school, they will go into the army. For many Israelis, the army is the time of their life, a welcome escape from home, and they relish the camaraderie. For others it is a nightmare they must avoid, or endure. But they must all confront it (unless they can claim exemption on religious grounds, for example). Their every minute is spent in a system that owns them, nurtures them, trains them, and protects them. They suffer together, and thrill together. They form lifelong friendships and powerful bonds of loyalty and mutual sacrifice.

One late night at a club in Tel Aviv, I listened to a young woman letting out her anger at the Israeli military system. I drank sangria; she ate the fruit. In her mid-twenties, she was a poet and wrote daily. Her skin was clear, her face serene, her eyes questioning, and limbs sensuously mobile. I thought about limbs like that clothed in army fatigues, and I thought about them mutilated and bloody, caught up in a suicide bombing. The men in the party grated at our conversation: why were we being so serious, why wouldn't we talk to them instead?

No, she said to them firmly, she wanted to talk to me and she wanted to talk about military service. She had served in military intelligence, her perfect English setting her up for listening in on Anglophone sources. "I resent the Israeli army for forcing Israeli youth into a system of killing and brutality. There's no space, no identity: no space to find your *own* identity. To be formed, at eighteen, into something you have no choice but to be formed by, measured by, valued by, and to have to do the things the army wants you to do without really understanding why any of it is happening."

"*Alicia*," one of the group broke in. "Phone call for you." She made a face. It was one of the British journalists she had met earlier that night, trying to lure her to a different club where, he promised, the dancing was better. She brushed him off: "Maybe later."

Starting again, she went on: "And then you read about things—I've become very interested in our history, and I'm reading, reading, reading. You read about the *Nakba*—do you know what that is?"

I nodded; she looked pleased that I understood her reference to the Palestinians' "catastrophe," when Israel was created on 78 percent of Palestine.

"When you read about the *Nakba*," she went on, "it all becomes so clear, so obvious, and you wonder *why* this hasn't been explained to us before, and then you think a little, and you realize why. And you travel and look for yourself, and of course you are strong, if you have survived the process of being in the army, not like the others you meet along the way from other countries where there isn't this molding. In London, especially, everyone said 'What are you *on*, Alicia? What is it? I *must* have some. Tell us.' And all it was was my *strength*, and that was forced on me."

"Alicia." Mark, the friend sitting opposite us, handed her the phone: the journalist had called again, persistent. And now Alicia wanted to dance.

After she had left I thought of all the telephone calls she must have listened to, and of the times when senior Israelis would let slip to Andrew and his UN colleagues that they had seen transcripts of UN calls. I pictured Alicia listening to Andrew's conversations, and remembered the Israeli who had warned one senior international official that he could no longer risk talking to him on the telephone. "You're just too indiscreet," he had said. "Do you really think Israelis won't know you're talking about Egypt when you say 'the country of the river,' or the US when you say 'our overseas friends'?" And I thought that the people Alicia had met along the way who wanted her strength, however unwillingly acquired, were probably people like me; people lucky enough to be unexposed for so long.

Serving in the Occupied Territories did open some eyes, sometimes immediately, sometimes during their service, but more often long afterward. Yet the majority of soldiers did not "see." One ex-soldier explained that troops live, eat, sleep, play, and work in barracks, surrounded by crowds of like-minded buddies. "They're put into army jeeps, driven somewhere—they might have no idea where—to do their job for the day. They find themselves standing at a checkpoint, still with little or no idea where they are, let alone why. They are told to obey their orders to keep 'the Arabs' from going here or there, and that the locals would use excuses x, y, and z, but not to forget that every one of them was a potential terrorist and that they would try anything to get through. The soldiers would find that everything their commanders told them was true. The locals did indeed try to get through the checkpoint, and they did indeed use excuses x, y, and z—like 'going to work' or school or hospital—and they did indeed try very hard to persuade the soldiers to allow them to pass. Everything was as their commanders described, and so they trust their commanders completely."

The "why they are there" and the "what for" was not their problem. I heard as much when I took the children to Neve Samuel one Sunday afternoon. Most Jerusalem skylines are crenel-lated with apartment blocks, but some of the hills are smooth, crowned only with monasteries or minarets. Neve Samuel sits high on a hill overlooking Jerusalem from the north and defines the skyline with a great mosque and minaret. Here God appeared to Solomon and gave him wisdom, honor, and treasure. Samuel was buried here, and from this high point the first crusaders, and later Richard the Lionheart, caught their first (and his only) glimpse of the Holy City.

The soldiers on duty were surprised that we wanted to look around. The thin line of visitors made straight for the sarcophagus without taking in the site: its courtyards, rooms, and stables cut straight out of the rock. Two of the soldiers showed us about, but they couldn't answer our questions about the place. Archie's fixa-tion with history and with the military put a long list of questions into his head. "What were those things that look like troughs—were they for the soldiers' horses?" "What road did the crusaders come along, and how many crusaders were there?" The soldiers were bemused. We trailed up a long unbroken flight of stairs to the roof to take in the view. It was difficult on the stairs and the soldiers helped the little ones, making sure they were safe. On the roof, watching the boys climb over the low domes of stone, the soldiers were frank, "I'm not interested in history," said one. "The past doesn't get me at all. I think about *now*. I don't want to know what all these old stones mean."

"Those guys down there," said the second, pointing to the black-robed Jewish pilgrims heading for Samuel's tomb, "they obsess about stones and history. What do I care? It's all bullshit now."

The "bullshit," however, remained powerful for many Israelis. The attachment to the West Bank—Judaea and Samaria—meant that soldiers, including those who wanted to put their country's past behind them, had to fight and sometimes die to hold on to them.

"We cannot get beyond our own sense of victimhood," explained a young Israeli in a Tel Aviv restaurant. "We've always been the victim. All we can see is this: that the Arabs want to destroy us. And so some of us say we must give them nothing because if we do they will think we're weak and then they'll want more and more and more. And others among us say we have to destroy them before they destroy us. Beyond that, there isn't exactly much on offer." It was force, or nothing.

Security was everything, he said. "Security means repression and violence on a daily basis that you see only if you are in the Occupied Territories, not in Israel, and definitely not in the US. And that daily diet of repression and violence is recycled into Palestinian violence, which we label 'terrorism.' And of course, we all know we have to fight terrorism."

My mother, ignoring all warnings from alarmists abroad, came to stay again. One Saturday we went to Caesarea to walk among the Herodian and crusader ruins. It was hot, but the buildings were magnificent. As we trailed past Herod's outdoor swimming pool carved into the rocks below his palace on the edge of the sea, Andrew took a call.

We walked on, well used to phone interruptions. But Andrew called me back, away from my mother and my children so they wouldn't hear what he had to tell me. His face was grim. Another mother, a friend's mother, had been shot dead. Lana was an official with the UN Development Program, and her mother, Shaden abu Hijleh, was a leading peace activist. Earlier that morning, she had been sitting with her husband on the porch of their quiet Nablus house, stitching an embroidery. Curfew, as so often, had been imposed on Nablus yet again.* Out of the stillness came two IDF jeeps. They stopped thirty yards from the house. "Wait," Mrs. abu Hijleh called to her son inside the house. "Don't come out."

Without warning, a soldier in the back of one of the jeeps opened the vehicle door and opened fire, hitting the front of the house. Lana's mother was killed.

A senior British intelligence officer happened to be in Nablus that morning. He saw the evidence at the scene and listened to eyewitnesses. The army said she had been hit by a stray bullet in a shoot-out, and that soldiers had fired in response to "disturbances" after Friday prayers. But no one was at prayer; no one was allowed out of the house—it was curfew. Later, army investigators acknowledged that the area had been quiet.

The *Christian Science Monitor* correspondent and our friend, Nicole Gaouette, reported the story in detail. Not only was Shaden abu Hijleh well-known, but her four children were all graduates of US universities, and determined that her killing should not be ignored as so many killings of Palestinians were ignored. Her

---

*Amnesty International recorded that from the beginning of August 2002, Nablus, home to around 120,000 Palestinians, was under strict 24-hour curfew for 106 consecutive days.

murder was raised in the UN Security Council and with the Israeli prime minister, Sharon, by US President Bush.

"This should be a turning point," said Akiva Eldar to the *Monitor*. "Sometimes people become symbols after their death to make sure it doesn't happen to others." The IDF's chief spokesperson, Brigadier General Ruth Yaron, held that Palestinian testimony was often unreliable—deaths were manipulated for political gain, many witnesses refused to cooperate, and on some occasions investigators had been ambushed while collecting testimony. By now at least 1,700 Palestinians had been killed, hundreds of whom were, by any criterion, civilian. Only twenty cases of civilian death had been investigated.* Eldar said: "For me this is the ultimate example of how the army gives soldiers the wrong message... The message now is that we understand the soldiers are very nervous, it's a war, and of course, they'll convey their condolences to this family. But to kill an old lady on her porch? Somebody should pay for this."[5]

Nobody did. Lana wrote to her friends vowing to bring those responsible to justice, hoping at least to "make the next Israeli soldier hesitate before pulling the trigger and killing one more mom." But justice was out of reach. Over the months soldiers talked increasingly freely of their experiences and of their feeling of immunity from action. Soldiers knew they could get away with murder.

According to a report by Alex Fishman and Guy Leshem (Yediot Ahronoth, 23 January 2004), between September 2000 and December 2003 the IDF counted 2,253 Palestinians killed and thousands injured. Seventy-two cases had been investigated by the Investigative Military Police, of which thirteen had resulted in indictments. Two of these cases had ended in convictions, the soldiers responsible given suspended sentences. One had his promotion stalled.

12

For the Peace of the Settlements

There was no one around and I felt like giving up. Sitting in my stationary car clutching a map, I was stalled in the West Bank, looking for a village a few miles from Ramallah. The village, which I was supposed to visit as part of my research into childbirth policy, was marked on the map and not far away, but I couldn't reach it. I had been trying for more than an hour. Like a novice in a sorcerer's maze, I was brought to a halt again and again by massive, impassable mounds of earth and concrete blocks that closed off the roads. I thought about driving off the road, around the mounds, but the IDF had thought of that, and blocked off that option too.

I kept doubling back and starting again. It was impossible. I either had to turn back and go home or start walking and ask for help.

I parked the car and clambered over the earth-mound, glad there was rarely any rain. Sliding down the other side, I looked along the tree-lined road of a hamlet but saw no one. I walked past a couple of square concrete houses, neat gardens bordered with big-leaved fig trees, banks of nasturtiums, and tiny fields of weed-free vegetables, and came across a group of men and children working on a car under a large tree. Two children were sitting on a wall, playing a word game. I went toward them, speculating on my reception in view of the preparations for war on Iraq and hoped they didn't think I was American. And then reminded myself that it wasn't so hot being British.

The men looked up from their work. I explained that I was trying to reach a nearby village. The first two spoke little English, but they laughed at the name of the village and made it clear that it was hard to get there. And yet it was so close: there were Israeli settlements around us but none between us and the village to account for the roadblocks. I brought out the map and we all peered at it together.

"You could go this way, around here, and then over that," said a third man. I didn't follow. I would have to go back almost into Israel, head north and then come east again. It meant a detour of many miles and would take too long. I had to get back to Jerusalem before dark.

"I know what," said a man who had come out from under the car. "It is easier if you start this side of the earth-mound, so I will take you in my car."

There was no arguing with him, or pointing out that he must have a hundred better things to do. I wasn't going to say that with the closures they were less busy than they would have liked. I climbed into the front seat of his car, and wondered if we would get there—the car was beaten up and rattled. But it chugged confidently along the narrow, disintegrating concrete of the lanes.

"I'm going to ask my cousin to help," the man explained. "He was born in America." I wasn't sure how this was going to help, but Deeb—he told me his name—was pleased with his plan. Weaving through the village, I could see children staring at me, wondering who the strange woman in Deeb's car might be. Among the fig trees there were baskets hanging under folds of honeysuckle, and old tractors—not the miniature green variety used in the confines of Hebron and the Old City but bigger, freer workhorses. Small birds in white cages were everywhere, reminding me of a morning on a psychiatry ward in London. On that occasion I had taken a history from a man who had drawn pictures of his budgerigar in a cage just like these cages. He had then eaten the bird—God had told him to. He sat perfectly quiet on a chair in the ward and described the sound of a somber clear voice, the stretching out of his hand into the cage and the feeling under his fingers as they clasped the bird. For him the voice was real. He heard God and obeyed, grateful for His direction.

Deeb was telling me about the crops and I had not been listening. He was saying how hard it was to make ends meet when more and more Palestinian land was taken by the Israeli army. We spent a long time looking for his cousin and a long time looking for the village I had set out to find, but we ran out of time. There were too many twists and blocks, forcing us to double back, start again, try a different route, find ourselves blocked and then begin again. Disappointed when I said we had to give up, Deeb refueled his car with two liters of petrol and took me to his house to meet his family.

Deeb's home was in a narrow, unplanned street, a concrete structure pinned to the side of a hill among a cluster of similarly pinned buildings. The children ran out and shouted happily at their father. Deeb grinned at his clan, led me into the living room and offered me a seat. "Welcome," he said.

I sat and, for want of anything better, continued the conversation we had started in his car. Deeb was worried about his little brother. In order to continue his education at Birzeit University, the young man had been obliged to leave home and live in Ramallah. It was too difficult to travel the short distance from home to Birzeit each day. Living in Ramallah was expensive for the family, and he was away from their influence and vulnerable to dangerous ideas, which made Deeb fret.

"I worry about him, but what can we do? If he stays here, he doesn't get a degree. Then what?"

Deeb's mother kept asking me, through Deeb, why it had to be so hard for her to get to hospital appointments. "She says why do the Israeli soldiers want to stop her seeing her doctor—do they think she's a terrorist?" he said, laughing.

Deeb's mother wasn't laughing. I could see from her shortness of breath and two small but edematous legs poking out from under her traditional black embroidered dress that she needed medical attention—not urgently, but soon enough, and at regular intervals to monitor her response to whatever medications were prescribed. I had nothing to offer her, not even transportation to her doctor.

Deeb's wife brought in a little tray with cups of coffee and a tower of saucers. She put it on a white plastic stool next to the velour-covered sofa where I was sitting and handed me a cup and saucer. Then she gave her husband and her mother-in-law a cup of coffee, sat herself down on a plastic chair and smiled at me. I looked down at the concrete, swept floor. The bareness of the floor merged with the bareness of the walls. The children's feet set up echoing scuffing noises as they bounded in and out of the room, wanting to stare at me, giggling. Every one of them was blond and most had blue eyes. The youngest was a boy of just over a year. He balanced on the arm of the sofa where I was sitting, fell off, and on to me. He was embarrassed and threw himself at his father, who hugged him.

I asked where the boy had been born. Deeb translated for his wife and she rolled her eyes. When she went into labor they had spent three hours on the road, trying to get through to the hospital. In the end they returned home and the baby was born "over there," said Deeb, pointing at the back of the house. It wasn't something his wife wanted to remember, or talk about. Her mother-in-law commented again, looking angrier than before, but this time Deeb left her untranslated.

There had been another raid by the army. These raids happened unpredictably but usually in the dead of night. Deeb's face clouded as he described how the Israeli soldiers herded his wife and children, even his mother, out of the house and, along with the other villagers, into the freezing night air. "My children were lying in their bed, then the soldiers pulled them out. They were all afraid and crying to me. But what could I do?" Once outside, they were forced to stand at gunpoint. Deeb and the other men were made to strip down to their underwear. The shame of this—in front of his children—made Deeb stop speaking for a moment. Then he went on, telling me how the women had tried to carry blankets outside to keep the children warm but that the soldiers had grabbed the blankets and sworn at the women, another humiliation.

After a couple of hours the soldiers left. Deeb assumed they were looking for "fighters." He said he thought they had been lucky. Often the villagers' property was damaged or destroyed in these raids. Sometimes the soldiers dumped belongings into the street; sometimes they forced the villagers to do it themselves. They think nothing, he said, of emptying the contents of the kitchen on to the floor, and they make a point of picking on the oil. "They know what our olives mean to us, they know what it means when they pour out all our oil."

I had spent too long listening. It would soon be dark and I had completely failed to find the childbirth data I had set out for. Deeb took me back to the earth-mound. He said he wanted to come with me to Ramallah, and I certainly owed him a lift. His car was, after all, not only in bad shape but on the wrong side of the earth-mound. We trekked off through the West Bank valleys, glancing left and right before daring to take a settler-only road for a few meters, then diving off it again on to an unpaved road that wound down into the bottom of a valley. On our way, a long convoy of battered vehicles following an ambulance swept past us. A funeral, Deeb said, for a little girl who had been shot by the IDF.

"It happens so many times."

Then we drove uphill again, over a dried-up watercourse and into another village. A large stone church stood on one side of the road. The greenness, the stone, and the church in the calm of the village, reminded me of Italy.

We had managed to bypass the checkpoints. When we reached the center of Ramallah, Deeb asked to get out. He told me that now that he knew I was safe he could go home. He had wanted to show me the route. I felt bad that I had brought him so far out of his way, on top of all the help he had given me. I knew he wouldn't accept anything in return, even when I asked him to please buy the children some toys. He refused. "No. This is what we do. I would help anyone," he said, "if they were American, British, Russian, or Israeli."

I drove home fast along the settler-only road, with words I had heard spoken in the past two years filling my head; words I had heard and had learned to expect. The bitter words of those who would see only the terror: "He says '*this is what we do*'?—no, what they, the Palestinians, do is kill. Look at the rows of Israeli dead, they bomb and maim and kill, they kill our children." And the harsh words of people who would say: "So, his world is shrinking—life's a bitch, this is war, get real, they lost their land. Get over it." The words of people who were free and self-sufficient: "I live my life, he lives his, I don't want to know how bad it is for him, I've got my own problems." And the so-frequent words of the fearful: "So he's a decent guy, so what, he's just one man—how can we ever trust them now?" And the despairing words: "This is not just about what kind of Israel the Israelis want—democratic, theocratic, Jewish, or apartheid—it's about what kind of world we all want. What kind of world do we really want?"

The following morning I took the dog for a walk. Coming to the end of one of the paths through the Forest of Peace I saw a billboard painted with a picture of red-roofed houses lining the steep hillside near our house. It was a sign announcing a new development: 500 new housing units in a valley where Palestinian families, 10,000 people, were crowded into 1,000 units. The new development would bring good roads, services, and streetlights to a place where there were broken roads, few services, no mail, no pavements, and hardly any streetlights. Most of the Palestinian families' land had long ago been declared "green space," meaning they were forbidden to build on it and any new buildings faced demolition for being built illegally. Now, somehow, all the necessary permits had been granted for someone else to build on their land. The settlement was to be for Israelis only.

The quiet war that imprisoned Deeb and that I could see that morning on the billboard had been obvious to many for a long time, but had been hidden from broader view by the visible war and by a many-faceted process of silencing. In the months of Intifada leading up to Operation Defensive Shield, I had seen the visible war: the violence, the struggle between occupier and occupied and the use of terror against civilians. It was hard to see beyond the violence. But now the silent war was coming into focus; witnessing the relentless building program in the Occupied Territories, the wearing down of the Palestinians and the increasing limits on their movement and access, particularly to Jerusalem, I began to understand. As many people were telling me, this was about buying time in order to complete Israel's physical control of the land.

Alicia, the dancing poet, had talked about the settlement where she grew up: Ma'ale Edumim. It lies far to the east of Jerusalem, in the waist of the West Bank. She liked to walk to the edge of the town and look out over the loneliness of the Judean desert, wanting to enjoy the caress of solitude and to escape the drug culture and the problems she had told me about at length: her abusive father for one. To almost every Israeli, this settlement was part of Israel. It was also a key mechanism for Israeli control of the land. It is a huge wedge in the middle of the future Palestinian state, intended to sever the connection between the northern and southern halves of the West Bank.

The city's architect, Thomas Leitersdorf, was under no illusions. Recruited by the government in the 1970s, he said "the strategy at the time was 'to capture ground'... the further inside the Occupied Territories we placed settlers, the more territory Israel would have when the time came to set the permanent international borders— because we were already there." He was given map coordinates and told to build a town. He studied the area and reported back: it was unsuitable. Putting an Israeli town there "was a government decision, and its location was accurately specified—'at the end of the desert,' the furthest place from Israel that was conceivably possible... Ma'ale Edumim's location was, without doubt, political." Despite the topographical unsuitability he was told to go ahead and build.[1]

As I was frequently reminded, there were layers and layers of complication behind the occupation. The occupation was not only a physical reality. It was also a mindset, a set of assumptions. Not only Israelis but many Jews in the diaspora had grown used to the idea—and were daily getting more and more used to the idea*— that the Occupied Territories were Israeli possessions; that, despite international law and UN resolutions, the Israelis' occupation of another people's lands was not a foreign occupation at all. To some it was a "fact on the ground," to others it was even a liberation.

Palestinians wondered how Israelis reconciled their professed desire for peace with their continued building on Palestinian land. Israel signed up to the Oslo accords and accepted, or claimed to accept, the famous UN Resolution 242. Yet successive Israeli governments, including that of the "peacemaker" Barak, not only continued to build Israeli settlements in the West Bank and Gaza Strip but accelerated the process. To the Palestinians, the peace the Israelis claimed they wanted seemed a strange sort of peace: a peace based on the willingness of a besieged people meekly to accept the fact of their conquest and the loss of much of their land.

Israelis asked similar questions, but the other way around. Palestinians asked, "If the Israelis want peace, why do they take even more of our land?" Israelis asked, "If the Palestinians want peace, why do they go on attacking and killing us?" Israelis were increasingly convinced that continuing acts of terror committed by Palestinians could only be explained by the fact that the Palestinians did not really want peace—that whatever their leaders might say, they did not want Israel to exist at all. "What possible explanation can there be," they wanted to know, "for bombing the very people you claim you want to make peace with?"

It was an exasperated westerner who concluded: "Neither side wants peace—Israelis would rather have the land and the Palestinians want justice."

If I asked Palestinians why Hamas and Islamic Jihad kept bombing—thereby making peace and a final settlement more

---

* As many Israelis as well as others noted, no Israeli government has discouraged the Israeli people from thinking of the Occupied Territories as their own.

difficult, and also giving Israel more time to seize and settle the land—the answer was twofold: that nothing but violence and force had ever made Israelis listen, and that the international community had made promises and resolutions and laws but had never kept them. If I asked Israelis why Israel kept building settlements knowing that doing so made peace increasingly difficult to achieve, I was often met with a shrug or an awkward silence.

After more than three decades, many of the settlements were not illegal in Israeli minds. The inner ring of Jerusalem settlements was integrated not only into the fabric of the city, but into a new concept of the city and the way Israelis imagined and visualized it. So much so that when an Israeli friend called Beni, who lived in a Jerusalem suburb, French Hill, built over the Green Line and therefore a settlement, asked Andrew if he knew any settlers, he was dismayed at the tough reply: "Apart from you, Beni?" Beni did not consider himself a settler and believed that the area he lived in, abutting Palestinian houses, was a template for coexistence.

From those who didn't just shrug or fall silent, there were a range of justifications for building settlements: legal arguments (Israeli[2] and international[3]), security arguments, tribal arguments, even "integrationist" arguments: "We have a million Arabs in Israel, why not some Israelis in the future state of Palestine?" Some accused the Palestinians of trying to ethnically cleanse the Occupied Territories. Occasionally someone would repeat the mantra: "Settlements are not the problem," as though watching your agreed share of the land being taken away from you was somehow acceptable.*

American Middle East activist Daniel Pipes held that the settlements were not an obstacle to peace, but a "political triviality." He was so aggrieved by Ariel Sharon's decision to evacuate those in Gaza that he wrote that settlements "might be a tactical and political liability, but they must be retained and defended. To do otherwise is to indicate to the Palestinians that open season on Israel has begun" (Jerusalem Post, 11 February 2004). Israelis often complained that pro-Israeli foreigners tried to block what the majority of Israelis wanted: to withdraw. The rationalization for not evacuating a single settlement— that this would give Palestinians encouragement to overrun Israel proper—was another popular justification.

Others flipped into anger and threw out old myths: the Arabs only just arrived, they're the interlopers, it's our land, and of course, God gave it to us. But mostly it was a shrug.

Israelis love sports. They watch hours of it—soccer and basketball particularly—and doctors would sometimes wrap up a caseload early so that everyone could go home and watch the match. Among many Palestinians and Israelis, the big events could also be political. Though no one stopped work, there was much speculation in the hospital and beyond about George Bush's speech on June 24, 2002. He stated clearly: he wanted regime change in the Middle East, not just in Iraq but in Palestine as well. And then the Palestinians can have a state, he said, the first US president to declare the intention to see a Palestinian state.

But, "don't forget it's a Western club," my Palestinian colleagues said to me. "There are conditions: we can have a state, but..." Bush had said, "Peace requires a new and different Palestinian leadership so a Palestinian state can be born." One doctor said angrily, "So, we obey Bush, dump our elected president, then what—a state?" Not quite: "When the Palestinian people have new leaders, new institutions, and new security arrangements with their neighbors, the United States of America will support the creation of a Palestinian state, whose border and certain aspects of its sovereignty will be provisional until resolved as part of a final settlement in the Middle East."

The president's people on the ground in Israel were amazed that he had demanded so much of the Palestinians with no reciprocal demands on the occupying power, Israel. Rumors went about that another speech had been planned, but it had been ditched when news came through that Arafat had blown it yet again in some unspecified way. One senior US diplomat made clear his feelings, that Bush's was "a foolish policy," and later paid the price for his frankness, finding his position precarious.

"What did I tell you?" said a doctor. "The people of East Timor have just been delivered from occupation. Did *they* have to check off a list of constitutional demands before they got their freedom?"

Israelis also expressed amazement—at President Bush being so compliant with Likud policy. Israeli papers joked that the delay in delivering the speech came from the White House being unable to find anyone to translate it from the original Hebrew. Soon afterward the Israeli Chief of Staff General Moshe Ya'alon, spoke at a conference; he praised the determination of the Americans and condemned the Europeans. The Europeans, in his view, were clinging to the narrative of the Palestinians, according to which they "are under occupation."

"Ah, so this is the problem," said another doctor. He laughed. "People like me live in a dream-world, thinking the Israelis are occupying us. Those Israeli roadblocks that held me up all along my way to work this morning, like every morning—I must have imagined them." He laughed again, adding an afterthought, "You Europeans had better watch out: pointing out the occupation to the Americans could be dangerous."

He made light of it, but many people, both in Israel and abroad, were in denial, unaware of the reality of the occupation. US Secretary of Defense Donald Rumsfeld, referred to "the so-called Occupied Territories." "What occupation?" wrote the Israeli journalist Doron Rosenblum sarcastically. "According to our official narrative—even when it is related from the depths of Ramallah and Nablus and from numberless outposts, blocs, and settlements—there is no occupation. There are only operations against terrorism. And we know that our official narrative, which bears the seal of Sharon's office, is the only one that counts."[4]

The occupation may have been a myth to some in Washington, but not to Ariel Sharon. To the astonishment of many, he was unequivocal, suddenly declaring in May 2003: "I think the idea that it is possible to continue keeping 3.5 million Palestinians under occupation—yes it is occupation, you might not like the word, but what is happening is occupation—is bad for Israel, and bad for the Palestinians, and bad for the Israeli economy. Controlling 3.5 million Palestinians cannot go on forever. You want to remain in Jenin, Nablus, Ramallah, and Bethlehem?"[5]

This remarkable admission meant facing frightening questions. Regardless of whether it had been legal or illegal to colonize these lands, and whether Israel's presence in the West Bank and Gaza Strip was an occupation or a dispute or a figment of 3.5 million Palestinians' imaginations, the Palestinians who lived there were just that—still there. And so, now, were the settlements. How had this happened? And what had the occupation done to Israel? Now that there were so many settlements crowning the West Bank hills, how were the Israelis to disengage? And, if they were not to disengage, how were Israelis to live among a people who felt dispossessed by them—unless they gave those Palestinians full citizenship? Citizenship? That meant the end of the Jewish majority, the end of the Jewish state. Or were the Palestinians, as some cabinet ministers suggested, to be removed?

The land that was occupied was in fact being "redeemed," according to an Israeli who asked for my advice on varieties of yogurt in the supermarket. We fell to talking, and he soon heard that I was British. "Oh," he assured me, "I know *all* about you British and colonialism, yes, I've seen *Gandhi* the movie." Israelis were not occupiers: "We're liberators," liberating the land from Arab intruders, giving it back to the rightful owners to whom God had given the land 3,000 years ago. When he told me that "the Arabs" had arrived in Palestine only a hundred years ago, like the Palestinian radiographer telling me there were no Jews in Israel when Jesus was born, I hurried away from the mythology.

The settlements kept growing, even now, with all the killing and with all the promises to stop. They crept outward, their perimeter fences expanding, swallowing the surrounding farmland, any land, any buildings. A no-man's-land pushed out in advance of the settlement fence. There must be a "clean" expanse, the argument went, so that no terrorists could get too close.

I was being shown this pattern near the settlement of Kfar Darom in the Gaza Strip: "The other day," my host was saying, "the director general of one of the PA ministries lost the last of his lands, and his house, to the settlers." He used to have greenhouses, farms, lands, and a big house where he and his grown-up sons and their families lived together. They weren't even given the time to get their clothes out of the house. Now he's sharing two rooms with his brother-in-law, and his sons are dispersed. He became like any other poor guy looking for work. He'd always been the employer, and he used to give thousands of dollars to charities, especially during Ramadan, and he'd leave trucks of seasonal vegetables for the poor in Dir al-Balah. "It's a killing feeling to see your land stolen. Millionaire to beggar overnight."

I was visiting healthcare providers in Gaza and staying with Basem, who lived in Dir al-Balah. He was a political scientist; his wife Atidal taught chemistry to sixteen-year-olds. Basem had driven me along the coast from Gaza City, where we had been working. The road had been choked with stretched yellow taxis, trucks transporting boxes of goods, and cars half buried under piles of fresh chickpeas, a mass of green foliage. He also wanted me to see where Salahadin Road, the north–south aorta of the Gaza Strip, had been closed.

Out of the traffic, we sat for a moment on the ghost-road that had once led south to Rafah, watched by IDF lookout towers. The expanse of dead concrete was scraped by drifts of rubbish and debris taking over; "The snipers have an unbelievable range," said Basem, as he turned the car around and headed away. "We call those bullets the 500s." A few days before, one of his friends had been hit and killed by one as he sat on his balcony.

In Dir al-Balah we passed a memorial. "That commemorates my two brothers," he said. "They were murdered by collaborators."

He talked about the collaborators and the consequent network of suspicion that threaded its way throughout the lives of the occupied. Collaborators were widely used by the IDF, which recruited hundreds of individuals by a range of methods: blackmail and bribery, threats and extortion. Sometimes simple but essential permits were granted on condition of handing over information—permits to pass through checkpoints or for building a house, for example. Assassinations by the IDF were widely believed to rely on information provided by collaborators. It was a brutal tool, and the response was brutal. When a collaborator was unearthed the result was usually his death, sometimes by lynchings fêted by ghastly demonstrations of public glee.

"Have you been in prison?" I asked Basem.

"Of course I have, everyone has been in prison here. But only twice—yes, I was tortured—but most people have been imprisoned many more times." So much of Palestinian experience was shared, Basem said: dispossession, bereavement, house demolition, prison.

We reached the house and Basem introduced me to his wife and sons. Atidal showed me my room—two of their three little boys had given up their room for me—and offered a hairdryer in case I hadn't one of my own. The boys were very young. The smallest was making a house out of cushions under the coffee table. The oldest, Mohammed, showed me his uncle's soccer trophy, a huge gold and silver statuette.

"He's obsessed with soccer," explained Basem. "And with his uncles."

"The ones who were killed?"

"Yes. That's them on the wall," he said, pointing to two poster-sized studio photos. There was another of a young Basem with a background of autumnal forest. The apartment was full of plants and light and solid wood. Atidal, the daughter of an imam, had made it a sanctuary against the dust and violence, but the noises of the street filtered in: traffic, the clip-clop and rumble of horse-drawn carts, the crackle and anger of a loudspeaker calling for demonstrations, this time against the PA's refusal to obey the Palestinian high court. Basem explained: the international community insisted on freezing PA payments to a branch of Hamas; the Palestinian high court said that was illegal. The people insisted that Hamas provides services they needed, unlike the PA, so they demonstrated.

"It makes me sick," said Basem later, as we were discussing the PA. "The world insists we must be democratic, but it doesn't allow us to elect who we want. When it looks like Arafat is going to win, the US—with the British—bans the elections."[6]

When I woke up the following morning I looked out of the window at the palms. "Balah" means palm tree, and Dir al-Balah is full of them. The bedroom window overlooked a field with olive trees and fig trees, all young, newly planted, and patterned in rows. A small road ran alongside, shaded from the sun by a single row of tall palm trees, and the quiet was very different from the noises of the night before: distant shooting, and not so distant.

We had breakfast before Basem drove me back to Gaza City. He and Atidal laid the table, piling it with *labaneh*, cucumber, fresh thyme, bread, and coffee. They asked me about my children and what they liked doing when they finished school each day, and we talked about their life. "It's the *daily* life living under occupation, this is what is really hard. It never stops." The invasions, the bombings, the infiltrations, and assassinations are one thing, but "It is the misery of every day that is so difficult to take, especially for the kids. It's impossible to explain to them why they can't leave the house or go to school because of curfew."

I said goodbye to the three little boys and wondered if they would play outside that day.

Basem drove me north along the coast. "I like to travel," he said, "and I used to travel a great deal." He slowed down to show me a point in the only remaining road that connected northern and southern Gaza, serving more than a million people. "Here," he said, "the road can be closed down in a moment, for hours, by a single tank. Then it takes five hours to go 300 meters. You can never hope to do more than two things in a day because of the closures."

The open sea on our left swelled green in the early light. On our right the bare patches and daubs of green were scabrous and shrinking. "It's all being destroyed by the IDF, gradually."

"The reason for closing the road at Netzarim used to be the settlers. When the settlers want to pass, all of Gaza's traffic has to stop and wait so the settlers can go by without waiting. Now the settlers have a overpass so there's no need to stop Palestinian traffic, but the soldiers still shut down the road, completely, whenever they feel like it."

Basem did not complain. He was wistful: "I like to smell history. Two of my favorite places are Cordoba and Bruges. When I'm there I can breathe in the past and I just love it." He talked about the two cities, and then pointed at the dunes leading down to the beach and the pounding surf. "You see there, that's the route my wife will walk when Israeli tanks close off the road. Like everyone, she insists on getting to work whatever the obstacles, even when it means walking for miles through the heavy sand."

I looked out to sea, but there were no fishing boats. "Not allowed," said Basem. "In theory yes, within a mile of the coast—Oslo said twelve, but that soon shrank to one—anyway, in practice the fishing boats hardly ever get out because the Israeli navy comes, and they get chased, shot at, and driven back. So we don't eat fish any more. Most Gazans can't afford the price of what fish there is, and those of us who can afford it feel bad about having fish when no one else can."

13

Between the Alaska Mosque and the
Columbia Checkpoint

We were at Fink's, a favored West Jerusalem den of journalists
and writers for many years. It is tiny, cramped, and mostly a
bar, but you can sit down and eat under the photographs of visitors
dating back decades, scrawls of writing and rows of bottles ranked
against mirrors. The problems nowadays were getting there, through
the most frequently bombed area of Jerusalem, and then sitting there,
wondering from time to time if it was an "unnecessary risk," if the
next person to walk in would be carrying a backpack of explosives.

My companion, Uri, wanted to explain Israel's right to defend
herself. "The world glares at Israel. Other Western powers have
done far worse." Uri, an Israeli businessman and a reservist, was
incensed: "How dare the West hold Israel to higher moral standards than anyone else?"

It was often uncomfortable talking to Israelis about the situation, in which so many suffered. I could always leave, get out, never
think about the place again. In theory. The impact of this conflict
goes far beyond just the Holy Land.

"Everyone is proud of their army, whatever the country," Uri
said. "Our pride is no different, except that our army goes far and
away beyond any other army's efforts *not* to harm civilians. We
don't kill those who are innocent of aggression. And if we do, it is
by mistake, and it tortures us when this happens."

I didn't raise the recent killing of Salah Shehadah. In order to
assassinate one man, the Israeli air force had dropped a one-ton
bomb on a civilian area of Gaza, killing sixteen people, nine of
them children, and wounding hundreds. Challenged by horrified
Israelis, the commander of the air force, Dan Halutz, rated the

operation as "excellent," and later, when asked about how it felt to
drop a one-ton bomb on a populated area, he said that the pilot
feels a slight shudder of the plane as the weight is released.

"We go so far, in fact, that we end up losing men because we
use ground troops where other armies would just bomb the enemy
from the air," my companion said. "Do Western journalists ever
admit that?" he asked. Did I know how many times operations
had been cancelled because the IDF had received intelligence that
there were civilians in the area? I didn't. Did I know how many
soldiers' mothers had shouted that their sons would be alive if the
IDF had chosen to use air power against the terrorists, instead of
ground units? I didn't, but I dreaded to think. One Israeli mother
had told me, twice, that "when your son becomes a soldier, every
soldier is your son." You feel and fear for every soldier, wherever
you stand politically.

I had ordered goulash, but found it unappetizing. I made the
mistake of pushing it around the plate. The manager of the bar
was offended and said, "Let me bring you something I *know* you
will like." He ignored my "No, really, thank you," insisting light-
heartedly, "You *will* like it. If you don't like it I'll eat it myself."
And he hurried off to place the order.

"We weep to see the suffering of other people," said Uri, "but
what can we do?" What Israel was doing was self-defense. That
was all. Defending herself against something that I should be able
to understand, after 9/11, a little more clearly. "They leave us no
choice," his voice rising slightly, "they make us do it."

More food arrived, a schnitzel. It lay, limp and orange on the
plate, taunting me. I hadn't had much appetite for the goulash,
and now the manager was watching me. I tried.

"Other countries have experienced terrorist campaigns—the
IRA campaigns on the British mainland, for example—without
giving in to extremism," I said to Uri.

"Very few of you were affected by that," he replied. I remarked
that Andrew's cousin was killed in an IRA attack on a troop of

cavalry in Hyde Park, my brothers' school friend was killed in a bombing by the IRA and my uncle was lightly wounded in the Harrods bombing, and did what he could to help the injured. This cut no ice. "It's not the same. These terrorists are out to kill us because of who we are."

Because of who you are, or because of what you're doing in the Occupied Territories? I wondered, struggling with the schnitzel, but I didn't have to ask.

"It's *because we're Jews*," he said. "They hate us and they want to destroy us. That's all there is to it. And it's spreading. It's a growth—the Palestinian terror breeds terror all over Islam, including al-Qaeda. We have to destroy the terror. We have to free the world from terror."

The manager came over, took the plate from me, and ate the schnitzel himself, standing beside our table.

A few days later I found myself stuck for longer than usual at Qalandia checkpoint. Hundreds of Palestinians stood in line. I watched, from my air-conditioned car, their daily ordeal in the heat, their ears and eyes and shoes dusted with the sand that was kicked up and swirled about, veils and keffiyehs wound across their faces, children on their hips until put down because they were too heavy, then looking up, dejected. After Qalandia, and then the next one, a-Ram, I thought I was finished with checkpoints for the day when immediately there was another—a temporary checkpoint—and we were stuck again. We had all been checked at a-Ram and now we were stuck for another hour and a half only 500 yards further on: a checkpoint just after you got through a checkpoint.

We made dinner that night for a group of friends. One of them, an Israeli public health researcher, talked about checkpoints and Closure. She was saying that people exaggerated their impact, then she suddenly brought it down to me: "You've never had any problems at checkpoints, have you?"

"No." I said. Then caught myself, shocked at what I had just done. I wanted to rewind, tell her the truth: "Yes, I have, I've had endless problems. We all have. Let me start with today..." But it was too late, the moment had gone, and the underlay remained: I am a coward. I dare not say how bad it really is, what it's really like: not just the checkpoints—the closures, the control, the shootings, everything. I can't begin to describe how shocking it is. Checkpoints are irritating for me, but they don't ruin my life: I have a British passport. I have nothing to complain about compared to the Palestinians. But I don't dare be frank about the situation. I don't want to be called "anti-Semitic" for objecting to what the Israeli army does to Palestinian civilians. I want to pretend, all the time—but especially when I'm with Israelis—that none of it is true, that there is no repression, no cruelty, that there are no children shot in their classrooms, no East Jerusalem families turned out of their beds at night—for ever, their homes taken over by settlers. I want to believe that there is a way out of this, that Israelis will be free and Palestinians will be free, and maybe we'll all be better off. But I'd let the smokescreen remain. I had said "no." It's easier.

A British magazine asked me to write a piece about life in Jerusalem during the Intifada. I sent it in, and the features editor emailed to say she liked the piece and that the editor was reading it. Later she phoned to say that the editor "didn't want the politics," she wanted to know who I saw and what my house was like, but not how the checkpoints hindered life. "Privately," the features editor said, "I wouldn't change a thing" but "the reality is, we have to think about the owners." So I cut out most of the checkpoint reality. The magazine was still hit with complaints—many similar to each other, part of an orchestrated campaign—especially after it came out in the US.

During a coffee break at a conference in Jerusalem, an Israeli talked to me about media bias against Israel. We had been discussing the importance of presentation, and the situation slipped in. "Jenin, for example," he said, "was not a campaign against a civilian population, it was a battle between Palestinian terrorists and the Israeli army. Almost all the Palestinians killed were terrorists, and we lost a lot of troops. And yet your British journalists called it a 'massacre.' We were condemned with no evidence to back them up."

"And," he said before I could say anything, "we're also condemned for the closures. The IDF put the checkpoints up in September 2000 to stop Palestinian suicide bombers from killing Israelis."

Two more conference-goers joined in. One, an Israeli, said the first was confused: the checkpoints came before the suicide bombs. The first man looked offended, and carried on: "What government would do nothing while its citizens are murdered? What would any army do about terrorists who use civilians as cover, and children to carry weapons—even as bombers?

"We're condemned whatever we do, however we respond. Even if we took to throwing stones we'd be condemned." He was irked by the fact that Israel has a free press "and helps the foreign media, while the Arabs don't even have democracy, let alone a free press." The PA manipulated the international press, he said. The foreign press has no objectivity—how could it, in the face of threats and kidnappings and when they were made to promise to push the Palestinian line? Anyway the media were more concerned about Palestinians' right to move around freely than Israelis' right to life.

I put in that good journalism and balance need an explanation of the context.

"Precisely. You have to remember it was a *defensive* war that gave us control of the territories—and you have to remember that the Arabs still want to annihilate Israel."* At this, one of the

---

* It is often said that the Six Day War of 1967 was defensive despite the statements of, among others, the then Chief of Staff, and another future prime minister. Yitzhak Rabin, chief of staff, told Le Monde, February 28, 1968: "Nasser didn't want war. The two divisions he sent to Sinai would not have been sufficient to launch an offensive war. He knew it and we knew it." Menachim Begin told the New York Times, August 21, 1982: "In June 1967 we again had a choice. The Egyptian army concentrations in Sinai did not prove Nasser was really about to attack us. We must be honest with ourselves. We decided to attack him."

newcomers muttered about peddling old myths not getting anyone anywhere, and moved away.

The first man pressed on: "Palestinians want the media to show only what that control feels like, how cruel it is. You can show cruelty in a TV report but you can't show context. You'll see scenes of women at checkpoints and endless shots of boys holding stones standing in front of tanks."

"I've seen a few, yes."

"Except it's not that simple. The TV doesn't explain that the checkpoints and the tanks are only in the territories to defend Israelis. When you see a Palestinian child in front of a Merkava, you react. This is all you Europeans see—the innocent against the occupier. And now look—rising anti-Semitism all over Europe. The two are related. It's Israel's right to exist that is being questioned."[1]

"You can't blame the media," said the one remaining newcomer. "It's *what* they're reporting, not how they're reporting it that's the problem."

The next session began, ending our conversation. We went back into the hall and I made a note of the conversation instead of listening to the speaker. Words had taken on a new sensitivity. Israelis loved free speech, and debate, but there were constraints, from the subtle to the forceful. As one Israeli diplomat frankly admitted, "If we hear words we don't like, like 'apartheid,' we stop talking, we won't listen any more." Beyond Israel too, the constraints were rigid. Mention the word "transfer" (the policy of removing Palestinians from the Occupied Territories as a solution to Israel's demographic problems) abroad and people clammed up: "That's absurd," a US diplomat who had served in Tel Aviv told me, "of course that can't happen," and closed the subject. All I had said was that in Israel, even for some cabinet ministers, it was a real debate.

On the way to school one morning Archie, aged eight, asked: "What's a fucker?" We were alongside a car pasted with stickers. Before Operation Defensive Shield began we had seen signs of a campaign launched by the minister of tourism, Benny Elon. He announced that he wanted to remind people of transfer and to remove the taboo. "It is intolerable that the Arabs should think that, every time, they can drain our blood and then we will negotiate with them." He recommended another *Nakba* as a solution.[2] The campaign included interviews on Israeli TV and in newspapers, billboard posters, bumper stickers, and fliers. Some were in English and therefore accessible to us: "No Arabs, No Problem" was a common one. Another stated plainly: "Only transfer will bring peace." On this car every variety of sticker glared. The one Archie had seen from the car window was: "Deport the Fuckers." The increasing talk of driving the Palestinians from the Occupied Territories was acceptable in some circles. Israelis I met were, for the most part, horrified.

Why did the prime minister not object to Elon's campaign? these Israelis complained. His spokesman, Ra'anan Gissin, said Sharon would like to expel the Palestinians but did not believe this could be carried out under the present conditions. "There is a difference between wishful thinking and realpolitik... If the Palestinians would have a change of heart and move elsewhere, okay, but Sharon realizes transfer cannot be done because of the stance of the Israeli public. What Elon is saying is not something that today seems possible."[3] Gissin was a man some Israeli journalists teased (one called him Sharon's "tea-boy") and some Palestinians welcomed as an asset to their cause. When I met him at a Norwegian embassy reception in Tel Aviv, he touched his tongue and said it was his best asset. "I'm a great talker," he added.

Paradoxically, talk, *hasbara,* and "information," were all-important in the business of silencing, extending through every sphere of life, the obvious being the media. There were "issues" at almost every stage of the media's work, with the result that, while journalists saw the injustices played out to both peoples, the Palestinian context was submerged to the point that many abroad were unaware of the military occupation.* Editors in the bureau, editors back home, were acutely sensitive to the supervision of every word and image printed or broadcast on the Israeli-Palestinian conflict. Influence was pushed at every level both at head office and in the field—visits, lunches, informal meetings, questions, friendly advice and not so friendly criticism, threats to withhold advertising, funding, promotion, career: a relentless, tireless program of monitoring and "guidance."

In London a senior editor admitted he had been "brought to heel" by his management, and financially he couldn't risk his position by including unacceptable—to management—balance. A radio journalist told me in Jerusalem: "When I do a Palestinian story my editors are all over me. They tell me I *must* have an Israeli story to balance it, but when I do an Israeli story, there is no such request." Sometimes the journalists applied the silencing themselves: "That editor's visit," said a *Times* correspondent, "was a waste of bloody time. Doing a story on the Palestinians, comes all the way to Israel, and refuses to go to the Occupied Territories. Still did the story though. From Tel Aviv."

One Jerusalem bureau chief was frank. "This is a machine," he said. "It's not just the individuals, the officials, the influential friends. There are endless arms of the machine. There's deciding who gets press passes, who gets recognition as a journalist. There's singling out individuals for criticism. There's pressure applied to individual journalists: complaints are made, accusations placed with the bureau or the paper back home. The journalist would know that he or she was a target and would have to deal with the pressure of 'surveillance' without jeopardizing either organization or career. The balance is tipped against the journalist if the organization is not supportive: the pressure and constraints are sometimes bad enough for journalists to resign."

A Glasgow University study of TV reporting between 2000 and 2002 found that among British students sampled only 10 percent were aware of the occupation. The Israeli perspective, particularly the government perspective, dominated.

The bureau chief went on, "And there's the department in the Ministry of Foreign Affairs set up with banks of television screens, to watch, count, time, assess, and report on each one of the networks 24 hours a day, seven days a week." He was matter-of-fact, "I don't know if the guys watching are actually using a stopwatch, but if they think that you give more airtime to the Palestinian stories than to Israeli ones, or if the way you present the information doesn't gel with their interpretation and the way they want the information to be seen, then they get on the phone or come and see you and tell you so. And then of course you have to defend yourself.

"It is endless. However professional we fancy ourselves to be—and we do, by the way—the result is that we are—how shall I put it?—more *careful* than anywhere else in the world that not one word is out of place, which can't be a bad thing. But on the other hand, it does affect what we put out and how we do it. Yes, of course it does."

As a result of the "carefulness"—the censorship and self-censorship—Andrew and I, and the children too, found ourselves saying unexpected goodbyes. One family moved back to Britain when the husband, Sam Kiley, quit a successful career with the *Times* as a result of wearying criticism and constraints during his Jerusalem posting. He wrote later that while in Jerusalem he was not to refer to "assassinations" of Israel's opponents, nor to "extra-judicial killings or executions," he was to call them "just 'killings,' or best of all—'targeted killings,'" if he had to write about them at all. His editors did not dispute that settlements were illegal under international law, but to refer to this was "gratuitous." On the other hand, "the leader writers," he wrote, "were happy to repeat the canard that Palestinian gunmen were using children as human shields." A story referring to Sharon's "hard-line government" and to a Palestinian village "hemmed in on three sides" by settlements was cut after the first edition: these terms were found unacceptable. And when Sam succeeded in tracking down, interviewing, and photographing the unit in the IDF that admitted to killing Mohammed al-Dura, the boy whose death was caught on camera at the beginning of the Intifada, he was asked to file the piece "without mentioning the dead kid."[4] It was at this point that Kiley decided he had had enough silencing and resigned.

Our second child, Xan, was miserable when his best friend Balthazar left in a hurry. His mother, Alexandra Schwartzbrod, was one of a number of journalists removed from their posts: she was the correspondent for *Libération*. For more than two years she filed story after story with no quibble or query from her editors. Then, suddenly, she was replaced and found herself back in Paris on an unrelated assignment. An investigation of silencing published in *Le Monde Diplomatique* found that one organization systematically accused her of inciting ethnic hatred and anti-Israeli propaganda, until, on July 14, a headline proclaimed: "Alexandra Schwartzbrod is leaving! Our friends at *Libération* have confirmed the rumor with some satisfaction, reporting the internal discussions which ended up with her recall..."[5] When Alexandra returned to Paris she questioned her bosses about why they had replaced her. They brushed her off, unable to produce anything substantive.

An Israeli journalist who worked for a foreign television network told me he found himself, and his wife and children, threatened with violence and death. The threats came from Israelis who despised the way he covered the Intifada. To protect his family he had to move from his house in Jerusalem to an apartment building with security—security from other Israelis, extremists who continued to threaten him and demonstrate against his coverage. He was worried, he admitted, about the state of Israeli society: "We're in a terrible place, morally, emotionally. It's complete confusion. I've never had any pressure from the network, only from Israelis."

Palestinian journalists had other worries, like being granted press passes. Many worked for foreign media and were often targeted. Their reporting was directly affected by the closures:

checkpoints made life so difficult for journalists that they became a real impediment to covering news. "We can't cover the stories because we just can't get there in time any more," said one. "Getting to Jenin has become an all-day journey—even somewhere as close as Nablus can be out of reach."

There was also intimidation. Some was actual: an attempt was made by Palestinians to kidnap James Bennett of the *New York Times* while he was covering an IDF assault on Gaza, and Josh Hammer of *Newsweek* was kidnapped there for a few hours in the first months of the Intifada. Some was manipulated in order to deter journalists from going to hot spots: reports would go out of threats from Palestinians against journalists who were working in the Occupied Territories, but on further follow-up the rumors were found to be baseless.

One Palestinian complained about some journalists' ignorance of context: "Some of these correspondents coming in on short assignments hardly know what region they're in, let alone the substance of what they're writing about. The other day one wanted to go to al-Aqsa and Qalandia. Except that what he said was "I wanna see the Alaska mosque and the Columbia checkpoint." She laughed angrily: "There you have it: between the Alaska mosque and the Columbia checkpoint, we are lost!"

From time to time we would head through Qalandia by night on our way to Ramallah, perhaps for a drink at the apartment of a French friend—all spartan minimalism and blocks of color—then dinner at an Italian restaurant buzzing with young Palestinians trying to lead normal lives, all of them ready in a second to decamp to another restaurant if the IDF started bombing. The atmosphere was not so different from the equivalent Jerusalem scene: in West Jerusalem with Israeli friends drinking and eating well in the quarter off Jaffa Road, its quaintness buzzing with young Israelis having fun. In both places, Ramallah and West Jerusalem, everyone wondering if we would be unlucky and get bombed that night.

For a safe bet, there was always dinner at the Maronite convent in the Old City: parking inside Jaffa Gate, walking through the narrow lanes, not far, around a dim-lit corner to the sound of our padding footfalls on the limestone, to ring a distant bell at a low door and into the fortress of the convent. The sisters' welcome in the courtyard would transport us a hundred miles from any trouble, and we would duck under the arched doorway and into a low vaulted dining room to sit at long tables overhung with bright neon lamps. A feast prepared by the sisters would involve plates of aromatic food, raw filet of beef that I couldn't eat when I had been pregnant, tumblers of illicit arak (aniseed and grapes, distilled somewhere in Lebanon), then rosewater tea—"white coffee"—in white china. Talk all the while, safe unhindered wise talk, from old hands who had watched the situation play out down the years, and finally perhaps an invitation to see the view from the bishop's roof. Then we were out again, into the dark, other, Jerusalem.

On the way back through the alleys, one of the newer hands pointed out a somber truth: getting editors to take a story from Gaza was much easier than getting them to take one from Congo or Rwanda. "Do you know how many blacks have to die before they'll print something back home?" he asked. "Hundreds. We know that every dead Israeli is news, but at least the Palestinians get in the frame in single figures, or tens at any rate." He was bitter, both for Africans and for Palestinians.

And 9/11 had changed the atmosphere for reporting on the Middle East conflict, sharpening racism from blinkers into blindness. It was not just that the bombing of Afghanistan was better television than yet more stories from Nablus or Haifa—"We try to find angles to make it new," said one journalist, "like the Palestinian kids who collect Intifada cards of the 'martyrs,' instead of soccer stars or Pokemon cards"—it was also the syndrome of "them" and "us." "We" had been attacked, and "they" were being bombed back. We, the West, against "them," the Muslims. Never mind that many of the Palestinians being bombed were Christian, not Muslim at all. This was a "crusade." Israelis were us: they looked like us and lived like us. They built skyscrapers like us and liked the beach like us; they liked the same movies and music and restaurants and shopped in the same shopping centers. And in those shopping centers, Israelis were being attacked by "them." "They," we were continually being told, had different values and morals, the lowest of motivations. And besides, they were just, well, *different.* Their dress, their music, the way they treated their children, their women, and the way they ate. They were different. Different from *us.*

Differences, even when superficial or not real at all, were played on, and likenesses ignored. When a suicide bomb went off, we could all see how vile a crime it was. The buses looked like our buses, the restaurants like our restaurants. When a Gazan refugee camp was bombed, things looked alien to some. Tragic, but alien—those twisted piles of concrete, women in long black dresses and veils beating their breasts and wailing, the dusty children, the old men in keffiyehs. Perhaps being "alien" to us, and similar to those targeted in "the war on terror," helped explain why such events often failed to register and were ignored. One Israeli cabinet minister, registering the effects of one wave of IDF bombing in Gaza, said that the scenes of old women and children picking through the rubble afterward reminded him of his grandmother (who had died in Auschwitz). He was excoriated for saying this.

All over the world journalists find much of what they see hard to take, but there was something else about this conflict. Journalists were sickened at the sight of dead Israelis—children, mothers, old people, youngsters, laid out lifeless in or out of body bags, depending on how soon after the event the journalist arrived; and they were sickened by the sight of buried, blasted, collaterally damaged, bombed, and shot Palestinians—children, mothers, old people, youngsters. But, they said, reporting the dead Palestinians was not as straightforward as reporting the dead Israelis.

I saw what they meant in September 2002 when Ramallah came under fire again: I did not get to the office for a while. Tanks invaded Arafat's compound again in response to two suicide bombings against Israelis after a six-week period of quiet. At least, the month and a half was *reported* as "quiet"—in fact 75 Palestinians were killed in IDF actions during this period. "Six weeks of 'quiet,'" muttered one colleague on the phone. "What Colin Powell and the Israeli government mean by 'quiet' is when no Israelis die. Dead Palestinians don't count."

As another example, in October 2003 Hamas suspended bombing. On Christmas Day, the "calm" ended for Israelis when a suicide bomb in a Tel Aviv suburb killed four Israelis, the first suicide bomb since October 4. For the *New York Times*, "The suicide bomb attack in Petah Tikva broke a tense sort of relative calm that has existed on both sides since October."[6]

Yet since October, during this "relative calm," the IDF had killed 117 Palestinians. They had also bulldozed nearly 500 Palestinian homes, leaving thousands homeless. Even at the beginning of the "lull," the IDF attacked Rafah with more than eighty tanks, armored bulldozers, and helicopters, killing eight Palestinians, including three children, wounding fifty-three and destroying seventy homes. In two assassinations a few days later, eleven people were killed (eight were passers-by, including a child and an on-duty doctor) and fifty wounded (eleven of them children). Within a few days the IDF opened fire on three people driving to a family Eid celebration: one and a half hours later the army allowed ambulances through, but by then two were dead and the third moribund. Israeli media said the car had been carrying weapons; the IDF admitted they were unarmed and had been killed by mistake. Only the day before the Christmas suicide bomb "broke the calm," the IDF attacked Rafah, killing nine, injuring thirty-seven (eight of them children), and making 116 families homeless.

Still, for media organizations this was "relative calm" or "quiet."[7] In nearly four years of the Intifada, the longest period when no Palestinian was killed by Israelis had been one week: July 9–15, 2003. Organizations monitoring the numbers injured and dead showed that Palestinians were killed or injured almost every day. The fact that the "calm," in which so many Palestinians were killed and injured ended only when Israelis were killed persuaded some Palestinians that in Western eyes the lives of Israelis were more valuable than their own.

14

Separation

There was a war coming, war in Iraq. As the killing around us went on, we escaped again. Jericho was a frequent choice: apart from visits to Val's house with the Mount of Temptation looking down on us, and ruins of crusader sugar mills and the walls of Jericho below, there was Sami Musallam's riding stables out toward Allenby Bridge, offering horses instead of trail nags, and Hisham's Palace with its famed tree of life mosaic and its star window. On one visit there the children and I met a young Palestinian archaeologist restoring the mosaics. He let us in even though the site was closed, and showed us around, explaining everything. The mountains of Jordan in the distance loomed blue exactly as in the David Roberts lithographs; the children ate tiny apple bananas we had bought in the central square and ran about the ruins in the glow of the late afternoon light, swiping at the green grass pushing through the stones, poppies, buttercups, and blue flowers too, and laughing at the jangling goat bells of the nearby grazing herds. And yet Jericho was also a sad, bewildered place, like so much of the West Bank, its population virtually imprisoned for months on end, its produce also, and therefore minimal incomes for everyone, with not much to do. It was semicircled by a two-meter trench dug by the IDF.

In the heat of the Middle Eastern summer, a couple of months after Operation Defensive Shield, the French consul general and his Cuban wife sent out a general invitation to expats, knowing that we were the only ones allowed through the checkpoints, to stay at a Jericho hotel with a pool and tennis courts. One guest, a consul general from Latin America, headed off like the rest of us, glad of the break and to be away from Jerusalem, but she and her husband, who was Palestinian, had to make a choice: should he ride in the car with his wife and risk being picked on by the checkpoint soldiers, or should he try to sneak into Jericho using the tracks through the desert, being made to feel like a criminal? I saw him later, at the party. I did not ask which option they had taken.

Andrew and I sped down the Jerusalem–Jericho road, the children and Julita in the back, the car thermometer registering the rising temperature as the signs on the blistered rocks outside registered our sinking below sea level. Along the plain to the lone checkpoint that holds in the Jerichites, the temperature was 114°F and the few cars in line weren't moving. In the distance, inside the ring of defenses, an out-of-place high-rise block stood like a giant molar against the soft dunes: the Jericho casino where Israelis had gambled happily before the Intifada, now empty and idle.

We waited twenty minutes, the heat sweeping in dry eddies around us. I got out of the car, in a hot summer dress that stuck to me and stab heels that were soon gritty with dust, and walked across the no-man's expanse toward the overheated soldier who motioned me to stop. It was the heat that dictated, not the soldiers. I walked on up to him and asked "What's going on? Why is no one being allowed through?" Boiled with sweat in his heavy fatigues, he reeled off the reasons: "It's our job, it's the rules, we have to do this." But he looked as unconvinced as I was.

I said, "Surely you could let some through?"

"Yeah," he agreed, wiping the lines of sweat with the back of his thumb as they tracked down into his eyebrows, "but at least we let the pedestrians through first because of the heat."

I looked around at the empty plain, the city hazy in the distance. The Jericho checkpoint was a long, long way outside the city. They were only pedestrians because the IDF wouldn't allow their cars through. By this time it was clear that I was neither a suicide bomber nor a Palestinian, so he said we could pass. "You should have come straight to the front," he said. "What about the others?" He shrugged. I wanted out of the heat, I had the right ID. There was nothing I could do.

We apologized to the other drivers sitting in their hot cars, knowing they would have to wait, perhaps for hours. They smiled back. "What can we do?" they shrugged. *Sumud* again. We slipped through the chicane. And the soldiers were not awful. What they have to do is awful.

Later, by the tepid pool, Xan appeared dripping with blood, his chin split. A Palestinian pool attendant, Khaled, had rescued him and wouldn't let go even though I explained I was his mother, and a doctor, and that I could decide if he needed stitches. He needed stitches. Khaled showed me the way through the quiet sunlit streets to Jericho's hospital, telling me about his career as an engineer. "Not many engineering jobs in Jericho these days," he said.

The hospital was out toward the checkpoint, set away from the desert road in a pool of sand and heat. A gift from a European government, it was new and crisp, but nearly empty. The corridors were slow, with linoleum and a small quiet crowd of people huddled at one end. Again the special treatment—we were guests. The red-headed Palestinian doctor left what he was doing and waved us into a yellow and gray trimmed dock. A couple of juniors watched the doctor, world-weary and dour, as he swung my boy on to the table and peered at his bleeding chin.

Xan all stitched up, I bought him an army hat from a startled stall owner in town—they were used to isolation—and we returned to the pool. It was, Khaled told me, the hottest day recorded since 1947. We sweated out our weekend, dancing in the dark moonlight, children fast asleep.

Back in Jerusalem, as the summer wore off we stuck to the Forest of Peace, with a walk in the first midday cool of the season, and a picnic on the lawn by the former Shabbat café. This had been a small place run by two young Israelis, Josh and his friend, who prepared minted lemonade and huge bowls of pasta for all-comers, Jewish, Palestinian, whatever, and open on Saturdays, hence the name. Then it burned down, mysteriously, leaving a charred shell on the edge of the lawn.

A Canadian journalist lived just above the café on the promenade. Her children were at the lycée with ours, and our boys often played together. One day she called to arrange their next encounter, and suddenly interrupted herself: "This Wall," she said, "is wicked. And guess what, it's Israelis who are saying so."

She had just returned from an assignment: "In the North there's a kibbutz on one side of the 1967 border and a Palestinian village on the other, inside the West Bank. They've had peaceful relations for years." When some of the Palestinian youths started running stolen cars through the kibbutz, the kibbutzniks built a fence along the '67 line, but this caused no ill feeling. In fact the kibbutzniks were proud of their example: "Coexistence is possible; it really works," they told her.

"But now," she said, "a wall must go up to separate the terrorists—all Palestinians are terrorists—from Israel." Okay, the kibbutzniks said, that's one way to deal with a problem, to fence the two sides apart—they had used this method themselves. "But the wall is not going along the '67 border, it must go three kilometers inside. It just happens to separate the Palestinian villagers from their fields, their olive groves, their livelihoods." And those trees and crops the villagers were not separated from were uprooted to make way for the wall itself. She used the word "wall." Later we learned to say "Barrier."

"You know, it's not Western journalists who are complaining about the placement of the wall," she said again, "it's the kibbutzniks. And they're not just complaining, they're mad." By depriving the Palestinians of their incomes, they told her, their own government was turning their neighbors into terrorists— "What else can they be now?" the kibbutzniks asked.

She had seen olive trees being pulled up to make way for the Barrier: "There are 'relocated' olive trees all over Israel," she said, referring to the practice of uprooting trees from the West Bank for replanting elsewhere. "You see the despair on the farmers' faces, and you don't have to imagine the hopelessness." The women and children were scrabbling among the remnants of their groves, wary of the bulldozers, trying to pick up as many olives—the last of their fruit—from the dust as they could. "The Israeli government officials," she said, "tell the kibbutzniks that they don't understand the political and security implications."

It was the first eyewitness story I heard about the Barrier. There had been talk for months, but so many other things had happened that it had been lost in the background, especially with the prospect of a war in Iraq. A year before Operation Defensive Shield there had been reports that Likud had a plan, proposed by legislator Michael Eitan, to erect high fences around Palestinian enclaves of self-rule. "We are not talking about ghettos, people will be able to enter and exit through a security gate," said one of his aides.[1]

The Security Barrier, or security fence, apartheid wall, terror fence—there were many names—grew out of a Labor plan for unilateral separation (in other words a separation without negotiation with the other side). Fostered by Israeli fears and the longing to prevent civilians from being killed by suicide bombs while trying to lead a normal life, the idea gained acceptance. In June 2002, after a spate of bombings that left scores of Israelis dead and injured, Likud accepted that it had not protected Israelis, and adopted Labor's plan to build a barrier, one between Israel and the Occupied Territories. It was to be, as far as possible, impenetrable to terrorists. Teams of specialists were recruited to design and build the structure, a combination of patrol roads, barbed wire, trenches, tracking zones, electronically sensitized wire fencing, and stretches of an 24-foot-high wall of concrete. It would be manned at intervals by soldiers in watchtowers, and monitored via the electronic paraphernalia. The Barrier would help ensure Israelis the "right to life." It would run along the Green Line.

If the last sentence had turned out to be true, the Barrier that Israel built would certainly have had the support of most of the international community, most Palestinians, and a great many Israelis. Instead, the Barrier brought a storm of bitter disagreement and a hearing at the International Court of Justice. Some Israeli commentators were in no doubt that the political and security implications, which the kibbutzniks had been told they did not understand, were straightforward. In their view the Barrier may have started as a security measure, but it became a tool for taking land.*

I saw the wall soon enough, on my first trip to Qalqilya, a small Palestinian town about 45 miles north of Jerusalem on the Green Line between Israel and the West Bank, to visit the hospital's obstetric department. My coworker Laura and I drove behind an UNRWA truck, partly to help us find the way, but also because we thought we might stand a better chance of getting into the town if we were with a supply truck.

It is not far from Jerusalem to Qalqilya but the journey time, as always, was dictated not by distance but by the closures. The cluttering of checkpoints along the direct route through the West Bank ruled out going that way. We followed the UNRWA truck as it went west into Israel toward Tel Aviv, then turned north. The road across the toes of the foothills was being superseded by a new motorway coursing north–south: Route 6, the vertebral column of Israel that would open up the interior to development. The old road, which had itself been the new road not so long ago, was spliced by roadworks for the new motorway. And every now and again there were ruins, remnants of unburied Palestinian villages along the way.

Once on the opened motorway, we found ourselves suddenly parallel with the wall. Here the Barrier can be called a wall because it is a wall. The vast concrete slabs towered over us, dwarfing even

---

The Barrier, declared Ha'aretz, *"hijacked the original idea of a security fence and twisted it into an invasive and provocative fence running deep into the West Bank," confirming that "the networks of settlements to be surrounded by the fence and situated deep inside the territories were always meant to prevent the formation of a viable Palestinian state."[2]*

For a Ma'ariv *commentator, "The pointless presentation of the fence route is part of Israel's general policy; speaking about security yet really intent on occupation, settlement, and annexation. As with the fence, so it is with the territories: Israel's friends would not criticize if it were acting in the security interests of its citizens, but they cannot stand actions like establishing settlements, land expropriation, and annexation."[3]*

the giant construction vehicles still at work on it, smoothing out the skirts of the wall. The skirts were swathes of cleared land, wiped clean of crops, sheds, houses, and humans in order to protect the wall. In some ways, the wall was like other sound barriers along motorways except that its height was so massive, so un-human. And at intervals there were watchtowers.

We began a dance, twisting back and forth. We knew that Qalqilya was on the other side of the wall, but we couldn't find a way in. The lead truck turned across the motorway and doubled back. The driver carried on for a while, then paused to make a call. He climbed down from the cab, raised his arms in a shrug at us, then asked directions of a work crew on the roadside. He listened, climbed back, started up and headed west, away from Qalqilya— then doubled back eastward.

I looked for signposts. There were plenty, but none said "Qalqilya." The map showed it as a big town, a splash of gray on white paper. It existed on paper, but the real town was hidden. We kept driving, wondering. Into the West Bank the road scaled down and became ragged. A checkpoint straddled the road. Settler cars streamed through to their jobs in Israel; all other vehicles waited. More road, and at last Qalqilya appeared, to our left beyond a gash of stripped land. We made a left turn, doubling back again, on to the one remaining road into Qalqilya.

The long arms of the wall had mutated into fence, and the wrists of the fence were tied together at a final checkpoint. This was the pore through which Qalqilya breathed. The IDF watched, controlled. In the line ahead of us sat a line of vehicles, trying to get in. A Frenchwoman left her NGO-marked car in the line and came over to talk to us. She had been there two hours already. "Medical work—they won't let us through. One of the soldiers is insisting." Aid organizations bringing supplies and help to the Occupied Territories were accustomed to being blocked and hassled, "and we're the ones doing the Israelis' job for them— keeping the occupied going," she said angrily. Just then the

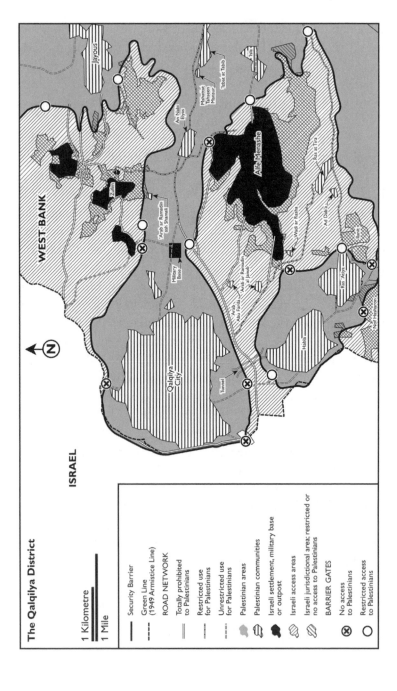

The Qalqilya District

1 Kilometre

1 Mile

Security Barrier

Green Line
(1949 Armistice Line)

ROAD NETWORK

Totally prohibited
to Palestinians

Restricted use
for Palestinians

Unrestricted use
for Palestinians

Palestinian areas

Palestinian communities

Israeli settlement, military base
or outpost

Israeli access areas

Israeli jurisdictional area; restricted or
no access to Palestinians

BARRIER GATES

⊗ No access
to Palestinians

◯ Restricted access
to Palestinians

UNRWA truck, laden with food and medicine, was called forward out of the queue, and allowed through the checkpoint. We made a bid for his slipstream, and eased through. The NGO worker was still trying to get in when we came back out again, hours later. The UNRWA hospital we were visiting was tucked away inside the town. The truck slipped into an improbably small alley, forced an oncoming car to reverse, almost scraping the buildings on either side as he went, and squeezed right, disappearing into a compound. We followed the truck, parked, and were greeted by the staff of the obstetric department. They showed us around the cramped wards and explained that a new wing was under construction. In the maternity ward grandmothers and fathers came up to us, handing out chocolates wrapped in stiff paper, celebrating their new babies' arrivals. Siblings sat by, enjoying the sweets and peering at the babies, then at us. We were finally led back to the head midwife's office. She sat us down and began describing hospital procedures.

Given the restrictions, their policies, procedures, and results were impressive. It was the conditions that were so hard. Many of the staff came from out of town, which meant living and working in the hospital for weeks at a time, hoping that at the end of their month-long shift they could negotiate a ride in an ambulance to get through the checkpoint and home to see their own children. One midwife, Fatima, explained that she lived in Tulkarem, thirty minutes away. Except that now, because of the roadblocks, it was six or seven hours away by five different taxis, and a two-kilometer walk for good measure. They were not complaining about conditions, they said; things were good for them compared with others, and at least the hospital, being an UNRWA institution, was adequately supplied so they didn't have the extra worry of running out of equipment and drugs. As long as the soldiers at the checkpoint permitted.

At one stage the head midwife, who had already spent the morning plying us with sweet coffee, suddenly had a thought. She leaned far out of the office window and called to some invisible person to fetch guavas from the market. They appeared minutes later, and the midwife smiled with pleasure. She sat, portly, homely, peeling the fruits for us, handing us slice after slice, fresh and scented, on the tip of her knife. The guavas we were eating were the last crop Qalqilyans would be harvesting, she said. The trees were on the other side of the Barrier.

The Barrier and the checkpoints ruled everything, she told us, and destroyed everything. It wasn't just the crops that were on the wrong side; it was also the many Palestinians who relied on Qalqilya for services. Cut off from its hinterland, Qalqilya had been condemned to death.

As we drove away from the hospital, I noticed an old signpost near one of the settlements. I could just make out "Qalqilya" printed on it, but someone had daubed swirls of black paint over the word to make it disappear, as though the town would take the hint and follow suit.

After dropping Laura at Damascus Gate, I went home and called Andrew. We arranged a weekend away. There is plenty of solitude to be found in the tiny land of Israel: north to the verdant Galilee or south to the Negev. The Negev sits in a wedge at Israel's base, dotted with remnants of ancient civilizations. Here the Nabateans plied their trade routes, building khans to shelter camel trains from the elements and wild animals as they wended through the desert, loaded with exotic goods, flocks trailing in their wake. Here stood great cities like Mamshit and Avdat, whose irrigation schemes had tamed the desert centuries ago, and now the desert was dry again. We slept in a Bedouin tent and watched the flies change shifts with mosquitoes and then swap back again the following morning.

Later that week Andrew came home in the evening and looked at me as I sat at my desk. He stood there, hand in his hair. I thought someone must have died. A plug of dread balled in my stomach.

"I have to leave."

"What?"

"I'm being sent away. To Senegal."

"Senegal?" Where was that exactly? But at least no one was dead.

UN Headquarters in New York wanted him to spend six months helping to set up its new West Africa office based in Dakar and covering sixteen countries, many of which seemed to be in constant crisis. And then he would return to his post in Jerusalem. So the rest of us would stay. Jobs and schools meant stability, and he would come back every month to see us and to keep his current unit on track.

Everything was changing. In its campaign to free the world from terror, the US administration was linking Saddam Hussein to al-Qaeda. The Israeli government was linking Iraq to the Palestinians, publishing reports of financial aid from Iraqis to Palestinians. Saddam and Osama, Saddam and the Palestinians, the Palestinians and al-Qaeda: all one confusing pot of terror to scoop into and stir about. We, in the middle, were receiving alarmist calls from family reacting to the foment. Time to think about moving back "home," they were saying, guardedly, but increasingly strongly. Being whipped up, they were whipping us up.

I went numbly to Nablus with Laura the next morning. The new posting had been confirmed: Andrew was to go to Senegal in two weeks' time. A civil war had just started in Côte d'Ivoire; there were problems in Liberia, Sierra Leone, and Nigeria. I met Laura at our rendezvous in north Jerusalem, outside a tiny post office on the old road that was now sidelined by the newly finished settler highway and stilled by checkpoints. We couldn't risk driving ourselves to Nablus—too many checkpoints. We would use taxis, and if checkpoints were blocked we would abandon the taxi, walk across, and take another on the far side, then on to the next. People buzzed about us as we waited for the first driver. The staff of the cab company brought coffee, and helped me park my car in an unobtrusive slot in a side street.

I sat in the taxi, thinking about being alone in Jerusalem. My head filled with separation, situation. Nablus is north of Jerusalem and Ramallah, not far, but for many it is an impossible journey. Another impossible distance, Jerusalem to Senegal. Maybe the whole family should move to Senegal for six months. There was a great deal of our research program left to do. The road to Nablus winds through hills of olive groves and almond orchards, pink in springtime with violets under the trees, but now dusty after the long summer. The conflict so visible: Palestinian villages in the valleys, Israeli settlements on the hilltops, squads of IDF vehicles on the road.

The driver, with typical insouciance, quipped: "What's going on here? Anyone would think there was a war on." Laura and I had foreign passports, but the driver, who had managed to get us so far, had no chance of taking us through the notorious checkpoint, Huwarra. We switched to another vehicle. *Senegal,* I was thinking. *It's so far away—and no direct flights.* No driver dared go too near the soldiers for fear of becoming another victim. Soldiers routinely picked on taxi drivers, who might end up beaten up, their keys confiscated, or their vehicle impounded.

Laura knew her way around Nablus, a lattice of the very old and the sharply new, lying in a valley with steep hills looking down on us. We found our way past shop windows of shoes and sheets and plastic toys, up two flights of concrete stairs and into an out-patient clinic. Women sitting with their babies and bellies, and nurses busying round them, looked at us momentarily. The doctors were stoical. They talked of the way the conflict had affected their patients. I wasn't concentrating. I had always thought medical terms were a code, a way of conferring uniformity on to a range of signs, symptoms, and syndromes and what to do about them so that everyone knew, with precision, what everyone else was talking about. Occasionally medical language was for obfuscation: to spare the patient too much frankness all at once. Fluency in the code gave entry into a club of sorts, a club of Latin and Greek roots and stems—why say "blood in the urine" when you can say "hema-turia?" *Senegal? Why did he have to be sent to Senegal?* Here the medical code was for obfuscation of another sort. By using terms like "maternal mortality," obstetricians were able to discuss the dead mothers without confronting the cause too bluntly, and when I tuned into our host, Dr. Salim, he was talking about the "decrease in prenatal care translating into increased peri-natal morbidity and mortality." This code gave him control over the anger he felt at the cruelty of the checkpoints and closures. It was part of a far broader barrier Palestinian doctors put up against their rage. Israeli doctors used the same tools to protect themselves against their anger when they were dealing with the maimings and mutilations inflicted by suicide bombers: the young woman turned overnight into a "monster," her face a patchwork of skin grafts; the children with stumps instead of limbs.

Medicine often means dealing with the cruelty of "nature," its brutishness and inevitability. Sometimes there is also "avoidability" to deal with: the consequences of road accidents, domestic violence, alcohol. But here dealing with the avoidable was exces-sively painful—the avoidability of suicide bombs; the avoidability of death by closure, checkpoint, and collective punishment. Dr. Salim's training and early professional life—in England, as it happened—had not prepared him for his patients dying before they could get to him, to medical safety, "because of the stroppy mood of some Jewish kid with a gun at a checkpoint." There, he'd said it. Then he flipped back into code.

"Pregnancy," he added at the end. "The minute the women here get pregnant they get worried. In Britain when women get pregnant they go shopping; in Palestine they get terrified."

At the main Nablus hospital the midwives were slumped on metal chairs in the delivery room. Six delivery beds were lined up along the oblong room, each had its curtains swiped back against the head of the bed. Two were occupied. The new mothers lay as they had delivered, a sheet pulled up over their pudendae—code again—legs akimbo. One was cradling her baby. Another newborn lay wrapped in pink on a shelf under a warming lamp.

"It seems like a quiet moment," I said.

"If you'd been here an hour ago," said one midwife, "we'd have had you with your sleeves rolled up. Every bed was full and only three midwives, all of us crazy—and it's been like that for I don't know how long."

A laboring mother was brought in and the midwives turned their attention to her. I left, and met a doctor in the corridor outside the room. He was leaning against the wall, holding his head.

"No, today hasn't been a good day," he said. "We had a mother come in at eight and a half months this morning. She had been tear-gassed at the checkpoint and the baby died in utero. I've no idea if this was cause and effect, but for her—well, she'll live the rest of her life hating the Israelis for killing her unborn child."

He told me about his years of training in Russia, and how eager he had been to come back to Palestine and make his contribution. "Now look at me. I haven't been home in a month—I haven't been out of this building in a month. If I'm lucky I might get a ride in an ambulance so that I can see my family. The only other way is to make a break for it across the fields—and I'm not trying that again."

"What happened?"

"Once I did that—me, a doctor—I was running and the army was shooting at me and I knew I was going to die. One hundred percent, I knew. And that very day a pregnant woman had been killed when the IDF fired on her ambulance—they claimed the ambulance hadn't stopped... and I just thought, what's the point?"

"Was it during curfew?"

"What are you talking about, *was it during curfew?* What's curfew?—I'm talking about a doctor trying to get home from work and a woman in labor trying to get to the hospital. In an *ambulance.* I nearly get shot, she gets killed. By what, why? This is our city. It's miles from Israel. They put on curfews so we can't move *in our own cities?*"

"Suicide bombers have come out of Nablus and attacked Israelis..."

His face opened in astonishment. "You find this amazing? Can you really be amazed if some Palestinians want to hit back at the occupation, the collective punishment, the daily killing? Every day they kill us, every day, and no one says a thing in your world." He looked at me. "Are you one of those who thinks Palestinian blood is cheaper than Jewish?"

"I..."

He didn't want to hear. "Come *on*, does anyone *know* what's going on here? Do people know? Tell me honestly. Do they understand *at all?*"

"They..."

"Where else in the world would you find a quarter of a million people *not permitted to leave their homes?* Sometimes we can't even leave one room—for day after day after day—in one room. In April we couldn't go near a window. We would be shot. *Think* about it."

Curfew... the thought of being trapped... Trying to imagine what it meant to be locked inside the house when the children were begging to go to school... or just begging to be allowed outside, through the door into the open air. What did they do, hour after hour, day after day? How did they survive the suffocating feeling, hearing the church bells calling them to prayer, or the muezzin from the minaret, putting a hand on the door to push it open and run out—but then stopping themselves? Knowing their families were a street away, or half a town away, yet trying to explain to the children why their grandfather would not be coming with the traditional presents and food for Ramadan. Explaining to my own children that their father would be going away for work, that was easy enough. But explaining to Palestinian children that Christmas had been canceled and there would be no celebration, no games or singing, no gatherings, because the IDF wanted them all to stay at home and not to leave the house, not even to get food, or to go to the doctor if they got sick?

Oh God, and on the other side, the Israeli children whose fathers or mothers or brothers, sisters and grandparents were dead, blown up. Or maimed, mutilated in the suicide bombings. All the avoidability. And the interminable suffering.

On our way out of Nablus Laura and I bought *shawarma*— lamb sliced off a spit into a fold of bread—in the market. We walked a little way into the kasbah to take in the ancient buildings, the heavy stone and delicate carvings,[4] then wandered about the fruit and vegetable market, found a *servees* taxi to take us out of town and rejoin our own taxi.

At the checkpoint one soldier was shouting with rage at anyone who tried to approach. No one was going anywhere. It is very hard to know what to do when you face a soldier in a fury blocking your route home. After all, you have to get home. Laura and I moved forward and he screamed at us: "When I tell you to WAIT—you wait, and you WAIT until I tell you to stop waiting. Do you understand!" Storming up to us, still shouting "Get back! You *cannot* pass."

Gently, I asked, "Until when? You see, I have to pick up my children from school..."

"Until I *say* you can pass! It doesn't *matter* what you have to do." His face was puce, his helmet bouncing in his rage. "Now GET BACK! Understand my words?" Not only his words: two vehicles driven by settlers sped through. We turned to go back but were beckoned forward by another soldier, who looked at our passports and gave us to understand that his colleague was having a bad day. A third soldier came up, calmed down the screamer and led him away, motioning for us, the foreigners, to pass through.

On our way home the taxi driver pointed out his village and its olive groves, and the fields along the way that were his but that he no longer dared harvest. Settlers had attacked him, his family, and his crops too many times and they had given in. "I cannot work my land now," he explained. "If I try to harvest my olives, the settlers shoot at me, and the army does nothing." Along the road we looked up again at the tops of the hills, at the settlements up there, looking down on us.[5]

There was one weekend left before Andrew left for West Africa. We flew to Istanbul and visited Andrew's cousins who lived there. I was still thinking about curfew. I had thought curfew was simple. Simply locked indoors. The Nablus doctor had said they were being shot at while in their homes, and a number of people had died that way, including Lana's mother. It wasn't just prison: prisons offer some safety. Here families were not safe even inside their own houses.

In prison, but you have to fend for yourself, forced to remain indoors for days at a time, a brief release for an hour or two, and then several days' curfew again. In the grinding heat of the Middle Eastern summer, a family of maybe fourteen people in two rooms, with no running water and no air conditioning, you run out of baby milk because the army didn't tell you how long the curfew would be, and anyway you have no money to buy food, or milk, as you haven't been allowed to work for months, and if you step out you may be shot on sight.[6] Then, if someone does fall sick, you have to hope they don't get too sick, because if they do then you *have* to risk breaking the curfew to get help. And the worry. And all the time the children scream because they are hungry and bored and just maddened with frustration.

The words of one Israeli woman came back to me: "You know what the Palestinians do under curfew?" she asked. "They make babies."

Andrew's cousins showed us some of the glories of the Ottoman Empire, the vast mosques and churches with exquisite mosaics. They gave us lunches in the souk and sumptuous dinners overlooking the Bosphorus. How was a curfew "lifted?" How did the message get through to each family that they had a couple of hours to stock up before curfew was imposed again for days on end? Palestinian TV stations were one way, but sometimes the IDF cut the electricity. There was word of mouth, but you couldn't move; mobile phone calls, but how to charge the batteries with no power and anyway the messages were often wrong. People missed the lifting, or went out when the curfew was still on. Some were shot getting to the shops. The Nablus doctor had laughed sourly: "You know when the curfew is on again because you get shot at in the street, or your water tank is pumped full of holes. The IDF can make it very clear like that."

Before we left Istanbul we had a drink with the historian Norman Stone. We chose arak (*raki* in Turkey) and sipped its aniseed strength as we talked. Curfew came up again—curfew that had lasted in some places for *eight days* without one break. Was he aware, I asked of any other curfew so draconian in the last hundred years? The professor thought it unlikely. "Maybe in Eastern Europe toward the end of World War Two."

Landing in Jerusalem again, we drove home and saw Sholto take his first steps—four of them—in the garden. He didn't like to try walking inside the house on the glassy marble tiles. He liked to be outside on the limestone flags. In the fresh air.

15

Days

I took Andrew to the airport. We made up nonsense about seeing each other again in a few days' time, and said goodbye as if that were true. We knew it would be at Christmas, six weeks away. Then we said goodbye again.

The children and I spent the rest of the day away from the house. I felt a sense of relief that almost outdid my sense of loss. Now that Andrew had gone, we could start to look forward to him coming home again. Was that it? He had been so loath to leave us; we had been so uncontrolled. The children said very little, as though questions and their answers might make his absence harder to bear. We hid our missing him at the house of an Israeli friend. Nothing could have been more peaceful than spending a couple of hours with Alison in the playground near her home, talking about the origins of an ancient Jewish festival, and wrapping ourselves against the descending cold. In the dusk we went back to her house, where her son pulled out a box of toys for my children, who played on the carpet. We drank minted tea, and threw ourselves into their normality.

In the village that evening, there was a gathering around *nargila* (hookah) and coffee. There had been another Palestinian attack, this time on armed settlers in Hebron. "Settlers," Alison had said to me, "but still, how stupid can the Palestinians be?" At Maha's house, the spools of *nargila* smoke hovering over the stiff chairs, the mood was angry: "The onus is always on us Palestinians."

I caught hold of our dog, who had appeared from nowhere, bouncing between the men and the bulbous waterpipe. Amer, with his pathological fear of dogs, joked as usual: "Dog, I'm going to cook you one day." I used rescuing her from Amer as my excuse to leave, and went down the few steps to Rasha's house to find the children drawing pictures with her and her sisters. We went down more steps to our house, read stories, and talked about Christmas. There was a late party that night; a French journalist, François, was turning forty. I had planned to stay away and be lonely, but then thought, what the hell: bury it. I arrived at a big vaulted room full of François' Palestinian, Israeli, and expat friends, and then dithered. Turning around to leave, I was swept up by a Palestinian friend, Shireen, elegant in black leather. Knowing that Andrew had just left and what I must be thinking she pulled me into a dance: "You're not leaving. Come on, stay and enjoy yourself."

Paul, a Palestinian-American friend, joined us. All three of us were hiding in different ways, and we buoyed each other. Shireen was being pursued by an American who found it hard to understand the constraints she lived under: divorced, living with her extended family. At the same time she had decided to send her children to boarding school in Switzerland, away from the situation. Paul was bemoaning the Palestinian leadership's reluctance to confront the meaning of "the facts on the ground."

"Why not put it to the Israeli people—head-on, no messing about—that Sharon's road leads only to a one-state, binational solution?" He was using code, political, not medical this time. As opposed to the two-state solution, the one-state binational solution meant creating one state, comprising Israel and the Occupied Territories, with the two nations, Israeli and Palestinian, living as one. "If Israelis could grasp that they are being pushed into the end of the two-state solution, and that they'll end up with us as the majority *and* with citizenship, wouldn't they change their minds?"

Another Palestinian sat down on a bench with Paul and me, watching the women drift in and out of the dancing. He added his frustration to Paul's: "The PA won't talk about the one-state solution because that means giving up on independence. The Israelis won't talk about it because it means the end of the Jewish state, and they say that this is what we have planned all along, using it as a cunning way to obliterate Israel. But, Christ, what choice is there now?

Thanks to the settlers and their infrastructure, we're locked so tight into the State of Israel we're like a bug in concrete."

Somehow I wasn't escaping at all; Shireen saw this and laughed at the men. "Okay, okay," they said, "let's dance," and we went back into the dark colors of the vaulted Pasha Room of the American Colony where François was smiling, dancing in a circle of women.

I went home very late, creeping in and hearing the baby cry as I closed the front door, feeling more grateful than ever to Julita for providing such consistent care and love for my children. I had heard Israelis and Palestinians debate a single state before. I had listened to people say that the one-state solution had always been the only equitable answer. To others who said they would not care what the country was called as long as they could return to their village and lands and their culture unfettered, and that they would defend these against anyone. I had heard Israelis and Palestinians reach bravely beyond the hate, beyond the challenges of nationalism, into a place where both would be permitted to join their neighbors and form an economic union or regional confederation.

Michael, an economist, wrote to me in an email: "What is it that is being silenced? The two-state solution (Israel and Palestine) was never a real proposition, it has just suited everybody to pretend that it was. Israel has never pursued policies that could help a 'viable' Palestinian state come about. And without Israel's help, how can any of us imagine the Palestinians can establish a proper state? The more thoughtful of the donor nations know this, yet this 'two-state solution' remains the main reason for providing billions of dollars in assistance. It has suited everybody—including the PA, who understandably wanted the money to keep flowing, even if they too have serious doubts that they will ever be allowed an independent, viable state—to maintain this fiction. Now," Michael ended, "we face the prospect of a unique experiment in human misery—Gaza—being replicated on the West Bank: huddles of human misery, kept alive. Hardly an independent, functioning state."

Within a few days of Andrew leaving for Senegal there was more killing and more impunity. Another suicide bomb exploded, this time on the outskirts of Jerusalem. Hamas dispatched a bomber to choose a bus bringing people into town during the morning rush hour. Obediently the suicide bomber timed his explosion with accuracy.

"Do you think he even saw that the bus was full of kids?" asked one parent at the lycée. "What kind of mind is it, taking out those innocents on purpose?" said another. The bus was full of people traveling to work and children coming to school. Eleven people were killed. One of the lycée children was among the fifty injured. He had recently arrived from France with his mother, new immigrants to Israel, and the explosion injured him horribly.

The teachers were angry and grieving: the boy was so badly wounded that he was not expected to live. The conflict had come deep inside the school again and set off waves of hate among the children, and then other ripples. One girl triggered a political row between two boys, one Israeli and one Palestinian, by telling one that the other had said, "This is what your people do." The teacher who sorted out the fracas let out a slip of bitterness, saying that the girl was "teasing" both of them (she was thirteen and a half). "She's a *salope*, like her mother," said the teacher.

The new French consul general's wife mobilized help and comfort for the wounded boy, and for his mother who was attempting to cope alone. The school switched its attention from trying to organize transportation for Palestinian pupils imprisoned behind barriers by the Israeli army, to coping with an Israeli child gravely injured by a Palestinian terrorist. And all the while keeping a lid on the roil of loathing in the schoolyard. Xan and his friend Freya, aged six, galloped up and down the school courtyard oblivious to the sorrow. Their older siblings were subdued, caught in the middle of something they didn't want to understand just yet.

The killing on both sides was close again. Later that day we heard that a senior UN official had been shot by an IDF sniper in

Jenin. The news that an expat had been killed spun around in the wake of the news of the boy injured in the bombing. The dead and wounded Israelis were, rightly, big news, splashed all over the world. The death of Iain Hook, a former British army officer, was barely covered by the US media: it made page 34 of the *Washington Post*.

Iain Hook was in Jenin trying to rebuild Palestinian homes razed during Operation Defensive Shield. IDF tanks, armored personnel carriers, and helicopters had attacked the refugee camp once again, and Palestinians had fired back. The IDF continued to fire into and around the local UNRWA compound even after the fighting stopped. An Irishwoman living in Jenin saw Mr. Hook after he tried to evacuate women and children from the compound. He had left the compound waving a blue UN flag. The IDF had shouted via megaphone: "We don't care if you are the United Nations or who you are. Fuck off and go home." The Irish witness then heard that a small boy she knew had been shot dead and others wounded by tank fire. She tried to field other Palestinian children away from the line of fire—they were throwing stones—while pleading with the army not to fire live ammunition at unarmed children. She was shot in the thigh. Some of the children dragged her out of the continuing Israeli fire.

Israel Radio reported that a soldier shot Mr. Hook as he came out of an alley from which Palestinians had been firing earlier because he mistook the object at Mr. Hook's ear, his mobile phone, for a hand grenade. Then the army said that two soldiers fired at him while he was inside the UN compound because they thought he was holding a gun. And that the gun battle had not ended at the time he was shot. In fact Mr. Hook was inside his office when he was shot. There were stories, rumors, about the red laser point of the sniper's sights homing in, but no one wanted to think too much, especially those who worked in the Occupied Territories. The UN reported that the IDF had delayed the ambulance for nearly an hour. The IDF denied this: they said they sent an ambulance immediately, and that he was already dead by the time it arrived. The Irish witness saw Mr. Hook brought into the hospital alive. He died a few minutes later.[1]

The IDF's invasions continued and Bethlehem's turn came round again. That same night a fundraiser was held for the town's Peace Center. I went dutifully to the Seven Arches Hotel in Jerusalem for the "Bethlehem Ball." There was a minute's silence for all the victims of the conflict. The room was full of people dressed in satin and lycra talking about death: the Israelis killed in the bombing, the schoolboy, the Palestinians killed in the retaliations, and the 50-year-old Briton. On top of the sadness hovered the usual questions about the inconsistencies of the IDF's stories, and why—*why*—a sniper would shoot a UN worker.

The dancing appeared frenzied, as though frenzy would erode the futility: fundraising for Bethlehem children on the day the tanks went in again. I sat between two British diplomats, both professional and both brilliant, neither immune to the despair. Not dispassionate or buttoned up: professionalism only sits so deep. People from Tel Aviv were appreciating the change just as we in Jerusalem liked to escape to Tel Aviv. "How nice not to see any of those fish we eat for breakfast," said one. I was missing Andrew, hearing his voice in my ear, feeling his thoughts in my head; friends asked if I was all right and to call if I needed anything, anything at all. Of course I was all right; I was fine. The whole point of everything was bleeding away. Our friend Michael saw all of this and led me away, on to the dance floor. Father Jerome Murphy O'Connor, leading Pauline scholar, known to everyone as Father Jerry, led me into a stiff ballroom posture, confronting me with his ample form and the question, how do you dance with a monk? My conversation slipping into carelessness, like everything else.

And then in the morning I switched for a moment to positive again, running up to Government House to hand in our passports for new Israeli visas and seeing the Dome of the Rock pour a gleam into the morning light, its Hebrew University backdrop in shadow. I let myself linger along the promenade, but was then downed again at the words of an early crop of American tourists. They were looking out across the valley, a valley full of hundreds of Palestinian houses, home to thousands, and then came the guide: "All this is Jewish land, as far as you can see. Don't let anyone tell you otherwise. They'll try, but it is *not* true." Silencing in motion. I had heard it so many times before.

That morning the children felt unjustly treated because of my down—how children despise unfairness. They were low. Every day each one asked: where is Daddy, when am I going to see him, when's he coming back? Catriona, three years old and pining, was the worst. I emerged from my room one morning to the sound of her quietly crying to herself, "Daddy, Daddy, I want my Daddy." It wasn't because I was listening—she didn't know I was there. Julita found her in the kitchen one day with the phone in her hand. Catriona explained: "I am phoning Daddy, because I want to see him. I'm going to be a good girl; I'm going to say hello to him all the time and hug him." She was blaming herself for his being sent away.

We went to the Old City thinking it could be diverting to hunt down white teeshirts for the school play and Turkish Delight dusted with confectioner's sugar, and to run in the narrow alleys and around the archaeological gardens. Instead we were coiled up in the crowds and had to push our way through, so we gave up on souk life and Byzantine ruins.

Hell, I thought, let's risk a movie. The boys and a schoolmate we picked up along the way were thrilled: *Harry Potter* at the cinema inside the Jerusalem Mall. The child's mother later ribbed me for costing her a ton of money, she said, by taking her son to the mall. Like me, she had a "no mall" rule because of the threat of bombs. As a result of my giving in, she had to let the boy's older sister go there too, but for shopping, not *Potter*. Many shekels later she and her daughter had left the mall, lugging bags of new clothes and shoes, and, like me, guilt at having taken the risk for no good reason.

I had dinner a few nights later with Alison and her family. Being Friday night, it was special for them, but not from a religious point of view. It was a gathering, a rhythm that they maintained each week, to sit down together and talk. Her husband Avi was more relaxed even than his normal relaxed self and played the fool, pretending he had done the cooking. We talked about risk, and the rules we laid down for ourselves to deal with the risk, and then breaking the rules of Israeli life, "You have to take risks, sometimes," he said. "We'd all go mad if we ruled out everything. For the kids, I agree, it's different."

And we changed the subject gently. Israelis were coming to terms with two terrorist attacks in Kenya and another at a Likud voting station. But, as Avi had said, when something happens you check that no one you know is involved, and then you carry on. Their oldest son talked about his day; he had attended the wedding of a friend, "religious people," he said. "It was full of joy and the usual wedding feelings, except that over all the wedding finery there were M-16s. That was odd."

It was not so odd. Not now. Israeli normality had been filled with guns for some time, even at weddings. We had been surprised from the beginning by the number of guns in everyday Israeli life, and not just handguns for policemen but machine guns in the hands of civilians. At every shop, bar, restaurant, cinema, theater, or club we opened our bags by reflex as we went in. The bag-check normality had become part of saying hello. "Shalom, here's my bag, how are you?" Security guards were a growing business, stationed outside any place a bomber might pick. Perched on stools outside the doors hour after hour, the guards had a lonely, dull life, except that it was sometimes deadly frightening.

As the days passed, the French-Israeli schoolboy injured by the suicide bomber held on to life. Parents followed his progress each day, hearing that he was breathing on his own, had setbacks, infections, then turned a corner again, enduring operations and more infections and pulling through it all against the odds. It took weeks, but he made it back to school: a triumph of courage and good medical care.

I had seen bomb injuries in Afghanistan, working with a team of mine engineers and medics in Baghlan province. The Afghan surgeon had been highly skilled, debriding the wounds the mines inflicted, usually to the feet and legs, which were frequently blown off. If he managed to get the patient stabilized, the most difficult and painstaking part of his work was cleaning out the particles of dirt and shrapnel forced up into the wound by the blast. Often the nursing staff were little help, and I would find him dressing wounds on the wards by himself, saying the nurses were "useless." Worst of all, he had little anesthesia and had to use products like ketamine, which was popular with vets in Britain.

On Bagram airbase I learned a little about mines and wondered about the minds that designed them, intending not to kill, but to injure. The calculus was simple. Injured men, I was told by ex-Royal Engineers who were training Afghans to clear mines safely, have to be picked up, transported, treated and cared for. Dead ones cost the enemy less time and effort.

In Israel there were no supply problems, and nurses were skilled. In this conflict both sides' operating surgeons dealt with particles of dirt and metal blown into their patients' bodies. And neither side stopped at mere destruction. Both had methods to maximize injuries: Israel's army sometimes used fragmentation, anti-personnel tank shells and flechettes (internationally banned in case of civilian injury)—once in Gaza they were fired at a group of boys playing soccer: nine were hit. And Palestinian suicide bombers and their handlers packed their bombs with screws, bolts, and metal objects to inflict as many injuries as possible. There were burns as well as blast injuries, and rehabilitation, years of fighting to achieve some normality again.

After the Bethlehem Ball I visited hospitals in Bethlehem and talked to more surgeons. Samir, my helper, had organized a list of doctors and my aim was to gather information about their current hospital policy and protocols. But they were not so concerned with obstetric or other protocols. Instead they were worried about caring for their patients under the continuing siege. "We haven't been able to give them fresh vegetables or fruit for days, and we haven't enough milk."

Samir and I dropped by the Church of the Holy Nativity and sat for a while in the ancient silence. A Greek Orthodox priest approached. I thought his concern was spiritual but I was wrong: he had come to check that I was not malingering. Very tall, very beautiful, with long flowing black hair and robes, he explained that he had had his fill of siege and refuge-seekers since the Nativity Church standoff during Operation Defensive Shield. At that time Palestinian fighters had taken refuge in Christ's birthplace, itself under siege, with civilians and activists who sneaked in under the eyes of the IDF and caused havoc. When a family had recently sought refuge in the church he refused: "*Not again*," he told them.

As he told the story—"They said they wanted to die here"— he stood up, he was a towering Hercules of a man, saying: "I asked them, 'Are you ready to die?' 'Yes,' they said, 'we will die here.'" Taking off his black cap and robes in front of me, he said, "I told them, 'Right then, I kill you *now*!' and I went like this..." lunging toward me, hands outstretched, aiming at my neck.

"They ran," he said. "They ran away, right out of the church and they have never come back." I was not surprised.

Samir took me away from the towering priest and the church and through the town to meet his cousin, a businessman in Beit Jala. The idea was to have a break from our day; instead it was a confrontation with yet more reality. In the store were dozens of chocolate items, all red and gold and Christmasy. I must get some, I thought, I'll never find them in Jerusalem. There were bells, stars, Father Christmases, and angels. Ranks of them. "That's nothing," said Samir's cousin. "Come up here and see the warehouse." We followed him up the wooden stairs, unhindered by banister or balustrade. At the top we stared: row upon row, pile upon pile, of chocolate figures. There were Santas by the candied dozen, angels in dark, milk, or light chocolate by the host, squadrons of red-robed melting elves and bell upon unchiming bell.

"Oh Hassan, what did you go and do?" said Samir, knocking over a mountain of chocolate money and starting an avalanche.

"Don't worry about that," said Hassan, steadying those elves that were still upright. "I ordered all this months and months ago. One of those American envoys was in Israel and I thought the Israelis would have to listen to the Americans and lift the siege and freeze the settlements. I thought there'd be negotiations again. I never thought the Israelis would be allowed to carry on and on and on like this. Believe me, I thought long and hard. I invested a fortune in this fucking chocolate. All of it. Then when I realized the Americans would give Israel the green light for anything—Operation Defensive Shield, remember—I tried to cancel the shipment, but they wouldn't let me. Italians. It arrived a few weeks ago, the shipment. Now I have to sell all this before it gets warm again—I can't afford to chill this much stock—and no one has any money. They can't even buy flour and rice."

Back in Jerusalem a week later everyone dropped their normal routine and assembled at UNRWA's depot in Jerusalem. There was to be a memorial service. People came from all quarters and organizations: diplomats, journalists, aid workers, religious leaders, politicians and water specialists, agronomists and doctors, nurses and teachers. Car after car drove in through the security gate, parking in the forecourt abutting the huge warehouses from which tons of aid were distributed to the holed-up Palestinian refugees. We stood in a semicircle in the open air in front of the warehouses.

The service was in memory of UNRWA workers killed in the conflict. Father Jerry and a Palestinian prelate led the prayers. Richard Cook, UNRWA's West Bank director, gave a short address.

"We planned this memorial for Iain Hook and two others, little realizing that by the time the memorial took place, three more UN workers would have been killed." He said how much it had meant to UNRWA and to the families of those killed that so many people had sent condolences. I felt guilty that the one time I had had a chance to give my condolences to the Hook family I had allowed myself to be talked out of it.

One American aid worker said he wished the UN secretary-general "would just come here and give a speech to both sides saying you cannot kill my people, you cannot do these things, or something, anything... There was such outrage at the killing of Daniel Pearl in Pakistan, but where is the outcry now," he asked, "when the IDF kills a Briton who's trying to help refugees?" His anger grew, "Those dumbfucks in Congress who think UNRWA sponsors terrorism—my God, their ignorance is outdone only by the damage their statements cause. Damage to Israel, if they only stopped to think."

The mood was bitter. Everyone felt the pointlessness and the injustice, the impotence. "But," said Richard Cook, "we will go on feeding the needy and helping them as much as we can. We will go on doing our job." All that the humanitarian workers were asking, he said, was that the IDF allow them to carry out their aid work in safety, without risk of being killed or injured. It was a short, very poignant service.

On my way home I stopped in a peaceful, untouched suburb of Jerusalem to do some errands. There was a cake shop run by an English émigré: her cakes were worth several journeys. I parked my car, which carried license plates marked UN"P," for personal vehicle, in a side street. As I got out a woman saw me, ran up, and started shouting in furious Hebrew. She appeared to be Orthodox, with her cloche hat and long, covering clothes. I didn't understand what she was saying and must have looked blank. This incensed her even more.

Then she launched into perfect American English, spitting: "You bitch! You dirty bitch. You UN bitch—get out of here!" Her rage was spraying all over me. In my head I was still at the UN memorial, thinking about the British family getting ready for

Christmas, without the dead father.

I said nothing and tried to disengage without engaging. I walked up the hill toward the main street. She followed me, cursing as she went.

"You BITCH! You *whore*! Dirty *dirty* bitch!" she went on, keeping up alongside me. I hurried; she went faster. By the main road she was trotting, breathlessly spitting out her insults. On the main street more people were about, and some began to stare, others walking on by, embarrassed. She didn't stop, but kept shouting that I was a bitch and that I should get the hell out. My heart was thudding, but the outer me was calm: her anger was so out of control that calm was the only thing to be, especially after the sadness of the memorial.

The cursing went on and on, building to the climax: "You kill our soldiers." She looked relieved to have spoken the words. But it was a surprise to me: unarmed UN personnel bumping off IDF soldiers? And I'd just been to a memorial for five UN humanitarian workers killed by the IDF. What was she thinking? I gently tried, but couldn't get an answer to how it was that she thought the UN killed IDF troops. All I heard was more accusations of whoredom and harlotry in my ear. She followed me all the way along the road, shouting more obscenities as she went. Those people who caught my eye looked sympathetic.

And then she said, "You UN are for the Palestinians. You love the Palestinians. You are for the Palestinians and *against* Israelis."

"No," I said, speaking for the UN for once. "The UN is for the Israelis *and* the Palestinians." I wondered whether to try to start... how to explain, perhaps, that one of the UN's mandates was to feed, clothe, shelter, and educate the Palestinians made destitute by Israeli military activity over the years, and continuing now. To lay out that there was a difference between UN *workers*—agronomists, doctors, water specialists, political scientists—and UN member *states*. That people who work for the UN don't represent or even share the views of the member states, and that even though a number of those member states took an anti-Israeli line, it was nothing to do with the individuals who worked for the UN.

But she had stopped, suddenly silent, quieted. Her shoulders dropped as her vitriol ebbed. She turned about and left me alone. Her anger had run its course, and she looked weary as she walked away. I listened to my own breathing and swallowed the gorge of frustration and emotion.

An Israeli who had heard the shouting came up to see if I was all right. "Perhaps she was related to one of the three IDF soldiers captured on the Lebanese border," he said.

"Maybe that was it," I said, glad of a reason. But the conflict again: how to explain that you can want to see justice for an oppressed people and still be pro-Israeli?

There was bitterness toward the UN dating from the original Partition Plan of 1947, though not from those whom the results had deprived of a state. It was Israelis who were angry with the UN, and it came out from time to time, as it had done to me just then.

"One reason many Israelis dislike the UN is because the UN's job is to protect the Palestinians dispossessed by the war of 1948–9." The speaker was one of the many young Palestinian lawyers recruited to help the PA prepare for statehood. "The UN is a constant reminder of Israel's violent birth," she explained. Some people, "perhaps forgetting the strength of a refugee's longing," she said with care, "argue that the refugee 'problem' would just fade away without 'the interference' of the UN and the Arab world." Lebanon, for example, could let the refugees integrate instead of denying them all rights and making them subsist in a pitiful state. "Israelis would like the issue of the Right of Return to just 'go away.' They say the world is full of refugees—history is littered with them—and eventually they blend in. But not here, and they say it's the UN's fault." UN resolutions uphold Palestinians' right to return to the homes they fled or were driven from and, according to this viewpoint, the UN perpetuates not only the refugees' misery but also violent anti-Israeli feeling.

Before we left New York we were introduced to a Russian-American couple who had lived in Jerusalem. "You will love the Israelis," they said. "Israelis like nothing better than a rip-roaring debate with criticism flying in all directions. Then at the end you all make up and go home friends again." They were right, even though I started with a disadvantage—I was UN by marriage, and many people saw the UN as an anti-Israeli institution. By the UN's very composition there is an automatic majority—the Arab states, Islamic countries—that uses it as a battleground to attack Israel. The result has been more resolutions passed against Israel than against any other nation—the 1975 resolution stating Zionism was a form of racism and racial discrimination, repealed in 1991, was only the most painful example.

"We can accept criticism," said one Israeli. "We welcome it. And given the Intifada we expect it. But we would like to see every other country subjected to the *same degree* of criticism. Do we really deserve more censure than Syria, than China?"

She went on: "When we see Europeans taking the same line as anti-Semitic countries—when we see Syria a member of the Security Council—when we ask ourselves where are the resolutions condemning suicide bombing, we see a problem with the UN. Don't you?" I did. She continued: "How can an organization with such an institutional bias against Israel play an honest role in promoting peace between Israel and its neighbors?"*

*Palestinians would also talk about bias, laughing in their resigned way about US impartiality. At a rundown exhibition of paintings by young Palestinians, with every canvas and installation a shout against closures and the director sitting in fear of another raid by the Israeli authorities trying to close down the gallery and commandeer the records, one artist had painted a US flag in among the debris. A small group looked at the work, talking about the role of the US. Most of the comments were bitter unsubstantiated jibes, but one was armed with fact. She made one point: that throughout the administrations of George Bush senior and Bill Clinton—twelve years in all—Middle East policy was effectively run by Dennis Ross. That he subsequently became head of the main pro-Israeli think tank in Washington, linked to its lobbying organization, AIPAC, was, she felt, as good an indicator as any of Ross's impartiality.

Apart from being the target of a steady trickle of harmless gestures, like printed posters held up by drivers at traffic-lights—"UN unwanted bodies—GO Home" was a typical one—UN personnel faced other aggression. Being picked on in airports, subjected to body searches, being held up unnecessarily at checkpoints especially if the UN worker concerned had an Arabic name, being pulled forcibly out of vehicles, despite Israel's according the UN diplomatic status, being searched and threatened, tires slashed and physical abuse—these were among the many things UN workers and their families put up with. One Italian living on her own in a smart area of Jerusalem was subjected to a long campaign of abuse and intimidation, including having bricks thrown through her car window and messages plastered to the glass accusing her of being a Nazi ("UNazi"), warning her to leave or face the consequences.

Most UN workers took these to be a result of the anger of a small minority of Israelis. The majority was friendly and helpful, especially if treated that way in the first place. I had just as many encounters with Israelis helpfully pointing out that I had a flat tire or had left a brush on the car's running board as with Israelis telling me to sod off or that I was unwanted because the car carried UN plates.

War and separation were testing, but the days' duties, errands, work, and routine were grounding. More nighttime parties that morphed into daytime stupors, or into daytime parties, that dealt with the evenings and momentarily blanked out the panic—war panic, separation panic, daily-danger panic. Julita was our strength and calmly refused to be panicked. Sholto, all of one year old, was found stirring the toilet with my cell phone; we presumed that was the end of that. Yes, said the agent at Orange in Talpiot, having tried his best to dry it out, I did need a new phone. Mr. Strinkovksy, the violin-maker, loaned us a violin after Xan tried simultaneous fiddling and roller-blading in an enclosed space. He spun on his wheels, flailed for a second, fell back, sat on his violin and snapped its neck. There were bikes at the shop and boys to pick up from soccer. Impressive match, the other parents said—except that Xan was being rough and had tackled a girl, switching to rugby instead of soccer, and then had carried on tackling when she was on the ground. The coach, Kim, was kind. She said it was because he was bored.

The pizza ritual had broken. It had become—or I finally accepted that it had always been—too big a risk to sit there, much as we liked to. Instead, I picked up takeout pizza in flat boxes from the pizza store—kosher—and talked to the boss. Shaven-headed and hardworking, he was affable, relaxed, and always welcoming. His wife had been pregnant at the same time as me, and we laughed that I had only just won the race to give birth. He understood when I guiltily explained why we weren't going to stay to eat our pizzas. He shrugged his shoulders and said he hoped we were wrong.

I met Julita and the children at Liberty Bell Park, where we ate the pizza and ran relays to the replica of the Liberty Bell in Philadelphia, symbol of independence and freedom from foreign interference. There were spaces for biking and roller-blading, courts for basketball and volleyball and a wooden ship to climb on, but tensions surfaced even in the playground. A bunch of older boys shouted at Archie in a language he didn't understand and he answered, "I don't speak Arabic." They, wearing kippas and clearly Israeli, though not to him, were furious as if he'd known what he'd said, and pushed him around, yelling, "Don't fuck with us, kid."

He took refuge beside me. We went home via the bike shop to collect the newly repaired bike and buy some oil to maintain it.

I couldn't get to work in Ramallah again. Curfew. I needed work.

Father Christmas came early. He carried six medium-sized cardboard boxes and one large plastic one. Each was marked with our name. The big one was for the baby. "What are they?" the children shrieked.

"Gas masks."

"Gas masks for Christmas?" said Xan. "Wow!'

He was too young to understand. Gas masks were being issued because of the coming attack on Iraq and the possibility of retaliation against Israel. There were so many out-of-the-ordinary things to explain to the children. It was as impossible as ever to prevent the children hearing stories. After more than two years of Intifada, they now asked why children and women were killed by soldiers as well as by the air force. They liked to have things clear in their minds; they liked lists, categories, and answers. And they were wising up to weaponry, becoming increasingly sophisticated. What weapons do the Israelis have now? Do they have more planes? Warplanes? F-16s? Tanks? What kind of tanks? Merkavas, Abrams? What weapons do the Palestinians have? Do they have planes now? Warplanes? F-16s? Tanks? Merkavas, Abrams? Why not? How many on each side have been killed? How many boys? How many girls?

They knew all about the suicide bombings, and they hated them. "Why do the Palestinians do this?" they asked. They knew that one of their schoolmates had been injured in the attack of mid-November and was critically ill. And they often talked about the bomber who set himself off right outside the school, his head landing in the schoolyard. "Not his whole body, Mum, just his head," they repeated. They knew about "martyrs": the Palestinians in their class often talked about martyrs. For them, martyrs were still superheroes.

I spilled one cup of coffee too many over my computer keyboard. After a piano lesson Archie and I headed to Rosh Ha'ayin near the Green Line to get a new one. The Apple dealer in Jerusalem had closed down: "It's the economy," the agent said, "there's not enough business these days." I had been told the store we were looking for shut at five o'clock, and it was a long way to go for a keyboard, but with no computer, no email, I was cut off. We reached the town and drew up alongside a pedestrian to ask for directions. She took pains to explain exactly how to get to the industrial zone we were aiming for.

The directions were good, but I didn't follow them properly. We swept down a slip road and found ourselves on the settler road heading for Ariel, well inside the West Bank. We were on the wrong road but there was nothing I could do about it—there was no exit: mile after mile without a side road or turning. We had been waved through a checkpoint just after the slip road and that was when I remembered that for once I hadn't brought my passport so maybe they wouldn't let me back through the checkpoint.

And this was a settler road for settler traffic, and settlers were a target for Palestinian gunmen. I had never been frightened in the West Bank, but now I felt afraid of being shot at, and I was sweating. Archie was lying across the back seat—that was something. He was reading, asking from time to time why we weren't there yet. The road went on and on with no way off or out, like a tunnel blanking out the land, taking us deeper into the West Bank, until we were almost in the settlement of Ariel. At last, there was a turning point. I turned around and headed back.

When we did finally arrive, the computer store was closed but there were three men left in the building. They took pity on me when they heard I'd driven all the way from Jerusalem. They tried to fix my keyboard (all their stores were locked so a purchase was impossible) and when they diagnosed that it was only the mouse that ailed they gave me one of theirs. And then when I'd left and was trying to buy Archie something to eat from a stall outside the store, they stopped their car beside us to make sure I was all set to get home.

16

Two Zoos

The winter frittered on, the chill, the damp, and the sluggishness overwhelming, but it was better than panic. Now that it seemed certain there would be war in Iraq, all we had to do was wait. I tried to take the children out of Jerusalem each weekend; if it was warm enough we plumped for the beach north of Tel Aviv because it was simple to organize and the children enjoyed the sea and the sand. When Andrew came back on leave we decided on a trip to a local zoo. We had toured the big Jerusalem version—the triumph of garden and Ark and biblical animals—enough times for it to have lost its edge. We had heard that Qalqilya, whose obstetric hospital I had visited, also hosted a small zoo. It would be less impressive, but it offered a picnic, a day out of Jerusalem, and a few animals, so off we went.

There were four carloads of parents, children, and singles, and we gathered at the central Jerusalem apartment of Peter the Australian and his wife, Penny. Peter reverted, uncharacteristically, to his military background and laid out a plan.

"Right, guys, listen up. I think it would be best, all things considered, if we all make our own way to the checkpoint on the Modi'in Road, and rendezvous there. We can then follow the lead car—better be me, I reckon—and head for Qalqilya after that."

The convoy of families headed away, around the West Jerusalem YMCA, through the rainy Jerusalem streets, up the old Nablus Road, and on to the new network of highways.

We passed through the checkpoint and parked on the other side to wait. Children swapped places and parents to neutralize the age/gender tensions and minimize the question of who listened to what music.

We waited some more. Where was Peter? Eventually someone

tracked him down on his mobile phone: "Hey, where are you guys?" he asked cheerfully. "*We're* nearly there." Despite his coordinating plan, he had taken Route 1, leaving the rest of the convoy waiting at the rendezvous—on the Modi'in Road.

He may have been nearly there when we called him, but he still hadn't found the way into the town by the time we caught up with him. A number of us had been to Qalqilya before, but it had been difficult enough to find it then and things had not improved: they were worse. We knew we were close but there were still no road signs to Qalqilya.

"Look, there's the zoo!" one of the younger children suddenly shouted. "There's the wall all around it. That must be to keep the lions in."

There it was: the massive concrete wall flanking the highway. It could have caged in King Kong. The children began a debate: what animal could get over such a wall? A giant kangaroo, a blue whale? "If you had wings you could get over it," said the smallest helpfully.

We found our way eventually. The red roofs of the Israeli settlements crowned the hills around us, and there, sheltering in their lee, was the old town and its minarets. As we followed the Barrier's great length and turned off the settler road toward Qalqilya, the children realized that the wall was not there to keep the animals confined. We soon came to a standstill in front of the fence, looking at the fortified gap.

The bald reality of the Wall/Barrier hit home again: the one way in and one way out for 45,000 people (and they were passing into and out of Palestinian territory) was through this single, Israeli, checkpoint.

The soldiers on duty manning the gap in the fence were an odd group alongside our gaggle of families on a day trip to the zoo. They could have said the same of us. Youthful soldiers were swamped by their heavy fatigues and all-in-ones for warmth against the cold, helmets lashed down on to their heads with thick chin-straps, machine guns over their shoulders. To pass the time while the soldiers checked our passports, we looked out of the car windows at the space around us. As we waited, people on foot came up to the checkpoint and asked the soldiers at the barricade for permission to pass. One by one they were told "No"—we didn't know why—and each of them turned round to walk slowly back again. One old man, on a donkey cart, had trouble persuading the donkey to retrace his steps.

The soldiers examining our papers were lodged behind a waist-high, concrete counter. Sometimes a more friendly soldier would foray out to meet the supplicant Qalqilyans. To reach the window of our car they had to emerge from their den for a moment. At one point a van loaded with cauliflowers drew up to the row of concrete cubes across the gap. The driver circled the van so that it was end on to the cubes. Another vehicle, a bigger truck, appeared from our side, the side of the outside world. This too reversed up to the cubes, so that the two trucks were end to end. Men emerged from inside the vehicles, leaped up on to the open back of the van, and began lobbing cauliflowers into the empty truck.

We were watching the IDF's back-to-back process: all goods came and went this way. This was also how Qalqilya was fed. No truck was permitted to enter directly. The now-loaded truck and the emptied van drove away, to the outside world and incarceration respectively. And then a soldier lumbered up to us and waved us through, handing back our clutch of foreign passports.

The road into Qalqilya was lined with clipped, drum-shaped laurel trees, giving an aura of wealth to a place that was not wealthy. The streets were lined with shops, now sealed up and silent. One or two, processing car parts, were still operational. Skeletal cars were banked up behind the streets, giving an end-of-the-world air to the place. All the cars had been run into the ground and would be broken down into smaller and smaller constituents, recycled until they were used up.

Further in, toward the center of town, there were restaurants, again mostly closed up. Before Intifada 2000, these restaurants had been popular with Israelis. Fear and the checkpoints would have made Palestinian towns off-limits to most Israelis even if they were allowed to enter the Occupied Territories. Two Israelis were murdered at one of these restaurants after the start of the Intifada. The many suicide bombings and other acts of violence made the idea of entering the West Bank unthinkable for most Israelis. Except for the settlers, to whom the West Bank was now home.

I thought of our home in Jerusalem—only that morning we had driven past a herd of goats grazing in the wild thyme, and horses being exercised along the tracks by small boys with smiles of freedom on their faces. A few days before I had seen young men riding jumpy Arab horses along the verge of the new Mount of Olives tunnel road, a tunnel to transport Israelis swiftly under East Jerusalem. The horses leaped from verge to tarmac; ignoring the rules that everyone else had to obey, they cantered along the road as though it weren't there.

And here we were, going to the zoo. First we took a closer look at the wall around the humans. It wasn't hard to find, its great height like a dam at the end of every street. On top of everything else, Qalqilyans said they missed being able to see the sun go down each evening. Val, who had known Qalqilya well over many years, had described how she had recently found herself stuck inside the town like a beetle trapped in a child's game, trying out one road after another only to come to a halt every time at the pitiless wall.

Qalqilya had been a market town, a hub of husbandry. The ring of concrete and wire had now been set tight around its perimeter, like a rigid collar hard up to the town's chin. There had been no question of fencing their land in with them; it was cut away. The flow of produce from the town had dwindled to a few loads every now and then. Even where there had once been nurseries near people's houses growing a range of shrubs, fruits, and vegetables, now there was only a barren emptiness, bulldozed by the IDF to protect the wall, their wall, their "security measure." There were moments living here, frequent moments, when you succumbed, not to the silencing, but to disbelief. The truth was so incredible that, even though it was happening right in front of you, it was still almost impossible to believe. So it was with the Barrier.

Some Israelis complained that it was Israelis who were being imprisoned. "What people fences itself in?" asked one member of the Knesset, "This takes us back to the days of the ghetto."[1] To mark the scale of the wall we walked up to it and gazed.

While we were gazing, we were shot at, twice. The shots warned us to move back. At first we didn't understand what was happening: bullets overhead don't always register to people unused to being shot at. Even living in Kabul, when the mujahedin fired rockets on the city almost daily, I had never actually been shot at. We lurched to a slow realization that there had been a noise from beyond our normal range, and from somewhere the notion sank in that it might have been gunfire. A second shot. Now the noise made sense. A Dutchman ducked involuntarily, leaving his arms where they had begun, his body dropping so that he looked for an instant like a rag doll hanging on a line, but a living rag doll, starting to run in the same movement.

We moved back and looked to see who had fired the shots. The area looked manless. A few children from town had watched us head for the wall, hanging back at some magic but now explained line. The wall stretched away in both directions, skirted by its attendant mud desert. But then we saw bulges in the body of the wall: the watchtowers. It was from these that the shots had been fired. The towers were rounded, lowering keeps, capped with low-domed concrete roofs, with narrow slits for the soldiers to peer out.

We gathered the children quickly and headed for the zoo, an ordinary, well-kept little zoo with limited space for the animals. It enclosed bears, leopards, a giraffe (there had been two, explained the keeper, but one had died in a cloud of tear gas during an IDF attack on the town), a lion, crocodiles, birds, and monkeys; the lion roared, the hippo came to the fence and yawned open her mouth to show us her vast, fleshy palate, and the giraffe stretched his head over the fence to be fed by the children.

Qalqilya too had become a zoo whose inmates also had to be fed from across a fence. Now that the Barrier divided the town from the outside world, farmers from their land, and the populace from their vegetable allotments and water supplies, thereby leaving citizens dependent on humanitarian aid, many had quit, often relocating to other Palestinian towns, all of them under closure and frequent curfew. "Voluntary transfer" was working: the mayor of Qalqilya reported that up to 20 percent of its citizens had already left. Those who stayed behind, often turning from belief in coexistence with Israel to Islamic extremism, survived thanks mainly to aid provided by the UN and the EU. These organizations were, in effect, subsidizing the Israeli occupation. The alternative was to let the Palestinians hunger behind what an Israeli commentator called "the Starvation Fence."

We retreated for lunch: a Palestinian national dish—falafel—from a café on the main square. It is also an Israeli national dish. So much closeness and yet, at the same time, such infinite separation. Each culture vying with the other for claims as earthy as the origin of foods; we once heard an Israeli exclaim that he had no idea that they had falafel in Cairo.

A van drove past selling gas canisters, ringing out its tinny call tune. At the falafel café I met a lab technician who could no longer go to his job in a nearby town because he couldn't get a permit to leave Qalqilya. "Now they are building this wall, they are slowly continuing all the time, flattening everything near it, all the gardens, all the homes. The Israelis have killed everything in Qalqilya: the businesses, the agriculture, travel, study, universities, and schools. And at our holy feast of Eid al-Adha they raided the town and killed three people. One was a boy, only eight years old."

As we left the town our nine-year-old asked if the ambulance we saw being searched at the checkpoint would be allowed through or not. I asked the soldiers. They spoke no English, but the two Palestinian ambulance workers looked at us and said that yes, they were being allowed through—today. "No problem," they smiled, and went on showing the soldiers the contents of their ambulance. My son turned to me and said, "You know, today was okay, I like animals. But zoos—I don't like zoos at all."

I looked out of the window at the checkpoint. "I know the Qalqilya case," one diplomat had said to me after my first visit. The Qalqilya "case": he was using code to distance himself. The "case" of more than 40,000 people locked inside a human zoo. And we were all hiding from the truth of it, the cruelty of it, by blocking it from view at best or numbing it when we had to confront it, with excuses and professional language.

Andrew left again, back to his new, African, world. The children learned to capitalize on my increasingly late nights—my distancing from the days. Knowing that I felt guilty at being up late in the morning, they would launch themselves at my bed, me slow and sleepy, with cries of, "Let's go to the beach!" which I could rarely face. Jerusalem's altitude kept it colder than both the coast and the Jordan valley: we lived on a spine of chill between two welts of warmth. One Sunday, instead of the beach we went to Nabi Musa, where Muslims hold that Moses was buried. It sits in the Judean desert, white-walled and square, with rows of low domes set off against the yellow dunes and stark blue sky. At Nabi Musa we met the bearded mullah who worked part-time there and part-time at the al-Aqsa Mosque. He showed us around, not minding that the children swarmed irreverently. We walked through the compound, inspecting his chickens and sheep as well as the tomb of Moses. He described to me the drug programs he was running, taking in addicts and rehabilitating many of them, slowly, carefully. Drugs were increasingly an issue for Jerusalem authorities.

Halfway through our tour the boys decided to be Catriona's horse, and disappeared into the desert. Archie carried his sister up and down the dunes around Nabi Musa, Xan in pursuit, two lanks of boyhood charging down the stony dunes clutching rocks that they were sure were rock salt. Xan clashed the rocks together, trying to create slates to write on.

I followed them away from the shrine, walking on into the Judean desert toward the scarp that looked down over the Jordan valley. The folds of rock rolled away, and the stillness settled around, broken only by the occasional war noise from the children. Some say the desert is the easiest place to find God, should you happen to be looking, and that it is no accident that the desert plays such a frequent role in religion: temptation, contemplation, mountaintops, and messages. Hiding away from the new and frightening, like the Essenes, just down there in Qumran, 2,000 years ago.* Was that what the Gush were doing now? Here in the dunes, scuffing soilless rock underfoot, separation looked appealing; running away from modern life, being protected by a different system of rules, rules you don't have to question. Here you can convince yourself that the land is empty, at least in tiny patches, and, if you want, you can exist in the biblical dream for a moment: the goatherds, the oases, the domes, the past. Then you turn your face, back to reality, and head into the new settler-only road system that bypasses the goatherds and the towns and villages where they live.

Israeli democracy was brewing elections again, two years after Sharon had been brought to power for the first time. The Labor party was fielding Amnon Mitzna, a former general who had served under Sharon—and had publicly questioned his military decisions—and was now the mayor of Haifa. Haifa was a success story, the beachside city that had proved coexistence between Jewish and Palestinian Israelis was possible.

I went to hear Mitzna speak in a conference room near Yad Vashem, the site of Jerusalem's Holocaust memorial. In the dark and the rain I parked the car and wound my way through the secu-

---

An ascetic sect originating in Babylon, who lived apart as a reaction to religious laxity and dedicated themselves to perfect observance of the law, the Essenes were the scribes of the Dead Sea Scrolls.

rity system. There were guards everywhere but nothing odd in that. The huge room was full of activists and journalists, recent immigrants and old hands, the occasional observer like me. It was an Anglophone meeting, but Mitzna's English was not spruce. There was no demagoguery, and he seemed misplaced on the political stage. He was a mild man up against the titan of Sharon: time, place, and politics against him.

"We must let go of Eretz Israel," he said carefully. "We have to take responsibility for what goes on around us. We have to separate ourselves from our enemies by building a fence... to prefer our own problems to occupying three and a half million Palestinians against their will... we must live in the real world. It is time to say 'enough.' If we don't separate, we will lose either our majority or our democracy."

There were no illusions in the hall: too many Israelis were too angry at Palestinian methods of resistance for Mitzna's message to penetrate the majority. We stood up at the end, and "Hatykva," Israel's haunting and beautiful national anthem, rang out, overpowering. Nahum Barnea, chief commentator for *Yediot Ahronoth*, greeted me on the way out; "No," he said, "I don't hold out much hope for anything these days. Things are really very bad."

A few mornings later Roni, the manager of the café near school, was making sandwiches and *'afurch* as he did every day. Some parents would come in—harried—before dropping the children, others would come in afterward, more relaxed, and would sit for a while. Some of us did both. We would take five minutes, or twenty, exchange news, take stock. The television always sat up high, playing either soccer or the news: the World Cup and the suicide bombings. The station was in Hebrew, and Roni would often translate for those with no Hebrew. This morning he saw a group of us sitting at a table with a pile of Hebrew papers left behind by another customer, trying to work out who was who in a newspaper tableau of Israeli politicians. It was just before the election and he decided to give us a course: Israeli politics 101.

We asked him, "Roni, come on, who're you going to vote for?" He ignored the question. Instead he picked out a photo of Sharon and said, pointing: "This guy is shit because he'll make me go in the army."

We laughed.

"And this guy," his finger on Mitzna, "is also shit because *he'll* make me go in the army. So I don't vote tomorrow. This country is shit."

"Come on, Roni, be serious." He shook his head, leaned over us and opened a newspaper. One by one he went through all the stories in the paper, explaining why he thought his country was shit. There was constant war and violence with the Palestinians; at this he simply threw up his hands in a gesture of hopelessness and exasperation.

Then, "Look at this," he said at the stories of domestic violence, "and this—and this," at the rapes and wife beatings. "You finish beating up the Palestinians when you go off duty and then you feel bad about it so you beat up your wife and maybe your kids as well."

There were stories of the economic crisis that had made so many people desperate: "You finish in the army and you get a job or maybe you don't and you land in shit and you can't even afford the shit you need." And a piece on the increase in suicides, especially among soldiers: "When the shit gets so much—too much to take any more shit—so you want to put an end to the shit."

And there were pages of sport: photographs, results, and reports. The obsession with soccer and basketball: "Because it's easier if we forget that everything else is shit except that."

Finally, on the back page for us, the front page for him, there was a photomontage of all the big names in the election. He pointed from one face to another, saying, "This guy is shit. This one is very shit. And that one—what a shit *he* is. This one is shit shit shit."

He was winding up the tutorial. "And *this* one," pointing to Effi Eitam,* "is the *shit* of the shit. He put me in jail in Gaza two

---

* *Ex-general and now a far-right Likud minister.*

times because he told me to break the arms and legs of the Palestinians and I refused. So he put me in jail one time for sixty days, and then another time as well." He finished with this, looking at us.

That night an Egyptian diplomat gave a party, typical of the parties that went on most nights, all for the same reason that the Israelis were so fond of soccer and basketball. Unlike other parties this one had a serious side to it: screening a documentary about the Palestinians. All the guests had to roll up their hedonism and sit somber to watch the video, which had been brought by an expat who managed to combine bacchanalian abandon with vivid, clear analysis of the political situation, and within minutes of each other. There were many who did both but most needed a few hours between the two to disengage the hats.

I found the video hard to watch. The facts were there: the occupation, the repression, the broader impact of the conflict. "What are you going to do, keep quiet about it forever?" asked a friend visiting from Rome, with all the new anger of a visitor seeing the situation, and the wall, afresh. I asked him not to be combative when he met my Israeli friends. A group of them were having a party later that night and I was taking him along.

"Living here has immunized you," he whispered. He accused me of seeing the reality up close, and railing against it, but "the process of immunization makes you tell yourself 'don't say it too loud,' speak gently, tell people what they *want* to hear, don't use words like 'ghetto,' keep on the right side, don't ostracize yourself by saying what they don't want to hear.

"And then one day you'll have had enough of being party to the injustice, of sitting opposite Palestinians, listening to their daily gruel and being unable to say anything except that you're so sorry they've got problems. Hiding what's happening does no one—Israeli or Palestinian—any favors."

The documentary was about the obvious, not the hidden. There was no code, and no hiding the context. There was also footage of tied-up Palestinians kneeling on the ground during the first Intifada. Behind them stood IDF troops and these troops were breaking their prisoners' arms. One soldier held an arm horizontal, another hit the arm with an implement, a gun butt or a large stone. But arms are difficult to break, they don't crack under the first blow or the second or the third sometimes. You could see the resistance, the elasticity in the living tissue. The soldiers had to hit harder, and harder, and then the bones would snap. And the Palestinians knelt in the dust without hope, pain screwed into their faces. What Roni had said was no longer just a story. There were the deformed arms and the faces deformed by pain. And I saw Roni's face, distorted with distaste, disgust, at what he had been told to do by his commander, Eitam.

Then, slam, came another suicide bombing, sent by Hamas, killing 17 people and wounding 53 in Haifa, en route to Haifa University. Now what about distaste and disgust? Broken bones and broken lives—hundreds of them. Two months earlier, on January 5, 22 people had been killed and more than 120 wounded in a double suicide bombing in Tel Aviv. That attack was carried out by two members of the al-Aqsa Martyrs Brigades, helped by Islamic Jihad.

Sometimes I talked to people to put out the reality, sometimes I kept things to myself, choosing not to join in the clusters discussing the looming war in Iraq and Bush and gas masks at the talking points in the rhythm of the day. The situation and its concentric rings remained wrapped around our family, always. I sent another email to Andrew, telling him the details of our life, commenting on the details of his life in his emails, touching on but not wholly understanding his liberation and how badly he wanted to share it with us, and ending feebly: "We miss you. When are you coming—Catriona wants to know."

17

Countdown

We were leaving. So much for having control of my life—it was entirely controlled by outside forces. Andrew had been dispatched to another job a continent away in a matter of days, and we had thought it was to be temporary. The decision to have him stay in Senegal took a while to filter through: he wouldn't be coming back to his post in Jerusalem. The West Africa job had become permanent, so it was now up to me to pick up the children and our lives, leave jobs and schools, and move ourselves out of Jerusalem to start again in Senegal.

There were troubles elsewhere in the world, after all. The fighting in Côte d'Ivoire had forced the evacuations of missions, embassies, and NGOs, mostly to Dakar, and the international schools had filled up with refugee children. There was no space for ours. I was going to have to "home school" three children for the summer term, and was staring at the prospect of being "*la maîtresse*" in a strange place where I knew no one at all.

I didn't want to leave Jerusalem. Not at all. Something about the place had burrowed itself into me and I had lost the desire to hurry off to a new life. It was absurd to think of not going. Andrew was counting the days, searching Dakar for a suitable place for us all to live. He looked at house after house, picturing us on the stairs or running into the rooms of each one until he found a house where the children would have space and that I would come to think of as "home," a home where we would be free from checkpoints, bombs, hatred, shootings. And there was war coming to the Middle East, imminently.

Yet I was loath to leave. I tried various delaying tactics. I wanted to finish my work and I wanted the children's upheaval to be as smooth as possible. Better to wait until the spring vacation, maybe the UN would send Andrew back to Jerusalem after all, there were essential things to complete, our *life* is here. The US administration's determination to remove Saddam Hussein was working against me and I was losing my campaign to draw out our departure: the security argument was taking over.

I didn't want to quit working at al-Makassed Hospital with Dr. Ibrahim. Our work was going well and I was learning from him. He was a Muslim who had heavy criticisms of Islam, followed the code but not the faith, and awaited independent Palestine. One day in the hospital canteen with the rain outside chilling the drafty room, he said, echoing so many other Palestinians: "It might take 3,000 years but we'll do it. We have Palestine inside us." He was a fine gynecologist and obstetrician and a good friend; we still sat and discussed cases, him teaching me from his broad experience of every imaginable complication, as well as many that were hard to imagine. My leaving meant we had to wrap up the current stage of the childbirth project and pass it on to Rita's team. I had to get it into a fit shape to hand over.

I explained this to Andrew. He didn't like the delay, but he understood. He understood things I didn't see about myself, and he had never believed in coercion. Perhaps he also understood what it was I felt but could not explain. He said that he had hated leaving for two reasons: leaving me and the children behind, and abandoning his work colleagues in Gaza who had no choice but to stay. What I did not yet understand was his sense of freedom, what he described as his "liberation." His flight out of Tel Aviv to his new posting was, he later admitted, his escape from what he knew was an ugly reality where truth, reason, and people's well-being played a role secondary to a mindset splinted by obsession and the desire to be seen as victor. And it had taken being pulled out of all this and dropped into a new job thousands of miles away for him to see this clearly. Like so many others, he had believed something would change, that the rule of international law would be upheld, for the good of both sides. Like so many others, he had left without seeing the change that he had thought must happen. Instead the situation was worse than ever.

Now our roles had reversed. We had a pact about danger and a pact about death, but we were still afraid. Now Andrew became the worrier. He called again and again to talk, and to check up on us, and emailed more frequently still. Once he called just before leaving Senegal for the Nigeria–Cameroon border, knowing he would be out of contact for two days.

"Where are you?" he asked, concerned.

I admitted I was in Ramallah. He was immediately alarmed, but then became distressed when he heard shots being fired in the background. "Please, get out," he urged.

"I'll call you back," I said, moving away from the source of the noise, but by the time I was back in Jerusalem and able to make the call, he was in-flight and incommunicado.

Family back in Britain also called, sounding increasingly nervous. At the beginning of February my mother-in-law said, "You must be packing up,"—but quickly enough for me not to have to answer. Then my father-in-law took over: "So, when *are* you leaving?"

"At the beginning of April," I said.

"Isn't that rather late? The balloon's about to go up." The Haj was ending on February 15, and the war would begin after that, maybe allowing enough time for the pilgrims to get home first... He predicted March 19.

I began to repeat what people had told me: that the risk of being hit by Iraqi missiles in Jerusalem was so small that some of the Tel Aviv embassies were actually relocating there. After all, even if the Iraqi regime had the capability to launch an attack on Israel, Jerusalem would be hit, said the military analysts, only if a missile went wildly astray. The risk of Iraq aiming anywhere near Muslim holy places was very low. Intelligence in Jerusalem also held that even if there were any biological or chemical weapons available to be launched, there wasn't much, if anything, to launch them on. What could there be—scuds? These had been old in the 1991 war with Iraq. Now, if they existed at all, they would be doubly old and buried in sand.

Families were being split up, sometimes for the second time. Governments and agencies were evacuating spouses and dependants, asking them to leave their jobs behind and pull their children out of school. Risk blended with fear: once separated, imagination and news reports would add to the crescendo of danger. After evacuation, being allowed back again was uncertain, and though the military campaign was expected to be brief, post-war planning was known to be unformed and the situation might therefore remain unstable. "We've been trying to get the Americans to think about the post-war phase," said one British diplomat. "They just aren't interested in what comes after."

The UN had paid a price for evacuating families at the beginning of the Intifada and their threshold for evacuation was higher as a result. Now I had a call from a UN security volunteer. Her message was specific: we were to evacuate the following week. She started by asking to speak to Andrew. As our warden, I thought she might have known that he had been posted to Senegal four months before. She was confused.

Closure of a kind was handed to me, at the hospital one Saturday. There was a deluge in Ramallah on what turned out to be my last day of work there. We had scheduled a meeting on a Saturday because it was the only time available that everyone could meet before Eid, and the threat of prolonged curfew hung over Palestinians. The meeting turned suddenly from work to farewell, with presents and thanks from the department.

"But I haven't—we aren't going," I said, pulling on the tassel of the embroidered cushion they had given me. "Not yet, at any rate."

Rita smiled, explaining gently, "But the war is coming. You'll be sent away immediately. And God knows what will happen to us all. It's best we say goodbye now, while we can."

The small study we had started together had turned into a three-year project. Laura, Rita, all the team, talked about the data on Caesarian sections at al-Makassed, the database we had compiled, the information on more than 10,000 births, and the possibility of ongoing studies. But, they said, even from afar I would be able to keep up some involvement. It was a strange feeling for me: I had had no idea that it would lead to this. It would be incorporated into a regional study on childbirth, they said, and all those long conversations with Dr. Ibrahim had helped set up a relationship with Birzeit University that would now carry on. They were building me up, easing my quitting, for my sake. Rita knew what it was I was leaving and understood. All the faces around me, what did they see? A coworker? A friend? Someone who could opt out and start again somewhere else at a moment's notice, passport in hand, life on hold, life in a set of packing boxes, but not a refugee? And what did I see, in the rain and apprehension, the walled-up future, and a blockade on academic freedom? I wondered who was helping whom; I was the one being looked after.

I went back on the DCO road: the longer route but one on which foreigners were given preferential treatment. All my colleagues were tramping back across the Qalandia checkpoint in the drenching rain, Scottish weather, unable to come with me in my dry car because they knew the soldiers wouldn't let them through in my vehicle, and *insisting* that I shouldn't go through Qalandia for their sakes because the lines were always so long. I could take the quicker, foreigners' exit out to the east. There, the plastic-covered soldiers were kind to me. One went to great lengths to inspect my passport while holding it out of the dripping weather inside the shelter of my window. He turned to the pedestrians behind me, sodden under failing umbrellas, and bellowed at them to stop and wait.

I paused on the other side of the checkpoint for a while and looked back at the soldiers making the pedestrians wait in the mud and rain, all the while letting the cars through first. The cars carried other expats, aid workers, diplomats, and perhaps even the occasional Palestinian with a foreign passport. Some of my colleagues had foreign passports but refused to use them on principle. Freedom of movement in a country, they said, should not be a privilege afforded only to foreigners.

Then, traveling the road on the way back, its undulations winding through the still-growing scars, the chunks of hillsides, missing contours, violated beauty, I paused. The rain had stopped, and the air, washed clean of every trace of dust, shivered in the cool. I stopped on the hard shoulder, as I had done before. I wanted to write something as a record, something to explain the sense of abandonment, mine, theirs, everyone's. Again an army jeep drew up beside me as I sat there. The soldier-passenger along-side my door muttered something in Hebrew.

"Shalom," I said. "Do you speak English?"

"Yes."

A pause.

"What are you doing?"

"Writing."

They looked. "OK." And they left me to finish.

Back in Jerusalem I picked up a friend who was alone with her half-written book. Her children were at my house and her husband was at work in New York. I brought her home; the children played with swords they had made out of sticks while we talked. My neighbor, Amer, walked into the kitchen carrying a steel-gray fish from the Sea of Galilee: fresh, bloody, straight from the water that morning. He and Julita prodded it and Catriona put in: "You can't cut his head off, he'll cry."

Eid approached. US and allied forces were poised to invade Iraq. Pilgrims were to have a chance to get home from Mecca, then there would be war.

I emailed Andrew: "You need to come back quickly for your round-up visit." Then the news came through that more health workers were dead: two nurses at work in a Gaza hospital had been shot by IDF snipers. This was one of the things that "didn't happen." Their names were Abdel Karim Lubad and Omar Hassan.[1]

So many things "didn't happen": historical "didn't happens" like ethnic cleansing[2]; guilt "didn't happens"—like the Palestinians being stateless, that's not our fault, that was their leaders' choice not to share Palestine when the UN partitioned it in 1947. There were Palestinian "didn't happens," like not making the right choices (not accepting the UN partition plan was, in retrospect, a disastrous error), not playing what cards they possessed appropriately (having international law behind them), not allying with helpful sponsors (e.g., choosing to support Saddam Hussein's invasion of Kuwait). And above all, not accepting or understanding that Israel also had existential fears, belonged in the Middle East, and that suicide bombings would only alienate support within and beyond Israel.

And Bertrand the French journalist wasn't shot. The IDF doesn't do that kind of thing.

There were other "didn't happens," as when Daniel and I had driven through Bethlehem and Beit Jala, hearing "We never shoot people who break curfew" from the checkpoint soldier. Perhaps he hadn't heard of the doctor shot dead by the IDF, despite having permission—from the IDF—to drive medical supplies through Bethlehem under curfew, of the numerous other cases, including Lana's mother, of people who were shot during curfew—while in their homes.

Another thing that "didn't happen" was settler violence. I ventured to one religious settler that it was hard to understand, for example, the practice of settlers taking Palestinian farmers' olives. "They don't." He was firm. "Settlers don't do that. Never."

"But groups like Rabbis for Human Rights help protect the farmers in precisely this situation."

"Let me explain to you what actually happens. Rabbis for Human Rights are—how shall I put it?—*in league* with the PA. What they do is they go into the villages and *incite*. They put it about that settlers are going to attack them, when the opposite is true. Then the Palestinians get all worked up, rush to their fields, and that's when the trouble starts. It just doesn't happen that settlers steal Palestinian crops."

In an article I wrote for the *Spectator*, I quoted the report by the *New York Times* journalist Chris Hedges in which he described IDF snipers shooting children.[3] The *Spectator* received a letter from someone who was adamant that what Hedges had seen, and published in *Harper's*, could simply *not* have happened, because "if it had, we would have heard about it."

Campaigns were launched to prove that Mohammed al-Dura was not shot by the IDF, that he was shot by Palestinians who had planned and staged the entire incident, no doubt also killing the ambulance worker who tried to rescue the boy and his father. "If only we were capable of that degree of planning," said Dr. Ibrahim. The campaigners were not content with saying that the boy had been murdered by his own people. In their enthusiasm they attested that he did not die, that he was not Mohammed al-Dura but an actor, even, for good measure, that he had never existed at all. "Can you imagine," said another doctor, "the outrage if there were campaigns to 'prove' that one of the dead Israeli children was killed by the Israelis in order to manipulate the media?"

The IDF bombed a warehouse in Gaza, destroying food for thousands of people who had very little food. I drove to school to pick up the children and pounding down the Hebron Road was a convoy of new UN trucks emblazoned with "WFP" (World Food Program). Food was running out in Gaza, the UN's warehouses for feeding a million Palestinians nearly empty. Two years before, UNRWA had fed only 11,000 people in the Gaza Strip, mostly widows and those with no means of support. Now those needing to be fed numbered nearly three-quarters of a million people, more than half the population. Despite the UN's massive feeding program, nearly one in four Gazans were by now malnourished, with child malnutrition comparable to that in Congo and Zimbabwe.[4] In Gaza, too, the cause was manmade.

Just two years before, the people we met who were working in Jerusalem for international aid agencies and NGOs had thought of themselves as helping to build, or at least work toward, a Palestinian state. From time to time individuals working for such agencies would be frank enough—perhaps above all with themselves—to admit that the only reason the Israeli authorities "kept them at the table" was to have them fulfill the task of feeding. At a dinner given by a glamorous French doctor, Bettie, and her husband, in their house, built a hundred years before in the newly expanding Jerusalem by one of its aristocratic Palestinian families and filled with Bettie's art collection from Swat, Damascus, Herat, Rajasthan, Iran, and Hebron, one aid worker spoke out. He put down his plate of delicately spiced lamb and pulau and leaned back against a pile of embroidered cushions.

"One day," he said, and he had not drunk too much, "we will look back on this charade with shame and ask 'how in hell was this allowed to happen?' We dress it up in shades of 'security'— what are we talking about? That's crap and we all know it. This is not about security. None of this is making anyone secure—the opposite is true, but we're not going to say so, are we? This is about annexation of territory and slow ethnic cleansing. It's making Israel less secure and a pariah nation on top of that. And we're playing along with it," he said, "pouring billions of Euros and dollars into keeping the occupied going, keeping their heads above water while they're boxed in like animals. '*Never mind, never mind*,' we say when the IDF destroys the things we've just funded. We'll just carry on and rebuild it all, pour more money in, waiting obediently for the next round of Israeli bulldozing and bombing. Oh, but don't let anyone hear you say it. My God, we're in trouble if we say it like it is. No no, we *must* toe the line, but why?"

The preparations for war in Iraq continued. More journalists were transferred to Baghdad, coming back every now and then to take a break from the waiting. The BBC said they were not expecting to be covering much in the Occupied Territories because it would not be newsworthy compared to what British troops were putting up with under fire in Iraq. Instead, BBC reporters would be covering what the Israelis were putting up with: scud alerts, air-raid drills, gas-mask routines. Palestinians were not issued gas masks. Should there be an anthrax-laden scud landing within the radius of our village, my children and I had the equipment to counter it. Maha and her children did not. They were Jerusalem residents, municipal taxpayers. "They shouldn't have supported Saddam Hussein last time around," I was told.

Snow and storms and warnings of imminent war became a part of the days. Archie and Xan threw snowballs with Hamoud and Basil at the other boys in the village until the snow became too soft to form into weapons. The morning school drop-off routine was wet with gray snow and grim with sarcasm about the roll of events. I was still trying to fill in gaps in our research data, but was thwarted regularly. Once I had to call off a planned trip to Qalqilya because a nine-year-old child had been shot dead by the IDF the previous day and the funeral would close everything down. As for peace, by now it was labeled the "road map": the plan for peace by the quartet of US, UN, EU, and Russia that Sharon insisted the US delay yet again.

One group of Israeli peace activists glumly predicted that the "international community" (by which they meant the UN, EU, and Russia) were so keen to remain at the top table, so keen that they should be seen to be "players" alongside the US, that, after the Iraq war was over, "the UN and the Europeans will okay the 42 percent solution.* Sharon will find a way to do it," they insisted.

Andrew applied a salve of long-distance sangfroid to my confusion about getting out but wanting to stay. He also knew that the build-up to war was diverting me from the fact that Jerusalem was only low risk. He and I took turns at worrying; our fears, once triggered, would overcome logic. I was unnerved by a gas-mask

---

* *42 percent of the West Bank.*

demonstration even though I knew an attack was unlikely. A Canadian soldier had shown me how to use the masks and give atropine injections in the event of a nerve-gas attack. The gas masks in their cardboard boxes with plastic shoulder straps had lain untouched in a corner of the house. Sholto's, more of a gas suit than a gas mask, was fitted with nipple attachments to deliver his milk during a chemical or biological attack—no need to flip the trapdoor of a lid that sealed him into the contraption exposing him to clouds of poison when he was hungry or thirsty mid-attack, just screw the bottle directly on to the nozzle. We had, the soldier explained, "to get him in it and have him not worry, let him play in it a while, just so as he gets used to the idea." The man's professional frankness unsettled me. Still, now that terror was to be disseminated big time, there was some comfort in being surrounded by Israel's missile defense systems.

Then when I arrived at school one day a big gathering of students and teachers met me in the courtyard. A boy of thirteen, another one recently arrived from Paris, had just been expelled for incitement, and the students were being given a chance to speak. He had set up a website foaming with hatred of Palestinians. One mother, normally unflappable, held her hand to her throat and whispered, "It is shocking, *shocking*." The French consul general and the Conseil Culturel had been pulled in, and the Quai d'Orsai consulted. The teachers were very upset, many of them in tears. But one announced that there was nothing wrong with what he had done, and that the boy should not be punished at all.

Now the conflict was inside the fabric of the school. One fifteen-year-old French girl had been asked by her Jewish friends to choose: "Which side are you on?" Her best friend was Palestinian. The teacher who monitored the playground said there was a pattern: the Israeli boys would provoke the Palestinian boys verbally and the Palestinian boys would respond with physical violence. The French boy's website had been discovered a few days before. His parents were confronted, expressed horror, and agreed that he must clean it up. But that day some of the Palestinian boys had looked up the site again, found it still vile, and rushed out of the library threatening to beat the French-Israeli boy senseless. Now the school had had to tell the website boy that he was no longer welcome, and that those who did not think that such incitement was wrong were not welcome either. Meanwhile, they were trying to sort out the children's feelings. For the last they had recruited psychologists. In order to sort out racial tensions between Jews and Arabs, German psychologists were on their way.

At a party later that night parents were still debating the effects on the children and the school. The spate of parties had turned into a rush, with families evacuating in anticipation of war. The swell of rumors of war, bitterness at leaving, longing to be reunited as a family, and looming evacuation had become overpowering. Two Palestinian friends were toying with predictions—when would the war begin, what would happen in the West Bank under cover of the war and who would notice—when they became suddenly angry at the arrival at the party of a particular Israeli.

"That guy," said one, "is supposed to be a peacenik but did he refuse to serve in the West Bank? No, he did not. His concession was that he didn't serve as a sniper. Some compromise."

"Are we really supposed to be okay about this? He may have killed some of us, but we say nothing and act like it's all happening in another world? I'm not staying here any longer. Let's go."

While others were succumbing to bitterness, I was finding that being even half-organized was a memory: I forgot an invitation from Amer and his wife Suker to lunch the next day. When I remembered, I rounded up the children—we were rudely late, but they understood. It was a fine afternoon as we walked down the track to the lower village and wound our way beyond where the road ended. The house was at the foot of a path lined with almond blossom and barbed wire.

For more than two years Amer and I had been friends. He had helped me out with flooding rooms, faulty wiring, hopeless heating systems, and countless other problems, lugging large gas heaters up the hill in the rain to keep Sholto warm when the power failed completely. And we had talked for hours, yet he had never told me his family's story. I had to prod to get him to tell me that his family fled their four-story villa in Haifa in 1948. He now lived in a small building that had been a stable. But he wouldn't complain, only apologized. Three of his siblings were doctors in the US and Europe. Amer's focus was on the future: he believed in the integration of Jewish and Palestinian futures, and chose not to look back. He was trying to teach his children the same approach.

My children watched as Amer wiped every surface cleaner still, moving chairs and arranging cushions for us, and his wife laid out the many plates of food they had prepared. Amer had less and less work because of the situation and took whatever jobs he could find. Job-hunting kept him away from home, and Suker felt estranged from him. The strain on the two of them showed in their turning away from each other, the unwillingness of one to listen to the other, to give each other space in their small home. The two children, dark-haired Mohammed and blonde Siwar, raced about the tiny paved courtyard and the rocky garden, seemingly unaware.

Later that afternoon our young neighbor, Rasha, came to our house after she had finished her studies. She had taken off her veil; I tried to remember if I had ever seen Maha wearing one. Catriona ran to her for a hug, not understanding what Rasha knew, that we would soon be leaving. Rasha had long since taken to calling her "my lovely girl," and did not want to say goodbye. She was working hard in her final year of school and, planning to be a journalist, had applied to university. We would often sit and talk about her ambitions. Her parents' support for her surprised me, as they were conservative in outlook, and I had imagined they would want her to marry early as her mother had done. She told me with quiet pride about her latest results, which were even better than the previous ones, and turned to Catriona: "Come, my lovely girl, let's go and see if Nur has had her foal yet." Catriona ran after her, taking hold of her hand and laughing at the dog who jumped up to lick them as they went past.

Andrew was returning one last time, and then we would all be leaving. I reread an email he had sent suggesting we live on the island of Goreé, just off the Senegalese coast. People kept saying I must be crazy to go and live cut off on an island. Senegal—what were the odds of Senegal being my next life? After storms and snow in Jerusalem and more snowball fights in the village, Andrew appeared from Senegal and stayed for a week. The sun came out and warmed the hills again, and we followed Father Jerry on one of his guided walks through the West Bank to the ruins of one of Herod's retreats, Herodion, and a fifth-century monastery high up a desert wadi.

Our convoy drove through the emptiness of the West Bank's desert, past ancient villages, herders with their goats and sheep, children running about in sand-covered clothes. Despite her 90 years Val climbed with the rest of us through the innards of Herodion and walked the long hike up to the cave monastery. We peered at the goat pen in the cave with its layer of earth and dung on the floor, taking Father Jerry at his word that underneath lay a perfect mosaic. We drank cold beer, pictured the hermit monks weaving their baskets or at prayer among the stones, and listened to the desert wind before heading back to Jerusalem. And then to Gaza, walking on the cold beach where horses were being hitched to makeshift carts, saying goodbye to colleagues, deserting them again. There were more farewell parties, so many that Andrew never even started on the cardboard boxes from the shipping company. He woke late on the last morning with a hangover after two hours' sleep and declared: "But I haven't packed." It was too late. He left again. Our tickets were reserved for ten days' time.

Now the edgy mood of the daily morning drop-off-and-coffee routine at school was cranking up. Every few days there were new departures with friends dispatched from their homes and lives, none of them knowing when, if ever, they would be back. Many

Israelis were beginning to relish the chance to "sort out Saddam" and the Iraqis—"let us at them," was the mood, and why even bother with gas masks—few Jerusalemites walked around town with a gas mask slung around their necks. Machine guns, yes, but then we were familiar with seeing settlers coming in from the occupied hills dangling their weaponry. "Familiar," but far from comfortable. I went to IKEA, a popular branch north of Tel Aviv, to stock up before the packers came, and underwent a rigorous search of my tiny bag to check there was no possible chance of even a ladies' penknife. Behind me came two settlers with Uzis over their shoulders. The guns seemed to give their owners inalienable rights. The settlers swept in without so much as a glance from the security guards probing my bag. We kept bumping into each other among the sofa beds and self-constructing kitchen units, and they would eye my concern with suspicion, though it was only that they were a little careless as to where their machine guns were pointing. It is disconcerting to adjust your focus from a beech wood countertop to the hard-eyed gaze of the barrel of a full-on automatic weapon.

Just two days after our last trip to Gaza an American girl was killed there. Her name was Rachel Corrie; she was twenty-three. She had been living in Rafah and was protesting against house demolitions. The IDF were searching for tunnels used by smugglers to bring weapons from Egypt to Gaza. Peace activists and international organizations, armed with aerial and satellite imagery, pointed out that this "search" hid a broader aim: to erase a broad swathe of Rafah in order to redefine the border between the Gaza Strip and Egypt.[5] When, nine months after she was killed, the IDF did eventually bulldoze the house Rachel Corrie had been protecting, no tunnel was found.

Witnesses said that the bulldozer, a vast machine, advanced toward her and ploughed her under. The driver then reversed, without raising the blade, crushing her again. Within seven weeks two more westerners, Britons this time, were killed or mortally wounded in Gaza. Student Tom Hurndall was shot in Rafah on April 12. And James Miller, a journalist, was shot and killed in Rafah on May 2.*

Misinformation flowed in. The IDF said the bulldozer driver did not see Rachel Corrie. Eyewitnesses responded that this was absurd: wearing an orange vest, she was the only object for many meters, directly in view of the D-9's elevated cabin. As the bulldozer advanced, Rachel was forced on to the mound of dirt it was pushing, elevating her so much that she was at eye level with the bulldozer's cab before she disappeared underneath.[6] The IDF said Hurndall and Miller were shot in "crossfire" accidents. Eyewitnesses and recordings testified that there was no concurrent Palestinian attack on Israeli troops on either occasion. Only Israelis were shooting.

Tom Hurndall was shot in the head by a sniper with telescopic sights. Wearing a Day-Glo jacket and carrying a camera, he was shepherding Palestinian children to safety at the time. It was broad daylight. According to his sister, "Three days before he was shot he saw a child shot in front of him. That is why he acted when he saw children being shot at and tried to protect them, he knew there was a chance they could be killed."[7] He never regained consciousness, and died ten months later.

The reaction to these killings was to try to silence: denials, removing evidence, failing to bring those responsible to justice without enormous pressure, campaigns to interpret the victims' presence as malevolent.[8] In the case of Rachel Corrie it was particularly distressing. The families of Tom Hurndall and James Miller received assistance from their government and eventually the soldier who shot Tom Hurndall was given a jail sentence for his crime. In contrast, a year after her daughter's killing Mrs. Corrie had to ask why there had been no move by the White House, the

---

*James Miller was making a documentary about Rafah. He was shot as he and his team tried to leave the place where they had been filming all day. Miller was shining a torch up at a white flag held by his colleague.

State Department, or the Justice Department to initiate a US investigation. Mrs. Corrie reminded those who accused her daughter of helping terrorists that Rachel "was an unarmed peace activist trying to prevent the demolition of the home of a Palestinian pharmacist, his wife, and three children... Rachel stood there to protect a home and family in Gaza because the United States and Israel rejected a UN proposal to send international human rights monitors there. International activists went instead. Rachel stood there protesting illegal home demolitions that the United States opposes on the record yet fails to stop—destruction that we support with billions in annual military aid to Israel for bulldozers, Apache helicopters, F-16s, and more."[9]

Others noted the double standard: when Palestinians attacked an American convoy and killed three US citizens in Gaza, the US government demanded immediate justice, threatening to withhold funds from the PA until they got it. For Rachel, killed by an IDF bulldozer, the US government demanded nothing.

Soon after these killings, the IDF began to demand that visitors to Gaza sign a waiver absolving the IDF of blame should they be harmed or killed.

We had seen so many leave. Now it was our turn. The packers arrived and parceled us into boxes. Every last thing was swept into cardboard and deposited in a truck that had inched backward up the little hill and blocked in our neighbors. We moved our suitcases to an evacuee friend's house for our last two nights. I left the children and drove the car to Ashdod to add it to our shipment. An American friend gave me a lift back to Jerusalem under grizzled skies. It was Purim, normally a colorful festival when children dress up and play games of the imagination. Now traffic and people were thinned out, the roads half-empty, schools half-full. Yet there were some Israelis braving the dusty rain, dressed as clowns and princesses, determined to ignore the war. The BBC ran a piece about the courage of Israelis, the young ones surfing in the Mediterranean swell, in the shadow of banks of Patriot missiles, trying to be oblivious of the coming war.

We said our goodbyes to the family in the village. Our dog rejoined her original family, looking betrayed, but we knew she would be far happier with them than if she were transported with us to Senegal. The mare had foaled at last, but died in the process. There was no choice but to cut up her body into pieces and drag them down the hill. She was too heavy to move otherwise. Amer helped. No one could speak about it. Rasha's father, Mahmoud, was especially silent; his finest horse dead, and the foal too. The rain sluiced down and we hugged goodbye, photos hurriedly taken, promises to return, and tears. Rasha was wretched.

The war machine was on the home stretch. British Airways suspended its flights to Israel. Other airlines did the same. Alitalia, with which we had reservations, stood firm for the moment. In Britain our family watched the preparations and knew the bombing was about to start. A group of singles and lonely spouses came to say goodbye and we drank champagne, talking about West African singers Youssou N'Dour and Alpha Blondy instead of Yasser Arafat or Ariel Sharon. Moving on. When they left I squeezed the last few things into our suitcases and wrote goodbye notes to our evacuated hosts for their return when the war ended, whenever that might be. Andrew called again, promising to call me later in case my alarm failed. I set my alarm, twice, and lay down to sleep for the hour and a half before the taxi came to take us to our 5AM flight.

The phone rang. My father. He had just heard that the Foreign Office had issued warnings to all Britons in Jordan and Israel. "The war's about to start, you've got to get out."

"We *are* getting out. I was trying to sleep before the taxi comes. There's nothing more I can do."

"Oh, thank God for that. Call me later. Go to sleep."

The taxi arrived. The children were deadened with sleep, lying in the large car I had requested, large enough to fit in the four children, Julita, me, and all our bags.

Down the hills we drove from Jerusalem for the last time, off
to another life, an unchosen life, and leaving so much behind. So
many people, trapped.

At 3AM in Ben Gurion airport I bumped into Orly, an Israeli
journalist.

"Hi, what are you doing here?" she asked.

"Heading west, Africa, to join Andrew. And you?"

"I'm going east, Iraq. The bombing's started, you know. Just
now." We wished each other luck and kissed goodbye. There was
a strange atmosphere of calm about everyone. It didn't make any
sense. As we boarded the plane I asked the Alitalia crew if they had
heard that the bombing had started.

"No, no, it hasn't started." The professional smile belied by
one eyebrow. "But let's hurry up just the same."

A long pause on the tarmac, watching the slivers of dawn
lighten our old home, thinking that maybe we were sitting in a
possible target. Then lumbering to take-off, the children excited.
Out of the dark and into the west, away from everything. We
floated through the separating hours, toward Milan for our
connecting flight to Dakar. The children excavated the insides of
their croissants, filled them with jam, and then lost them in a
tangle of clothes and airline blankets. As I left the plane, the crew
member who had denied the start of the war looked down at the
sticky children, then up at me and said, "The bombing, the war—
yes, it had started. Of course."

Epilogue

Out of the Night

Andrew was waiting when we emerged from the airport into the warm sweep and mosquitoes of the Dakar night. He drove us along the coast road, the Atlantic waves lashing the shore beside us, to begin another new life. But we watched the bombs landing in Iraq and we watched "the situation." It is hard to let go of Jerusalem. Of all the lives we had lived so far, Jerusalem was the one that clung to us and that we took away with us when we left. We felt the shadow of Jerusalem and found that even the sand-filled wind followed us. Now it had a different name—the *hamarteen* instead of the *hamseem*—but it was the same breath of yellow dust and it covered us with the same longing.

Even far away in Africa the situation was there in front of us. Andrew had hidden from it but we brought it back to him. The children's new teacher asked where we had come from and frowned at the answer: the war, Iraq, dead Muslims, rumors— "lived in *Israel*?" Senegalese pilgrims coming back from the Haj were full of brotherhood, and angry. The ebullient head of UNICEF in West Africa heard that we had lived in Jerusalem and out came her story: her family one of the thousands who fled their West Jerusalem houses in 1948, her uncle one of more than eighty people killed in the bombing of the King David Hotel by Jewish terrorists.

Not long after we had settled into the quiet of Gorée a couple of miles off the Dakar coast, President George W. Bush paid the island a visit. Gorée is a common pilgrimage for world leaders who pay homage at the main tourist attraction, the House of Slaves, and the islanders were blasé about the visitors who walked among them, talking and pressing flesh: Mitterrand, Mandela, Clinton, Pope Jean Paul II. The coming of Bush was different. It was the Senegalese's first taste of post-9/11 security, and this time there was no walking among or pressing flesh. At dawn on the day of his visit almost the entire population of the island was herded into pens and held there, hot and thirsty, until the afternoon once the President had left. A privileged few, us included, were locked inside our houses under armed guard. We watched the President's speech on television, the man himself a few meters away in a place emptied of people, bar security and a few screened guests.

"Today," he said, on the platform Goréans had built for him near the old rose-stuccoed prison, "we can see the advance of human liberty... after the agonies of slavery.

"But," he went on in the heat, to the tiny cluster of guests, "the spirit of the slaves *did not* break. Instead, the spirit of the captors was corrupted... As Christian men and women became blind to the clearest demands of their faith, turning into hypocrites, still they could *not* crush the desire for freedom... Blacks' struggle for equality was resisted by the powerful for a long time... But our destination is liberty and justice for all... History moves in the direction of justice, therefore these problems *will* be overcome... We have," he concluded, "an untamed fire for justice."[1]

Listening to his words transported me straight back to so many conversations with Israelis and Palestinians who had also talked of the desire for freedom, of the same corruption of the occupiers' spirit, and with the same fire for justice, much of it untamed. There was no escaping Jerusalem.

The occupation persisted. IDF re-invasions, land expropriation, and settlement building continued.[2] So did the closures and curfews and the building of the Barrier. And Palestinian violence went on, though diminished: conditions were so grim that most Palestinians' priority was to improve their daily lives, favoring a permanent ceasefire and the collection of arms from militants.[3] Not wanting to lose support, and with many of its leaders assassinated, Hamas imposed another *hudna*—truce—in February

2005.* Yet since 2001 there had been no return to negotiations. Without government-driven talks to find a solution, Israelis and Palestinians tried negotiating for themselves: in 2003 Ami Ayalon and Sari Nusseibeh put together a plan backed by tens of thousands of Israeli and Palestinian signatures; more Palestinian and Israeli moderates met in Geneva to sign peace accords based on the Taba negotiations.[4] Many people abroad welcomed these accords, including US Secretary of State Powell, who was lambasted by American hardliners for encouraging them.[5] The international community still had its "road map," the staged route to peace put together by the Quartet (US, UN, Russia, and EU). Sharon had accepted the road map, but with fourteen crucial qualifying conditions. His successor, Ehud Olmert, declared that Israel's very future depended on the establishment of a genuinely viable Palestinian state, but not until after he had lost the power to try to effect that reality.[6] Arafat's successor, Mahmoud Abbas, continued the tradition of falling short of Israeli demands to control Palestinian violence and militias and Qassam rockets; meanwhile the Occupied Territories grew yet poorer and even more desperate.

In the spring of 2004, at the height of criticism of the Separation Barrier's route and just before the hearing of the International Court of Justice on the Barrier's legality,[7] Sharon had announced a historic decision: the unilateral removal of all Jewish settlements from the Gaza Strip and four from the West Bank.

"Disengagement," as it was called, was opposed by those who wanted to keep every inch of the Occupied Territories, and welcomed by some others as a brave first step. More withdrawals would inevitably follow: once started, we would see that dismantling settlements need not lead to civil war between Israelis and the

---

*From the start of the second Intifada in 2000 to October 2005, according to the Middle East Policy Council, the dead numbered 975 Israelis and 3,695 Palestinians. By November 2008, these numbers had increased to 1,065 dead Israelis and 5,200 Palestinians. Operation Cast Lead (December 2008–January 2009 in Gaza) added 13 and more than 1,300 respectively.

diehard settlers. When the time came (August 15–September 12, 2005), Israeli forces evacuated the remaining settlers with sensitivity and gentleness. The policing of the withdrawal was exemplary.

But others predicted that the plan was to finalize control of the land: by withdrawing from settlements it didn't want to keep anyway, the government could say it had made painful concessions, point to the inevitable chaos in Gaza after disengagement and thereby hold on to the West Bank indefinitely. Sharon's gamble was that "the world would be grateful to Israel for quitting Gaza and for a few years at least lessen its pressure for solutions to other territorial demands. Gaza would save the West Bank."[8]

Sharon himself explained the strategy: "The Palestinians understand that this plan is, to a great extent," he said, "the end of their dreams, a very heavy blow to them,"[9] and that the "current arrangement [with the Americans] determines for sure that Israel will not return to the 1967 borders" in the West Bank.[10] The US administration—Israel's partner in the disengagement process—changed decades of US policy by accepting previous Israeli expansion into the Occupied Territories. "In the light of new realities on the ground, including already existing major Israeli population centers," said a presidential letter, "it is unrealistic to expect that the outcome of final status negotiations will be a full and complete return to the armistice lines of 1949."[11]

Sharon's long-time right-hand man, Dov Weisglass, went further, stating that disengagement from Gaza was designed to "freeze" the peace process. "Although by the way the Americans read the situation, the blame fell on the Palestinians, not on us, Arik [Sharon] grasped that this state of affairs could not last, that they wouldn't leave us alone, wouldn't get off our case. Time was not on our side… The peace process is the evacuation of settlements, it's the return of refugees, it's the partition of Jerusalem. And all that has now been frozen… *what I effectively agreed to with the Americans was that part of the settlements would not be dealt with at all, and the rest will not be dealt with until the Palestinians turn into Finns.*" And all this "with a presidential blessing and the ratification of both houses of Congress." This was to be "formaldehyde," he said, for a Palestinian state.[12] The day after the withdrawal of settlers from the Gaza Strip Shimon Peres blithely admitted that its 38-year occupation and settlement—and attendant misery for millions of victims—was a "historic mistake."[13] But he also warned that Sharon's disengagement strategy would only perpetuate the conflict; Israel must provide the Palestinians with a viable and contiguous state and "give up all of the land that it captured in the 1967 Middle East war." "If you keep 10 percent of the land," he had admitted, "you keep 100 percent of the conflict."[14]

The experience of the Gaza Strip post-disengagement showed that, while the Israeli web of control remains over this unchosen land, no peace plan will bring peace.[15] While much of the world celebrated the beginning of new optimism for peace, behind the Gaza Barrier the 1.5 million Palestinian inhabitants were coping with total, asphyxiating closure, exacerbated by a new tactic: terrifying sonic booms breaking the sound barrier overhead throughout the night, night after night.[16] The 5,000 settlers and soldiers were gone (so only Palestinian eardrums could be damaged by the tactic); Israeli control remained. Control not only of borders, airspace, and territorial waters, and over all movement of people and goods in and out of the Gaza Strip, but also of the Strip's electricity, water, gas, and oil, of the collection of customs duties due to the PA, of the issue of Palestinian ID cards and all population data—births, marriages, deaths. All Palestinians must still be registered with the Israeli interior ministry. Following the withdrawal, Physicians for Human Rights-Israel and medical NGOs on the Palestinian side appealed to the international community for—at the very least—essential medicines to be allowed into Gaza and for sick patients trapped at the borders in inhuman conditions to be permitted to pass.[17] Most of the time, these appeals were ignored, as medicines continued to be blocked.

So much for quitting Gaza. The former head of the World Bank, James Wolfensohn, the UN Special Envoy to the Quartet, likened post-disengagement Gaza to a giant prison.[18] Nahum Barnea, Israel's leading commentator and another of those who saw the reality, wrote, "We delude ourselves, that we have disengaged from Gaza, that the occupation is over, that they go their way and we go ours. All we have done is taken our hand out of the cage, leaving the keys in our hands."[19]

I went back to Jerusalem as often as I could, and I saw the effects of the freezing process and the political formaldehyde, a fluid used to preserve dead bodies and remnants of the still-born or once-living—Weisglass knew what he was talking about. Life was much improved for Israelis, much worse for Palestinians. I heard from Israelis about the hope that had been ignited by the withdrawals of settlements and of Israelis' weariness with those settlers who were determined to remain. I saw my friends Jeff and Shoshana, who also talked, though less confidently than President Bush, about history moving in the direction of justice. There were still slivers of the old fears, and the resentments: "I hate being Israeli sometimes, I feel like an animal in a zoo," said one girl. "People come and look at us to see what we're doing, what cruel things us Jews are up to now. And they watch us, without understanding." Israelis felt like an exhibit for the old colonial world, a remnant of those countries' own dabblings in subjugating other peoples. "Europeans went home after their colonial experiments," Alison told me. "We have no home but here. And now we've built ourselves into a pit with our settlements and it is more dangerous for Jews here in Israel, our refuge, than anywhere else in the world. How ironic is that?"

I sat in a West Jerusalem café with Nahum Barnea and watched Jaffa Road go by: busy, thriving, normal again. Suicide bombings had tailed off, the economy was recovering, tourists were back, the hotels all full. People were getting on with their lives: the fear that had been so overwhelming only a few years before was in retreat. We talked about Arafat, who had died in October 2004, about Sharon, felled by a stroke in January 2006, and of Israel's genuine fears about Iran developing nuclear technology.

"This is our worry now, not the Palestinians," said Nahum. "As far as that conflict goes, we have normality again, and that's pretty good." Other Israeli friends talked of the same freedom from fear, the same welcome return to normality, and of the majority view that the future looked better than for some time. Many now gave the situation no thought at all.

In East Jerusalem and Ramallah and the rest of the West Bank, there was no normality. As for Gaza, life in the Strip had been desperate enough in the autumn of 2005, but it was to get far worse. Under absolute control, there could be nothing approaching normality. And in the West Bank the cementing of Israeli control continued, seemingly faster than ever, with more settlement building, more roads for Israelis only, while for Palestinians there were continuing raids, house demolitions, land requisitions, and still tightening closures. Despite all assurances to the contrary, the numbers of barriers to movement in the West Bank increased. Even when some checkpoints were removed under international pressure, others replaced them, in greater numbers. By August 2005, the number of "obstacles to movement" in the West Bank numbered 376; by May 2009 the number was 634.[20]

For Palestinians, conditions were worse than ever: people less able to move, more cut off, more restricted, more imprisoned and, above all, increasingly denied their holy city. And all this more unseen than ever. Again and again the words of the young journalist and artist telling a group of friends of the latest unreported IDF raids on Ramallah came back to me: "It's easier to reach heaven than the end of the street." Her pale and beautiful Semitic face wore the strain of closure all too clearly. But all this was screened off from the rest of the world.

And then, just as Israelis were enjoying their normality, Palestinians' despair brought Islamic fundamentalists to power. In exactly the same way that moderate Israelis had complained in February 2001 that Palestinian violence had given them Sharon, now moderate Palestinians complained that Israeli violence and policies had just led to the election of their own extremists: Hamas won a majority of seats in the Palestinian legislative assembly.* These moderates pointed out that a majority of Palestinians had voted against Hamas, and that the party's victory was more of a vote against the corruption of the PA and its failure to deliver services let alone an agreement with Israel. But there was Hamas—in power—and Israelis now found themselves facing a democratically elected organization with a bloody terrorist past and a sworn opposition to Israel's very existence. All this at a time when Iran's president was questioning the Holocaust and had called for Israel to be "wiped off the map."

"Where's the big surprise?" asked one Fatah member in Jerusalem. We were sitting in a café next to the Damascus Gate, drinking fruit juice that the owner had crushed for us from the baskets of oranges spilling over in the corner. "We've had nearly forty years of occupation. We've tried everything—international law, nonviolent resistance, violence, and force. Nothing has brought us our rights, our freedom." He grew angry. "The opposite. At every step Israel puts up new demands and conditions—now it insists we become democratic—and all the while it carries on taking yet more of our land and making our lives unbearable, unlivable. And what does the West do? Says little and does nothing." Offering me more juice, he went on, "Instead everything is *our* fault, and they, the US and the EU, arrogantly tell us what to do and how often we 'disappoint' them. All this builds up the Islamists and undermines the moderates—Fatah, Abbas— who're punished for not protecting Israelis from our violence but

* On January 25, Hamas won 74 of 132 seats in the PLC, with 44.4 percent of the vote to Fatah's 41.4 percent. The remaining 14 percent was won by other secular parties supporting the two-state solution.

are not allowed to protect us against Israeli violence. Of course our moderates have no hope of being heard.

"So we hold elections—we shouldn't be amazed when the winners are those seen as the greatest resisters to the occupation, the least corrupt and most likely to do something about social conditions. We made our democratic choice, but we're told it doesn't suit Israel or the West. Israel says: 'Look, here's proof that Palestinians don't recognize Israel,' cuts all contact and stops handing over our money—taxes that they collect 'for us.'" I remained silent. He was venting the resentment of so many Palestinians.

In joining the democratic electoral mechanism, as opposed to boycotting the elections as it had in 1996, Hamas had made an all-important statement about abandoning the tactics of violence and signing up to the political process. Instead of embracing that shift and building on Hamas's new political responsibilities, the international community declared that, even though it deemed the election "free and fair," it did not approve of the electorate's choice and would now seek to overturn it.

Astounded, the Palestinian people watched as the international community clapped sanctions on them for electing Hamas, sanctions described by the UN special rapporteur as not only "the first time an occupied people have been so treated" but also "possibly the most rigorous form of international sanctions imposed in modern times."[21] And all for exercising democratically (and certifiably fairly) their right to vote for a party that happened to be one of which Israel and its friends disapproved.

In our old village Maha was as cheerful as ever, but her sister's Jerusalem house had been demolished and the family now lived in a tent against the cold, and all the while the new Israeli settlements in the valley were surging ahead.[22] Maha's daughter was hoping to be a doctor, but how, she asked, was she to study now that their university—on the West Bank side of the Wall—was cut off from Jerusalemites? "Who knows how often student permits, if we can get them, will let us through." She had no choice but to start learning Hebrew and to apply to the Hebrew University. Ghassan, the computer engineer, was still struggling to see his wife and son, separated from them by the Wall. Even praying was still difficult: in an East Jerusalem Friday rainstorm I sat trapped in a car while mounted Israeli police charged down Muslims trying unsuccessfully to reach al-Haram al-Sharif to pray. Two drenched little boys looked at me from behind their father's sheltering hands, stepping back to avoid the horses' clattering hooves.

Zahi, still denied Israeli customs clearance for his own company's equipment (it had now been sitting at the docks for more than five years) talked of the thousands of tons of produce, including millions of flowers blooming for Valentine's Day in Europe, all rotting, blocked for weeks at the one gate, Karni, where produce could leave Gaza. Ostensibly there was a bombers' tunnel underneath Karni, but nothing had been found after three separate attempts to locate it.[23] "The gates are closed against us more frequently than ever now—especially when there's a crop harvested and ready to sell. We can be economically strong, if only we are allowed to get our produce to a market." On the way to Ramallah I saw the new "terminals" to control Palestinian movement, with cattle-crush turnstiles just like a market.

Inside the city, beyond the turnstiles and the lines of imploring women, my friends and colleagues were less free to move than ever before.[24] They were increasingly filled with anguish, at the closures, and the loss of Jerusalem, and despair—among some—at the ascendancy of the Islamists. Career women wondered what restrictions Hamas would now place on them, and why the West had undermined civil society programs, thereby encouraging Hamas. I drove a rented car, fearful but unhindered, through the waving green flags and heady shouts of a Hamas demonstration in Manara Square, and then on to Bili'in, a village to the west where Israeli peace activists stood side by side with Palestinians protesting at yet more land being taken from them. The tear gas flew and the police cudgels wheeled about our heads and the crowds went slowly home. On my way back I gave a lift to a settler called Yisrael who explained again that the West Bank is all Jewish land and that Palestinian resistance is all just about *jihad*—the desire to destroy—nothing more.

I joined a party of North American clergy being shown the Barrier by Jeff Halper in his peace-activist role. We began at Abu Dis, where the Wall stands across the middle of the main road, severing one half of the community from the other. The bus disgorged us at the stump of road that once swept through the town and on down toward the Dead Sea. These are ancient routes, ancient names. One of the sawn-off districts is al-Azariah, a corruption of "Lazarus." Palestinians jested that Jesus would be hard put to raise Lazarus now, with the Wall in His way.

The North American clergymen looked up and gasped at the structure dividing Palestinians from Palestinians and at the wraiths of the once-thriving community. We looked across the Palestinian valley to the Forest of Peace and the village where Andrew and I had lived and where Maha still lived, at the work going ahead on the new Jewish settlement on Palestinian land. Another settlement would soon fill the near side of the valley. Israeli West Jerusalem was far away to the right, over the next hill. The clergymen, having heard the argument that the Barrier was supposed to divide Israelis from Palestinians, were mystified.

Jeff responded in his kindly way, explaining that the Wall was not just about security but also about Israel holding on to occupied Palestinian land, including all of Jerusalem.

As we stood at the foot of the Wall I heard the clerics' disbelief, so characteristic of those who witness the facts on the ground: "How do families on that side get to the hospital? How do they get supplies, food, fuel? How do they get to see their relatives? The convent here—how do the sisters look after the community now? How does anyone... What do the kids... where do... This," the Canadian priest said, "is an obscenity."

And the justification of an American Israeli in the group: "You don't understand terror, not unless you live here. The Palestinians want to kill us. They're terrorists. It's as simple as that."

"What, all three million of them?" asked another cleric.

The Israeli was offended: "Like I said, you don't understand. Nothing will stop the terror because it's in their nature, but the Israeli left will never admit it."

In front of the Wall you confront both the fear and the agenda. The Wall is both protection and annexation. It is the Israeli dilemma in solid concrete: the longing for security *and* the desire to hold on to the land *and* the need to maintain the Jewish state *and* to remain democratic—and the impossibility of having all this and peace with the people who share that land.

In the gargantuan Wall and its scale and blankness you see the desire to block out the suicide bombings that have taken so many lives. The slabs of Wall are memorials unwritten, monstrous blind tombstones, reminders of the ruin wrought by the killings. On a background of racism and misunderstanding the killings have etched lines with the colors of cruelty and brutality.

The Wall is a testament to cynical alliances[25] and unquestioning support: those who might not have agreed with settlement-building but who nevertheless refused to criticize Israeli policy or to admit that one day the settlements would entrap both peoples; those who failed to encourage Israel to make the most of a Palestinian partner who had not only bought into the two-state solution but could sell it to his people, or to welcome the Arab League's peace plan; those who said that any objections to Israel's expansionism were an attempt to deny Israel's "right to exist"— even while this expansionism threatened Israel's future security and denied Palestine's right to exist.

And the Wall is also a winding monument to the tens of thousands of lives broken by its route, those of the Palestinians now consigned to poverty and bitter dependence. There were many ways this was put into effect. In October 2003, for example, the OC Central Command declared a new "closed military area," comprising all the land between the Barrier and the Green Line. By military decree 90,000 dunams of Palestinian land were instantly rendered out of bounds for their owners—unless, that is, they applied for, and were granted, a permit from the Israeli Civil Administration. Villagers were told that if they were to be away from home overnight—as many were, for study or for work, nurses on night shifts, for example—they could be defined as "not permanent," and lose their right to live in their own homes. If they chose not to bow to the new permits, they would not be allowed to leave their village at all. Or, if they did leave, they would not be allowed to return.

By taking a scalpel to thousands of acres of the best Palestinian agricultural land—the "fertile basin" of the West Bank—the Barrier, or Wall, cuts away these lands from the Occupied Territories. "Behind the separation fence are thousands of personal tragedies, which are entirely invisible to the Israeli public," wrote an Israeli commentator. "This kind of occupation perhaps doesn't kill. Not right away, anyway," he wrote. "But it does destroy the soul." In the verdict of a right-wing settler, "The fence is a death sentence for the Palestinians... This fence is a mistake, it will only exacerbate the problem... you are creating more hatred instead of the possibility of living together."[26]

The clerics and I moved away from the part of the Wall where some of my Israeli friends had recently protested alongside throngs of Palestinians. "The Wall crept up on us," one Israeli friend had told me. "Our government never admitted what it was really doing, and now suddenly it's here in the middle of East Jerusalem and carving up the Palestinians' lives and taking their land from them." I pictured my friends arm in arm with long-robed Palestinians and other Israeli peace campaigners, keeping one wary eye on their own troops.

The group and I then climbed to a high point overlooking the settlements growing around East Jerusalem: the spacious Jewish areas, with their clean lines and neat rows, red roofs and green gardens abutting the crumpled Palestinian areas, with the Palestinians denied the right to develop their own city or build housing units for their own growing families,* and forced out in search of cheaper accommodation. The Wall was blocking Palestinians out of Jerusalem in perpetuity.

Beyond the more heavily built-up parts of the city, the Barrier was descending like a giant cookie cutter to slice more Palestinian areas out of Jerusalem and out of their society and kinship, dropping more steel loops around villages, with an exit, or maybe two, and if those inside could get permission to pass through one exit, they might make their way to the next, and eventually to Ramallah, or to the nearest town with services, or to school. Some of the new but as yet unevacuated islands would connect to other islands by way of tunnels burrowing under settler roads. Ten-minute drives had become senseless loops of 20 or 25 miles in the wrong direction, with sometimes fatal consequences. And there would be three gates—"terminals"—to allow the few permit-holding Palestinians into Jerusalem.

"How long," asked one of the reverend tourists, "could anyone continue living like this?"

As we looked at the Wall and the settlements, the settler-only roads, the industrial areas built to keep the land-robbed Palestinians busy, and listened to Jeff explaining their effects and the severing of Jerusalem, the other Israeli, distressed, protested: "None of this is true. None of what Jeff is telling you is true," he said.

"But we're seeing it," said the clergymen, "there it is."

There, stretching away into the distance, was the occupation's matrix of concrete and control. The settlements, the roads, the "terminals" and the Wall were like a net thrown out over the hills

---

* The Deputy Mayor of Jerusalem, Yakir Segev, revealed that in 2008 only 18 permits were issued for building in the Palestinian parts of the city, home to some 270,000 Palestinians. It was the Municipality's policy of granting so few permits that was driving Palestinians to construct illegally. "To get a construction permit in East Jerusalem you have to be more than a saint," said Segev.

and valleys of the West Bank, and the Palestinian areas choked in between. "There it all is," said one of the clergymen. "Right there in front of all of us."

Right in front of us, visible but unseen, is the web of concrete and denial that, by keeping control of the land and its resources, makes real peace for Israelis and Palestinians impossible. In March 2006 former US President Jimmy Carter observed that, "The preeminent obstacle to peace is Israel's colonization of Palestine." Noting that settlement building had expanded after 1977, despite this policy's condemnation by Presidents Reagan and George H.W. Bush, and especially under President Clinton, regardless of his "strong efforts to promote peace," Carter observed that Israel's best official offer to the Palestinians so far was to withdraw a mere 20 percent of the settlements. He also warned that the "5 percent" figure given for the amount of land taken up by existing settlements, "is grossly misleading, with surrounding areas taken or earmarked for expansion, roadways joining settlements with each other and to Jerusalem, and wide aerial swathes providing water, sewage, electricity, and communications. This intricate honeycomb divides the entire West Bank into multiple fragments, often uninhabitable or even unreachable."[27]

Like the American clergymen, I wondered how long Palestinians could put up with such constraints on their lives. *Sumud* is strong: despite the conditions, they are determined not to give up, saying, "We've learned the lessons of '48; we'll never leave our lands again." I heard from Israeli friends, as I had heard so often, that progress toward peace is being made. "We're doing really well—why does the world give us such a hard time when we're finally getting somewhere? Things are much better than they used to be—if only the Palestinians would face up to their responsibilities."

"The Palestinians will have tunnels to connect between their areas. They'll have their cities. And factories to work in." My Israeli friend, a diplomat, always did his best to look on the bright side.

"So they'll have to drive around this settlement bloc or that settlement bloc to get across the valley—that's not *so* bad." I was looking doubtful. "Of course the gates will always be manned, some of them. If a Palestinian needs to get a sick child to the hospital, you bet the soldiers will let them through. There won't even be any soldiers most places." He preempted me, quickly: "And they'll get used to not having East Jerusalem. The Arabs lost. They just have to accept that."

But for how long, ask other Israelis, those who know what life is like in the Occupied Territories, for how long can the Palestinians accept their gated, shut-down lives and be kept quiescent? One Israeli demographer spoke of the future candidly in an interview: "When 2.5 million [Palestinians] live in a closed-off Gaza... those people will become even bigger animals than they are today, with the aid of an insane fundamentalist Islam... So, if we want to remain alive, we will have to kill and kill and kill. All day, every day. If we don't kill, we will cease to exist. The only thing that concerns me is how to ensure that the [Israeli] boys and men who are going to have to do the killing will be able to return home to their families and be normal human beings."[28]

We returned to New York from Gorée in 2006. The situation remained unaddressed. The following year, 2007, the fortieth year of the Israeli occupation, began with ongoing intra-Palestinian skirmishes that looked like the onset of civil war.

Alongside continuing human rights abuses, the humanitarian suffering deepened to crisis level: nearly half the population of the Gaza Strip was food insecure and increasingly malnourished. Strikes were held in protest at the sanctions, and at Israel refusing to hand over Palestinian tax revenues: government employees went without salary and the supplies with which to work for months on end. An Israeli human rights NGO reported that since the settlers were evacuated, Israel's control over Gaza "has tightened in ways that have crippled civilian life."[29]

People used to tell me that part of the problem was the vitri-olic hatred, dating back decades, between Arafat and Sharon—the two archetypes of the old way of thinking, the old, violent way of doing things. By the spring of 2006, one was dead, the other moribund. New elections had brought new people to power on both sides.

Yet the numbers of dead continued to rise. In 2006, Palestinians killed six IDF soldiers and seventeen Israeli civilians: thirteen in the two suicide bombings of that year. In the same year Israeli forces killed 660 Palestinians, 141 of them children. Palestinian militants fired hundreds of primitive Qassam rockets from Gaza into Israel, killing two Israelis and bringing down thousands of IDF missiles in return, as well as full-scale re-inva-sions (e.g., Operation Summer Rain in June 2006, Operation Autumn Clouds in November 2006).* Gaza's infrastructure was pounded and its sole electricity plant destroyed when one Israeli soldier was kidnapped and two killed during a military raid. The destruction left much of the Gaza Strip with no electricity—even to pump water or power hospitals—for months.

The world paid little attention to the suffering in Gaza, even less when Hezbollah provoked Israel by an attack from across the Lebanese border in July 2006. Israel responded on a massive scale, bringing down rocket attacks on northern Israel. And this at a time when Iran was cranking up its anti-Israel language, its Holocaust denial, and, most ominously, its uranium enrichment program. Ordinary Israelis grew increasingly concerned. Benjamin Netanyahu, speaking Israelis' deepest fears, warned: "It is 1938, Iran is Germany, and it is about to arm itself with nuclear weapons."

Late in President George Bush's second term, the US admin-istration, mired in Iraq, looked about for a policy success in the

---

* Humanitarian officials were not alone in commenting on the cynicism of these operation titles—"summer rains," for example, with its gentle and verdant imagery, actually signi-fied a rain of artillery shells and missiles.

Middle East as well as for support from its Arab allies, and the Israel–Palestine issue became for a time a focus of attention. American plans did not include Hamas, however, and Hamas played into this by refusing the Quartet's demands to "recognize Israel," "renounce violence," and "adhere to agreements already signed by the PLO." Pointing out that no reciprocal demands were being made on Israel, and no delineation of Israel's final borders was proposed, Hamas continued to refuse.

The US armed and trained Fatah forces in preparation for a civil war in which Fatah would defeat Hamas, thus setting aside the unwanted, by the US, outcome of their push for democratic elections in the region: a radical Islamist party in government. Civil conflict duly began in late 2006, with more than 90 Palestinians killed, mostly in Gaza. Saudi Arabia stepped in to halt the killings and forced Fatah and Hamas to form a unity government. President Mahmoud Abbas and Hamas leader Khaled Meshaal signed the Mecca Agreement, angering both the US administration and Israel, for whom intra-Palestinian violence was apparently more congenial than the prospect of a Palestinian national unity government.

As usual, the drama of events helped silence the underlying reality: the steady erasing of a potentially workable Palestinian state. But there were significant voices raised in alarm, both in Israel and abroad. Two American professors, Stephen Walt and John Mearsheimer, opened a new debate on the role of the Israel lobby in US foreign policy. Ex-US president Jimmy Carter warned of the choices in a new book, *Palestine: Peace Not Apartheid*, saying bluntly: "It will be a tragedy—for the Israelis, the Palestinians, and the world—if peace is rejected and a system of oppression, apartheid, and sustained violence is permitted to prevail."[30] Campaigns of vilification were launched in the US against both the professors and Carter. Critics of Israel's policies were increasingly accused of damaging Israel, putting Israel's very existence at risk, and anti-Semitism. Most strongly criticized were Jewish voices pleading for Israel to consider the consequences of creating a "failed state" on its borders.

In return visits to Jerusalem I heard Israelis say, "Everyone knows what the solution will be": borders based on the Geneva Accord, the Nusseibeh-Ayalon Plan, and the Clinton parameters; both capitals in Jerusalem, and a mutually agreeable land swap to compensate for Israel keeping some settlements. It was just, people said, a question of how to get to that point and of how much damage was done before that inevitable point was reached. "You only have to look at Gaza now," said one moderate, "to see what we're creating in the West Bank." The Gaza Strip, purged of moderation, was seen as an uncontrolled ferment of terror, armed via tunnels supplying weapons from Egypt.

Despite the Arab League's renewal of the Arab Peace Plan, offering peace and full recognition in return for withdrawal from the Occupied Territories, Israelis' profound insecurities were now even more sharpened. But most Israelis, having been through so much, were unwilling to trust Palestinians, especially after quitting Gaza and being rewarded with Qassam rockets in return. The Palestinians I spoke to, in their growing despair, warned me that the Israelis had a chance with Abbas but gave him no concessions that would convince Palestinians that they could trust Israel—so the Israelis got Hamas. "Now they refuse to deal with Hamas and they'll get al-Qaeda." Killing hope and moderation, they said, had opened the door to the worst sort of extremists.

Palestinians I spoke to talked endlessly about separation and barriers in every aspect of their lives, about being cut off from the next village, their family, their local town; about the hundreds of IDF military raids, the almost daily bombings or killings by IDF assassination squads; about more and more Palestinians being denied access to their homes, more new measures to keep Palestinians abroad out of the West Bank and to put barriers between family members, even spouses. Thousands of Palestinians, and thousands of foreign citizens married to Palestinians, often businessmen, overwhelmingly moderate and pro-peace, now faced being permanently separated from their children, spouses, and enterprises because of new policies to refuse them entry to the West Bank.

The Wall continued to wend its way through Palestinian territory, cutting off 42 villages from their lands; Bethlehem, throttled by an eight-meter wall that chokes its life away, its water fiercely rationed as it is the rest of the West Bank; and Jerusalem, with its mosques, hospitals, churches, and businesses, now impossible to reach for most Palestinians. But most alarming were the settlements—expanding still, despite the pleas for peace, and even as it was revealed that the majority are built on private Palestinian land, and therefore illegal even under Israeli law.* And the settlers from those settlements were increasingly violent against Palestinian farmers, villagers, and schoolchildren, and increasingly unrestrained by Israeli forces.

On my visits back, I met teachers who had resorted, like so many Palestinians, to subsistence farming on the plots of land remaining to them. I met farmers who had been promised access to their lands on the other side of the Wall, but who were denied the (Israeli) permits to pass through. "Even when we do get permits," they explained, "the gates stay locked most of the time, and they don't open them when they say they will." And Israeli peace campaigners try to help the farmers get through the gates but the soldiers say "no," or confiscate their hard-won permits, on any pretext. One Israeli activist said: "No one can understand what it's like, not unless they see it. It's a living death for them. But how many of us are prepared to accept that they deserve anything more?"

Despite its severity, the "diet" Dov Weisglass had outlined in 2006 was not working. "The idea is to put the Palestinians on a

---

* Commissioned by the Sharon government, the Sassoon Report (March 8, 2005) revealed the depth of government involvement in settlement and outpost construction in "blatant violation of the law" and concluded that "drastic steps" were needed to rectify the situation.

diet," he had said, "but not to make them die of hunger." The hunger was designed to persuade Palestinians to force Hamas to change its attitude toward Israel and submit to Israel's terms, or to throw Hamas out of government. Gazans, however, are no different from any other people. During this time, we had dinner in an Italian restaurant on the Upper East Side with Ethan Bronner, a *New York Times* correspondent, his Israeli wife, and another Israeli, one of my closest friends. My husband, a historian by training, asked the rest of us: "Can any of you think of a nation—or even an individual for that matter—that has ever become more moderate as a result of being starved? Could anyone really imagine that a people who have suffered so much, as we all agree those in Gaza have, will become less angry, or less extreme, after being deliberately made hungry by the same people they attribute their suffering to? What this policy will do is make people more extreme—and believe me, it will help ensure that Hamas stays in power." No one demurred.

The outcome of Palestinian civil strife was the violent takeover of the Gaza Strip by Hamas in June 2007 and the collapse of the Mecca Agreement's Palestinian national unity government. The Israeli government declared Gaza Strip an "enemy entity" and limited still further the already inadequate amounts of supplies—despite signed agreement—they would permit into Gaza. Soon Israel began limiting fuel to the bare minimum to keep the Strip's only power plant operating at subsistence level. Power was limited to a few hours each day. As the inflow of all supplies slowed, the humanitarian situation became "alarming," according to ICRC, an organization not known for exaggeration.

By January 2008, the economic blockade was all too clearly ineffective at halting the firing of Qassam rockets fired both indiscriminately and in response to ongoing raids and military incursions in the West Bank as well as Gaza. The increase in Qassams duly led to Israel sealing the border completely. The tunnels connecting Egypt and Gaza that were the conduits for both military and humanitarian supplies were used to capacity. Within a few days the world watched extraordinary news footage as tens of thousands of Palestinians walked from Gaza into Egypt through breaches in the fence that normally held them captive (militants had planted explosives to demolish parts of the barrier to let the people out) and then returned laden with essential, and non-essential, supplies. After ten days, Egypt sealed up the breach with steel and barbed wire, and the Palestinians had to revert to using tunnels to augment their scant supplies.

In June 2008, Hamas signed a truce with Israel with both parties agreeing to abjure violence against each other. Hamas would stop firing rockets at Israeli territory and prevent militants from doing the same, and Israel would cease military incursions and targeted assassinations. Although by Israeli intelligence agencies' assessments Hamas had performed well, IDF attacks continued, and on November 4, 2008, the military invaded Gaza, killing six members of Hamas. (This went virtually unreported in the US.) Nevertheless, Hamas offered to renew the six-month *hudna* (truce) if Israel would ease the blockade of Gaza. Israel refused. The blockade worsened.

By the end of December 2008, Israelis were exasperated by the nagging fear of incoming rockets fired from the Gaza Strip. Sixteen Israelis, four of them children, had been killed by Qassam rockets since attacks began in 2001. Over 4,500 rockets had been fired, terrorizing the population within their striking distance. Many had fled.

By the end of the IDF's response to the militants' rockets, Operation Cast Lead, in which Gazans came under fire from the unleashed force of Israel's arsenal, but with no option to flee, more than 1,400 Palestinians had been killed. More than 300 of the dead were children. Thirteen Israelis were killed, four by friendly fire. Six months after the offensive, thousands of Gazans remained without running water and homeless, with Israel refusing to allow entry of basic foodstuffs like pasta and other essential supplies into Gaza, let alone building materials to rehouse the bombed and homeless. No exports were allowed out. And rockets were still falling on the Israeli town of Sderot, though in diminished numbers.

Operation Cast Lead looked different from New York. The coverage we saw and read there appeared to be that of a wholly different war from the war being described by email, blog, local correspondents, and any media other than most American sources. This was nothing new; it was the filter through which people in the US are normally shown the conflict. The filter filtered not just the military campaigns, it also distorted the ongoing policies engendering Palestinians' despair and preventing peace, if any of that was covered at all. The accelerating campaign to cement Israel's hold over East Jerusalem,[31] for example, which threatens that aspect of final status negotiations, was covered in the *New York Times* by a story about the creation of parks out of "wastelands" in East Jerusalem without mention of Israel's policies that prevent Palestinian communities from developing their city.[32]

It was not just the details of the military campaigns: the restraints on media coverage, the justifications of self-defense, etc., the build-up and ultimate trigger point provided so obligingly, and unseeingly, by Palestinian militants, the blocking of ambulances and relief to the wounded, the rewriting, both at the time and afterward, or the block on independent investigation of possible war crimes. It had all happened before, most dramatically with the attacks on the West Bank, the IDF's Operation Defensive Shield, in April 2002. Only this time there were so many more dead and injured, and the extent of devastation was so much greater. Gazans had been bombed many times in the past but now the outcries abroad against the reports of the IDF firing on ambulances, shelling hospitals, using white phosphorus in civilian areas, and of whole families left to watch each other die in bombed-out buildings were loud and impassioned, as were the voices raised in denial, defense, and justification. Truckloads of medical supplies, many assembled by

Israeli humanitarian groups, were sent through the gates into the Strip to help the wounded, but this only emphasized that the recipients were a people locked inside a veritable cage, dependent upon those whom they regard as their jailers to feed and supply them, and unable to find any shelter when those who hold the keys decide to bomb them. Not only unable to find any shelter, unlike any other war-affected population the world over, they were unable to flee the bombardment, owing to the barbed wire and minefields that hem them in on three sides (the Israeli naval blockade taking care of the fourth). And predictably, the passivity of the international community was so destructively the same.*

And considerable resentment on both sides exists toward the international community. One Israeli diplomat pointed out the self-perpetuating nature of the situation, singling out those on the international peace conference circuit "whose career is built on the conflict and therefore don't want it solved because they'll be out of a job. Much of the international machine is like this—have you thought how many people will be out of a job when the conflict is over—it may be only subconscious, but it is a factor." Greg, a Palestinian political scientist, was more specific, "There's a failure of international law, yes. So many Palestinians say, for example, 'After the International Court of Justice ruled that the Wall was illegal, we ask—what happened? All 25 members of the EU endorsed the ruling, but Israel carries on building the Wall, and settlements are expanding faster than ever, and the economy's worse than ever because of internal closure.' You can understand the guy in the street saying, 'Look, when will you *ever* understand, this thing you call the language of law and justice, it doesn't apply to us. The only time people see us is when we make noise.'"

---

* In 2007 one former Israeli foreign ministry official told me that during the 2006 bombardment of Lebanon the ministry had waited for the international community to call a halt to the bombing. "We kept saying, 'Surely it will come today, surely.' But it never came," he said, in amazement.

The smokescreen suited us all because it is too uncomfortable to contemplate what we are watching—helping—set up. Easier to concentrate on more immediate problems. But hiding behind smokescreens does not help Israelis or Palestinians. After two Intifadas most Israelis are convinced that the occupation is not good for them and they want an end to it.

One balmy May morning I drove to Ramallah to see my friend Rita before leaving the "situation" once more, as it is only too easy to do if you have a foreign home to go to. The air in the city was strangely still, despite the heavy bustle of people and vehicles. Rita looked out of her office window at the near hills and the Israeli settlements spreading over them. Music was playing across the street. She reminded me of the inequality between the sides and of how well it was hidden. Of course, everyone wants peace. "But, before peace can come we need justice, and the formula that every-one talks about in the West is peace without justice. There can be no peace without justice: recognizing that my mother's narrative is actually correct, that we were kicked out of our homes, that she wasn't lying. Saying 'I'm sorry.' And then we can look at issues in rational ways so that, for example, the 'right of return' is not actu-ally to Haifa, or the village of our forefathers, but a symbolic and practical one."

She was echoing the words of an Israeli friend of mine, now a member of the Knesset, at dinner in Tel Aviv the previous night. He had gone further: "Israel—the government—is not yet willing to recognize that the Palestinians are here to stay," he said. "It's carrying out a policy of ethnic cleansing, and is unwilling to look within, to realize there's a problem inside Israeli society. As long as the US supports this, it is, ironically, giving support for the destruc-tion of Israel—and the Israel lobby is certainly not to the benefit of Israelis. The Palestinians gave up so much already and even that is not good enough. They at least have learned, painfully, that Israel wants land, not peace."

"Only an outside force for peace can work, and an outside force means the Americans. I tell you, American inaction has been criminal to Israel, and anyone involved in this obstruction of peace is doing harm to Israel, and to Israeli kids, and to Israeli soldiers and to Israeli mothers. Bush, Elliot Abrams, all the big shots were part of this bloodbath of Jews and Arabs. As long as we have the American shield, we can just tell the world: 'go to hell.' It's not just a tragedy, it's a sin." His anger reverberated, but was cut off by the appearance of our waitress, who recognized my friend, and they bantered flirtatiously until he asked her, "What about the future, what do you think?" Her young face fell, and she said sullenly, "There is no future," and walked away.

In Ramallah a flurry of cultural events was in evidence: concerts, plays, operas, and visiting choirs, Mozart's *Requiem*. "Yes," said Rita, "it's about solidarity, the outside world coming to perform, saying we know you're here, suffering, but you're not unheard." She described a production of *The Magic Flute*: the Ramallah audience was mixed, some were long-time opera lovers, but many others came for the solidarity, knowing nothing. "The place was packed, and there was a standing ovation like I've never seen after any opera anywhere in the world. There was such heady excitement, such exhilaration that events of such good quality were happening again, right here in Ramallah."

"Siege, isolation, incapacitation, we all feel them. A small proportion of us go into a black area of stress-related disease, but the rest of us are both highly distressed and highly resilient. We depend on each other; resilience is collective. Every day is highly stressful, every day you wake up and you don't know if you can get your child to school, if you can get yourself to work. In the afternoon you don't know if your child will get home safely. It's grinding. My way out is music. I don't know what I'd have done without music, and YouTube—there's this one tenor from the fifties…"

I left Ramallah after visiting Rita and a couple of other equally resilient friends, and drove the short distance back to Jerusalem.

There I caught up with a number of Israelis working tirelessly, and despite real dangers, to end the occupation. One, Amiel, was a professor at Hebrew University who still carries an IDF bullet inside him. He had been demonstrating, peacefully, against settler attacks on Palestinian farmers in the West Bank when he was shot, but was unable to bring the shooter to justice because of a "lack of evidence." Another, Ezra, was a plumber who was later found guilty of "assaulting" two Israeli police officers while in the West Bank defending a Palestinian farmer's home from demolition by the IDF. When 140,000 letters in his defense and supporting his anti-occupation activities were sent to the Israeli Ministry of Justice, the only justification that could be found for his accusal and conviction was that he "provokes local residents." For these "provocations," always nonviolent, he has been repeatedly threatened, beaten, and arrested, and even outed as a gay man.

Mikhail, someone else I went to see, was a clean-cut, handsome man in his late twenties. A former IDF officer, he is now an official in Breaking the Silence, an organization that strives to explain the problems underpinning the conflict as they, the fighters on the front line, have encountered them. "Israelis, and maybe the international community, are not aware of the gravity of the problems, not only on the Palestinian side, but also on the Israeli side. Like, what does 'occupation' really mean? It's much deeper than any map. A majority of Israelis don't understand the meaning, or aren't even aware, of the facts. I was very much the victimizer, part of the 'shooting and crying.' It's often said that we have no choice. That's just not true—we're *obligated* to refuse if an order goes against our conscience. The whole idea of this country was so that we could be in charge of our own destinies. I want to burst the bubble that I was sent to defend Israel—I wasn't. Whether we like it or not it's our call—we're the occupiers." He smiled wearily, adding, "Obviously it's a bit more complicated getting out than it was getting in."

The author, lawyer, and human rights activist Raja Shehadeh, whom I had visited in Ramallah, emailed me to say he was irritated by a conversation I had told him about with Amos Oz. The writer had been eloquent to me about "the wonderful spectacle of debate in Israel; the arguments about the real significance of Jewish heritage, morality, and political and metaphysical good and evil." It was never just about land, he said. "The occupation only evolved the argument. There are as many blueprints and master plans as political individuals—that's the beauty of it. There was never the one dream of the founding fathers and mothers. When I look at what we have, I see a warm-hearted, temperamental, materialistic, noisy and passionate people, culturally vivacious, bursting with creativity, guilt-ridden, and endlessly argumentative. I love it. Self-righteous and hypocritical, feeling sorry for itself—about the occupation—yes, our share in it." But Oz's recommendations of economic assistance for the Palestinians were characteristic, in Raja's view, of "a classic liberal's position akin to a white South African during apartheid proposing that the South African situation could be resolved through keeping everything as is [the apartheid system] and just infusing enough money to make everyone happy. It is so typical of people who want to feel good while remaining faithful to the establishment; refusing to see the cause of the problem and looking for solutions that retain the evil edifice while appealing to the largesse of others (America) to finance the poor and silence their resistance." He bemoaned the widely touted theory that, "With money they will forget their inferior status, and what they lost, and all will live together happily ever after. It is simply so annoying. In a way regimes such as Israel's would not be able to survive without the likes of Oz constantly beautifying all that is ugly and blurring the truth by fine distracting words."

My final journey in the West Bank was to the south. "If you want to see the future for Israel," Mikhail had advised me, "go to Hebron." Here, Genesis tells us, Abraham bought the cave of Machpelah as a burial site for his family; Abraham was buried there, as were Isaac and Jacob. "Hebron," Mikhail said, "is where it all began."

And here, he said, is how it might all end as well: "The settlements are destroying Israel." I wondered what he meant, since Hebron is almost unique—apart from East Jerusalem—in that Israeli settlers in Hebron are living in the heart of a Palestinian community.

An Israeli friend, Ari, offered me a ride. We drove toward the ancient city through the fertile West Bank valleys along roads prohibited or restricted for Palestinians, past the 24-foot-high wall strangling Bethlehem, beside perfect vineyards, laden donkeys, and scores of young children.

Once inside the city we visited a vast Herodian edifice, the Tomb of the Patriarchs (Abraham, Isaac, and so on). Inside, a young Israeli soldier sat awkwardly on a metal chair, absorbed in his hand-held electronic game. He replied cheerfully to my friend's questions: no, he didn't know anything about the tombs he was guarding. Around him, other Jews prayed alone or in groups, whispering their invocations. Beyond a dividing wall, Muslims were also praying.

Outside in the warm spring air all was quiet. Unearthly quiet. A couple of Israeli policemen at their watch post eyed Ari and me with weary stares until we tried to leave by way of the wrong exit. "No, no, that's for Palestinians," they objected.

My companion, who was 82, explained in Hebrew that there could be no harm and we would end up in the same place even if we did go the "Jewish" way around. They were immovable. We walked around.

As we did, we saw that the street was boarded-up and dead. "This can't be the street I remember," said Ari, and he headed off to ask a soldier, holed up in a concrete pillbox, the name of the street. The soldier had no idea: "I don't know the name of the street. All I know is that the Arabs have to walk on one side, the Jews on the other. And I have to keep them apart."

But it was the street that Ari remembered. "They've killed it," he said, shocked. "They've killed this town."

We walked through more empty streets, every storefront shuttered in metal and bolted, splashed with burns and graffiti. It was unnerving, standing in the stilled meat market, knowing that not long ago there was a noisy community of thousands living, working, and thriving here. But now it was empty and abandoned, partly demolished. Even more unnerving, in the stillness, was knowing that there were many unseen eyes—and cameras—on us: settlers wondering whose "side" we were on, Palestinians locked inside their houses, soldiers knowing they have to keep everyone apart, and international observers—officials, church groups—who watch and monitor, but cannot intervene.

The revered Palestinian negotiator and physician Dr. Haider Abdel Shafi had told me how he had lived in Hebron as a child and would light candles on the Sabbath for the Jewish family who lived next door. The Jewish and Palestinian communities of Hebron maintained essentially good relations until the advent of Zionism, of which the Jews of Hebron were not a part. But in 1929, 67 Jews were massacred by Palestinians in the ongoing wave of nationalist struggle taking place in Palestine at the time. The remainder of the Jewish Hebron community was evacuated by the ruling British, and most of their descendants have decided not to return.

Not so, however, a small group who established a "return" after the 1967 war. Since then, relations with the Palestinians of Hebron have been violent and lawless, causing repeated problems for the Israeli government.

A system of "separation" was instituted after Baruch Goldstein, a settler and Brooklyn doctor, murdered 29 Muslims praying in the Tomb of the Patriarchs in 1994. The Israeli government almost removed the tiny settler community from the city of 150,000 Palestinians, but then rejected the idea. Instead, "sterile buffer zones" were created—that is, zones that are "free" of Palestinians—which widen with every clash, allowing the gradual takeover of territory.* Apart from enforcing segregation, the IDF in H2 uses various methods of control to keep the peace, including boarding up Palestinian houses and shops and imposing curfews. It has been impossible to maintain economic life under these conditions.

Curfews may last for two weeks before the army allows a two-hour break to let Palestinians out of their homes in order to stock up with supplies before curfew is slapped on again. Between 2002 and 2003 there were 500 days of curfew. The Jewish community is not put under curfew.

When there is violence between the communities—well documented, largely by Israeli organizations, since the 1970s—it is up to the Israeli army and police to intervene. Unlike Palestinian violence toward settlers, settler violence toward Palestinians rarely results in arrests, let alone prosecutions. The latter is a frequent, and distressing, occurrence. I met the headmistress of a Palestinian school that comes under regular attack from settlers, especially young ones: she described the failure of the Israeli police to protect her staff and students, and how they have to rely instead on support from Christian volunteers from abroad.

All along one street the IDF has barred and bolted every door—all to Palestinian homes—from the outside. When they need anything the inhabitants have to climb out of the top floor and clamber over the roofs at the back of each building in order to reach the outside world. If someone is ill, medical help has to come the same way. The dead too, are carried out over the roofs.

As a result of the separation, the control and repression, and the violence in the context of two systems of law, 30 to 40 percent of Palestinians have left this part of Hebron during the last ten years. Some would call this ethnic cleansing.

---

* Under the 1996 Hebron Agreement the city was divided into H1, under Palestinian control, and H2, under Israeli control. H2 is home to 500 Jews and 40,000 Palestinians.

"There is a military policy that is causing the Arab population to leave the center of Hebron," Haggai Alon, an advisor to the Israeli defense minister, said in an interview with *Ha'aretz*.[33] "But that is not the policy of the State of Israel. The problem is that under military rule the spirit of the commander is stronger than anything else."

Alon's job, he told Israeli journalist Meron Rapaport, "is to ensure that the official statements made by the Israeli government regarding its policy toward the Palestinians are in fact implemented." Instead, he says, "the IDF is setting a route for the fence that will not enable the establishment of a Palestinian state and is allowing itself to evade High Court orders to change the route. The army is carrying out an apartheid policy that is emptying Hebron of Arabs, setting up roadblocks without anyone knowing where and how many, Judaizing the Jordan Valley, and cooperating openly and blatantly with the settlers."

We met the Hebron settlers' spokesman, who immediately said that he recognized Ari. Ari Rath, editor of the *Jerusalem Post* for 15 years, had given a lecture in 1974, in which he had talked about repentance. David Wilder, the settler spokesman, reminded him. Behind the spokesman's head was a map. Its subtitle asked, "Don't the Arab states have enough land of their own?" The shaded "Arab" areas on the map included Iran and Turkey.

We listened as David explained: "The Arabs are trying to exterminate us," and that "all this acquiescence only encourages them to take more and more. I believe in the two-state solution," he said: "We get Israel. They get something else. If peace is so sublime why doesn't Egypt give the so-called Palestinians the Sinai?" Like Mikhail, he too saw Hebron as a model, but from a different point of view: "if Jews aren't allowed to live here in Hebron, why would the billion Arabs, who don't want us, leave us alone anywhere?"

Ari tried to reason with him. In doing so he mentioned the right of return, whereupon the response was a furious, "That's post-Zionist nonsense. The Arabs in '48 packed their bags of their own accord. For us it was all about survival. There is no connection." Ari said later that he could have cited all the evidence about the Palestinian exodus, or the moral issues, or the legal… but he didn't. It is easier to leave extremists to the comfort of their mythologies.

Ari drove me back to Jerusalem. He played Verdi's *Requiem* and we talked, full of gloom, about Mikhail's prediction. Ari was taken aback by the vehemence of the settlers' views, and their impact. Israel had celebrated its 60th birthday in June 2008. If Hebron is the future, with its dual system of law, separation, oppression, and ethnic cleansing—and the fragmentation of the West Bank makes this outcome virtually inescapable—what will Israel's 70th birthday look like?

The year 2000, when we arrived in Jerusalem, was a key moment. Peace, however fictional, still seemed realizable. The situation was simmering but had not yet blown up, exposing fully the failure-myths of Oslo. We walked into it a month before the situation declared itself at crisis point, and watched flurries of last-minute attempts to respond before the diehards and extremists at home took hold. What I had done was witness one dramatic chapter in an ongoing process. Like so many others, I had thought I was seeing something new, and I thought that I would see things change, but I was wrong on both counts.

As long as it remains easier to reach heaven than the end of the street—or the field, or school, or hospital, or the next-door village, let alone Jerusalem, the City of God—then no security measure yet devised will stop people seeking a gruesome shortcut to end their hell on earth. As Rita said, there can be no peace without justice, but the willingness to make peace exists. It's real, but drowned out.

Now, with a new president in the US, there is hope that the situation will be addressed at last. Not just the smokescreen of events and the accompanying excuses and delaying tactics that have become so familiar, but the real situation that lies behind it. How many times do Israelis and Palestinians have to prove themselves unable to reach peace alone? How many more times will the international community allow the bar to be reset knowing that the setting is designed to be unreachable and therefore only a ruse to prolong the process? For how much longer is peace to be a "process" only, and all the while entrenchment on both sides, both in concrete and in hatred, allowed to fester, making peace ultimately all the harder?

Days after President Barack Obama's inauguration a bilateral group of ten high-level former government officials, including Brent Scowcroft and Zbigniew Brzezinski, presented to him a report entitled, "A Last Chance for a Two-State Israel-Palestine Agreement." There can be no understating the importance of its title, timing, and intent.

This is surely the last chance indeed, if it is not already too late. If such an agreement is not reached, the prospects for Israelis and Palestinians are grim: a continuation of the status quo, the "microcosms" General Gilad had so genially described back in 2002, putting people into pens and screwing down their lives, is palpably unsustainable. At best, this would mean a series of mini-Gazas in the West Bank, centered on the main Palestinian cities, isolated from one another and from independent life, existing on handouts from Israel or the international community. And throughout, especially where the enlarging settlements encroach on Palestinian homes, the ordeal of "Hebronization" would be imposed.

Dr. David Kimche said to me in 2007: "The two-state solution is the one thing that can save us from the eventual end of Zionism. We have to be told in the plainest language possible that the two-state solution is US policy *and* that the US will do everything possible to achieve it. Not just an afternoon tea sort of speech made by President Bush, but a statement of US policy; that they *want* to achieve it, and in order to achieve it the US will really push for it." Dr. Kimche, diplomat, scholar, and writer, was once deputy head of Mossad. "The majority of Israelis would welcome action by the US on this. The problem with that majority is that they don't believe it's possible. That's the crux of the problem. Neither we nor the Palestinians think the other will ever make peace. The US could make it possible. And it could be solved by an active policy by the international community. Our government would object, in all probability, but it's important enough for the international community—the US in particular—to insist on doing it. It's not just a question of helping Israel or the Palestinians. Quieting down this region goes far beyond the issue of the Israelis and Palestinians."

As advised and as Dr. Kimche hoped, President Obama has indeed launched a concerted drive to resolve the conflict. From the start of his term in office, he has engaged the issue. On the first day of his tenure as president he contacted the leaders of the Palestinian Authority, Israel, Egypt, and Jordan. Naming Senator George Mitchell as his special envoy, on day two, the president signaled that his intentions were serious. In interviews with Arabic media, visits to the Mideast, and a powerful speech in Cairo, Obama pronounced a shift in US policy toward evenhandedness that has been widely welcomed across the world.

He has moved on to a list of demands: of Israel, an end to settlement building; of the Palestinians, a return to negotiations; of both sides that the terms of the road map and the conditions of the Quartet must be met; and of the Arabs concrete gestures toward normalization and to build on the Arab peace initiative. He has made clear the conviction that advancing the peace process and bringing about the establishment of a Palestinian state is essential to Israel's welfare and security. It is self-evident that the same applies to the Palestinians.

One *Jerusalem Post* writer pointed out that although settlements had neither ensured the dream of Jewish sovereignty as far as the Jordan River, nor prevented the world—or the majority of the Israeli public—from accepting the inevitability of a Palestinian state, they had succeeded in making the implementation of the two-state solution as difficult as it has ever been. But, he added, "Obama's is the first US administration to see it for what it is, rather than be blinkered by the 'freeze' terminology sold to it by Israeli officialdom."[34]

Indeed, fully aware of the blocking techniques, President Obama confronted the settlement question squarely, insisting on a total freeze. As pointed out by many Israeli commentators, the official US position on settlements has always been clear: "Obama did not invent a new American policy. The United States has long held that the settlements are illegal; the same is true for the status of East Jerusalem and the Golan Heights…" readers read in *Ha'aretz*, "The Americans are sticking to the same road map drawn up seven years ago, it's just that Israel apparently didn't notice that the Palestinians have fulfilled the first article in the document almost completely. Military action against Israel has stopped, even from the Gaza Strip, and an increasingly effective Palestinian force in the West Bank is taking action against terror organizations. Israel, in contrast, has not met its road map obligations and continues to argue over the terms of the agreement—as if it never adopted it…"[35]

Opposition to Obama's strategy, inevitably, has already mobilized. The Israeli prime minister, Benjamin Netanyahu, objected strongly to Obama's demand to stop settlement building, and even more so when the administration objected to Israeli construction of settler apartments in East Jerusalem, after which American officials said that Washington does not differentiate between East Jerusalem and unauthorized outposts.[36] In the US, Obama will confront strenuous opposition. Henry Siegman, director of the US Middle East Project in New York, predicts that Obama "will face growing criticism from pro-Israel pundits and publications, and politicians who depend on campaign contributions from Israel's backers will press him to moderate his stance. Many of Israel's supporters will defend the special relationship because they believe that the two countries' interests are synonymous, and because they believe that even mild pressure on Israel might jeopardize its security." Difficult though the task may be, President Obama could benefit from recent domestic shifts. Whereas the American Jewish community is overwhelmingly liberal and progressive, its leadership has not necessarily reflected the views of the majority on the question of Israel and the Palestinians—those who are supportive of Israel, but not of "Greater Israel" or its territorial ambitions. Until now, those moderate voices have not been adequately represented. A recent poll found that a majority of Jewish Americans (approximately 70 percent) support President Obama's moves, and a two-state solution that includes a Palestinian capital in Jerusalem with some limited "right to return." In addition, a strong majority opposes settlement construction. Increasingly, Jewish Americans see the truth of Ehud Olmert's words about Israel's future when he warned that if there is no two-state solution Israel will "face a South-African-style struggle... and as soon as that happens, the state of Israel is finished." New and existing pro-peace organizations are now providing the forum, structure, and voice of this majority: J Street, Americans for Peace Now, Brit Tzedek v'Shalomare and the Israel Policy Forum, all of which are committed to a two-state solution and support strong American leadership to end the conflict, urging Israel to change tack before it's too late.

With all these encouraging developments within the US can we now, with a US president who not only sees the realities but seems to be prepared to act on them, dare to hope for a just solution? And if a just solution is agreed upon, will it be implemented and enforced?

Or will the cowardice of the past decades that we have all demonstrated, myself included, continue to block us from confronting the conflict with honesty? And, if so, at what cost to Israelis and Palestinians, and their children?

Notes

Introduction

1 Interview with author, 3 May 2004.

2 "NO EXIT," *Harpers Magazine*, 2 January 2004 (Interviews with Israeli soldiers, identified by pseudonyms, conducted by Israeli journalist Uri Blau and first published in *Kol Ha'Ir*, a Jerusalem weekly, in September 2001. Translated from the Hebrew by Tal Haran).

1 A Forest of Peace

1 For the allocation of the refugees' property in Israel, see, for example, Tom Segev, *1949: The First Israelis* (New York: Henry Holt, 1998), Chapter 3.

2 "All Changed, Changed Utterly"

1 Shmuel Ben-Ruby, spokesperson of the Jerusalem District of the Israeli Policy Forum (IPF), in a telephone conversation with B'Tselem on 4 October 2000.

2 "Peril in the Palestinians' Territories," Committee to Protect Journalists report, 9 November 2000.

3 "Events on the Temple Mount," B'Tselem Report, 29 September 2000.

4 See Amnon Kapeliouk, *Ha'aretz* 23 November 2001, and Eyad El Sarraj, "An Encounter with Arafat and back," *Palestine Chronicle* 18 January 2004.

5 The commission, initiated at the Sharm el-Sheikh summit meeting, convened by President Clinton in October 2000, reported in April 2001. The chief recommendations were resumption of negotiations, confidence-building measures, security cooperation, and cessation of violence. Also recommended: the government of Israel "should freeze all settlement activity, including the 'natural growth' of existing settlements."

6 Quoted by Amnon Kapeliouk, *Ha'aretz* 23 November 2001.

7 "Tacit Consent," B'Tselem Report, March 2001.

8 *Ha'aretz* 5 October 2000.

9 Graham Usher, "The al-Aqsa Intifada," *Middle East International* 13 October 2000.

10 Akiva Eldar, "Military intelligence presented erroneous assumption on Palestinians," *Ha'aretz* 10 June 2004. Similarly, from interrogations of Palestinians arrested during Operation Defensive Shield it emerged clearly that "during the ten days following Ariel Sharon's visit to the Temple Mount, the disturbances were utterly spontaneous—an emotional response by field activists whose hearts contracted at the sight of 'the storm trooper of the Lebanon War' arrogantly trampling the sanctity of Islam underfoot. This was accompanied by a feeling of despair at the spread of the Jewish settlements in the territories and the frequent closures, as well as a feeling of disgust at the corruption among Arafat's people who control the mechanism of the PA. These field activists came mainly from Fatah, but also from the opposition organizations, and they had not received orders from above, from Arafat or from those who do his bidding. They inflamed their disciples, who from the outset shared these emotions. Only at the end of ten days, testified those who were questioned, did the PA and the Fatah leadership—who until then had been in a state of confusion, and mainly silent, in face of the seething street—'take charge,' give orders and provide funding. And that with the aim of fanning the flames... That is, since the spring of 2002, the defense establishment and the Prime Minister have known for certain that Arafat did not initiate the disturbances at their outset, and that it was only later that he joined the fray and exacerbated the situation." Emmanuel Sivan, "What the General is allowed," *Ha'aretz* 14 June 2004.

11 "Peril in the Palestinians' Territories," Committee to Protect Journalists report, November 2000.

12 Tanya Reinhart, "Don't Say You Didn't Know," *Indymedia* (www.indymedia.org) 6 November 2000.

13 Kathleen Christison, "The American Media Spin," *Middle East International* 10 November 2000.

14 Baruch Kimmerling, "The Right to Resist," *Ha'aretz* 27 March 2001.

3 "The Only Real Option"

1 Ari Shavit, "Sharon is Sharon is Sharon," *Ha'aretz* 12 April 2001.

2 Benny Morris, *Righteous Victims* (London: John Murray, 1999) 341.

3 Cited by Israel Imperial News, London, March 1968, quoted in Nur Masalha, *A Land Without a People* (London: Faber and Faber, 1997) 82–3.

4 Masalha, *A Land Without a People* 93.

5 For example, Military Order 58 deemed any Palestinian titleholder not at home—for whatever reason—at the moment of the war an "absentee," and gave the Israeli government the right to take over that property. This measure provided land for settlement building. It allowed, for example, 40 percent of the Jordan Valley to be expropriated by 1978. See also Morris, *Righteous Victims* 339.

6 Avi Shlaim, *The Iron Wall: Israel and the Arab World* (London: Penguin, 2000) 459.

7 According to B'Tselem, 160 Israelis were killed by Palestinians and 1,162 Palestinians were killed by Israelis during the first Intifada, between December 8, 1987 and September 13, 1993. Five of the Israelis and 250 of the Palestinians were children. Three hundred and fifty-nine Palestinians were killed by Palestinians, mostly accused of collaboration with Israel. One estimate gives 15,000–20,000 Palestinians injured by Israelis during the same period. (Mark Tessler, *A History of the Israeli-Palestinian Conflict*, Bloomington: Indiana University Press, 1994: 701; quoted in Morris, *Righteous Victims* 596.)

8 "Thirsty for a Solution: The Water Crisis in the Occupied Territories and its Resolution in the Final-Status Agreement," B'Tselem Report, July 2000.

9 César Chelala, "Stop demolishing Palestinian homes," *International Herald Tribune* 8 May 2003.

10 At a press conference on June 29, 1999, then Assistant Secretary of State Martin Indyk commented on "security cooperation, which the Palestinians have done a good job on... We have always said that the Palestinians have done a good job on some of the issues, particularly on the security cooperation issue and combating terrorism. We weren't the only ones to say that; Prime Minister Netanyahu, at one point, called Yasser Arafat and thanked him for the efforts that he'd been undertaking." Similarly, Ami Ayalon, then head of the Israeli secret service, announced in a government meeting on April 5, 1998 that "Arafat is doing his job—he is fighting terror and puts all his weight against the Hamas." *Ha'aretz* 6 April 1998.

11 In November 1988, at the meeting of the Palestine National Congress (PNC) in Algiers, Arafat won a majority for the proposal to recognize Israel's legitimacy, to accept all relevant UN resolutions from November 1947 on, to adopt the two-state solution and issue a declaration of independence for a state in the West Bank and Gaza Strip

with East Jerusalem as its capital, thereby abandoning the claim to the whole of Palestine enshrined in the PNC (Shlaim, *The Iron Wall* 466). In 1993 Arafat wrote to PM Rabin after the signing of the Declaration of Principles, confirming "the PLO's commitment to recognize Israel's right to live in peace and security, to accept UN Security Council Resolutions 242 and 338, to renounce the use of terrorism and other acts of violence, and to change those parts of the Palestinian National Charter that were inconsistent with these commitments" (Shlaim, *The Iron Wall* 518). On December 14, 1998, witnessed and applauded by President Clinton, the PNC voted "to lay to rest the PLO goal of destroying Israel," and there was a renewed cancellation of the offending clauses of the Charter. Six days later the Israeli government suspended implementation of the second pullback stipulated in the Wye River Memorandum whose course the Palestinians had "scrupulously adhered to" (Shlaim, *The Iron Wall* 604).

12 Figures given by B'Tselem, Jerusalem.

13 *See* Hussein Agha and Robert Malley, "Camp David: The Tragedy of Errors," *New York Review of Books* 9 August 2001; Charles Enderlin, *Shattered Dreams: The Failure of the Peace Process in the Middle East, 1995–2002*, trans. Susan Fairfield (New York: Other Press, 2003); Deborah Sontag, "Quest for Middle East Peace: How and Why it Failed," *New York Times* 26 July 2001; Clayton E. Swisher, *The Truth about Camp David: The Untold Story about the Collapse of the Middle East Peace Process* (New York: Nation Books, 2004). Quoted in Tamara Cofman Wittes, ed., *How Israelis and Palestinians Negotiate: A Cross-Cultural Analysis of the Oslo Peace Process*, United States Institute of Peace, Washington, DC, 2005: 39.

14 The Allon Plan, named for Israeli cabinet minister Yigal Allon, was presented on July 26, 1967. The plan proposed incorporating into Israel most of the Jordan Valley, most of the Judean Desert, a large part of greater Jerusalem and the Latrun salient. It included as few Palestinians as possible, recommended building permanent settlements and army bases to strengthen Israeli control of the land, and giving local Palestinian leaders autonomy over what land remained, which would be linked economically to Israel. This was neither accepted nor rejected by the Israeli cabinet. "It was to remain the unwritten platform of Israel's Labor-led governments down to 1977, and of Labor in opposition thereafter" (Morris, *Righteous Victims* 330).

15 Baruch Kimmerling, *Politicide* (London: Verso, 2003) 130–131.

4 A Sense of Closure

1 Chemi Shalev, "Bone in the throat," *Ma'ariv* 23 June 2003.

2 Ibid. Sharon, says Shalev, "deployed the settlements in strategic locations, the length and breadth of the land, and set the Israeli presence in the territories deep in the ground, with iron stakes, and concrete." He "thought of everything—except the possibility that probably seemed fantastic in his eyes at the time, that one day, of all people, it would be him who would want to leave, at least partially, and find himself unable to do so, because it's too late."

3 Since the start of the Intifada four months before there had been five bombings, killing six Israelis ("Suicide and Other Bombing Attacks in Israel since the Declaration of Principles," Israeli Ministry of Foreign Affairs website, www.mfa.gov.il).

4 Jeff Halper, "The 94 Percent Solution, A Matrix of Control," *Middle East Report* 216 (Fall 2000).

5 See, for example: Meron Benvenisti, *Sacred Landscape: The Buried History of the Holy Land since 1948* (Berkeley, CA: University of California Press, 2002), or Mahmoud Darwish, *Unfortunately, It Was Paradise* (Berkeley, CA: University of California Press, 2003).

6 *Ha'aretz* 8 January 2001; letters page, *Ha'aretz* 17 January 2001; "Soldiers taking photographs of themselves with their victims [battered Palestinians], holding their heads by the hair like hunting trophies," Lee Hockstader, *Washington Post* 19 September 2000.

5 It Can't Get Worse

1 The plan to topple Arafat, known as "Fields of Thorns," which had been prepared as far back as 1996, and was then updated in early 2000 once the Intifada began, was reported by Amir Oren, *Ha'aretz* 23 November 2001.

2 *Shamgar Commission Report in the Matter of the Massacre at the Cave of the Patriarchs* (Jerusalem, 1994) 157–200, 250–251, quoted in "Impossible Coexistence: Human Rights in Hebron since the Massacre at the Cave of the Patriarchs," B'Tselem Report, September 1995.

3 "At a welcoming ceremony for the Pope, Mr Assad said: 'We see them [Israel] attacking sacred Christian and Muslim places in Palestine ... They try to kill the principle of religions in the same mentality in which they betrayed Jesus Christ and tried to kill the prophet Mohammed.' The Israeli President, Moshe Katsav, said it was 'surpris-

ing that the Pope did not find it appropriate to correct Assad's statements.'" Ewen MacAskill, "Pope makes history in Syria, and angers Israel," *Guardian* 7 May 2001.

4 Ghada Ageel and Suzanne Goldenberg, "Baby's killing fuels hatred," *Guardian* 8 May 2001.

5 "Border patrol fired at reporters' video shows," *Ha'aretz* 17 May 2001.

6 Middle East Policy Council statistics.

6 The Head in the Yard

1 Haim Shalev, *Ma'ariv* 1 August 2001.

2 Chris Hedges, "A Gaza Diary: Scenes from the Palestinian Uprising," *Harper's Magazine* October 2001.

3 The army's audit department sent four senior undercover officers on a tour of checkpoints. The officers were "treated to negative, arrogant, and insulting behavior." The report concluded that most checkpoints were "not organized to stop hostile elements," "the checking of cars is done randomly," and they "harm the Palestinian population by creating friction between soldiers and Palestinians, with the former victimizing the latter." "Checkpoints don't work, says internal IDF report," *Ha'aretz* 2 November 2001.

4 Naomi Klein, "The Likud doctrine," *Guardian* 10 September 2004.

7 In Bethlehem?

1 The PFLP's victim, Rehavam Ze'evi, was a member of the Israeli government. He held views that many Israelis found repellent: he had headed a political party whose name alone—the Transfer Party—was shocking to many, and he was the foremost exponent in Israel of ethnic cleansing. Mr. Ze'evi had believed that all Palestinians should be expelled, not just from the West Bank, but also from inside Israel, in other words the expulsion of one fifth of Israeli citizens. He was a celebrated user of racial incitement, referring to Palestinians as "vermin" and "lice," and had publicly demanded the assassination of PA leaders.

2 "Two weeks after the invasion, it can be said that never before—throughout all the sieges and closures that were imposed and lifted in the past—has the paralysis of civilian life been so harsh as it has been in these past two weeks... Their suffering intensifies their hatred. They see themselves as victims of a collective punishment, of revenge for revenge's sake. And naturally, their support for those they perceive as

resisting the arbitrarily vengeful punishment only increases."
'Withdraw from the cities," editorial, *Ha'aretz* 2 November 2001.
3 Physicians for Human Rights-Israel Report, 25 October 2001.
4 Ibid.
5 Sara Leibovitz-Dar, "Half-truths and double-talk," *Ha'aretz* 25 January 2002.
6 Alex Fishman had reported in *Yediot Ahronoth*, "Nothing of what has happened in the last few days is by accident. It was all written down, black on white, in a document that was published on the eve of the elections and then immediately after the elections, under the headline 'The Dagan Plan...' The plan came from Sharon's unchanging view that Arafat was a murderer not to be negotiated with, and the Oslo accords were "the greatest disaster in the modern history of the people of Israel, and therefore everything must be done to eliminate them." As a result, Fishman reported, Israel had "spent the past weeks doing everything possible to prevent progress in the political realm and 'succeeded' in torpedoing Zinni's mission." Alex Fishman, *Ha'aretz* 19 October 2001.
7 Danny Rubinstein, "Who must stop the violence?," *Ha'aretz* 26 November 2001.
8 Rosenblum wrote: "When he served as the peace-torpedoer in the Shamir government, Sharon... stuck to three no's: 'no negotiations with the PLO, no Palestinian state, and no settlement freeze.' Since he had become Prime Minister, a new three no's had taken the place of the originals: 'no division of Jerusalem, no right of return and no dismantling of settlements.'" Sharon was still wedded to the old set of no's, said Rosenblum, who invited Israelis to "Ask yourselves, and give an honest answer: Are there negotiations with the PLO today? Is there a Palestinian state? Is there a settlement freeze?" Doron Rosenblum, *Ha'aretz* 30 November 2001.
9 "Whoever gave a green light to this act of liquidation knew full well that he is thereby shattering in one blow the gentleman's agreement between Hamas and the Palestinian Authority; under that agreement, Hamas was to avoid in the near future suicide bombings inside the Green Line, of the kind perpetrated at the Dolphinarium [discotheque in Tel Aviv]. Such an agreement did exist, even if neither the PA nor Hamas would admit it in public. It is a fact that, while the security services did accumulate repeated warnings of planned Hamas terrorist attacks within the Green Line, these did not materialize. That cannot

be attributed solely to the Shabak's impressive success in intercepting the suicide bombers and their controllers. Rather, the respective leaderships of the PA and Hamas came to the understanding that it would be better not to play into Israel's hands by mass attacks on its population centers. This understanding was, however, shattered by the assassination the day before yesterday—and whoever decided upon the liquidation of Abu Hunoud knew in advance that that would be the price. The subject was extensively discussed both by Israel's military echelon and its political one, before it was decided to carry out the liquidation." Alex Fishman, *Yediot Ahronoth* 25 November 2001.

10 *Ha'aretz* 28 December 2001.

11 Charles Glass, "The scene is set for another Lebanon," *New Statesman* 10 December 2001.

12 "How," the former deputy mayor of Jerusalem wondered, "can we explain the series of military actions whose only purpose was to humiliate the Palestinian collective, deny its legitimacy and destroy its infrastructure?... What pressing security need was there in the destruction of [Arafat's] helicopters...? What vital operational need was there in the barbaric break-in to the Palestinian Authority's Central Bureau of Statistics, stealing its data...? The excuses expose the ideological goal, not the security needs, of the Israeli government... It's not a war on the articles of the [Oslo] agreements. It is the very recognition of the PLO as the national movement of the Palestinian people that Sharon is still fighting." Meron Benvenisti, "A Footnote for the future," *Ha'aretz* 13 December 2001.

13 Thomas O'Dwyer, *Ha'aretz* 7 December 2001: "When the Real IRA tried to bomb the Northern Ireland peace accords to hell and back—including the unbelievable atrocity of the Omagh car bombing—did the British government dig up Dublin airport because, as a nationalist republican entity, the Irish state must be responsible? Did it wipe out the very police stations that were expected to hunt for the terrorists? Did it assassinate a senior IRA leader on the eve of American envoy George Mitchell arriving? Send F-16s into Derry? Time and time again, the British government... proclaimed it would not allow terrorists to set the agenda."

14 Ze'ev Schiff, *Ha'aretz* 4 December 2001.

15 Quoted in Henry Seigman, "Israel: Palestinian moderation isn't what Sharon is seeking," *International Herald Tribune* 4 January 2002.

16 Private conversations with IDF officers.

17 Hatem Lufti, "Israel halts peace march," *Jerusalem Times* 4 January 2002.

18 Regarding the *Karine-A*, one of Israel's leading novelists, David Grossman, wrote: "What proof has been obtained here? Proof that if you oppress a people for 35 years, and humiliate its leaders, and harass its population ... this people will try to assert themselves in any way possible? And would any of us behave differently from the Palestinians in such a situation? And did we behave any differently when for years we were under occupation and tyranny?" *Ha'aretz* 6 January 2002.

19 Zbigniew Brzezinski, "Wanted: A US blueprint for a Middle East peace," *International Herald Tribune* 26–27 January 2002.

20 Hemi Shalev, *Ma'ariv* 15 January 2002.

21 Uzi Benziman, *Ha'aretz* 18 January 2002.

22 Phil Reeves, "Israel sends in its death squads and more bulldozers," *Independent* 15 January 2002.

23 Danny Rubinstein, "Karmi's assassination has already and directly cost lives of the ten Israelis who died in last week's murderous terrorist attacks," *Ha'aretz* 21 January 2002.

8 "When We Are Destroyed"

1 Joss Dray and Denis Sieffert, *La guerre israélienne de l'information, désinformation et fausses symétries dans le conflit Israélo-Palestinien* (Paris: La Découverte, 2002) 87.

2 Nahum Barnea, "Against another," *Yediot Ahronoth* 4 March 2002.

3 Ze'ev Schiff, "On the brink of chaos," *Ha'aretz* 9 March 2002.

4 Human Rights Watch interview with Efrat Ravid, age twenty, Maale Adumim, 12 June 2002 quoted in "Erased in a Moment: Suicide Bombing Attacks against Israeli Civilians," Human Rights Watch Report, October 2002.

5 Ibid. 76.

6 *New York Times*, 4 April 2002, quoted in "Erased in a Moment: Suicide Bombing Attacks Against Israeli Civilians," Human Rights Watch Report, October 2002.

7 Human Rights Watch interview with Rachel Klirs, daughter of Clara Rosenberger, Jerusalem, 2 July 2002, in "Erased in a Moment" (see note 4).

8 PM Sharon's address to the nation, 31 March 2003.

9 "The Limits of Force," *New York Times* editorial, *International Herald*

Tribune, 1 April 2000. The editorial pleaded for a political solution, since the military solution could never end the conflict. Israel's decision to build the settlements "and then pour billions into protecting and defending them, has been one of the biggest obstacles to reaching a workable, two-state solution. Israel must make clear that it recognizes the need to relinquish the bulk of the territories it took in 1967... there is no guarantee that a retreat from the West Bank and Gaza Strip and the construction of a secure border will end Palestinian terror. But it will greatly reduce it and give the Palestinians a reason to control their own terror groups."

10 The army had long-established plans to reoccupy areas administered by the PA and to destroy its infrastructure, see for example, Tanya Reinhart, "Field of Thorns," www.nthposition.com, April 2002.

11 B'Tselem Press Release: "Humanitarian Crisis in Jenin Escalates," 6 April 2002. Two years after Operation Defensive Shield, Israeli writer Elyakim Haetzni was rightly outraged when Egyptian authorities delayed the passage of ambulances and equipment crossing the border to help Israeli victims of the bomb attack on the Taba hotel in Sinai: "Who knows how many wounded paid with their lives for that," he asked. He also said: "If Jewish victims had experienced such attitudes anywhere else in the world, everyone would be talking about anti-Semitism. In Israel, there's another element—hatred for the Zionist state. The fact that the cruel Egyptian behavior is not perceived here as the enmity of an enemy and toward the Jew, as it appears on their TV stations, says something about the depth of the psychosis in the Israeli soul. It is difficult for it to understand, even after 100 years of Zionism, that the goy still regards the Israeli as a "Jew" in the most "Exile-like" meaning of the term, easily debased, not worthy of any respect." Elyakim Haetzni, "Settling Accounts with Egypt," *Yediot Ahronoth* 11 October 2004.

12 Interview with Jenin hospital staff by UN personnel.

13 Neta Golan, "The world just watches," *International Herald Tribune* 5 April 2002.

14 *Yediot Ahronoth* poll.

15 Prime Minister Ariel Sharon's political address to the Knesset, 8 April 2002.

16 Amos Harel and Amira Hass, "Peres calls IDF operation in Jenin a 'massacre,'" *Ha'aretz* 9 April 2002.

17 IDF Brigadier-General Kitrey announced that the "degree of resistance

was beyond our expectation." He said that after the ambush the "Palestinians refused orders to remove bodies or to treat the wounded. They were acting on orders from the terrorists inside the camp, who wanted to create the impression of a massacre. Gunmen shot at ambulances. The difficult fighting," he said, "proves clearly there was no massacre." Briefing by Brigadier-General Ron Kitrey, IDF spokesperson, 9 April 2002.

18 Nahum Barnea, "Jenin, a temporary farewell," *Yediot Ahronoth* 20 April 2002.

19 Anat Cigelman, Amos Harel, and Amira Hass, *Ha'aretz* 12 April 2002: a report that the IDF intended to bury Palestinians killed in the West Bank camp. They estimated that 200 Palestinians had died in clashes with the IDF. Two infantry companies, along with members of the military rabbinate, would enter the camp to collect the bodies: civilian dead would be taken to a hospital in Jenin, and then on to burial, terrorists would be buried at a special cemetery in the Jordan Valley. One Israeli source said that the burials were to prevent the Palestinians using the bodies for propaganda.

20 ICRC activities on the West Bank, 16 April 2002.

21 "The Massacre that Wasn't," editorial, *New York Post* 17 April 2002.

22 Fareed Zakaria, "Colin Powell's Humiliation," *Newsweek* 29 April 2002.

23 Colonel Didi Yedidya, Israel Radio, 19 April 2002. In 2004 the IDF accused UNRWA of transporting Palestinian homemade rockets in an ambulance, publishing photographs as evidence. On closer examination, the IDF admitted, it was clear that the long thin object the ambulance worker was holding in one hand was a rolled-up stretcher.

24 Briefing by Major Dr. David Tzengan, Jenin Brigade doctor, 22 April 2002: "The IDF took risks to avoid harm to civilians—but civilians provided cover to terrorists and sent their children with bombs." The camp—of between 13,000 and 15,000 people—Dr. Tzengan believed, "was not civilian, rather a centre of terror. We are talking about 400 terrorists, this camp sent many suicide bombers... We called for civilians to leave. The civilians that remained, many of them were used as a human shield by the terrorists... The army went from house to house so as not to harm civilians. In total we lost 23 soldiers, excellent people. Several of them I knew and it was very difficult. This was because we chose not to bomb the camp from the air... The UN levels accusations at us with no connection to reality. There was no damage

caused to the hospital in Jenin... every doctor knows that there was not even one bullet fired. We never stopped ambulances from passing through... All those that wanted entered... Four days afterward there was no smell in the camp and there was no situation where burial was not allowed. Within five days we found 25 bodies. The accusations of massacre couldn't be further from reality." When journalists asked him why the IDF closed the camp for so long, Major Dr Tzengan replied, "The camp was full of explosives in every direction, there were booby-trapped bodies, we are talking about a place full of armed terrorists and we could not take a chance that innocent civilians will be injured. Every Palestinian that needed help was given help by our best people. We never prevented the giving of assistance."

25 Tsadok Yeheskeli, "I made them a stadium in the middle of the camp," *Yediot Ahronoth* 31 May 2002. Gush Shalom, the Israeli human rights organization that circulated the article, commented that the man was a fanatic soccer fan and a self-confessed troublemaker who begged his commanders for a chance to take part in "the action." "His story may be extreme, and this man must answer to many serious questions, but Moshe Nissim is not much different from thousands of other frustrated and violent soccer fans, who terrorize cities in Europe after a soccer match. But then again, of course, it is inconceivable that the British army would send a drunken and frustrated Manchester soccer fan into Belfast riding a D-9 bulldozer. What kind of army puts a 60 ton, multi-million dollar demolishing tractor in the hands of such a person, who has not operated one before? How could his rampage go on, without being stopped by any of the officers? How can this army insist it is the 'most moral army in the world'?" Gush Shalom, 31 May 2002.

9 Sumud and Corruption

1 Story via William Dalrymple.

2 *Ha'aretz* 25 January 2002, cited by Aluf Benn and Amos Harel, *Ha'aretz* 9 April 2002. The Israeli press had buzzed with outrage that "one of the highest ranking Israeli officers in the territories" had publicly recommended that Israel should study the Nazis in the Warsaw Ghetto. In order to prepare properly for the campaign he said it was essential to learn from every possible source, "even, however shocking it may sound, how the German army fought in the Warsaw Ghetto."

3 Yoel Marcus, "He who rides on the back of a tiger," *Ha'aretz* 30 September 2002.

4 UNSCR 242, 338, et cetera.

5 For many Palestinians, the PA had long since lost all credibility. In the seven years of "self-rule" since the return of their leaders from exile in Tunis, Palestinians had been plagued by repression and betrayal from their own side. Corrupt, disconnected from the people, and jealous of their individual positions—whether related to their finances, their power base, or their proximity to Arafat—above all, jealous of each other, the PA had made itself so unpopular that by April 2000, 71 percent of Palestinians believed PA institutions were corrupt, 65 percent felt unable to criticize the PA without fear, and only 22 percent saw anything positive in Palestinian democracy. Palestinian Center for Policy and Survey Research, Public Opinion Poll 48 (April 2000) www.pcpsr.org/survey/cprspolls/2000/poll48a.html.

6 The new Russian immigrants, whatever their religion, were now some of Sharon's most unquestioning supporters. There had been a pivotal moment when the Dolphinarium nightclub was bombed in the summer of 2001. Many of the young victims had been Russian, and there were reports in the Israeli press about Jewish authorities disputing the parents' rights to bury their children in Jewish cemeteries as they were not properly Jewish. This, and the Russians' terrible losses, had helped integrate the newcomers; they had suffered too.

10 Living with Terror

1 Noam Ben Ze'ev, "A maestro who fights against loud noise and silence," *Ha'aretz* 10 May 2004.

2 Shlomo Lahat, "Breeding grounds for hatred," Opinion (Israel), *Ha'aretz* 5 January 2004.

3 When a lone sniper shot and killed ten IDF soldiers manning a checkpoint at a settlement and then escaped, there were rumors that he had been trained by the IRA, even that he was Irish—no Palestinian marksman could be that good, some Israelis said. One of the ten soldiers killed was a 29-year-old peace activist who opposed Israel's presence in the Occupied Territories, but who reported for reserve duty because he did not want to set a bad example to his students. After he was killed his mother left her job to join 500 other grieving Israelis and Palestinians. In October 2002, the Forum for Bereaved

Families and the Parents Circle, which promoted Israeli-Palestinian peace, launched a telephone hotline for coexistence, "Hello Shalom-Hello Salaam." Ghazi Brigieth was a Palestinian member. His brother was stopped at a checkpoint outside his village near Hebron: when he asked why he was being stopped, he was shot in the head at close range. Brigieth joined the group "to prevent death... for other families, it doesn't matter whether Israeli or Palestinian... When you lose someone close to you, you think of revenge—but this is our revenge, not with guns but with our mouths."

4 Lara Sukhtian, "Israelis Help Rebuild Palestinian's Homes," Associated Press, 3 June 2004.

5 Shay Shohami, former head of the country's civil aviation administration, explained: "This is a matter of humanity; they are human beings like us. We know how this will hurt them. If their livelihoods are going to be destroyed we have to do something. We can't just sit here and accept an atrocity by our government." Donald Macintyre, "How Sharon's giant fence broke down the barriers of suspicion," *Independent* 19 March 2004.

6 A Machsom-Watch volunteer witnessed a Palestinian doctor attacked and head-butted by a helmeted IDF soldier at a checkpoint. Complaints by Machsom-Watch and PHR-Israel led to the soldier and his sergeant being given prison sentences of 35 and 21 days respectively. There had been many complaints of soldiers' violence, but demands that the IDF investigate the incidents and bring the perpetrators to justice were typically refused, often on the basis that "the details of the incidents are unknown." This time was different because there were Israeli witnesses. Their persistence forced the brigade commander to bring the soldiers to justice. Physicians for Human Rights-Israel Update, 24 February 2004.

7 Maia Ridberg, "Israeli Women's Group Eyes Soldiers at Checkpoints," Reuters, 27 November 2003.

8 Linda Grant, "Checking on the checkpoints," *Guardian* 2 February 2004.

9 Ben Lynfield, "Israeli Women Keep Eyes on Army," *Christian Science Monitor* 24 February 2004.

10 Ishai Menuhin, "Saying No to Israel's Occupation," *New York Times* 9 March 2002.

11 Arik Diamant, "Immoral ethical codes," Opinion (Israel), *Ha'aretz* 2 March 2004.

12 Yigal Shochat, "Red Line, Green Line, Black Flag," *Ha'aretz magazine* 18 January 2002.

13 Conal Urquhart, "Elite Israeli commandos take heat for refusal to serve," *Chicago Tribune* 11 February 2004.

14 Justin Huggler, "Israeli Colonel Resigns Over Army's 'Immoral' Actions," *Independent* 5 January 2004.

15 Charles Sabine, "Unofficial Mideast Peace Plan Gains Ground," NBC News, 14 November 2003.

16 Aluf Benn, "The Shin Bet chiefs did it," *Ha'aretz* 13 October 2004.

17 Alex Fishman and Sima Kadmon, "Four Directors, one room," *Yediot Ahronoth* 14 November 2003.

18 Catherine Cook, Adam Hanieh, Adam Kay, *Stolen Youth, The Politics of Israel's Detention of Palestinian Children* (London: Pluto Press, 2004) 115.

11 "Only God"

1 For example, in the first three years of the Intifada, the 198,000 Israeli settlers in the Occupied Territories beyond East Jerusalem increased to 232,000. While the rest of Israel struggled with economic depression, the Israeli Interior Ministry gave settlements twice as much financial aid as Jewish communities inside Israel—three times as much as Palestinian Israeli communities. Yulie Khromchenko, "Study: Settlements get more aid money than other towns," *Ha'aretz* 20 October 2004.

2 Michael Ben-Yair, "The war's seventh day," *Ha'aretz* 4 March 2002.

3 Israel Harel, "One act of self-restraint too many," *Ha'aretz* 10 October 2002.

4 One notorious case was that of an eleven-year-old boy shot dead in the summer of 2001. He had been playing soccer in Rafah and was resting after the game with his friends. They were splattered with his blood and brain when he and two other boys were hit: a twelve-year-old in the leg, and a ten-year-old in the abdomen. Some distance away, other children had been throwing stones at an IDF position. Following up on the case, B'Tselem received a "standard reply from the office of the Military Prosecutor explaining that no regulations were broken and no further investigation is felt to be necessary." However, someone had put the IDF's internal investigation file inside the envelope by mistake. As a result, B'Tselem read the army's real conclusion: that the shots

which killed Khalil al-Mughrabi and wounded his friends were probably fired against regulations and, since there had been no threat to the
soldiers' lives, there was no justification for shooting the children. And
yet, despite the army's own conclusions, the military advocate general
chose not only to exonerate the soldiers but also deliberately to present
a version of the events that she knew to be untrue. "Whitewash, The
Office of the Judge Advocate General's Examination of the Death of
Khalil al-Mughrabi, 11, on 7 July 2001," B'Tselem Report.
5 Nicole Gaouette, "Attention Builds over a Slain Civilian," *Christian
Science Monitor* 10 January 2003.

12 For the Peace of the Settlements

1 Rafi Segal and Eyal Weizman, eds, *A Civilian Occupation: The Politics of
Israeli Architecture* ("the banned catalogue") (London & New York:
Verso, 2003) 152–3.
2 By declaring tracts of the Occupied Territories "state land," Israel says it
breaks no laws when building settlements. In the 1970s Israel's
Supreme Court forbade expropriating private Palestinian property for
settlements; if the land can be called "state land" this ruling is not
broken. Similarly, the Israeli government promises the US not to
expropriate territory for settlement construction, claiming that desig-
nating areas as "state lands" is not expropriation. Along with
international lawyers, Israeli NGO B'Tselem is not won over by these
arguments, seeing Israel's "state land" strategy as "a complex legal and
bureaucratic mechanism to take control of more than 50 percent of
the land in the West Bank. This land was used mainly to establish
settlements and create reserves of land for the future expansion of the
settlements. The principal tool used to take control of land was to
declare it 'state land.'" "Land Grab," B'Tselem Report.
3 International law states that "the occupying power shall not deport or
transfer parts of its own civilian population into the territory it occupies"; Israel argues that the settlers moved into the territories of their
own accord.
4 Rosenblum asked: "When do we begin to suspect that he [Sharon] is
deceiving us?... How long will we recite the mantra that 'Arafat is to
blame for everything'? Where is the conceptual alternative? How long
will the holiday taken—whether from desire or from fear—by skepti-
cism, doubt and a critical approach last? They all went on a lengthy

sabbatical two years ago, following the outbreak of the Intifada, and in America a year ago, after 9/11... the more time that passes, the less we know, but the more determined we are in our ignorance; and the more we are called on to cling to the official narrative and the hazier the facts it is based on become." Doron Rosenblum, "Doubt takes a holiday," *Ha'aretz* 18 August 2002.

5 Ariel Sharon, 26 May 2003.

6 For example, May 2004. *See* Jackson Diehl, "Why Not Palestinian Elections?" *Washington Post* 24 May 2004.

13 Between the Alaska Mosque & the Columbia Checkpoint

1 Later the Israeli government's Global Forum against anti-Semitism reported that the increase in anti-Semitism was due to media bias. In 2004 France had the highest rate of anti-Semitic violence with 96 attacks; in Britain the number was 77. When verbal assaults, damage to property, and daubing swastikas were included, the total number of incidents in Britain rose from 163 a year earlier to 304. An advisor to Mr. Sharansky on anti-Semitism said: "You can't brainwash people for four years that Israel is an illegitimate country and that Israelis are like the Nazis and that Israelis are monsters and expect that nothing will happen to Jews." The spokesman for the board of deputies of British Jews, Jason Pearlman, accused the BBC of "unrelenting anti-Israel bias." "The British media has portrayed Israel in a very unfair light," he said. "It's what's not said as much as what's said: the fact that most Palestinian attacks on Israel are not reported in the British press, and the fact that almost all the attacks on the Palestinians are reported." Chris McGreal, "Rising UK anti-Semitism blamed on media," *Guardian* 25 January 2005.

2 Ben Lynfield, "Israeli Expulsion Idea Gains Steam, The Moledet party's media blitz for the mass expulsion of Palestinians is gaining momentum," *Christian Science Monitor* 6 February 2001.

3 Ibid.

4 Sam Kiley, "The Middle East's War of Words," *London Evening Standard* 6 September 2001.

5 Dominique Vidal, "Les alliances douteuses des inconditionnels d'Israel, Au nom du combat contre l'antisemitisme," *Le Monde diplomatique* 6 December 2002.

6 *New York Times* 5 December 2003.

7 CNN took the opportunity to recap on Israeli victims without mentioning the 117 dead Palestinians. On Christmas day CNN's website said that the Palestinian attack "was the first suicide bombing in Israel since an October 4 attack in Haifa. That incident killed 21 people. There has been a relative calm since the Haifa bombing." A front-page *Los Angeles Times* headline the following day declared "12-Week Lull in Mideast Ends," and that the "back to back spasms of violence... shattered more than two months of relative quiet and dealt a fresh setback to peace efforts." And the *Chicago Tribune* reported that "Coming less than an hour apart," the December 25 "attacks broke a lull that had lasted more than two months and raised fears of a slide into violence."

14 Separation

1 Ben Lynfield, "Israeli Expulsion Idea Gains Steam, The Moledet Party's media blitz for the mass expulsion of Palestinians is gaining momentum," *Christian Science Monitor* 6 February 2001.

2 Editorial, *Ha'aretz* 6 January 2004.

3 Rafi Mann, "Fallacious exhibits," *Ma'ariv* 26 February 2004.

4 During Operation Defensive Shield the IDF had destroyed many of the buildings, and when the *Art Newspaper* reported on the damage and was accused of disinformation and anti-Semitism, they sent in a specialist reporter, Robert Bevan, to investigate the damage. He concluded that, yes, the initial report had been wrong; the damage was far worse than they had stated. This led to an apology from Dr. Martin Weyl, the former director of the Israel Museum: "I apologise for all the aggravation that I have caused you. I was evidently misled by my army sources." Anna Somers Cocks, "Israel-Palestine conflict also poisons press relationships, the *Art Newspaper* responds to accusations of anti-Semitism," *Art Newspaper* November 2002.

5 For a firsthand account of incidents of settler violence and peace groups' efforts to intervene, see David Shulman's *Dark Hope: Working for Peace in Israel and Palestine* (Chicago: University of Chicago Press, 2007).

6 "Lethal Curfew, the Use of Live Ammunition to Enforce Curfew," B'Tselem Report, October 2002.

15 Days

1 Caoimhe Butterly, as told to Annie Higgins, "Israel's Killing of British Citizen Iain Hook, UNRWA's Project Manager in Jenin," www.ElectronicIntifada.net, 22 November 2002.

16 Two Zoos

1 Hai Asher, Aryeln Bender, and Amir Rappaport, *Ma'ariv* 24 July 2003.

17 Countdown

1 Press release by al-Wafa Hospital for Rehabilitation in Gaza, 6 February 2003.

2 Palestinian participant Akram Hanieh described the denial during a session about refugees at Camp David: "[The Refugee Committee] was the most difficult committee because it was the reality committee, ruled by history... It placed Israel in front of her direct victims, in front of the witnesses to its crimes. It was strange because Israel continued to deny its crime. There is a complete denial of the *Nakba* and of the Israeli responsibility in causing it... When the Israelis were presented with the memoirs and the testimonies of their own generals, they rejected them." Akram Hanieh, *The Camp David Papers* (Ramallah: Al Ayyam Press, 2000) 46.

3 He wrote, "Children have been shot in other conflicts I have covered—death squads gunned them down in El Salvador and Guatemala, mothers with infants were lined up and massacred in Algeria, and Serb snipers put children in their sights and watched them crumple onto the pavement in Sarajevo—but I have never before watched soldiers entice children like mice into a trap and murder them for sport." Chris Hedges, "A Gaza Diary, Scenes from the Palestinian Uprising," *Harper's Magazine* October 2001.

4 Chris McGreal, "Food running out in Gaza as aid appeal fails," *Guardian* 11 February 2003.

5 On Israeli radio in September 2000 General YomTov Samia had said of Rafah: "The IDF must raze all the houses within a strip of 300–400 meters in width... Arafat must be punished, and after every incident another two to three rows of houses must be razed... we must employ this very extreme instrument... I am happy it is being used. Sadly in steps which are too small. It must be done in one operation." Quoted

in Jeff Halper, "Rafah: Holding Israel Accountable," 14 January 2002 (www.fromoccupiedpalestine.org).

6 Four eyewitnesses describe the murder of Rachel Corrie—Tom Dale, Greg Schnabel, Richard Purssell, and Joe Smith, International Solidarity Movement, http://electronicIntifada.net/v2/ article1263.shtml (19 March 2003).

7 Sally Pook and Nicola Woolcock, "Tom Hurndall was a young man with a dream, he paid for it with his life," *Daily Telegraph* 15 January 2004.

8 For example, in March 2004 an Israeli journalist implied that Rachel Corrie's death didn't happen as reported, and wrote: "On the first anniversary of her death, I wanted to thank Rachel Corrie for providing her organization, the Palestinian-sponsored International Solidarity Movement, with the opportunity to release a manipulated photo sequence 'showing' an Israeli military bulldozer deliberately crushing her. (I would also like to thank AP and the *Christian Science Monitor* for taking up the baton and immortalizing this cynical ISM stunt.)" Ruhama Shattan, "A 'Tribute' to Rachel Corrie," *Jerusalem Post* 1 March 2004.

9 Cindy Corrie, "Seeking Answers from Israel," *Boston Globe* 18 March 2004.

Epilogue

1 Notes made by author, George W. Bush speech on Gorée, 8 July 2003.

2 See Peace Now Settlement Watch reports, at www.peacenow.org.il.

3 Henry Siegman, "It is time to take Palestinian opinion seriously," *Financial Times* 18 November 2005.

4 www.geneva-accord.org, and, e.g., Qadoura Faris, "Looking for a realistic way out of the current despair: Why the initiative is so significant," *Le Monde diplomatique* December 2003.

5 Charles Krauthammer, "Geneva Sellout," Opinion, *Washington Post* 28 November 2003.

6 Aluf Benn, "Olmert's epiphany is too little, too late," *Ha'aretz* 2 October 2008. "At the age of 63, just moments before his departure from premiership, Ehud Olmert has reached an extraordinary epiphany. In order to make peace with the Palestinians and the Syrians, Israel must withdraw from 'nearly all the territories, if not all.' As he told *Yedioth Aharonoth* in a holiday interview, even East Jerusalem must be given to the Palestinians."

7 The International Court of Justice issued an advisory opinion calling for the barrier to be removed, and for Arab residents to be compensated for any damage done: "The Court finds that the construction by Israel of a wall in the Occupied Palestinian Territory and its associated régime are contrary to international law." See www.btselem.org/English/Separation_Barrier/International_Court_Decision.asp.

8 Nahum Barnea, *Yediot Ahronoth*, "Woe to the victors," 7 May 2004.

9 As for dreams, after Operation Defensive Shield the Israeli writer Aviad Kleinberg had bemoaned Sharon's policies of repression, saying bitterly, "Palestinian dreams are dangerous because, as weak as they may be right now, their dreams could give them strength. So Israel has to make sure the Palestinians give up their dreams, that they reach total despair." He explained the thinking, "Their complete surrender of any ambition is more important than tanks or territories. It means that the Palestinians finally have accepted Israeli mastery. Then they can love their masters, because we will be good masters. When they give up their national ambitions—because we hit them, because we dice up their land with thousands of settlements, because we kill off their leaders, and because they will be absolutely dependent on us—then we can show our humanitarian side, renovating their schools and water wells, and granting them passes to work in our cities." Aviad Kleinberg, "The scent of the pines," *Ha'aretz* 1 October 2002.

10 Aluf Benn, Interview with PM Ariel Sharon, *Ha'aretz*, Pesach supplement 5 April 2004.

11 Letter from President Bush to Prime Minister Sharon, 14 April 2004 (www.whitehouse.gov/news/releases/2004/04/20040414-3.html).

12 Ari Shavit, "Top PM aide: Gaza plan aims to freeze the peace process," *Ha'aretz* 6 October 2004. Emphasis added.

13 Shimon Peres interviewed on *Israel Radio* 12 September 2005.

14 Barry Schweid, "Peres: Israel Has No Claim to West Bank," Associated Press, 24 February 2004.

15 See report of John Dugard, UN Special Rapporteur on Human Rights, quoted in "Settlers Terrorize Palestinians: UN Expert's Report," Associated Press, 9 March 2006.

16 Sara Roy, "Dubai on the Mediterranean," *London Review of Books* 3 November 2005.

17 Gaza Mental Health Program press release, 10 October 2005.

18 Donald Macintyre, "Gaza in danger of becoming a giant prison," *Independent* 14 November 2005.

19 Nahum Barnea, *Yediot Ahronot* 21 October 2005.

20 OCHA AMA Reports August 2005 and May 2009.

21 Report of the Special Rapporteur on the situation of Human Rights in the Palestinian territories occupied since 1967, 9 May 2006, Office of the UN High Commissioner for Human Rights, 2nd Session, document symbol: A/HRC/2/5.

22 Comparing Israeli settlement activity during periods of peace and violence, one authority notes: "During the Oslo peace process (1993–2000), a period of relatively little violence, Israel increased its settler population by more than 72 percent and housing units by 52 percent. According to Israeli reports, the decrease in the rates of expansion of settlements from 7 to 9 percent in the 1990s to 4 to 5 percent in the past few years was due, in part, to violence. Israel's unilateral, as opposed to negotiated, evacuation from Gaza reinforced this message. What, then, is the message about the rule of law and violence?" Stephanie Koury, "West Bank Road vs. Peace," *Washington Post* 19 November 2005.

23 "Economic and Humanitarian Impact of the Karni Crossing Closure," UN OCHA OPT, the Gaza Strip Situation Report, 31 January 2006.

24 For details of impediments to movement, and a comparison with August 2000, see "Restrictions on the movement of people and goods within the West Bank," UN Office for the Coordination of Humanitarian Affairs, November 2005 (OCHAPT_frictionAnls_Nov05.pdf).

25 Christian fanatics aligned with the Israeli right knowing that their own aim was to see all Jews "convert or burn in hellfire." In their drive to see biblical prophecy fulfilled, one priest told me apologetically, "some Christian true-believers back home" were "ignorant of the doctrine and details, and ready to sacrifice Christian beliefs and principles" as well as the rights of their Christian brethren in Palestine. In April 2004, US election year, an umbrella group representing millions of US Christians wrote to George Bush informing him of potential political fallout among Christians if he supported the Israeli government plan for disengagement from Gaza: it could, warned the letter, "fail your own presidency." Michael Freund, "U.S. Christians Lobby against Gaza Retreat," *Jerusalem Post* 8 April 2004.

26 Meron Rappaport, "A wall in the heart," *Yediot Ahronoth* 23 May 2003.

27 Jimmy Carter, "Colonization of Palestine Precludes Peace," *Ha'aretz* 17 March 2006.

28 Interview, *Jerusalem Post* weekend supplement, 21 May 2004.

29 Gisha: Legal Center for Freedom of Movement, "*Disengaged Occupiers: The Legal Status of Gaza,*" January 2007.

30 Jimmy Carter, *Palestine: Peace Not Apartheid* (New York: Simon & Schuster, 2006).

31 See EU Heads of Mission Report, March 2009.

32 Ethan Bronner and Isabel Kershner, "Parks Fortify Israel's Claim to Jerusalem," *New York Times* 9 May 2009.

33 *Ha'aretz* 20 May 2007.

34 David Newman, "The Myth of a Settlement Freeze," *Jerusalem Post* 27 July 2009.

35 Zvi Ba'rel, "Painting Obama as an enemy will hurt Israel badly," *Ha'aretz* 26 July 2009.

36 *Ha'aretz* 20 July 2009.

Glossary

abu   (Arabic) father

al-Aqsa Martyrs Brigades   A group of West Bank militias affiliated with Yasser Arafat's Fatah movement. The al-Aqsa Brigades carry out the same sort of attacks on Israeli civilians as the religious fundamentalist groups Hamas and Palestinian Islamic Jihad, but the group's ideology is rooted in Palestinian nationalism.

aliya   Immigration to Israel by members of the Jewish diaspora

al-Quds   (Arabic) Jerusalem

Ashkenazi   Jews of European or Western origin

Ayyubid   Dynasty of rulers over Egypt and Palestine founded by Saladin

beit or *bet*   House

B'Tselem   Israeli human rights organization

Closure   The control by Israel of Palestinian movement within and at the limits of the Occupied Territories, by physical (e.g., checkpoints, earth mounds, barriers, ditches, gates) and administrative (e.g., permits) means. Introduced in 1993.

collective punishment   The imposition of punitive military measures on a community; curfew is one of the most detested.

DCO   District Coordinator's Office: responsible for issuing passage permits and travel permits to Palestinian residents of the Occupied Territories. Sixteen Israeli DCO clerks are responsible for all the residents of the West Bank—approximately 2 million people. Three additional DCO clerks are responsible for health in the West Bank and three more for Gaza, with a population of about 1.2 million. The Palestinian DCOs cannot issue permits. "The Bureaucracy of Occupation," report by Machsom-Watch and Physicians for Human Rights-Israel, 16 May 2004.

deir   Convent

djellabah   A loose hooded woolen robe

dunam   Four dunams to one acre, or one tenth of a hectare

Eid   Muslim festival

Eretz Israel   Land of Israel, often refers to "Greater Israel"

expat   Foreigner, neither Israeli nor Palestinian, nor any of the many other nationalities who live in Jerusalem: Armenian, Greek, Assyrian, etc.

facts on the ground   Israeli construction in the Occupied Territories—

including settlements and areas for their expansion, roads, industrial estates, military bases, and control of aquifers, electrical grids, sewerage, etc.—all of which is intended to give Israel permanent control of a large proportion of what would be the land for a future Palestinian state.

Fatah Acronym of Palestine Liberation Movement, main faction of the PLO

flechette An anti-personnel weapon fired from tanks. The shell explodes in the air and releases thousands of metal darts 3.75 mm in length, which disperse in a conical arch nearly 1,000 feet long and about 300 feet wide. Given this dispersal it is difficult to avoid injury to those not involved in combat. The use of flechettes was banned by IDF Central Command in the West Bank, but not by IDF Southern Command in the Gaza Strip.

Green Line The armistice line of 1949 dividing Israel from the remainder of mandatory Palestine. Also referred to as the '67 border.

Gush Bloc as in Gush Etzion (Etzion Bloc)

Gush Emunim Bloc of the Faithful, Israeli nationalists advocating Jewish settlement on the West Bank and Gaza Strip and opposing evacuation of any of these settlements

Hagganah Underground Jewish force established in 1920

Haj Pilgrimage to Mecca

hafouch (Hebrew) coffee (meaning upside down or turned over)

Halacha Jewish religious law

Hamas Acronym meaning "zeal," the Islamic Resistance Movement, established in 1987

hamseem Wind blowing in off the desert

Haredi Ultra-Orthodox Jew

hasbara Information, propaganda

Hassidim Main movement of ultra-Orthodox Jews

IAF Israeli air force

ICRC International Committee of the Red Cross

IDF Israel Defense Forces

Iftar The evening breaking of the fast during Ramadan

Intifada Literally, a "shaking off." First Intifada 1987–1992; second Intifada or al-Aqsa Intifada, sparked off September 28, 2000

IPF Israel police force

Irgun A right-wing pre-independence militia responsible for terrorist actions, most famously the bombing of the King David Hotel (July 22, 1946) and the massacre of Deir Yassin (April 9, 1948)

keffiyeh   Traditional male Arab headdress

kippa   Traditional male Jewish skullcap

Kyria   Israeli defense ministry complex in Tel Aviv

labaneh   salty cream cheese

Law of Return   The Israeli law of 1950 granting any Jewish person, anywhere in the world, the right to "return" and settle on land in Israel.

Magen David Adom   Israel's national emergency service, associated with the International Movement of Red Cross and Red Crescent Societies

machsom   (Hebrew) checkpoint

Mamluk   Rulers of Egypt and Palestine, 1230–1516

mukhtar   (Arabic) village elder/leader

Muqata   (Arabic) headquarters

MK   Member of the Knesset (Israeli parliament)

Nakba   (Arabic) catastrophe; at the founding of the State of Israel when three-quarters of a million Palestinians lost their homes and lands and became refugees

nargila   Water pipe or hookah, for smoking tobacco. The tobacco is often flavored with fruits

NGO   Non-governmental organization

outpost   Precursor to an Israeli settlement, usually established by individuals or a group with the hope of government backing to help form a fully fledged settlement. Often just a hut or trailer, and not always inhabited.

PA   Palestinian Authority

Peace Now   Israeli NGO advocating coexistence and justice

pey'ot   Long sideburns worn by Hassidim

PFLP   Popular Front for the Liberation of Palestine

PHR-Israel   Physicians for Human Rights-Israel

PLO   Palestine Liberation Organization

PNC   Palestine National Congress

PRCS   Palestine Red Crescent Society

Quartet   US, EU, Russia, and the UN, formed in 2001 as a diplomatic tool and forum for advancing the Middle East peace process.

Qassam rocket   Crude, inaccurate rockets put together by the Palestinians and fired at the Israelis. Hundreds have been fired from the Gaza Strip into Israel.

Rais   (Arabic) president

Refugee camp   The war of 1948–9 resulted in hundreds of thousands of people fleeing their homes in Palestine. These refugees (more fled in the war of 1967) were housed in refugee camps in Jordan, Lebanon, Syria, the West Bank, and the Gaza Strip. They or their descendants remain there still. Some hold that Israel bears no responsibility for the plight of the Palestinian refugees. Rather, this was the fault of the Arab leadership, both for their rejection of General Assembly Resolution 181 (the UN partition plan) and for the ensuing war, during which Arab leaders were thought to have called for the inhabitants to flee to avoid hindering the progress of the Arab armies. Others point out that although in retrospect the UN partition plan would certainly have been the best possible deal for the Palestinians (giving them 46 percent of Palestine instead of 22 percent), extensive research has shown that there were no calls to flee by Arab leaders, and that, following such events as the Deir Yassin massacre, the refugees fled out of one overriding motivation: fear.

Resolution 194 etc.   See under UN Resolutions

Right of Return   The right claimed by Palestinian refugees to return to lands and properties abandoned in 1948. Since the land in question is now in Israel, and since there are millions of refugees (or their descendants), the Right of Return would, if taken up, radically alter the demographics of Israel.

Sayeret Matkal   Elite commando unit of the IDF

servees   Large communal taxi

settlements   The first Israeli settlement in land captured and occupied in 1967 was constructed in 1968. Settlement construction has continued since then. The entire international community, including the US government, regards these settlements both as a contravention of international law (the Fourth Geneva Convention, by which an occupying power is forbidden to transfer parts of its own civilian population into territory it occupies) and as an obstacle to peace. These settlements, in which only Jews are allowed to live, are usually built on land confiscated from Palestinian villages. All of them are constructed on the 22 percent of Palestine that was not held by the

Israelis until 1967 and which the Palestinians envisage as their future state. The Israeli government claims that the transfer of Jews to the West Bank was entirely voluntary, and that the land is not "occupied." Nonetheless, successive Israeli governments have invested billions of dollars in these settlements, partly in order to encourage Israeli families to move to them. It is on the future of these settlements that any peace will depend.

Shabbat Day of rest, from sundown on Friday until sundown on Saturday

shawarma Slices of marinated lamb cooked on a spit, carved, and stuffed into pita bread

Shin Bet Israeli counter-intelligence and internal security service

souk marketplace

sumud Being steadfast in the face of all difficulty

TIPH International monitors, the Temporary International Presence in Hebron, installed after Baruch Goldstein gunned down 29 Palestinians at prayer

transfer Euphemism used among far-right political parties in Israel, for the expulsion of Palestinians from their lands and homes. *See also* voluntary transfer.

Two-state solution Two independent and sovereign states: Israel and Palestine

UN Resolutions These include:

General Assembly Resolution 181, 29 November 1947 The partition plan of Palestine, creating two states with an economic union

General Assembly Resolution 194, 11 December 1948 "Resolves that the refugees wishing to return to their homes and live at peace with their neighbors should be permitted to do so at the earliest practicable date, and that compensation should be paid for the property of those choosing not to return and for loss of or damage to property which, under principles of international law or in equity, should be made good by the Governments or authorities responsible."

Security Council Resolution 242, 22 November 1967 Calls for an end to the conflict based on the concept of "land for peace." Noting the "inadmissibility of the acquisition of territory by war and the need for a just and lasting peace in which every state in the area can live in security," its basic premises were "withdrawal of Israeli armed forces from territories of the recent conflict" and "the termination of all claims of states of belligerency and respect for the acknowledgment of the sovereignty, territorial integrity and political independence of every state in the area and their right to live in peace within secure and recognized boundaries free from threats or acts of force."

Security Council Resolution 446, 22 March 1979   "Determines that the policy and practices of Israel in establishing settlements in the Palestinian and other Arab territories occupied since 1967 have no legal validity and constitute a serious obstruction to achieving a comprehensive, just and lasting peace in the Middle East."

Security Council Resolution 1397, 12 March 2002   Affirms "a vision of a region where two states, Israel and Palestine, live side by side within secure and recognized borders."

unilateral separation   Separation imposed by one side (Israel) without negotiation

UNRWA   United Nations Relief and Works Agency. A relief and human development agency, providing education, healthcare, social services, and emergency aid to Palestinian refugees living in the Gaza Strip, the West Bank, Jordan, Lebanon, and Syria. The refugee camps, which developed from tented cities to rows of concrete blockhouses to urban ghettos indistinguishable from their surroundings, house around one third of all registered Palestinian refugees. They also provide facilities in other areas where large numbers of registered Palestinian refugees live outside recognized camps. UNRWA does not run any camps, has no police powers or administrative role: it simply provides services to the camps.

voluntary transfer   "Asked on Israel radio what he meant by 'voluntary,' Benny Elon, head of the [National Union] party and a minister in Mr Sharon's cabinet, said unapologetically that life would be made so unbearable for Palestinians in the West Bank that 'they would want to leave.'" Henry Seigman, "In Israel: Palestinian moderation isn't what Sharon is seeking," *International Herald Tribune* 4 January 2002.

wadi   (Arabic) small valley

WFP   UN World Food Program

ya'ani   Arabic expression with various meanings, e.g., "and so," "you know," "up to a point," often used at the end of a statement or question for emphasis

Yesha   Hebrew acronym for "Judea, Samaria, and Gaza"; i.e., the Occupied Territories of 1967

Acknowledgments

Many people helped me while I wrote this book, but I'll thank only those to whom I am most indebted. Professor Anthony King read, commented, steered, suggested, and guided me with extraordinary kindness and unwearying attention to detail, turning me from caution to confidence—no small task—and I am enormously grateful. Julita Arsenio looked after my children and gave me the time and space to write; without Julita there would have been no book.

Boris Johnson and Stuart Reid repeatedly published me in the *Spectator* in not the easiest of circumstances for them. Phil Reeves of the *Independent* and Nicole Gauoette and Cameron Barr of the *Christian Science Monitor* kindly helped me to get started in their respective papers, while Marie Colvin suggested a long article for *Vogue*. Patrick Bishop of the *Daily Telegraph*, Xan Smiley of the *Economist*, and Mandy Cunningham of the BBC were also key in this process. At Bloomsbury, Victoria Millar and Rosemary Davidson were gentle and supportive editors at every step. Asif Khan, Omar Dajani, my father-in-law Ian Gilmour, brother-in-law David Gilmour, Kim Keating, and Michael Keating all read the text and gave excellent suggestions. Nihad Rafeh was inspirational.

David Shearer was very helpful with the production of maps and with advice. The staff of the office he heads, the UN Office for the Coordination of Humanitarian Affairs in the Occupied Palestinian Territory, was also unfailingly helpful. Nahum Barnea of *Yediot Ahronoth*, Jeff Halper of the Israeli Campaign against House Demolition, Daniel de Wolff, Raffaella Iodice, Peter Bartu, Andrew Kuhn, Jesse Norman, Shoshana Halper, Bassem Khaldi, and Dominique Roch all gave me generous support and help whenever I asked. Laura Wick and the Institute of Community and Public Health, Birzeit University, were wonderful partners and coworkers.

David Godwin suggested the book and nurtured me through a long process with endless patience and good humor. Before I left New York in 2000, Nina Train Choa gave me a laptop, and this allowed me to begin writing down all the details that found their way into this book.

I owe Andrew above all others and for everything, and our four children, who generously remained happy, healthy, and understanding while all this was happening.